The Riddle of Erskine Childers

The Riddle
of Erskine Childers

ANDREW BOYLE

HUTCHINSON OF LONDON

Hutchinson of London
3 Fitzroy Square, London W1

London Melbourne Sydney Auckland
Wellington Johannesburg and agencies
throughout the world

First published 1977
© Andrew Boyle 1977

Set in Monotype Garamond

Printed in Great Britain by
The Anchor Press Ltd, and bound by
Wm Brendon & Son Ltd, both of
Tiptree, Essex

ISBN 0 09 128490 2

920
CN1

CONTENTS

ILLUSTRATIONS

Between pages 176 and 177

PREFACE

It would be idle to pretend that this book directly owes its conception and birth to its predecessor, *'Poor, Dear Brendan' The Quest for Brendan Bracken*; yet the latter certainly inspired and interacted on the former in a way which was more than merely coincidental. For, up to a point, the two works developed in tandem. I was a boy of twelve when I first stumbled on the baffling enigma of Erskine Childers, through reading his classic spy story, *The Riddle of the Sands*. Perhaps I was beginning to experience the first pains of a would-be biographer at a precocious age. For I can distinctly recall my keen sense of disappointment at being unable to prise from the tight-lipped masters at my Scottish school any plausible explanation for the disappearance from the literary scene of so extraordinarily gifted a writer who eventually came to a violent end at the hands of an Irish firing squad about the time I was emerging from infancy and learning to talk. To suggest that the downfall of Childers continued to trouble me as I grew up, or even when I started to write, would, however, be an absurd exaggeration. Not until I was threading my way slowly through the tangled darkness of Brendan Bracken's boyhood background did the original seed of inquisitiveness about the fated Childers begin to take and sprout. What, I wondered, had induced this mysterious Englishman to turn his back on his homeland virtually at the moment that the mischievously elusive Bracken was moving off in the opposite direction? Was Childers a failed Byron, a traitor, a double agent, or what?

I posed such questions in a disinterested, wholly academic spirit. For I was busily trying to solve other and more hilarious conundrums. I was aware, too, that Erskine Childers's life-story had already been consigned to the capable hands of A. P. Ryan, the author of *Mutiny at the Curragh* and an assistant editor of *The Times*. The fact that Ryan happened to be the same person who, in his previous capacity as Head of the BBC's News Division, had been instrumental in my being offered a job after my discharge from war service in 1947, struck me as no more than just another coincidence. Then Ryan died suddenly and unexpectedly. I learnt that the Childers family were on the look out for another biographer. My claims were pressed by Sir Robert Lusty, at that time chairman of Hutchinson. On my next visit to Ireland in search of Brendan Bracken's carefully concealed beginnings, I was invited to break my journey in Dublin and meet Erskine Childers's elder son and namesake. At least half a dozen other writers, he informed me, were being considered for the task. All of them appeared to have far better credentials than myself, as my host was quick to emphasize. Had I not confessed at the start of our conversation that my knowledge of Irish history was broad, oblique and anything but detailed? Yes, I replied; but, paradoxically, that must surely give me the edge over my rivals. As a Scot who had spent all my adult life in England, and whose dispassionate attitude to the theological nuances implicit in every line of the Irish struggle for freedom could not be gainsaid, perhaps I might be a better-equipped candidate than any number of committed Irish historians? After some thought, my host took me aback by conceding the point. In due course, the family trustees commissioned me to write this biography and generously offered me an entirely free hand.

President Childers, for such my host that evening subsequently became, did not live to see its completion. Over the dinner-table one night, less than two months before his untimely death, the President of the Irish Republic was asked by Harold Harris, editorial director of Hutchinson: 'What was your father really like?' He answered with disarming simplicity: 'I'm waiting to read Andrew's book and find out.' To the late President Childers and his widow, Rita, I am indebted for help, advice and encouragement in the early stages when I was their occasional guest at the old Viceregal Lodge in Phoenix Park, Dublin. I must record my gratitude also to Erskine Childers's younger son, Robert, and his wife Christabel, for the constant interest they have shown since. The main source to which the Childers family gave me unconditional access were the voluminous personal papers of the first Erskine Childers, a vast, uncatalogued collection of letters, diaries, logbooks, notebooks and other records which had been locked away in four heavy trunks for more than half a century. This had been arranged deliberately by Mary Childers, the widow of my subject, in order that the inevitable passions of hatred and bitterness, the Dead Sea fruits of all civil wars, might meanwhile be partially allayed and the life's work of her victimized husband judged in calm perspective. If I am convinced now that this was a prudent decision, I am less certain that she proved herself altogether wise in handling the papers during the years of her long widowhood. According to members of the family, Mary Childers worshipped unceasingly at the shrine of Erskine's memory with a zealot's unqualified devotion. In her own mind and heart she had canonized Erskine from the moment of his death as an Irish martyr of heroic stature. Nothing could have been more natural; but she refused to leave it there. Making herself the solitary exception to her own fifty-year rule, she compiled interminable commentaries on remembered episodes and turning points. Not content with that, she went so far as to excise or otherwise delete from the record as it stood certain parts which seemed to detract from the immutable image she had formed of him.

I could understand and even sympathize with her aim: Mary Childers wished to ensure that posterity would share her private, idealized picture of the man she deeply cherished and idolized, so that no hint of any disagreement or passing estrangement between them would ever sully the pages of his definitive biography. I should add that, as a reasonably experienced researcher, it was not unduly difficult for me to trace and repair the damage caused by such pious singlemindedness. Mercifully, only fractions of evidence, mostly from personal letters reflecting her early disapproval of Erskine Childers's resolve to settle in Ireland and immerse himself in the struggle for independence, had been wilfully tampered with; and I have succeeded, thanks mainly to the firsthand testimony of other witnesses, in piecing the whole picture together. Compared with the premeditated plan of Brendan Bracken to shake off all biographical pursuit by leaving written instructions that his personal papers should be indiscriminately burned within twenty-four hours of his death, Mary Childers's editing was little worse than child's play.

Of the many books on the period of the Irish Treaty talks of 1921, which brought Erskine Childers's curiously chequered career to its melancholy climax, the most valuable in my judgment is Frank Pakenham's *Peace by Ordeal*. Published over forty years ago, this sober, scholarly yet dramatic study of the conflicting personalities and attitudes of the Irish delegates who attended the London Conference, from which emerged the new Irish Free State, remains as indispensable a source as *The Whitehall Diary* of Tom Jones. The Earl of Longford, to give Pakenham his present title, has placed me further in his debt by offering sound guidance and several useful recollections of his own. I am obliged to him and to the late Robert Barton, the sole surviving member of the 1921 Irish delegation during my opening months of research, for their unstinted cooperation.

My investigations into the *dénouement* of my subject's brief but poignant involvement in Irish politics were lengthy and far-reaching. I have relied primarily on a mass of hitherto unpublished evidence in the Childers Papers, but must record my gratitude also to scores of individual writers and personal witnesses, Irish and English, whose written or oral evidence recurs in the pages that follow. To single them out by name would be invidious. Either in the text or in the listed notes on sources at the end I have tried to pay them due tribute, but to A. P. Ryan who preceded me and helped to smooth the path for me by his own preliminary groundwork I owe more than the usual and perfunctory expression of thanks.

The documents cover in detail not only the brave and frequently hazardous duties performed by Erskine Childers in the roles of air navigator and officer aboard coastal motor boats during the 1914–18 war, but earlier adventures of exploration through the wild seas about Germany as a skilled amateur yachtsman, as well as the relatively unclouded span of boyhood and youth at Haileybury and Trinity College, Cambridge, as a typical product of the English upper-middle-class from which he sprang. Indeed it should be said that, while Brendan Bracken left far too few clues about himself, Childers left too many. He threw nothing away; and his addiction to writing down nearly everything that

mattered, and much that did not, was not calculated to ease a
scrupulous biographer's task. For discreetly embedded in the
mountain of words there always lurked the complex spirit of an
ardent, diffident romantic of high ideals, rare intellectual quality,
and stubborn integrity. Talleyrand was talking sense when he said
that the love of glory can create only a great hero whereas the
contempt for it creates a great man. Glory did not concern
Childers in the slightest; and at the end of his days he sought
merely to clear his good name from calumny and falsehood.
Being somewhat accident-prone, possessing also an unerring
knack for standing in his own light, Erskine Childers appeared
foredoomed to live and die in the way he did: but the fascination
exerted by so eccentric a nature lingers on still, like a field of
magnetic force. I believe it will always do so. For destiny cast
Erskine Childers in no common earthly mould.

My final words of thanks must go to Harold Harris, my
publisher, to Graham Watson, my agent, to Andrea Scott, and,
as ever, to Christina for producing a legible typescript.

PROLOGUE

It was a condemned man's privilege to while away the slow hours of waiting in the guardroom at the end of the echoing, stone-flagged corridor, but Erskine Childers seemed quite content to forego it. He chose instead to stay alone with his thoughts in the death cell. The warders had frequently remarked on the courtesy and quiet self-composure of this unusual prisoner. What a contrast he made with that other 'damned Englishman', David Robinson, who had occupied the adjoining cell in Portobello Barracks for several days and had never ceased complaining about the food, the service and the slovenly ways of the staff. An old friend of Childers, with swashbuckling manners more befitting an eccentric British ex-cavalry officer of the old school than a wartime tank commander, he had a glass eye set in a long, pale, beaky face, a keen sense of the absurd, and a preternaturally soft heart. He knew that Erskine would have to die, having lived with the premonition for many months past; yet the blind vindictiveness of the authorities who sought to liquidate this man had caused David to heap abuse on their harmless lackeys, the jailers, until Childers was removed to Beggars Bush Barracks, Dublin.

Even the prison commandant there could not easily reconcile the unaffectedly calm demeanour of his prize captive with the reputation for indiscriminate ghoulishness that the name of Childers conjured up. Could this slight, grey-haired, prematurely aged man, who limped when he walked, be the same legendary wolf of the battlefields? Was this the fiend among tacticians whose destructive skills had prolonged the civil war between the lawful forces of the Irish Free State and the rebellious rump of the once unified Irish Republican Army? Why, the Provisional Government's Minister for Home Affairs had publicly denounced Childers on the very day of his secret trial as 'a leader of outstanding wickedness'. Yet the sole charge against him was that he had been caught in possession of a tiny automatic; and because that offence conveniently carried the death penalty, the authorities could safely leave the larger allegations to the public imagination.

Perhaps here lay the explanation of Childers's repeated requests for newspapers, ink and writing paper. Whenever a warder peered through the judas-hole, the prisoner seemed always to be hunched over the table, scribbling incessantly with the regulation pen. Only David Robinson, behind his languid exterior, could fathom the agonies of mingled doubt and self-reproach which Erskine Childers had endured after their capture and arrest together on 10 November 1922. Robinson had done his utmost to console and cheer him until they were parted. The discovery of a small communicating hole through the party wall, at floor level, had enabled the two men to converse together discreetly at intervals. According to Robinson's later account to Frank O'Connor, it had also encouraged them to improvise a time-killing game.

They were both passionate chess-players, so they 'chalked chess boards on the floor, made chessmen out of newspapers, and played . . . there is nothing in nature more removed from the imaginative boy than the grown man who has cut himself apart from life, seems to move entirely by his own inner light, and to face his doom with equanimity. . . . And yet again and again, in my own imagination, I have had to go through those terrible moments with him almost as if I were there: see the slight figure of the little grey-haired Englishman emerge for the last time into the Irish daylight, apparently cheerful and confident but incapable of grandiose gestures, concerned only lest inadvertently he might do or say something that would distress some poor fool of an Irish boy who was about to level an English rifle at his heart.'[1]

Altogether, when assessed in steady retrospect, the past twelve months had piled pathos on tragedy and failure. Exactly a year before Childers had been in London. There, as secretary to the Irish delegation, he had failed to prevent the signing of a treaty with the British which, in his view, did more than bring the Act of Union to an end. It destroyed forever the unity of Ireland, and also betrayed the Republican ideal for which thousands of Irishmen had died. Happily, de Valera had fiercely opposed the terms, and Childers with him; but the Dáil had voted narrowly in favour of them; Arthur Griffith became President in place of de Valera; and in March 1922 the British transferred power to the new Provisional Government. By then the signs were pointing towards the awful probability of open conflict. For the Irish Republican Army had split on the doubtful merits of a Free State, even one which gave Ireland a larger measure of independence in twenty-six of its thirty-two counties than O'Connell, Parnell or Redmond had ever dreamed of: complete autonomy in finance, justice, administration and education, with three 'treaty ports' reserved to the British for naval use as part of a compromise deal on defence. Erskine Childers, a powerful critic of these arrangements in the Dáil until June 1922, had lost his seat in the elections of that month when, despite an electoral pact between supporters and opponents of the London Treaty, chicanery and the intrusion of other candidates at the polls had led both to the confirmation in office of Griffith and to the outbreak of hostilities between the two factions of the IRA.

Frank O'Connor had served with Erskine Childers and David Robinson in the disorganized phase of small skirmishes, sudden ambushes and piecemeal withdrawals which characterized the fighting to the west of Cork during the summer months of 1922. There was, he surmised at a distance as vividly as did Robinson at close hand, something horribly unreal in the efforts of the Irish Provisional Government to destroy the character of Erskine Childers. For while the latter had been seized and overpowered with a toy gun in his hand, a keepsake from his old friend Michael Collins, Robinson had actually led a column of his own, displaying a panache and daring that struck terror into his foes. Not so Childers. His active campaigning had ended on Armistice Day 1918. His military superiors, mostly amateurs at the game of war, had invariably discounted his tactical ability and left him to pursue the business of counter-propaganda in the field. On the few occasions he had seen the Republican Irregulars in action, Childers was present on sufferance and purely as a passive observer, though undoubtedly he would have unpinned the pearl-handled pistol from his braces to defend himself if attacked, as he had tried to do that morning when soldiers of the Irish Free State burst into Glendalough House and disturbed his troubled sleep, capturing David Robinson and himself.

About five o'clock on the afternoon of 20 November, exactly ten days later, the officer of the guard unlocked the cell door, moved in with an awkward creaking of the leather holster at his side, and stood towering above the condemned man. The message he brought from military headquarters in the block beyond the barrack square was terse; the execution, he said, would be at dawn next morning. Childers thanked him gently, his worn face suddenly bright with relief. Then he asked the visitor for more sheets of notepaper, waited for the heavy door to clang shut, and settled down to a concentrated burst of scribbling.

Beloved wife, [his farewell letter began] I am told that I am to be shot tomorrow at 7. I am fully prepared. I think it is best so, viewing it from the biggest standpoint, and perhaps you will agree. To have followed those other brave lads is a great thing for a great cause. I have belief in the beneficent shaping of our destiny – yours and mine – and I believe God means this for the best: for us, Ireland and humanity. So in the midst of anguish at leaving you, and in mortal solicitude for you, beloved of my heart, I triumph and I know you triumph with me. It is such a simple thing, too, a soldier's death, what millions risk and incur, what so many in our cause face and suffer daily. There is this, too, that living I was weighted with a load of prejudice, unjust but so heavy that it may be I was even harming our cause. Dead I shall have a better chance of being understood and of helping the cause. I am, as I sit here, the happiest of men. I have had nineteen years of happiness with you. No man ever could claim so great and precious a blessing as that. But for you I should have foundered; and died, younger possibly, possibly older, but an unhappy man, a dwarfed soul, not understanding love, the secret of all, and not grasping life like a man. You redeemed me. I understand dimly the cult of the Blessed Mother, through you, with your divine intercession leading me to God, for through you I reach him. There is a mystery here. Isolated, direct personal communication with God I think I do not know. I go to him hand in hand with you, as it were part of you, with you interpenetrating me, and so, one with you, find him.

I could have been better for you. How I wish I had been. I have failed in serenity in spite of our treasured motto – and failed in much more. I do not ask you for forgiveness, for you know and forgive all and when all is said the sum of our love is infinite. You have never failed me. In these last years you followed me nobly and loyally into the hard, rugged path that has brought me to this cell. Together in vital communion, as comrades and apostles, we have followed conscience, honour and duty. Oh will this nation soon understand and pay reverence to what actuates our comrades in the cause and ourselves! If only I could die, knowing that my death would somehow – I know not how – save the lives of others, arrest this policy of executions, and – . . . . They say this letter cannot go to you today or any message. I will add to it at the last, therefore. Anyway I feel that instinct will tell you when the hour comes. At that moment we shall be supremely and eternally one. It came to me yesterday that I would be saying when they fire: 'I fall asleep in your arms, God above blessing us.' This is only an earthly metaphor expressing an idea but I caught at it somehow. Till then my spirit was somewhat confused, after that clear, and ever since I have been repeating it to myself and getting little lifts of happiness and security and serenity – serenity yes, I have that at last if never before. . . . I die at peace with all men, asking all to forgive me for wrongs I have done, and in my turn bearing ill will to no one. Personal things merge in something much bigger. I see big forces rending and at the same time moulding our people in affliction. I pity and hope without bitterness and I die full of intense love for Ireland. . . . I hope one day my good name will be cleared in England. I felt what Churchill said about my 'hatred' and 'malice' against England. Don't we know it isn't true and what line I ever spoke or wrote justifies the charge? I die loving England and passionately praying that she may change completely and finally towards Ireland.[2]

Childers's letter broke off abruptly at this point. For the second time that evening the key jangled in the lock, the creaking holster of the captain of the guard and the firm, following footsteps betokened the delivery of another message from the prison commandant. No sooner had the cell door clanged behind the officer in his dark-green uniform than the writer added the words: '10 p.m. My execution is "postponed". That's all I know.' He was swift to guess the reason for the postponement. When arraigned before a secret military tribunal in Portobello Barracks Dublin, on 17 November, he had at once refused to recognize the authority of the court:

'He recognized the authority only of the Irish Republican

Government,' ran the written statement submitted by his legal advisers. 'He has been taken prisoner in war. He is an officer of the Irish Republican Army, and he claims that if he be detained at all by an army whose legality he repudiates, he should receive the treatment of a prisoner of war. His own Government, the Irish Republican Government, has accorded to the troops of the Provisional Government, while not recognizing its authority, belligerent rights, and he demands reciprocity on behalf of himself and his fellow-prisoners.'

The senior Free State officers judging him had dealt summarily with his case. No verdict was delivered on 17 November. Childers, whose face still bore marks of bruising from the rough handling of interrogators after his capture a week earlier, was driven off in an armoured car to the cell at Beggars Bush Barracks, which also happened to be the General Headquarters of the Irish Free State Army. His warders, as he admitted, were uniformly 'kind and considerate' to him. Having failed to extract from him by violent methods any admission of alleged misdeeds or any information about his former comrades-in-arms, the authorities appeared prepared to let him wait for death in relative comfort. Then the wholly unexpected had happened.

In a Dublin evening paper that same day, 17 November, Childers read with dismay that four unnamed soldiers, Republican volunteers like himself, had been marched out and executed at dawn. Their offence, like his, was that firearms had been found on them when captured. Childers had no fear of facing death himself. He had repeatedly risked his own neck as an air navigator in British uniform against Germany and her allies during the First World War. What shocked and sickened him now was the certain knowledge of the bloody consequences that would flow from this policy of callous vindictiveness. Thus, when his lawyers implored him to apply for a writ of Habeas Corpus himself, so that the lives of eight other unnamed men also under sentence might be spared, Childers pondered anxiously, swallowed his scruples, and reluctantly agreed. It was, he realized, because the formal application had at last come before the Master of the Rolls that the Free State authorities could not yet oblige him with a firing squad at dawn. For the vestigial relics of discarded British justice continued to operate nominally in the

Irish Free State, and would so continue until the new constitution came into force.

'How strange it all seems', he wrote, resuming the interrupted letter to his wife.

I think of those four lads and the eight unknown, linked with me in this postponing business. Oh, I hope it is understood that my honour is unsullied, that I refused to act alone, and that by direction – orders – that I have acted at all for the eight as well, as it was by direction in the Black-and-Tan war in capital cases. There was no possibility of a test save on my specific case.

He would have felt dishonoured if in consequence his own life had been spared; but, for reasons best known to themselves, the military authorities had set his mind at rest on that score by sending him a copy of the official report on his trial. It pleased him to reflect that

there is no earthly chance of our executions being stopped, or at any rate my own, owing to my sworn statement and I don't recognize the Provisional Government and claim treatment as a prisoner of war. So I say to myself 'Then let it come quickly and end the tension,' and then again 'But it is giving me another day on earth with Molly, able with my mortal senses to commune and write to her and hear about her as I have from the Dean.'

They had allowed the Reverend Edward Waller, a friend since Childers's boyhood and now the Protestant Dean of Kildare, to call on him. Childers's request for visits from his wife, from the pro-Republican Capuchin priest, Father Albert, and from Dr Browne of Maynooth, had all been refused:

He tells me they drove him up to you [after Waller's first visit to the death-cell] in the Adjutant-General's car – good of them. He gave me your message and it was something to see and touch the hand of someone who had seen you and touched yours. He was very kind and nice, said at the end that he supposed I would not care to have him say a prayer. I said 'Pray – we are all one. In such a case as this there is no theology.' He said a simple and beautiful prayer, we two on our knees. He is stopping up in town on the chance of being allowed to come here before they execute me.

Childers could not trust himself to describe to his wife the contempt he felt for the remarks in the Dáil of that ill-disposed Free State minister, after Labour members had expressed their shocked concern at the judicial killing, without parliamentary consultation, of the four unnamed soldiers. An assiduous reader of such newspapers as were permitted, Childers was so upset by the slanderous references to himself that for the next twenty-four hours of grace his colloquy with Molly had to take second place. First, he asked for more writing paper. Then he composed this detailed and considered rejoinder. In due course, it was smuggled out to friends by one of his lawyers:

I wish to draw serious attention to the following matters. I was tried by a military court, sitting in camera, on November 17th. The sentence was not given out and I have not yet been informed of it. On the day of the trial, November 17th, there was a debate in the Provisional Parliament on four executions which had taken place that morning. In the debate Mr Kevin O'Higgins, Minister for Home Affairs, is reported by the *Irish Independent* to have made the following statement:

'Kevin O'Higgins, Minister for Home Affairs, said they should consider the end in view when the State or the Government took such action. This particular punishment was not vindictive. It was taken because it was necessary to take action of that kind if the Nation were to live. It was taken in the hope of deterring those who are killing the Nation. The Nation's life was worth the life of many individuals. If these were merely average cases it might perhaps have been because it were better at the first to take average cases, to take cases which had no particular facts about them to distinguish them from the cases of thousands all over the country who were bleeding the Nation to death. *If they took as* their first case some man who was outstandingly active and outstandingly wicked in his activities, the unfortunate dupes throughout the country might say that he was killed because he was a leader, *because he was an Englishman,* or because he combined with others to commit raids.'

I draw attention specially to the last sentence. . . . To the minds of all readers of newspapers, to the minds of the deputies present, the words 'An Englishman' would be taken as meaning me. I am the only member of the Republican Party or Army to whom the name 'Englishman' has been applied. It has been habitually, though incorrectly, applied to me, and often before by Mr O'Higgins, who, in a speech some months back, made I think in the debate when the Parliament authorized the Military, called me 'the able Englishman, who led the irregular movement', or words to that effect, and said I was bent on the total destruction of Irish life, statements which were untrue and grossly unfair.

When his speech was made on November 17th, my case, so far as I know, was still *sub judice*. . . . No evidence was adduced at my trial to show that I was outstandingly active or outstandingly wicked in my activities. Nothing was produced by witnesses beyond my identity and capture and the possession of an automatic pistol. . . . I understand that technically, at any rate, military courts are wholly under the Army and that the civil authority has no control over them – or rather has delegated its control to the Army – but Mr O'Higgins spoke as though he himself were, as a member of the Government, responsible not merely for authorizing the Army to execute but for the policy of actually carrying out particular executions at a certain time. . . . The impression left on the mind was that so far from the Army having sole and autocratic discretion, the policy of carrying out executions was a Cabinet matter in which Mr O'Higgins himself had a voice as well as General Mulcahy [Minister of Defence]. So that, in addition to the possibility of adverse influence upon the minds of those delivering or at any rate officially reviewing my sentence, it seems possible that public reference to my 'outstandingly wicked activities', not a word about which was brought in evidence against me, would prejudice the case and show bias in the decision.[3]

Childers the wordsmith, the rigid logician, the impulsive idealist, the romantic patriot, the recent arch-propagandist of the Irish Republican cause in a bitter war of brothers, had come to accept too late how passionately his enemies hated him. His notoriety on the battlefield, they asserted, was positively diabolical. Too long cut off himself from the real world, except through the columns of selected and censored newspapers, he could cling now only to the slender hope that future generations of Irishmen would read his testimony and judge him with detachment. It astounded and distressed him to learn that ministers as intelligent as Kevin O'Higgins and Ernest Blythe could have absorbed their own propaganda. They obviously believed, or pretended to believe, that Robert Erskine Childers, the non-combatant staff captain responsible only for countering the war propaganda of the Provisional Government, had instead blown up the transatlantic cable station at Valencia, organized the few successful rebel counterattacks in the Limerick countryside, and masterminded a campaign of wilful sabotage elsewhere. The assumption

of Childers that the Irish Cabinet rather than the Free State Army
had already reached a unanimous decision on his death was
equally accurate. Indeed, according to Mr Ernest Blythe, the last
surviving member of that Cabinet, 'it was a quick decision – and
rather ironically it was the much-maligned O'Higgins, arriving
late, who held us up by arguing in favour of finding some other
way; since no alternative deterrent existed, O'Higgins had to
concur'.[4]

On the British side of the Irish Sea, one politician of renown
had meanwhile vehemently condemned the prisoner. On 11
November, the day after Childers was arrested in the corridor
outside the bedroom of his Barton mother's home at Glendalough, Mr Winston Churchill had declared in a speech at Dundee:
'I have seen with satisfaction that the mischief-making, murderous
renegade Erskine Childers has been captured. No man has done
more harm or shown more genuine malice or endeavoured to
bring a greater curse upon the common people of Ireland than
this strange being, actuated by a deadly and malignant hatred
for the land of his birth.' The words had cut the condemned man
to the quick, as has been shown above in the early passages of his
farewell letter to Molly. Childers referred to Churchill's words
again as 'another indirect factor' which must have influenced the
minds of his enemies.

'To speak thus of an untried man when your words carry
round the world is grossly indecent, and would be a gross contempt of court if I were being tried, literally, as a "renegade" in
England for "murder". But Mr Churchill speaks more than as an
Englishman. . . . He has had personal charge of carrying out the
Treaty for his Government, and has been in constant and intimate association for that purpose with the Provisional Government and especially, among others, with Mr O'Higgins' . . .

Despite the pain of knowing that all slander and ignominy must
go unrefuted until long after his death, Childers steeled himself
against despair by reopening his soul once more to Molly:

November 22nd. Another day. Oh my beloved, I long to die and feel
you longing it too. Why should fate have chosen me for this? – To have

to compromise personally in the general interest and in the general policy in this case of the death penalty as under the Black-and-Tans! Oh I hope our friends will understand. Even now I cannot speak my thoughts to you for fear the censor may not allow it. It is no longer a case of life and death for me. Plainly the judge will dismiss the case and I shall be shot and probably the others too. It is a question only of my honour and when I read the thing in cold black and white and the case for the other side against me, I cannot control a shuddering . . .

5 p.m. I have seen an evening paper and liked what dear old Comyn [Mr Michael Comyn, KC] said, but the judge would not let him explain fully why *I* came to be party to the action, saying, materially, I suppose, that he would only hear argument on law. My request, made yesterday, to see my solicitor again has not been granted. So I have been unable to give any fresh instruction. Have been allowed to receive a cablegram from Henry [Childers's elder brother] – I enclose. It touches me because – well, I never expected it. He hated even Home Rule and must have detested all I have been doing for twelve years past – and then this climax. I have a note for him . . .

November 23rd. 7 p.m. Yet another day and the last. The case [before the Master of the Rolls in the King's Bench] ended as I expected. That it should have been useless to the other eight men is sad, but regrets are useless. I only hope that my memory will not be clouded and so hurt you my beloved. – I have just been told it is to be tomorrow at 7. Asked to see you. Told 'not at present' – a hard answer because ambiguous. In case proceedings at my trial are never known I meant to say that (NOTE TO CENSOR: IF THE FOLLOWING IS OBJECTED TO PLEASE OMIT PAGE) I asked all the witnesses questions to show that a shooting-fight in the passage outside my door, when taken, would have endangered two women there, and that is why I didn't use my pistol and only tried to force a way through. They admitted it was the fact. Normally, of course, I should have put up a fight. The pistol was in my hand. . . . Beloved, I am here only in a strange, figurative way. My spirit is with you and I will be with you always . . .

Pacing up and down the guardroom this last hour (how many miles I have paced there these last few days) I have been retracing and reconstructing passages in our lives these wonderful nineteen years. I mean continuously, I have been doing it off and on subconsciously all along. The lighter things are so exquisite – the drive at Rapallo and the rows (the *frutte di mare*?), one at Perugia, do you remember how you were *desillusionata*, the careers with the bullock, one at Florence and at Boars Hill and Glendalough. Each field and gate I remember – and you, love, browsing while I dug. And the enchanted adventures in the yacht – do you remember the night on the way to Finland and the overwhelming mystery of the heavens and the marvellous Danish fiords, and above all the Howth gun-running days and nights – and the storm and the run back to Holyhead and peace. And the tremendous things – that night on the lake, the crisis of our lives, and the hour that followed vision [when] you redeemed and consecrated me; mother's inspired mothering; Daddy's death; the coming of Erskine and Bobby; your operations; the decision to leave the House of Commons; the decision to join the Republic; the partings and meetings in the Great War; the crisis of the Treaty and this civil war. And all through, how do I see you? There are no words for it, the syllables stumble – oh God that they would let me clasp you once more! – but always serene, selfless, heroic, pouring out your rays of love like the inexhaustible radium not only upon me but upon all, invincible in your mastery over pain – feeding, lifting, inspiring, teaching – oh but all this is poor words . . .

The guard was relieved at eight and the men going off all said 'Goodbye and God bless you' and I to them. They wanted souvenirs but I have very few – the books you sent and some signatures. It will be the same with the present lot in case I am not able to record it: all privately and infinitely considerate. So we 'Children of the universal Mother' touch hands and go our ways in the very midst of this way of brothers. This is all disjointed but you will not mind. I have read in the paper some captured IRA letters with comments. I can only say, thank God I am dying, thank God. I never sought not to, and now I *leap* to it . . .

It is 6 a.m. You would be pleased to see how imperturbably normal and tranquil I have been this night, and am. It all seems perfectly simple and inevitable like lying down after a long day's work . . . . I enclose a lock of hair. Smile now. It must be washed! . . .

Childers had no need for the traditional hearty breakfast. There were so many Irish friends, on both sides, to be remembered to; and 'so few English, alas', that the pen was still between his fingers when the Dean of Kildare and the prison commandant came to summon him. He just found time to add:

Now I am going. Coming to you, heart's beloved, sweetheart, comrade wife, I shall fall asleep in your arms, God above blessing us – all four of us. Erskine. [2]

The Chief of Staff's office grudgingly complied with the prisoner's final request: to face the executioners' bullets nearly an hour later than specified, so that he might see the sunrise once

more. The squad stood at ease as the short, spare figure of
Childers limped across the square, ahead of the escort, to pass
through a gate in the main barrack wall to a prisoners' recreation
yard beyond. The firing party was waiting. Whispering to the
commandant, Childers suddenly detached himself from his
escort and moved slowly down the line of riflemen like an in-
specting officer, stopping momentarily in front of each man to
shake hands. If there was nobility in that natural gesture of forgiveness, the man who made it seemed at once to regret its possible effect on simple soldiers with a harsh duty to perform. He
tried to wave away the proferred bandage for his eyes, but the
sergeant-major insisted and bound it on very tightly. Then the
Englishman drew himself up and spoke his last words on earth
to the squad:

'Take a step or two forwards, lads. It will be easier that way.'

Childers gave the prearranged signal and the volley rang out,
shattering the stillness of that damp, new November day. His
bullet-riddled body slumped to the ground while startled pigeons
scattered overhead. Waller, the Protestant Dean, was not alone in
his feeling of sad wonderment. For he noticed the hands of
riflemen furtively wiping away tears when the word of command
was given and the squad marched past him into Beggars Bush
Barracks.[5]

The Irish Provisional Government thus wiped out the unlikeliest
of all revolutionaries even in that tragic land of turmoil and
endless paradox. Ministers had persuaded themselves, wrongly as
time would prove, that the execution of Erskine Childers would
serve the cause of Irish freedom by discouraging others: deter-
rence by bullet would surely bring defiant rebels to their senses.
In fact, Childers was only one of seventy-seven men whose deaths
in the next few months inscribed fresh names on the roll of IRA
martyrs. Yet the case of this 'damned Englishman', as the first
President of the Provisional Irish Free State Government, Arthur
Griffith, once called him to his face in the Dáil, has remained a
tantalizing source of mystery and confusion on both sides of St
George's Channel, and throughout the English-speaking world,
from that day to this.

For there was something at once wayward and ludicrously Christlike about the outlook of this son of an Ascendancy mother and an English intellectual father, something which had occasionally led Whitehall to regard him balefully in his climactic revolutionary phase as a man who was betraying England, his native land. Yet Erskine Childers's reputation equally gave rise in the country he had adopted only in the fiftieth year of an intensely adventurous life to suspicions that he might well be a double agent working for the British. The enigmatic spirit of Erskine Childers had always led him bit by bit to extremes; and if others shrank from accepting the conclusions of his hair-splitting logic, he did not and could not. In the words of a contemporary who loved him for his intrinsic goodness, while foreseeing to what ends the arrogance of such logic would lead him: 'It was his sniff that got him killed.'[6]

David Robinson and Frank O'Connor, however, touched the root of the matter in acknowledging that Childers was still more ill-advised to heed the call to arms in so chaotic a war of brothers. O'Connor's description of the extraordinary scene at Macroom, the rebel army's headquarters for a brief spell after the Republican evacuation of Cork, without a fight, in the high summer of 1922, deserves to be quoted at length:

'David Robinson, who had retreated in excellent order from Ballincollig with horses and field kitchen, gave us lunch on the lawn before Macroom Castle. It was a queer party on the lawn before the castle with its crude Renaissance doorway; David Robinson putting everyone at ease exactly as if he owned the place; members of the hungry disbanded army looking on; and exotic-looking women with queer accents arriving from Dublin with despatches, warning us that the members of the Free State Government were determined on killing Childers. He was talking to Hendrick and me when one of them came up and said earnestly: "You know, they will kill you if they catch you, Mr Childers," and he turned away and said wearily: "Oh, why does everyone tell me that?" Robinson was the only one who took the report seriously. He realized, as we didn't, that in a family row it is always the outsider who gets the blame. He took Hendrick and myself aside and asked if we would join him in hiring a fishing boat at Bantry and putting Childers ashore in France! To me it sounded like all the adventure stories of the world rolled into one, and even Hendrick, who made a point of not being demonstrative, looked enthusiastic. But we got a cold reception when we tried to explain Robinson's fears to members of the staff. "*Staff-Captain* Childers is under my command," said one of them, pulling rank on us, and though probably no one but Robinson suspected it, Childers' fate was decided that afternoon'. . .[1]

It hardly mattered anyhow. For Erskine Childers, if invited, would certainly have refused to go. The streak of stubbornness in his proudly romantic nature ran deep, reinforcing the zealous faith of a revolutionary convert who seemed to thrive on misunderstanding. George Russell believed that Childers's first and worst mistake was entering Irish politics; yet, allowing for 'AE's' understandable desire not to hurt a grief-stricken widow, the letter he wrote to Molly Childers shortly after the execution did underline one facet of a complex character which only a mystical poet could have perceived:

'I think there are souls who imagine all that they are going to do before they are born and who – from that altitude – can see more clearly the moral effect of their deeds in their own spirit and on their country; and with such self-predestined characters there is no argument which can stay them . . .'[7]

None of his remaining friends sought to write an epitaph for Childers. They were merely seeking, perhaps too soon after his death, to account for a twentieth-century mystery that has so far not been solved. The purpose of this biography is to unravel the riddle of Erskine Childers, once and for all.

1. THE BOY

Tragedy, never a respecter of age, class or status, first struck at Erskine Childers's heart when he was a small, helpless boy just a month past his sixth birthday. A happy childhood has, of course, no history. Yet it is worth noting here that in later years, when a sublimely good marriage had transformed him in spirit and outlook, Childers was fond of declaring that life had begun for him only in his thirty-fourth year. He was mistaken. For the facts contradict the romantic assertion. Indeed if a distinct point of departure can be established in the doom-laden career of Childers, it must be traced back to the chequered years that preceded and followed the death of his own father on 25 July 1876.

Like most grown men looking back, Robert Erskine Childers retained only disconnected and fragmentary recollections of his early childhood. He remembered it as a period suffused by a bewildering sense of uneasiness. This was especially true during the lingering illness of a parent whom he had loved with filial devotion but knew only as a shadowy presence. Mainly by piecing together the asides and scraps of adult conversation not meant for a Victorian child's ears, the precocious boy could dimly appreciate the increasing worries of his mother, to whom he would remain firmly attached by stronger threads of memory. To the end she hoped against all reason that her husband would throw off his chronic 'chestiness'. She would have wished away the bronchial infection eating steadily into his dwindling stamina, causing him distressing and uncontrollable bouts of coughing. Fortunately, perhaps, Robert Caesar Childers's ancestors had bestowed on him a mental toughness and a splendid indifference to fate which would one day characterize the behaviour of his own younger son under stress.

No matter how restlessly he tossed all night, disturbing the household with his wheezing, the scholar would be up early next day preparing himself for lectures and university meetings, or settling down without complaint to his work on the Pali dictionary in the book-lined study downstairs. Even when their second son first saw the light of day on 25 June 1870 Robert and his Irish-born wife, Anna Barton, might have been excused for silently wondering how the baby would ever surmount, unaided, the severe handicaps which had already begun to weigh them down. Nobody, least of all the husband's redoubtable father, the Reverend Canon Charles Childers, would have dreamed of accusing them of mere self-indulgence in producing a child every eighteen months for wealthier kinsmen to support. Besides, it had not quite come to that, so far. For Canon Childers's eldest son and heir was already earning a reputation in academic circles as one of the leading Orientalist scholars of the day; and he was still only thirty years old.

The names given to the new Childers baby at his christening lacked originality. That his father should choose to call the boy Robert went almost without saying. The decision to add Erskine, for good measure, sprang from the good-natured insistence of the mother. Anna Barton came from Glendalough, County Wicklow. She was descended from a long and quietly prospering line of Anglo-Irish landowners, wool-smugglers, slave-runners, merchants in wine, soldiers and lawyers. There were innumerable Roberts on her side of the family, too, including Robert the Bruce if one pushed back far enough through the thickly intertwined upper branches of the gigantic ancestral tree. One single Erskine, however, stood out above the rest, making all his Barton descendants feel distinctly proud of the pedigree. This was Thomas, born in Edinburgh halfway through the eighteenth century, while the Childers were still managing their estates and breeding their race-horses near Doncaster in Yorkshire; and Thomas Erskine had risen to become Lord Chancellor of England and one of the finest advocates ever to speak at the Bar.

His forensic skill in securing the acquittal of Captain Baillie, the Lieutenant-Governor of Greenwich Hospital, on a seemingly indefensible charge of criminal libel, had been matched by equally spectacular defences, in turn, of the court-martialled Admiral Lord Keppel and of Lord George Gordon, the instigator of the notorious Riots. Something of a maverick in his political sympathies, Thomas undid much of the favour he had won in high places by openly supporting English 'friends' of the French Revolution. His acceptance of a retainer from Tom Paine led the Prince of Wales to relieve him of the office of Attorney-General. Nevertheless the judicial authorities had to swallow their bile and admit that his speeches on behalf of Paine, Frost, Hardy and Horne Tooke were brilliant in the extreme.

Many loyal hearts were grieved when the Prince of Wales later revived an ancient office and appointed Erskine his Chancellor in 1802, a deft move which threw the recalcitrant counsel into the arms of the establishment. Raised to the peerage and the woolsack four years later, Erskine quickly grew bored and retired into private life. He was only fifty-six. He sired eight children. The youngest of his four daughters, Mary, married a Master in Chancery called David Morris; and Thomas Erskine's granddaughter, Frances Morris, was wooed and won in 1830 by Thomas Johnston Barton, the Master of Glendalough House, Wicklow, and the father of Anna. Was it altogether surprising that she, in turn, should have handed down to her second son, Robert, the resounding additional name of Erskine?

By contrast, the ancestors of Canon Charles Childers had been solid, landowning Yorkshire gentry since the early sixteenth century. The first occupant of Carr House, the fine country home which remained the family seat for the next two hundred years, was Hugh Childers, a successful banker, who became mayor of Doncaster in 1604. Like the Bartons, the Childerses had originally emerged as small squires of East Anglian stock. Only one member of the family, Leonard Childers, had acquired national fame, not as a politician, a writer, a lawyer or a soldier but as a bloodstock breeder. Spurred on, no doubt, by friendly rivalry with his St Leger neighbour at Park Hill, Leonard produced and trained a hunter which, because of its exceptional courage and speed, was transferred to the turf and eventually purchased by the Duke of Devonshire. 'Flying Childers' won the Five Hundred Guineas at Newmarket in April 1721, and according to family legend the horse once ran the Beacon course – a distance of 33 furlongs, 138 yards – in the record time of seven and a half minutes.

The Canon's father, Colonel John Walbanke Childers of the Light Dragoons, had served as ADC to the Duke of York in the Flanders campaign while Thomas Erskine was pleading eloquently at the bar for miscreants who befriended the King's enemies. Of Colonel John's five children, all sons, two took holy orders, one bought a commission in the Army, another joined the diplomatic service and the eldest, also called John, married the sister of a neighbouring Yorkshire squire who was to become the first Lord Halifax. Prosperity poured on the Childers family when, in 1797, Colonel John gained the hand of Selena, the youngest daughter and the co-heir of Sampson Lord Eardley. In her veins ran good Sephardim Jewish blood. Rowland Gideon, her paternal grandfather, had fled to England from persecution in Portugal before the close of the seventeenth century, setting up in London as a merchant and money-lender. Rowland's son, Sampson, did even more to consolidate the Gideon fortunes. One of the founding fathers of Jonathan's Coffee House, from which the Stock Exchange later developed, he was a skilful financier whom Walpole did not disdain to consult in times of embarrassment. Because he clung to his Jewish faith, Sampson was disqualified from receiving any title or honour; only when his son, following his mother's expedient example, was baptized into the Church of England did this young Etonian earn the ennoblement denied to his father, taking the title 'Lord Eardley'.

None of these hereditary factors distracted the Reverend Canon Charles Childers, perhaps the most powerful single influence on the brief London childhood of his grandson, Erskine. At Eton and Christ Church, Oxford, this aspirant parson had proved himself a tasteful classical scholar. With no desire to teach, no temptation to enter politics, he had no ardour either for service as a soldier. Of a somewhat indolent disposition, Charles could hardly have been described as a young man aflame with desire to spread God's Kingdom on earth. In this respect he differed from his closest friend, the solemn William Ewart Gladstone, with whom he shared a love of learning and little else. Though not averse to new ideas, Charles considered that Gladstone's earnest enthusiasms were liable to lead others astray. However the pair remained good companions at Oxford and corresponded for years afterwards, the final parting of the ways coming, not without recrimination, when in his first term as Liberal prime minister Gladstone introduced a Bill to disestablish the Church of Ireland. The break took place barely two years before the birth of Erskine Childers.

Because Eardley's delicate health obliged him to seek an incumbency in the sun his rich and well-connected mother helped him to secure the chaplaincy to the small, select English colony at Nice on the French Riviera. Eardley, who had married his first cousin, Maria Charlotte, died in office there prematurely, leaving an only son, Hugh, and was succeeded as chaplain by his brother Charles. Shortly after graduating at Trinity College, Cambridge, Hugh had settled in New South Wales where he held various administrative posts, finally being instrumental as a member of the first Cabinet of the State of Victoria in introducing the secret ballot. His heart, however, had never really left England. So when he returned to London at the age of thirty as Agent-General for Victoria, Hugh Childers decided to stay and enter English politics. As far as Uncle Charles Childers could see from his sinecure at Nice those politics appeared to be definitely of the wrong colour. Contesting the Pontefract seat in the Liberal interest at a by-election, the Canon's nephew defeated his Tory opponent and was returned to the House of Commons in 1860.

Robert Caesar Childers admired this older cousin's unaffected panache almost as much as the Canon deplored it. The latter, on his rare visits to London, refused to speak to any relative so intimately associated with the accursed Gladstone. He was inclined to blame Hugh's eccentricities on his immigrant Sephardim ancestors, wholly overlooking the Gideon blood throbbing in his own veins. He often boasted quite illogically that Dulcibella, his own wife, came of impeccable English stock, since this daughter of Sir Robert Chester, he alleged, could trace back her line to the troubled times of Edward II. The foreign-sounding 'Caesar' part of the Chester family name had been passed on by a certain Sir Julius Caesar, the son of a physician who had arrived in England from Treviso, near Venice, in 1550. His skills came to the notice of Queen Mary who appointed him her personal doctor. A volume of his recipes can be seen to this day in the

B

Sloane Museum. Precisely why Canon Charles Childers thought so highly of the Chester–Caesar connection, and so little of the Jewish Gideon strain, must be ascribed to an element of unreasonableness in his nature which was also handed on to his descendants.

These, then, were the mixed antecedents contributing whatever qualities of mind, heart and physique Robert Erskine Childers assimilated at birth. What worried the family at the christening was the sickly state of the baby's young father. The symptoms of what was still a fatal affliction, tuberculosis, were already suspected by Anna, Robert's wife, when their second son, Robert Erskine, joined a two-year-old brother, Henry Caesar, in the first-floor nursery of their town house at 60 Mount Street in the heart of London's elegant Mayfair district.

Robert's marriage to Anna Barton, whom he had timidly proposed to after a short acquaintance, had brought him profound happiness. The couple tried not to look too far ahead, accepting each day as it came; and in his ground-floor study at home the new child's sickly father worked away assiduously at the roots of the language and sacred literature of Ceylon. Some of the letters he wrote to his parents while serving as private secretary to Sir Charles McCarthy, the Governor of that country, emphasize a born scholar's fascination with the ancient tongue of the eastern sages: 'A Buddhist priest now gives me lessons. . . . I get on with him very well though he does not speak a word of English. . . . I am working hard and steadily and hope to pass creditably. . . . I have also spent a week in a Singhalese village.'

With the homesickness of an immature and unambitious young man who had come to dislike the routine as much as the climate, he had no compunction in telling his parents how deeply he missed them. The chance of being soon reunited with them, not at Nice but in Colombo, disappeared when Canon Charles Childers declined an episcopal mitre:

'I am sorry you did not accept the bishopric of Colombo,' his eldest son admitted. It would have been 'a capital thing',[1] especially if the old man had decided for once to follow Robert Caesar's unwelcome advice and rule the diocese in celibate splendour until the others joined him. Unquestionably the main obstacle was the worsening health of the Canon's wife. Their son had already been invalided home from Ceylon and was slowly recuperating when she took to her bed and died of a fever in 1865. The grief he felt slowed down his own recovery, causing his philosophical father considerable anxiety and intermittent annoyance. So the son never took kindly to his father's casualness in swiftly courting the mature widow of a clergyman and marrying a second time.

Robert and Anna Childers lived quietly in their Mayfair home. They had a housekeeper, a cook and a parlourmaid. For the care of two baby boys upstairs, there was a nurse in residence. They enjoyed entertaining but avoided the resplendent social whirl of mid-Victorian London. In 1869, the year before the birth of Erskine, their second son, the young couple duly celebrated the publication of Robert Caesar's first learned article on the abstruse subject in which he had started to specialize in Ceylon. His English translation of the *Khuddaka Patha* appeared side by side with the original Pali text in the *Journal of the Royal Asiatic Society*. Never before had a portion of the Buddhist sacred books appeared in print; and, encouraged by the accolades of oriental scholars elsewhere in Europe, the young man undertook a far heavier commitment. No grammar or dictionary of the Pali language then existed in any European tongue, and without these essential tools the contents of the age-old Buddhist books could not be made available for the study of comparative history and religion. 'These works', in the words of the scribe who assessed them later in the *Dictionary of National Biography*, 'Childers set himself energetically to work to supply, though the task was one from which any scholar less enterprising and less self-sacrificing would have shrunk.'[2]

The first volume of this monument to a frail young man's dedication was issued in 1872, when Robert Erskine Childers had learnt to walk. The India Office responded to the acclaim of the Pali dictionary by offering its author the nominally paid post of a sub-librarian; the academic world presently honoured him in a more fitting manner by creating a new Chair of Pali and Buddhist studies for him at University College, London. Fellow-orientalists in Paris, Berlin and elsewhere acknowledged his learning; by a singular irony of timing the much coveted Volney Prize for excellence in scholarship was unanimously awarded to him by his French peers in 1876 during the closing weeks of his life. He descended briefly from his bedroom for the forced gaiety of a family party on 25 June that year when Robert Erskine, his second son, reached his sixth birthday. Only Anna, his wife, shared the anguish of knowing that the doctors could do nothing more for him.

It was exactly a month later, on 25 July 1876, that the scholar died suddenly in his sleep. Anna was not at his bedside, to her intense remorse. For in his desire to avoid needlessly burdening anyone with vicarious pain, her husband had slunk away to a quiet hotel at Weybridge and spent his last hours alone.

Even at this relatively short distance of time, a mere century later, it is extremely hard to convey how superstitiously irrational were many otherwise sophisticated Victorians on discovering the presence of an infectious disease in the family. That these maladies, nearly all of them still incurable, persisted in killing off annually tens of thousands of the Queen's loyal subjects without respect to age, sex or class, had long been an accepted truth. That the majority of Victorians, in the memorable phrase of Florence Nightingale, 'deserved the VC for cool intrepidity in the face of facts' cannot be gainsaid either. Of the infectious diseases then prevalent, tuberculosis seems to have been the most feared, was certainly the most misunderstood and was possibly the least well treated.

'Up to quite a recent period', declared Dr Arthur Ransome in the Milroy Lectures of 1890, 'not only was consumption supposed to be incurable, it was also regarded as almost inevitable. Families in which existed a taint of the disease were supposed to be doomed to lose some of their members from this cause. Insurance offices still refuse to enroll upon their books those who have lost a father and mother from the disease; and even collateral relatives, who have died from it, are judged to have an influence upon the candidates for assurance. The fate of the consumptive himself was also generally regarded as hopeless.'

In drawing attention to what he called 'a strong family predisposition' to contract this and other ailments, Dr Ransome, a Manchester consultant who specialized in the diagnosis and treatment of the disease, likened the deadly inroads made by tuberculosis to those of leprosy in an earlier age.[3]

When Anna Childers finally admitted that she had been nursing her tubercular husband without reference to them, the family elders could not contain their indignation and horror. Nor did they condone her guilt. How could she prove that Robert had not passed the infection on to her? What could she say to persuade them that it had not been passed on again to her own two small sons and the three baby daughters who had joined them in the nursery, one by one, at eighteen-month intervals? Anna found it impossible to convince them that her one aim had been to spare Robert the intolerable wrench of being separated from his work and his loved ones. The temptation of confiding her fears to these relatives who would, quite heartlessly, have consigned the patient to an isolated room in a remote sanatorium, was one she had wilfully spurned. She was prepared to pay that same price, and pay it Anna did. Before the end of 1876, the family elders informed her that the only practical, dispassionate solution of their dilemma was one which she, in her headstrong fashion, had wished on herself. The five children must be separated from her. She must go into a home for incurables.

It was a brutal verdict. There is no evidence, however, to suggest that the spirited Anna sought to resist it, much as she may have resented the concerted views of medical advisers and family elders. The effect on her two eldest boys, and especially on the highly sensitive Robert Erskine, was harsh and lasting. A note in his own handwriting by Robert Barton, the younger cousin of my subject, testifies how much it affected every member of the rising generation, both at the time and in long retrospect:

'It was a tragically poignant incident. . . . The goodbye to five small children was for ever, and she could not even hug them as they left for Ireland and the guardianship of their uncle and aunt, Charles and Agnes Barton. Imagine what it must have been to the children but still more to the doubly stricken mother. She was going herself soon; her late husband had opened the door first; yet already it was closing on her little brood, none of whom she would see again. Could any loneliness be more heart-rending?'[4]

For the young Robert Erskine Childers there was one mild recompense in crossing the Irish sea to Glendalough House, after the sorrowful, yet unnaturally restrained farewells. The parting stirred in him the precocious hope that he might slowly acquire his mother's undimmed passion for this, her childhood home. His first glimpse of the long, plain greystone eighteenth-century mansion in its beautiful setting of rolling lawns and woodland helped him to understand why she had always loved the place so much. It did nothing to ease his longing for her. The Bartons did their best to compensate for the loss, bound as they were to this branch of the Childers family by double ties of kinship, since Aunt Agnes Barton happened to be the dead Robert's younger sister. The boy struck both Agnes and her husband at once as an unusually grave little fellow for his tender years, reticent about his own feelings, solicitous for his three younger sisters and largely indifferent to his own comfort. They were somewhat concerned to hear the dry, hard cough that sometimes racked his thin frame during the early months at 'Glan', the Barton diminutive for Glendalough. From the start they treated him more as an adult than as a child of six. How could he find words in return to confide how terribly that living death to which his mother had been condemned would continue to haunt him? Already the boy was teaching himself ways of steeling his heart, for everyone's sake, so as never to betray his thoughts.

Though he secretly went on grieving for his mother, and never wholly succeeded in reconciling himself to her banishment, the idyllic beauty of his new home helped to blur and gradually soften the edges of his sadness. More imaginative and thus more vulnerable than Henry, his elder brother, he could not overlook the simple fact that, though already an orphan in all but name, letters from his mother in England still arrived regularly. Each one reduced him to the verge of tears which had to be stifled back; and to every letter he dutifully composed the kind of stilted reply which would cause no fuss and rouse no comment. The burden of thus responding fell on him virtually from the beginning.

When Uncle Charles Barton had still been courting Aunt Agnes Childers, the boy's parents were both alive. Agnes, the

Canon's fifth daughter, frequently visited the London home of
her ailing brother, latterly with the man to whom she had become
engaged. It was not many weeks after their marriage at Laragh,
Co. Wicklow, in the vicinity of Glendalough, that the five forlorn
children descended on them. No arrangement could have been
more natural, since the two families were thus doubly held together. At the time the ageing master of the house, Thomas
Johnston Barton, was still in charge of affairs, though it was
already clear that responsibility would soon pass to Charles.
To some extent, therefore, the unfamiliarity of life in a new land
had been relieved from the start by the thoughtfulness of this
aunt and uncle.

Under a governess in the large, bright room where the children
of previous generations had studied, the two Childers boys
learnt the rules of English grammar and the rudiments of
arithmetic. Both could already read and write, and Robert
absorbed the rules with the speed of a child possessing a tidy mind
and a prehensile memory. Henry, in contrast, had less appetite for
mental discipline. He was in his element showing off his physical
prowess, whether it happened to be riding, running or sailing
under supervision on Lake Dan, the deep, dark, expanse of water
within walking distance of the house. A special 'Childers' room
was set aside, furnished with tables and chairs and a book-case
rescued from their parents' old home in England, to be theirs
exclusively. The families shared the same Tory and Unionist
prejudices, worshipped the same God in accordance with the
accepted tenets of the established Church, and held the same
suspicion of all pointless changes in the natural and political
ordering of things. For good measure, the Bartons felt naturally
superior to the native Irish over whom the Lord had set them in
authority.

Being a quiet boy and an intent listener, Robert Erskine
Childers picked up a store of loose information and impressions
of this odd country called Ireland that had become his home.
And because custom prescribed that children should be seen, not
heard, he learnt by observation the social differences between
himself and the sons of men who tilled the land or otherwise
served the family. His Barton uncle made reasonable allowances
for his English nephews and nieces, seeing that they said their

prayers at night and sometimes reading to them from Grimms' fairy tales in the nursery before the oil lamps were put out. They were exceedingly fortunate orphans in comparison with countless others in humbler circumstances who had no generous soft-hearted relatives to fall back on; yet 'Perk', as the lisping Childers girls nicknamed their favourite brother, still reserved a corner of his heart for the gracious, sickly ghost of his dying mother. The boy grew up secretly pining for her. Perhaps, one day, when he was sent to school in England, there might be a chance of meeting her once more before she vanished forever.

Henry's name had already been entered for Harrow. In due course, after spending three years at a private preparatory establishment, he went there in 1881. The Bartons had decided meanwhile, after consulting the knowledgeable Canon and other relatives, that a recently opened public school near Hertford might be more suitable for their younger nephew, who lacked the robustness of the older boy. Haileybury had once been a training college for young men aspiring to join the East India Company, and for many years the gloomy Dr Malthus had instructed students there in political economy and modern history. The college had closed its doors after the Indian Mutiny and the demise of 'John Company', but in 1862 it began life afresh in response to the growing demand of local English middle-class parents for the education of their children at fee-paying public schools. The first headmaster of Haileybury happened to be a friend of Canon Childers who clearly thought highly of a fellow-clergyman who had once worked under the great Dr Arnold of Rugby. Besides, Robert Erskine's mother wanted her younger son to attend a school that incorporated the best of the service in which her late husband had spent himself. It had also been warmly recommended by her friends, the Kenyons, whose judgment she valued because of their close ties with her favourite poet, Robert Browning. If these were poor reasons for ignoring the superior claims of Eton, Harrow or Rugby, they were good enough for the Childers and Bartons who, despite ample means, preferred to make their own mistakes in such matters.

So while Robert Erskine was in his second year as a boarder at

Bengeo, a preparatory institution on the outskirts of Hertford, his name was entered for Haileybury. By contrast with the Harrow reports on Henry, those from Bengeo on the younger boy confirmed that he had a natural aptitude for English literature, for writing compositions and for absorbing Latin and French grammar. Only two of his letters from Bengeo survive. Written to Dulcibella, the sister to whom he was most attached, they disclose nothing of his true feelings. The tone is mannered in the lighthearted way of a nine-year-old schoolboy only too well aware that the grown-ups would be shown what he had written:

'I hope you are quite well', the first letter began.

I hope that proud Ashrocka and beautiful Patch [ponies] are quite well. I hope your garden is getting on all right. Did you go to Church this morning? Tharpe [a school friend] has not come back yet. We had a game of cricket yesterday and unpacked our playboxes. Give my love to Wicks and tell her that the vest I put on this morning smelt most awfully of mice.

No hint of his own troubles was thinkable or permissible to a boy so hypersensitive to the likely effects on those he loved. 'My darling Baa,' he wrote to Constance, his youngest sister, in 1884 towards the end of his first full year at Haileybury. 'Thank you so much, darling, for that lovely bookslide you sent me – and your letter. I liked them so much.'[5] Significantly, he was still using the black-edged notepaper he had procured nearly six months earlier when the headmaster had summoned him one bleak, January day and gently broken the news of his mother's death. It abruptly reopened the inner wound which had been festering since his father was buried eight years previously. An orphan now in fact as well as name, he did not seek to share his sense of desolation with anyone else.

The head boy of the school, Hubert S. Arkwright, fortunately proved to be specially protective. For Arkwright happened to be the last but by no means the least effective link in the chain of helpers who were responsible for Robert Erskine Childers's presence at Haileybury:

'I had a large, comfortable study as Head of the School,' he recalled. 'I was asked by some friend or relative of the Childers family to keep an eye on Erskine as he was delicate. Of course, I gave him the run of my study and he seemed to enjoy it and became great friends with my younger brother, Ernest.... He was a delightful boy and I grew very fond of him. . . . I think [Erskine] had two sisters who were also delicate and it was my mother [née Kenyon] who, I think, helped them to get abroad to a better climate. . . .'[6]

Thanks to Arkwright's determination to shield him from bullying, the first year passed in unnatural peace. It was not altogether a happy situation: particularly during his second year he was put severely to the test by seniors as well as contemporaries who had looked askance at someone unfairly enjoying a favourite's privileged treatment. Childers endured the ordeal without flinching, and it was probably during this awkward period that he forced himself to overcome the gnawing fear of trying to clear unfamiliar obstacles. In order to build up his stamina, for instance, he obtained permission to go off alone on long, arduous cross-country runs from which he would often return, his lungs almost bursting, his pale face red, and his clothes drenched with sweat.

'Who is the present Chancellor of the Exchequer?' the master in charge of Childers's form, Lower Middle One A, had asked the class at large within days of the start of the first school year. Nobody seemed to know the answer. Whether through bashfulness or an inbred reluctance to draw unwanted attention to himself, Erskine Childers held his tongue until Mr M. Vaughan, drily refusing to accept such collective ignorance, finally pointed a finger at the smallest and most sickly-looking of the new boys:

'Don't you know, Childers, who the Chancellor is?'

'Yes, sir. My cousin, Mr Hugh Childers.'[7]

Undoubtedly Childers enjoyed himself most during his final year. The change for the better in his mood was accompanied by an imperceptible change in his handwriting which became firmer and to some extent less consciously neat, as if by now his pen had to hurry to overtake his streaking thoughts. He had felt a thrill of relief, as he admitted to Constance, when selected to play for the first fifteen.

I now shine resplendent on the football field in red and white, the school colours. . . . Do you remember Henry and myself playing a football match with the men on the place [at Glendalough] against the Laragh men? Well, I have written a description of it which is coming out in the next number of the *Haileyburian,* our school paper; I am becoming quite a literary character, aren't I?[5]

Erskine's normal place in class was just below the middle, on average twelfth out of twenty; suddenly, he began to show his paces. Swiftly developing powers of concentration, especially in subjects sufficiently well taught to command his interest, gained him many prizes. He won the Brisbane-Butler award for Shakespearean criticism in 1888, the Pratt award for Greek iambics, the Hudson for his Latin prose translation, the Butler for an English essay, the Jackson for his study of art.

It is part of the conventional wisdom of the English public school system to claim too much on behalf of its sons. The vogue was followed by Ivor Lloyd-Jones nearly half a century later, when Childers had met his violent and tragic death. This devoted Haileybury friend and contemporary wrote that 'Erskine Childers' intention to devote his life to the service of his country [was] acquired not from his parents, who were dead, and not from his holidays, which he spent at Glendalough in the hills of Wickow, but from his years at Haileybury'. The evidence of Childers's schooldays indicates that he lacked that touching, conformist quality which warms the cockles of all headmasters' hearts, enabling them to utter the expected clichés on speech days. In fact, while slowly coming to terms with himself, Childers was already groping hazily for ideals of his own which the Haileybury establishment would probably have regarded as dangerous.

'I did climb with you to the Acropolis by the ancient way but I never got to the top,' he wrote some years afterwards to his great Aunt Flora.

What a mystery the growth of one's personality is. It is well nigh hopeless to distinguish native impulses from stucco crusts imposed by environment. . . . I believe I want action more than anything. It has always been best for me . . . [5]

The glories of Greek and Roman culture exercised only a limited hold over him during the closing period of his schooldays; the regime of Haileybury impressed itself on him hardly at all. While it certainly gratified his vanity to take his turn at reading the lessons in the college chapel, where, in accordance with the unbending ordinances of the Reverend J. Robertson, the headmaster, attendance at morning service was compulsory, Childers paid only lip-service to religion. The articles of faith to which his ageing grandfather, Canon Charles Childers, still subscribed, as if it were as natural a thing as breathing, simply stirred the sceptic in him. Being the tolerant kind of youth who would never dream of upsetting others by scoffing at or arguing with them, he prudently kept his own counsel. To what extent Childers had been influenced by the cruel decision of otherwise kindly relations, the Canon leading the rest in his capacity as a venerable old man of the cloth, to condemn his mother to the living death of banishment, it is impossible now to say.

One early and tolerant witness to his religious scepticism was the Reverend Edward Waller, a Church of Ireland clergyman who was appointed Rector of Annamoe, the village at the entrance to the Glendalough estate in 1888. As Childers's only surviving cousin, Robert Barton, put it: 'Edward and his wife were very good friends of "Perk's", in spite of the disparity of their views on religion and politics. Both being goodnatured men, they agreed to disagree and seldom argued hotly. Perk's views were more liberal than those held by the Wallers, but it was Edward Waller whom Perk was allowed to have present at his execution.'[4]

He became attached to Haileybury without being enslaved. He loved the spaciousness of its buildings and the unspoiled rural beauty of its grounds. Of course, like everyone else he found fault with the spartan amenities and the sometimes harsh routine. Without drawing unnecessary attention to himself, Childers endured uncomplainingly occasional beatings by masters and prefects in his early and middle years until, as an upper sixth-former invested with prefectorial authority himself, he broke out of the expected mould. The unwonted tolerance and kindness he displayed towards younger boys in trouble was exceptional.

'We all liked him and thought him absolutely fair,' recalled one of his younger contemporaries at Haileybury. 'As a matter of fact I don't think that he fraternized with anyone though he was friendly to all. He was peculiar in liking to go for long runs by himself. We were a little daunted by his extreme conscientiousness, to which we hardly dared to aspire, but we chiefly admired the way he played his games, particularly as three quarters for the school fifteen.'[8] Because he detested cricket as a fussy and unnecessarily tedious ritual and had neither the taste nor the skills to make a batsman, bowler or fielder, Childers set solitary fashions of his own 'pounding across the fields in all weathers' and 'sailing strange craft on the Lea', in the phrase of another school-fellow.

'I see around me nothing very interesting', he wrote in the facetiously mannered vein that characterized most of his letters home.

The prefectorial staff of Trevelyan House is grouped around the fire in various attitudes of repose or deep study, their noble Head is wrapt in dignified silence as he pens this epistle to his youngest sister, alas how unworthy a recipient; There is a general sleepiness beginning to pervade everything – Ah! there's eleven striking. Time all decent citizens were in bed, and as I count myself among the latter class, – and as, moreover, I cannot go to bed while I am writing a letter, of necessity I must say Goodnight.[5]

Whether or not Haileybury left its mark on Erskine Childers by implanting that 'steady intention to devote his life to the service of his country', he certainly used a red-hot poker to brand his initials on the door of his study for successive generations to note his passing. Until Trevelyan House and its small, single rooms were converted into one long dormitory some years after his own death, there it remained.

Perhaps the most valuable clue to the developing mind of Childers during his final year can be seen to this day at Haileybury in a large, leather-bound volume known as 'The Headmaster's Book'. Containing the best work done by the school's senior pupils, it includes one prize essay of striking maturity by the boy whose cousin was one of Gladstone's ministerial colleagues. Hugh Childers occasionally visited him at school; and the politician's discreet advice may well have influenced Erskine's decision early in 1887 to apply for admittance to Trinity College, Cambridge, where the older man had once read law himself.

As First Lord of the Admiralty, Chancellor of the Exchequer, Chancellor of the Duchy of Lancaster, and later Home Secretary in successive Liberal administrations, Hugh Childers was always worth listening to. His political ideals were invariably rooted in common sense, a quality his orphaned second cousin envied and tried to reproduce in the prize-winning essay. Written to coincide with the centenary of the storming of the Bastille and the outbreak of the French Revolution, its clarity of style revealed both an infatuation and an impatience with all the Conservative certainties voiced by the great Disraeli in his recent heyday:

'All eyes were turned towards one country: that country was France. There thought was freer, more logical, more aspiring, than elsewhere; consequently development was more rapid, perhaps too rapid. A growing feeling against terrible social and political evils; a growing appreciation of the natural rights of man, which must some day revolutionize the world, culminated in one conclusive and premature effort, that great landmark of European history, the French revolution. . . .

'In England we see a colder, more practical race, building up by slow degrees a constitution for itself, unconsciously respecting its own conservative sentiments, never violently offending them, hard-headed for the present, cautious for the near-future, but, above all, never ignoring the past. Hereon rests the whole theory of modern conservatives; they recognize, and truly, what have been up to this, and under different conditions, English characteristics; they respect and take full account of them; but what they do not always see is that now more than ever, "Forward" is the word; that in accordance with a general law even those deep-rooted characteristics must change and develop; that this rationalistic spirit, and this democratic spirit, and this mighty evolution of the individual, are all unconquerable tendencies, and that to thwart them is ruin. In a word, they must realize that glorious, incomparably glorious, as our past has been, yet the requirements of the future advance a still higher claim, and call for their attention with a more terrible earnestness.'[9]

It would be tempting to conclude that Childers's plea for a Tory renewal was inspired by something more than the competitive resolve to win the school's English Essay Prize. Yet he gave few signs to his friends of any passionate concern with the political controversies of the day. Perhaps the one positive result of his intermittent exchanges with his Gladstonian kinsman Hugh was to make him question the easy assumptions of all his Conservative mentors, notably those in the family. Just as he had learnt through a childish feeling of injustice to doubt the fundamental teachings of the Established Church, so now that same sceptical distemper was extended to the natural rulers of Britain, the Conservatives. So far as Ireland was concerned, Erskine had no sympathy with the early Home Rule predilections of Hugh, regarding the Lords' rejection of Gladstone's first Bill to give Irishmen a limited measure of self-government as inevitable and right. Yet when, in February 1886, the Haileybury debating society discussed the topical proposition 'that Home Rule would be the best form of government for Ireland', and turned it down by a majority of nearly two to one, the inscrutable Childers did not once open his mouth.

From his study of the classics Erskine Childers had derived pleasure and not a little moral comfort. The stoic virtues of the ancient world evoked an instant response in him. With a pen between his fingers, he could abstract himself from the present and relive the epics and tragedies of legendary heroes, so that a touch of true delicacy may be glimpsed in these last two lines of one of his translations from the original Greek which the headmaster also pasted intact in the prize-winners' book:

No, to none has heaven given perfect happiness below
Each must have his share of sorrow, each must taste the cup of woe.

The words meant much more to the translator than a faithful echo of some ancient poet's thoughts: they sprang from the heart of a companionable, sensitive, slightly lonely but already self-sufficient youth who could well have adopted them as his personal motto. A certain dry detachment of mind, combined with an unfashionable belief in the force of destiny, kept him aloof from all but a handful of his contemporaries. Cheerful, approachable, outwardly conventional but inwardly at odds with the sumptuous and superbly self-confident Victorian world in which he had attained the use of reason, Erskine Childers baffled many who crossed his path. Companions in the upper sixth like Basil

Allen and John Hodgson had no doubts as to where their futures lay. Indeed the majority of them ended up as churchmen (including one bishop) or civil servants. The ideal of serving God and country, a logical and no doubt loftier extension of the lessons taught to aspirants in the days of the East India Company, produced impressive results at Haileybury. Because a single year's difference in age invariably tended to create a chasm even between boys in the same house, younger pupils such as Patrick Cadell, later to become a distinguished member of the Indian civil service, and Lionel Curtis, destined to deal blow for blow with Childers in the prolonged duelling of the Irish Treaty exchanges in London some thirty years afterwards, hardly knew him at all in their school days. For Erskine Childers, despite an understandable tendency to dark introspection, had not yet come fully to terms with life.

His mood turned to one of fleeting euphoria when, in June 1889, he heard on speech-day that he had won a place as an exhibitioner at Trinity College, Cambridge. Hugh Childers, in congratulating him, could not conceal his delight; Erskine's sisters were as pleased for him as his guardians, though his elder brother, Henry, who had already left Harrow for Sandhurst, could not forbear expressing ironical regret that Erskine should have inherited such an unreasonably large portion of their late father's awesome powers of concentration.

2. THE DABBLER

During the long vacation of 1889 Childers suffered an unnecessary accident which ruled out all rugby and long-distance running for the future. He spent most of the summer in Ireland, leaving Glendalough in August for an exhausting trek across country to the wilds of Connemara. Because he neither sought nor desired companionship on these walking expeditions, Childers tended to disregard ordinary creature comforts, on occasion throwing elementary caution to the winds. So completely was he enraptured by the untamed scenery as he marched down empty roads, over moorland tracks and round the edges of treacherous bogs, toiling up steep hillsides and letting gravity speed his steps down the far side into green valleys, that he had no thought to spare for the weather, still less for his own health. Armed with map and compass, he pushed on steadily, intent on covering the thirty miles a day he set himself.

One day it rained so hard that he was quickly soaked to the skin. Foolishly he persisted, struggling on through the downpour according to plan. Then, instead of stripping off every stitch of his wet clothes at the inn where he spent the night, Childers sat up talking. The chill he caught was bad enough. That he threw off, but he felt less happy about the pain in his left foot. When at last he reached Glendalough neither hot baths nor treatment with liniment seemed to relieve it. The family pronounced him an idiot. Specialists in Dublin could not promise to mend the damage. In the words of his cousin, Robert Barton, by now a bright, observant boy in his eighth year: 'Erskine, it turned out, had contracted sciatica. The nerve was affected to such an extent that nothing could be done to cure the lameness. As a result he went through the remainder of his life with that limp.'[1]

Lloyd-Jones noticed it at once when Childers first walked into his room at Cambridge after the holiday, but the victim was not in the least sorry for himself.

'It's nothing,' he said. 'It may stop me playing rugby, but it can't prevent us walking together.'

In one of his mildly teasing letters to Dulcibella at the start of the University term, he excused himself on grounds of pre-occupation with the unfamiliar for his dilatory performance as a correspondent:

If you had any idea of the bewildering amount of things to be done, purchases to be made, unpacking to be got through, exams to cram for, you would forgive me. I have just been for a long walk with Jones by way of clearing myself up from stuffiness. This is the first afternoon we have not had an exam. I am sitting in the Union, a de-lightful sort of club with every convenience, which I expect I shall patronize largely.... I'm on a strictly economical tack and don't order any extra from the kitchen except for visitors and occasions! Mrs Juler [his landlady] offers to cook simple things for me like bacon, eggs etc. without sending to the College kitchens. After the exam I shop or work for the next one or visit fellows, then a simple lunch and another exam, then more shopping, reading, tea or visiting, and at 6.30 p.m. dinner in the College Hall. The chief point that strikes me about the latter ceremony is precipitate haste; the waiters conduct their operations with frenzied rapidity. Afterwards coffee at home, or with someone else, then working, letter-writing, account-making – bed.

A young man already well attuned to the discipline of a fixed routine, Childers went up to Cambridge determined to enjoy himself without neglecting his work. He was not in the least disturbed to be assigned lodgings at No. 5 Bridge Street, a short stroll from the Great Gate of Trinity through All Saints' passage. On the contrary, he cheerfully accepted living out as part of the entrance price that any sensible freshman had to pay. Erskine Childers, partly as a result of childhood sorrows, was developing into a reserved and rather abstemious character who, without being a prude, had no appetite for the ostentatious and riotous living in which richer and idler undergraduates indulged. Yet he made a number of friends outside the small tight circle of his Haileybury contemporaries, notably Walter Runciman, the son of a wealthy North Country shipping magnate, who gradually fired him with a love of the sea and the beginning of a lifelong passion for sailing, and Eddie Marsh, the future secretary and companion of Winston Churchill, whose wit, knowledge of art and unusually wide aesthetic interests, intrigued and captivated Childers. These two, together with Charles Trevelyan and Lloyd-Jones, formed a quartet of close comrades: without their inspiration the self-sufficient Erskine would certainly have become intellectually and spiritually the poorer.

By no means all the ghosts of Trinity's long past haunted him, pleased as he was to boast openly of his descent from Thomas Erskine, whom the College had once nurtured and now honoured as England's most brilliant Lord Chancellor since Thomas More. To what degree this subtle tie with a remote forbear indirectly influenced Childers's decision to stay on for a fourth year and read law after taking his Classical Tripos it is difficult at this late date to establish. The fact that he was not in the first rank, quietly acknowledged it, and settled for second class honours, may have helped to clinch the matter, since Childers lacked the will and the inclination, if not the patience, to teach. His still nebulous ambition, fostered by the example and advice of Hugh, his political elder and second cousin, was eventually to strike out and find a career in politics. He had no vices. His one addiction, then and later, was to poetry, in particular the writings of Trinity's most distinguished alumnus, Alfred Lord Tennyson, the poet laureate.

'Read the *Talking Oak*', he urged his sister, Constance:

It is simply charming. And read Ulysses. There are some splendid lines in it and every word is exactly the best and most beautiful one –

> 'The long day wanes: the slow moon climbs the deep
> Moans round with many voices. Come my friends
> Tis not too late to seek a newer world.'

These lines always send a strange thrill through me and are half responsible for any longing I ever have to desert civilization and 'wander far away – on from island unto island to the gateways of the day' – and so on. If ever I disappear for a year or two, you will know what sent me.[2]

The demands of university statutes and college rules were reasonably unexacting. He observed these with a casual grace.

Because he had always found true pleasure in books and in the society of students bursting with artistic and aesthetic lore which he did not possess, Childers had no difficulty in winning over his tutor, the gifted Dr James Glaisher. Nor did the Master of Trinity, Dr Montagu Butler, a still youthful and perceptive individual, fail to recognize in Erskine a more malleable spirit than the elder brother Henry, whose indifference to work under Butler's recent charge as Headmaster of Harrow had left much to be desired. Beneath the deceptively easy-going exterior there already burned in Childers, the Cambridge undergraduate, a fiery resolve to equip his mind thoroughly for life without abandoning the pursuit of simple, conventional pleasures. These, of course, in accordance with the strict public school ethos to which he subscribed with no regrets, did not include associating with young women.

Acquaintances and college dons assumed as a matter of course that, for any kinsman of Hugh Childers, the shrewd administrative factotum who had long served Gladstone, the choice of a career was already predetermined, despite the young man's noticeable allergy to current political controversies. The kindness shown by Hugh to his second cousin did not end with Erskine's arrival at Cambridge. Hugh Childers, as it happened, had known and corresponded with Dr Montagu Butler for many years and continued to pay him occasional visits. The young man liked and respected his kinsman less as a politician than as a person, though he also took pride in his social standing and the national recognition he had earned. When Disraeli's failing health had obliged the Tory leader to conserve his energies and seek elevation to the Upper House, a false legend had been propagated in the Childers clan. It concerned Hugh's reminders to the Queen and Mr Gladstone about an imaginary family precedent that enabled Disraeli to get his earldom. The facts did not bear out their wishful thinking.

'I have been told', Gladstone wrote to Hugh Childers from No. 10 Downing Street on 27 October 1869, 'that, when a peer, he (your ancestor) was of the Jewish religion, which raises a constitutional point of some interest so that I do not write from mere curiosity when I beg you kindly to inform me whether there is any truth in the account thus given me.'

In his reply, Hugh Childers removed the Prime Minister's uncertainty without managing to destroy the family myth:

'One of my great-great grandfathers was a Jew, a Mr Gideon, who made a large fortune in the city and was confidential adviser of Sir R. Walpole, Mr Pelham and the first Mr Pitt. He guaranteed the rebellion loan of 1745, and for the following fifteen years was uniformly consulted at the Treasury on all financial questions. Mr Pitt offered him any honour he wished, but he steadily refused. He, however, accepted for his son (then a boy at Eton) a baronetcy, and the letter from the father to the son announcing this is a great curiosity. The son, so made a baronet, at (I think) fifteen, was Sir Sampson Gideon. But he was brought up as a Christian from infancy, to the great indignation of the Portuguese Jews of whom Mr Gideon was one.'[3]

What Erskine most admired about Hugh was his common sense, his robust optimism and his altruism. It was agreeable to discover, for instance, that he had drawn on his experience of North American business methods, as became a former chairman of the Great Western Railway of Canada, to introduce to Whitehall a strange device called the telephone. As for the development of Liberal policy towards Ireland, Hugh Childers's personal initiative proved to be greater and more decisive than either Gladstone or John Morley, the Grand Old Man's future biographer, would ever admit. It must be added that few of his in-laws paid him any credit either, so that even Erskine Childers's elder son and namesake, the late President of the Irish Republic, maintained that his father 'really owed nothing to Hugh in the growth of his own ideas on the difficult question of Irish freedom'.[4] As will be shown, the truth was quite different.

Childers's allowance was fairly generous, so he had few complaints. Such rituals as putting on a white tie for dinner parties and for debates in the Union were as natural as wearing heavy boots for country walks. They appealed to him as much as the scenery he would drink in on his long bicycle rides down country lanes, winding at speed towards the trackless, open fens. If it irked him to be no longer nimble enough to compete for his rugby blue, Childers soon hit on a simpler way of keeping his physique in trim:

'What makes you think I'm grinding myself to death with mental and physical labour, dear?' he enquired pointedly of his sister, Dulcibella.

Rowing couldn't hurt anybody. It is rather dull because it is such machine-like work, but for that reason isn't so very tiring. I often wish it gave one *more* exercise. . . . I chose rowing [because] if one does well this term, one gets rowing in the Lent and May terms. There is no football in those terms; and I don't play cricket and can't run now a bit . . .[2]

Surviving photographs of Childers taken at this period provide a startling contrast to the haggard, tortured likenesses of the man in middle age. The face of the boyishly slim undergraduate was round, if not exactly chubby. His upper lip was covered by a neatly trimmed moustache. He evidently smiled and laughed a good deal; and, despite his lame foot, regular rowing had helped to broaden his shoulders and harden his muscles. He gave the impression of being a goodnatured young man without a care in the world.

There was, he realized, a time and a place for everything: the Union every week, Trinity's 'Magpie and Stump' debating society on each alternating Friday evening offered outlets to sharpen his mind on the public controversies of the day. Childers had joined the Union at once; but he hardly ever spoke. Duly elected a member of the Magpie and Stump on 15 November 1889, at the very next meeting he proposed the notion 'that this house should petition Parliament in favour of the Channel tunnel'. In all forums dedicated to the exchange of ingenious or outrageous ideas, there are invariably speakers – and speakers. The University records show that Erskine Childers never ran out of steam yet seldom produced a single vital spark of originality. He was far too earnest in debate to let his imagination soar, let alone stand reality on its head. A respect for the facts held him immutably to the narrow path of logic. Charles Trevelyan, the future Liberal and Labour politician, happened to be the principal opponent of Childers's motion about the imagined advantages of a Channel tunnel. Trevelyan demolished, in four minutes flat, what it took

Childers fully quarter of an hour to develop in his dry, logically systematic manner. The motion was unceremoniously defeated. On the Irish Problem, Erskine Childers conformed instinctively to the family's Unionist line. When still a preparatory schoolboy, just past his tenth birthday, his stout, bearded kinsman, Hugh, had paid a brief visit to Glendalough in the course of an extensive fact-finding tour of the distressed districts of Ireland, North and South. In such a Unionist household, where the disruptive activities of their Wicklow neighbour, Charles Stewart Parnell, had long been frowned on, the visitor from Whitehall was not exactly at ease. His host, while maintaining the normal civilities, had made plain his own fears that Gladstone's kid-glove treatment of Parnell and the Land League agitators would lead to worse troubles. As for new-fangled Home Rule concepts of giving Irishmen a share in the management of their own affairs, that way lay ultimate disaster.

Perhaps the somewhat frigid atmosphere had induced the young Erskine to feel perversely for Hugh, the victim, though not for many years did he discover how original, practical and dispassionate had been Hugh's approach to the Irish question. Even as a Cambridge undergraduate he did not know or care why Gladstone, a firm upholder of the Anglo-Irish union until the dissolution of Parliament in 1885, had suddenly been converted to the cause of Home Rule. If it were true, as the family elders asserted, that the Liberal leader had 'ratted' on his own colleagues so as to win the support of Parnell, whose Irish Nationalist followers then held the balance of power at Westminster, the question left young Erskine cold. The fact that almost alone among Gladstone's colleagues Hugh Childers rejoiced at the Liberal leader's change of heart did not cause his young second cousin to rejoice with him. One Home-Ruler in the family was already one too many for comfort. A memorandum came to light, after Hugh's premature death in 1896, which demonstrated how deeply he felt the practical need for giving the Irish a larger say in their own affairs:

'Towards the close of the Parliament of 1874,' he stated, 'I began to be impressed with the hopelessness of getting through the work of the United Kingdom with one legislative body sitting at Westminster. I was present during the greater part of the long debates of that Parliament when Ireland blocked the way; and I was in the chair for half that all-night sitting in committee on the South Africa Bill, which clearly showed how an over-worked House of Parliament could be still more crippled in its powers of work.

'All this set me thinking whether time for adequately discussing at Westminster the often neglected affairs of the Empire might not be better obtained by relegating to inferior legislative bodies the purely local affairs of the three kingdoms than by artificial constraints on the liberty of debate, always distasteful to Englishmen, which had begun to be suggested in many quarters. . . .

'These impressions gained more and more power over me, and were strengthened by what I saw during annual visits to the United States and Canada: I had special facilities for watching the action of Congress and the State legislatures in the former, and of the Dominion Parliament and the provincial legislatures in the latter. Again and again I asked myself how it is that our race in the great Republic and in the greatest of our colonies requires and fully occupies all this parliamentary machinery (between forty and fifty legislative bodies, most of them with two chambers each), while we imagine that we can adequately transact the business of England, Scotland and Ireland, and the Imperial affairs of the whole Empire, with one Parliament only. . . .

'Before, however, making up my mind finally, I determined to visit Ireland again. . . . I returned to England convinced that in a plan of federal Home Rule lay the salvation of Ireland. Whether Scotland would demand the same (Welsh Home Rule had not then, I think, been heard of) I had no power to estimate. But that Ireland should be placed in the same relation to the United Kingdom as Massachusetts to the United States, or Nova Scotia to the Dominion of Canada, or Bavaria to the German Empire, seemed to me reasonable, feasible and highly expedient while, for Imperial purposes, the Union should be stoutly maintained.'[3]

Hugh Childers felt sure enough of himself to tell Gladstone in the autumn of 1885 that he intended to air these ideas as part of his campaign for the forthcoming general election. The Prime Minister, however, counselled caution; so Hugh Childers toned down the keynote speech on Home Rule, the first ever delivered

by any British politician in favour of a federal solution of the
Irish problem. It did him no good whatever. The Liberals held
on precariously to power but Hugh lost his seat at Pontefract to
a relatively unknown and untried Tory after twenty-six years as
the local MP.

The death of the Liberal member for Edinburgh South fortunately created a vacancy for Hugh Childers almost at once;
early in 1886 he contested and won the seat with a substantial
majority. Erskine was glad to see him back in harness, this time
at the Home Office; but slowly Hugh's satisfaction ebbed, since
he found himself almost completely ignored by Gladstone in discussions on the all-important Liberal plan for Ireland. Not until
March, when suddenly presented with a draft Bill prepared by
Gladstone alone, did Hugh bestir himself and threaten to resign
from the Government. Once assured that 'all the obnoxious
features of the Bill' would be struck out, Childers withdrew his
threat and agreed to speak in its support. He spoke in vain. When
the Commons divided on 7 June, Gladstone's Home Rule Bill
was defeated by thirty votes. The Liberals themselves were hopelessly split, Joseph Chamberlain and his faction having joined
forces with Lord Hartington and the Whigs; Gladstone yielded;
and in the subsequent appeal to the country the Conservatives
regained office under Salisbury. On the new Opposition front
bench Hugh Childers exercised a waning influence in preaching
to the unconvertible. It was small wonder that the soft heart of
Erskine, his kinsman, increasingly warmed to him. Heedless and
hazy he might be on the nuances of Anglo-Irish difficulties, but
the frustrated sincerity of the older man forced the younger to
listen and relearn the lessons of the recent past whenever they met.

To some extent Childers was that common phenomenon among
Cambridge undergraduates of his day, the mild-mannered
political and religious agnostic who had far better things to feast
his mind on than the muddled and often hollow aims of contemporaries who aspired to become the statesmen and churchmen
of tomorrow. The Union was their natural sounding-board. He
used it mainly for its amenities. Childers did not speak once until
the beginning of his third year, when he had become well-known
in the University and had shed any lingering inhibitions about
the repulsive sound of his own voice.

An insouciant ignorance, tempered by prudence, had served so far; but such qualities hardly sat well on a third-year-man who enjoyed writing and had been made editor of the *Cambridge Review*. Unlike the *Cambridge Observer,* a relatively shortlived if much livelier periodical to which his friend Eddie Marsh contributed regular theatre notices, the magazine demanded some awareness of what was happening in the outside world, sound judgment and a fair degree of organizing ability. These attributes Childers clearly possessed. Nearly six years after his death, on 26 October 1928, the *Cambridge Review* would celebrate its half centenary. It fell to the future editor to recall its purpose:

'The aim from the first was to act as "a journal of University life and thought", and the seriousness of its intentions aroused considerable scepticism. . . . A galaxy of literary celebrities such as *The Review* can claim is in itself a title to respect; to name but a few, Sir Edmund Gosse, A. C. Benson, G. K. Chesterton, 'F. Anstey', Rupert Brooke, Flecker, Sir Walter Raleigh, Quiller-Couch, E. V. Lucas, Erskine Childers and Archibald Marshall. . . . Childers [was] editor in the Michaelmas term of 1892.' The routine business of chasing likely writers for topical articles kept Childers abreast not only of all activities in the University but of significant events in the world beyond. Yet the months he spent in the editor's chair did not open his eyes to the glamour allegedly hidden away in the recurring crises of politics. Though he believed broadly in the predestined role of the British Empire, under the Crown, as a dispenser of freedom and civilized values among distant peoples who had not yet seen the light, he felt no compulsion to weigh the merits of Tory methods against Liberal methods in securing those ends. A few lines of Kipling could tell him more about the glories and the agonies of Britain's crusading mission than any number of dusty constitutional tomes.

A sensitive yet stubborn young man, he had privately resolved to make his own way as a prospective politician with the minimum of assistance from Hugh Childers, who had already announced his intention not to stand again for Parliament. The accidental beneficiary of Hugh's enforced leisure was, of course, Erskine, whose quickening interest in politics, combined with a reluctance to be rushed into the political arena, earned the old man's approval.

To what extent Hugh filled the gaps in the other's still sketchy knowledge of the Irish question must remain a matter of conjecture, but one crucial point did hold him. Hugh's endless reminiscing about the details of his threatened resignation over the Home Rule Bill of 1886, the fate of which had been quite predictable long before a divided Cabinet presented it and a hostile Commons rejected it, led Erskine Childers to wonder at Gladstone's mulishness in trying once more in 1892 to force through a thinly revised version of that unacceptable measure. Hugh Childers seemed to have no faith in it whatever. 'An old man in a hurry', was the label pinned on Gladstone when he asked the Queen to dissolve parliament after his Home Rule setback six years earlier. The controversial patriarch of eighty-two summers seemed to be in too big a hurry now to bother about any pitfalls. The second Home Rule Bill, which would have guaranteed Irish representation in the Imperial Parliament, fared no better than its predecessor. This time the Lords threw it out. For the sentiment of most Englishmen, Scots and Welshmen, quite apart from Ulstermen and Anglo-Irish Unionists, was strongly against it. Erskine saw no reason to disagree with Hugh Childers on that score. He would have thrown it out himself. It is oddly ironical that once again death and the pains of bereavement, factors of palpable significance in the early shaping of Erskine Childers's character, drew him closer to his older and wiser relative at this time. Charles Barton had died suddenly in October 1890, and Hugh's response had gone far beyond conventional expressions of condolence. Having originally put himself out to help Erskine after the death of the boy's father, he lost no time now in treating the young man with genuine paternal solicitude.

It was in the spring term of 1892 that Erskine Childers attained fleeting notoriety far beyond the gay confines of Cambridge through an unsuccessful but imaginative attempt to secure his election to the presidency of Trinity's Magpie and Stump Debating Society. He had been secretary and treasurer of that body in turn. As a rule, the final step to president was an uncontested formality. But, this time, a rival candidate came forward with the powerful backing of college dissidents who demanded that the appointment be put to the vote in a genuinely democratic way.

His opponent was a Scottish Tory dandy called George Hamilton-Gordon, a son of Lord Stanmore who had once served as President of the Union himself. An ex-Wykehamist of eccentric outlook, a good oarsman and a passable golfer, the rival candidate was also an amateur linguist then engaged in mastering Russian purely because it happened to be a difficult language to learn. Defeating Childers in a properly conducted ballot would, according to Hamilton-Gordon, be a much easier task. Securing fair play and a free vote did not constitute the sole objectives of the Hamilton-Gordon rebels. They opposed any would-be president who suffered from the long-windedness of Childers, a tedious man who never seemed capable of coming to the point. The posters and placards which appeared on walls and in windows all over the college proclaimed the fact: 'Which do you prefer? Mr Gordon's common sense or the intolerable gas of Mr Childers?'

To such provocative slogans the official candidate responded with a relatively succinct message of dignity: 'Vote for Mr Childers – the Constitutional Candidate and Legitimate Successor.'

The mock poll created quite a stir. Even the *Pall Mall Gazette*, a London newspaper which then exerted some influence, drew attention to what was happening at Trinity College, Cambridge, noting acidly that the Childers–Gordon duel had more to offer than the current English county council elections. Before the poll, the self-styled 'constitutional candidate' addressed one large and ribald gathering from the window of his room in New Court, and a second in the bar of a public house. Order was maintained by the chairman, a champion of Childers called Thomas Fisher, later to grace the bench of Anglican bishops. However, neither speeches nor witty circulars could cut the ground from under the feet of an anti-establishment rebel intent on destroying what he termed 'the gas monopoly'. When the votes were counted, Gordon won by a narrow majority, celebrating his triumph with a spectacular fireworks display in the Great Court of Trinity. No doubt because of the ensuing horseplay, which led to a few fines but no broken bones, the affair went down to posterity in the college annals as 'the Gordon Riots', 1892 style. The defeated Childers did not suffer unrewarded. Hamilton-Gordon, honour and pride satisfied, proposed that the unsuccessful candidate should be appointed his vice-president, a post specially invented for him. And at the end of the summer term Childers duly stepped into the victor's shoes. He would never be a Demosthenes or even a Gladstone; so said his friends. An ingrained distrust of the artificial flourish, of the appeal to the heart, of wit as a weapon, ruled that out. He was altogether too fair and reasonable. He always played the game in strict conformity to the rules – and he always lost it.

Yet certain matters almost too deep for utterance had the instant power of kindling his spirit so that his tongue and pen would spontaneously catch fire. When Alfred Lord Tennyson breathed his last in October 1892, mourned by the Queen, by the nation at large and by the more appreciative men at Trinity, his old college, Childers characteristically let himself go:

'There is nothing to grieve for in Tennyson's death', he assured his sisters at Glendalough.

His death seems to me to have just added the perfecting touch to his almost perfect life. . . . He just went out on 'such a tide as moving seems asleep, too full for sound or foam, when that which drew from out the boundless deep, turns again home'. You and I owe more to him than even we are faintly conscious of, I think. For my part there is hardly a good aspiration or a good motion in me which has not either been heightened or originated by him. Now he has died there seems no change – there are his words and his music still, only just with the added touch of perfection and consecration. Oh, I think such a life, such a life's work, and such a death are a treasure of unimaginable value to all English-speaking people. I send you one of the best personal records I have seen yet. It is by the musician Stanford and appears in this week's *Cambridge Review* which I am editing.[2]

In his heart of hearts, and without disrespect to Hugh or anyone else, Erskine Childers would, like Dr Faustus, gladly have bartered his soul for the loan of Tennyson's mantle of spun gold. Political ambition might be stirring slowly within him, but a thwarted poet with a romantic vision was struggling hard to get out as well.

'Childers has turned us all into fishermen,' Eddie Marsh informed R. C. Trevelyan in July 1894, some twelve months after Childers had gone down. A small group of Trinity friends were spending a week in Wales on a reading-party, one of those fashionable, late-Victorian intellectual distractions which is scarcely conceivable in the age of television. 'I had my first try yesterday and became perfectly brutal when I'd seen three trout knocked on the head. I was quite ready to put a worm on the hook, if I'd been asked to. I got one fish out of the water but (by no fault of mine) it awoke to its position before I could land it and rejoined its wife and family.'[5]

This isolated incident is only one of many in which Erskine Childers can be glimpsed, adding to the gaiety of likeminded friends, among whom, on that Welsh outing, was another called Bertrand Russell. Yet the same young Childers preferred at other times to walk alone, a remote and almost alien figure, buried in his own private thoughts. The burning of midnight oil in frantic preparation for his finals lay comfortably behind him as a memory. He could congratulate himself on the miracle of passing his Law Tripos and getting his degree. Ireland's country life, shared with his sisters, with his brother Henry, with handpicked friends like Lloyd-Jones, Walter Runciman and William le Fanu, appealed to him now far more than in his boyhood. He might well have been inhabiting an ancient manorhouse in the English home counties, so cut off was Childers from the ordinary people outside Glendalough's broad and well-marked boundaries. The place was an agreeable oasis; it was also an illusion of real Irish life, though that did not strike him for years to come. Thus he could hardly have been expected to notice, still less grasp the significance of, an event which virtually coincided with the defeat of Gladstone's second and abortive Home Rule Bill. This was the founding in Ireland of a new cultural body, known as the Gaelic League, by Douglas Hyde, a Protestant clergyman's son, and by a comparatively unknown scholar named Eoin MacNeill, their chief aim being to revive the ancient language and culture of their compatriots.

As he grew to manhood Childers felt himself to be Anglo-Irish in fact as well as in name. The adopted son of the Bartons thus became a sort of displaced patriot with his head in the clouds and his heart lost to that lovely garden of Ireland which lies below the sheltering flanks of the Wicklow Hills.

'"Perk" had a gentle disposition,' his cousin, Robert Barton recalled. 'He was considerate of everyone but could be very firm when aggrieved. He was always cordial in his approach to strangers as well as friends, and my general impression is that wherever he participated there was happiness and gaiety. My mother depended very much upon the advice and help "Perk" gave her (after my father's death) in solving the many problems that faced her, including decisions about our education. . . . When thinking seriously upon any subject, "Perk" was prone to go into a brown study and pay no attention to what was taking place around him. This concentration, known to us as his "vagueness", was so deep that his sisters could even induce him passively to accept another helping of food while he remained unconscious of their action. Once, when he came to and looked at his plate, he exclaimed:

' "Oh, how could you make me eat a poached egg when you know how I hate them!" '[1]

In returning to 'Glan', the childhood home of the mother he still mourned, Childers seemed almost to be returning to the womb. In bidding the enchanted place farewell at the end of a long stay, he had to pinch himself awake and rub the sleep from his eyes as part of the process of coming to terms with the harsher world beyond. Usually he had made the necessary spiritual re-adjustment by the time he was stepping off the mail-boat on to the quayside in England.

A lean, soft-spoken young man of twenty-three, who dressed well without consciously seeking to become a glass of fashion, Childers led an adventurous life in the imagination only because no other was practicable for the present. To a limited degree which would grow larger with time, he 'became what he beheld', in the sense used by Blake. From Walter Runciman, a wealthy young man of conventional outlook and tastes similar to his own, he had recently acquired an enthusiasm for sailing; from Ivor Lloyd-Jones, a paragon of concern for others, a vague yearning to serve his fellow-men, especially those worse off than himself; and from Eddie Marsh's circle of literary aspirants and aesthetes, which included traditionalists like R. C. Trevelyan and Maurice

Baring, and brilliant individualists like Bertrand Russell and later Lytton Strachey, had come the prospect of alternative if less easy worlds to conquer. While he admired Strachey and Russell for their caustic wit and knowledge, he preferred the wide-eyed innocence underlying the sophistication of Marsh, whom he would continue to cherish after losing sight of these more forceful iconoclasts. Meanwhile he had a living to earn and three sisters to encourage and maintain, since they had reached the age at which Glendalough and its rapturously sleepy mode of life no longer satisfied *their* inchoate hopes and longings. He formulated the plan of inviting them to stay with him in London, but only when he was in a position to support himself. His ageing cousin Hugh's repeated advice had not fallen on inattentive ears: a clerkship in Parliament appealed to him as a simple unobtrusive way of entering the political sphere by the back door. Thomas Erskine May, whom Hugh had once known well, was held up as positive proof that a clerkship could be a distinguished career in itself; but the young Erskine Childers saw it rather as the means to a higher end, that of sitting at Westminster as an MP.

So in January 1894 he crossed to London and enrolled as a student at W. B. Scoones, one of the best known cramming establishments of the day, in Garrick Street, just off the Strand. The place was bleakly functional and expensive. The victims of its force-feeding methods were mostly graduates like himself, driven to work for good marks and high places in competitive examinations to various branches of the Civil Service, including the Foreign Office.

'I was one of five competitors for a clerkship in the House of Commons,' wrote H. F. McClintock. 'We were all working together at Scoones. The successful one, who passed top, gaining the appointment to nobody's great surprise, was Erskine Childers. Among the others was a young man called Massingberd, and a sister of his later married General Montgomery from Blessingbourne, County Tyrone. Oddly enough, another sister of the same young man was to marry Montgomery's brother, a soldier who took the name of Montgomery-Massingberd and rose to the rank of Field Marshal and Chief of the Imperial General Staff between the two world wars.'[6]

Childers celebrated his success by renting and furnishing his

first home, a pleasant flat in the Temple at No. 2 Mitre Court
Buildings, a brisk fifteen minutes' walk along the Embankment
to his future place of work at the Palace of Westminster. Hugh
Childers would steal time from his duties as chairman of a Royal
Commission recently set up to examine the financial relations
between Great Britain and Ireland. He guided his young cousin
through the maze of corridors, showing him the sights of that
labyrinthine place and introducing him personally to the Chief
Clerk and the assistants in the committee rooms. It thrilled the
young man to test the chair behind the desk where he would soon
start earning his keep. The salary for beginners like himself was
not princely, but Childers drew a reasonably steady income from
private investments to eke out the modest £100 per annum on
which he would otherwise have had to manage.

'I wonder if, in your sternness with that business self of yours,
you could manage to visit us in Ireland in September, say about
the 12th or so,' Childers wrote to Walter Runciman. 'We should
be delighted to have you. I suppose you are starting yachting
now and I hope you will have a jolly cruise. Come South.'

It is clear from the letters that passed between them that
'Runcy' and Childers went cruising together whenever they could,
and that Childers had acquired his first yacht. She was called
Sheila,

a nice little eight tonner which we're going for a cruise in. We start
Saturday next, Herbert Jones with us, from Fort William at the top of
Loch Swinhe in the West of Scotland. . . . I didn't wire the idea because I thought it unlikely that anyone in your responsible (?) position
could get away at such short notice. . . . There is plenty of room on
board for four. . . .[2]

The passion for the sea grew apace, helping to placate Childers's
wistful if still fitful craving for adventure. He had quickly learnt
the essentials of good seamanship. If there were any substance in
the Gospel story, which he doubted, that the wind and the waves
on the storm-swept Sea of Galilee had become calm in response
to Christ's command, Childers had already grasped the simpler
truth that real sailors respected the elements and sensibly co-
operated with them rather than tilting madly against them. Basic
skills and sudden emergencies apart, the sheer pleasure he derived

C

from sailing stirred him to the depths of his being. It made him feel good to be alive.

A further extract from the letters he exchanged with Runciman portrays Erskine Childers in a more conventional guise, that of acting Anglo-Irish squire and country sportsman:

That camp of yours on the moors sounded delightful but I'm sorry the shooting was bad. We have had a very fair season – and finished with a drive the other day, in which we got fifty-three brace and a lot of hares.[2]

It would be a splendidly Wodehousean exaggeration to suggest that hares and game birds were incomplete, in Childers's book, without leadshot lining their innards. He was, of course, quite handy with a gun; and as one who behaved in accordance with the style to which he had grown accustomed, Childers did not disdain picking off birds in the season. He was imbued with the zeal of his late Uncle Charles who had the sound landowner's intuitive appreciation of how best to conserve – and when to destroy. Besides, game birds, even hares for that matter, provided food. And not only Runciman but Herbert Jones and many other visitors would say their goodbyes at Glendalough weighed down with parcels of the delicacies they had helped to harvest in the woods and fields of the estate.

Childers's initiation to parliamentary ways was as effortless as breathing. The minutiae of Westminster procedure fascinated him; the legal mechanics of turning complex ideas into formal Bills by skilful drafting was something which attracted his tidy mind. As one of the junior men in an office where polite informality reigned, he was expected to learn routines by understudying senior colleagues; and by the summer of 1895, within six months of arriving, Childers felt that he had mastered it to his own and their satisfaction. The one book of rules by which everyone swore, Lords and Commons and Clerks like, was the Bible according to Erskine May, that late friend of Hugh Childers, whose indispensable treatise on the *Law, Privilege, Proceedings and Usage of Parliament* had already reached its tenth edition in 1893, nearly half a century after its publication. Erskine May proved to be the supreme authority whom none could lightly disregard; so Erskine Childers applied his mind diligently to absorbing the Master's ritualistic wisdom. He gradually grew proud of belonging to a small select, almost exclusive team of experts; and the sense of pride quickened his wits and sharpened his competitive spirit. A clerk in any branch of the commercial or administrative world of the City or Whitehall usually connoted ill-rewarded and dull drudgery; but a clerk in this legal and procedural workshop of the Mother of Parliaments, still the most powerful democratic forum on earth, shed an untarnished lustre on the title which had been borne proudly in medieval times by learned men in holy orders. Sir Reginald Palgrave, Erskine May's latest successor, quickly took to Childers. A dignified and kindly person, who was something of a specialist on Cromwell, he also kept a protective eye on the two other recruits, F. C. Bramwell and John Scott Porter.

The atmosphere, a cross between an old-fashioned law office and a senior common room, was very much to Childers's taste. He did not mind the numerous inconveniences lurking behind the pretentiousness of Barry's architectural handiwork; the ornate arches, the frescoes, the statues of dead leaders, the numerous staircases, the long, high corridors, the tall, elaborately decorated ceilings, and the high book-lined rooms, all this impressive fussiness of design made it virtually impossible to keep out draughts. In the winter months coal fires roared away in big, open grates, sending most of the heat straight up the chimneys. If insulation against the cold was poor, the sanitary arrangements in what was then an all-male establishment, from which women were virtually barred, left still more to be desired. Chamber pots, embossed with the royal coat of arms, suitably screened off from matching china jugs and basins which lined the walls of the toilets, had to be emptied regularly by servants. Only the catering and dining facilities were on a scale, and of a quality, higher than is known nowadays.

When Parliament reassembled on 5 February 1895 Childers found a Liberal government under Gladstone's successor, Rosebery, clinging tenaciously if somewhat precariously to office. Though a newcomer he had little difficulty in first recognizing, then in getting recognized by, MPs on both sides of the House. Because the Prime Minister sat in the Lords, the leadership of the

Commons was exercised, seldom effectually, by the Chancellor of the Exchequer, Sir William Harcourt. No representative of the Childers family sat on any side of the House, the retirement of Hugh some three years previously having severed an ancestral link with Westminster which stretched back to the early years of the great Queen's reign.

Erskine Childers kept a detached eye on the current standard-bearers of Liberal policy. Bit by bit he pieced together the background of factious difficulties besetting the party's new leaders. He could well believe the common assertion that the mighty Gladstone's final departure from Westminster, as a stubborn old man of eighty-three, had created a fatal vacuum in which these relative pygmies were ingloriously floundering.

For the next few months Britain was ill-served by what amounted to rival governments and their squabbling partisans, Rosebery and Harcourt usually communicating with one another through papers conveyed in the red despatch boxes or through chilly exchanges in the Cabinet room. While the Prime Minister sought, without benefit, to interest his rival in curbing the powers of the Upper House, Harcourt fulminated against the 'forward policy' advocated by Rosebery's Foreign Secretary, Lord Kimberley. Indeed it was in a conflict of views on Imperial questions that the ill-fated Liberal administration at last foundered. The watchwords of 'Peace, Retrenchment and Reform' may have suited such old-fashioned followers of Harcourt as Morley and Campbell-Bannerman; they did not suit Liberals of the younger generation like Asquith, Haldane and Grey, who preferred Rosebery's new brand of Imperialism. They at least were not ashamed of the Empire and its challenges.

There were minor triumphs for Harcourt if not for Rosebery during the brief span of five months from the day of Childers's arrival until the Liberal administration petered out. The downfall of Rosebery came, without great lamentation, after a successful Tory motion to cut the salary of Campbell-Bannerman, the Secretary of State for War, for failing to equip the Army with sufficient supplies of cordite, the smokeless powder then in use. Two days after that adverse vote, which any stronger-willed Prime Minister could easily have reversed, Rosebery explained his government's inadequacy in one terse sentence: 'June 23

[1895], Harcourt came to see me spontaneously before dinner: the first time since I have been P.M.'

The Clerk's officials were shrewdly well-informed in assessing the weaknesses of political leaders and unfailingly discreet in preparing for the worst. The frustration Childers felt in having to scrap piles of unfinished parliamentary business, only to start afresh at the command of whichever party won the next election, was keen enough. His one consolation lay in the reflection that no better system of fulfilling the people's will had yet been devised. Lord Salisbury came back to power with a substantial majority of 152 seats, proof indeed of the fall from favour of his divided opponents. Nor was the new Prime Minister lacking in guile when it came to selecting his Cabinet. Into it he brought for the first time some Liberal Unionist leaders, including Joseph Chamberlain. They had forsworn their old allegiance because of Gladstone's magnificently stubborn if futile attempts to settle Ireland's problems at a stroke.

So for the next four years, from that memorable summer of 1895 until the outbreak of the Boer War in October 1899, Childers settled down to serve Salisbury and his ruling party with the impartiality he had been schooled to display towards Rosebery and his wrangling Liberals. On the surface he looked the part for which he had been cast, adapting himself naturally to think and speak in the detached manner of the well-trained Whitehall administrator until this became second nature. He differed from his colleagues in the Clerks' Department in one notable respect. So diffident was he about expressing an opinion, so given to plunging into one of his 'brown studies', that he acquired an understandable if undeserved reputation for absentmindedness. His closest friend in the small, compact group of assistants to Palgrave, the Commons' clerk, was a young man called Basil Williams who had joined the staff in 1893. Williams, later to become Professor of History at Edinburgh, remarked on these traits without malice or surprise:

'Few realized that the unobtrusive little man with the glasses and the sciatic limp was leading a double life. He let none of us know – until the information tumbled out one day, quite by chance, – that his weekends were spent in the Thames estuary, sailing singlehanded a scrubby little yacht.'[7]

His four years of formation at Westminster might have been more fruitful had he devoted himself singlemindedly to his work as a junior assistant committee clerk and as an aspirant to the political game. As it happened, the deaths in 1896 of the two family patriarchs, who, in their wholly contrasting ways, had been the most decisive influences on his youth and early manhood, set Erskine Childers free to go his own way. Canon Charles Childers, that ultra-conservative and somewhat fearsome spectre of childhood days, had died during February of that year, less than a month after the body of Hugh Childers was laid to rest among the headstones of their common ancestors. Not every link with the past had been broken; but there were signs of change which suggested that the salad days of the Victorian epoch might soon be drawing to an end.

By sending the able but ambitious Joseph Chamberlain to the Colonial Office, Salisbury had virtually guaranteed that there would be no peaceful solution of the political problems left unsolved for a generation in South Africa. Gladstone's granting of partial independence to the Boers in 1881, after the humiliating defeat of the British at Majuba, had settled nothing. The discovery of gold in the Transvaal in 1885 had since encouraged a wild rush of Britons to the goldfields. The Boers resented the presence of the prospectors; their President, Paul Kruger, had retaliated in 1890 by raising the period required for white immigrants' naturalization from five to fourteen years. Even Chamberlain had no illusions about the weakness of the British case for securing the voting demands of the immigrant prospectors. Whatever the nature of Britain's suzerainty over the Boers, it certainly did not include the right to determine the suffrage. The ludicrously badly organized Jameson Raid in December 1896 hardened the attitude of extremists on both sides, and thus the drift towards an unnecessary war gathered pace. In July 1899 Queen Victoria wrote in her journal:

'Lord Salisbury came to see me. . . . Talking of events in general he said the one cause of anxiety was the Transvaal. This country, as well as the Cabinet, excepting perhaps Mr Chamberlain, were against a war.'[8]

3. THE ADVENTURER

The life-style of any well-connected English bachelor of independent means could not fail to be more leisured and agreeable in the 1890s than in any decade since. Because Erskine Childers happened also to be conscientious and fairly abstemious, without being mean or prudish, he valued the freedom which his parliamentary duties and social status assured him. Not that he was totally oblivious of the wretched, poverty-stricken existence endured by so many of his fellow-countrymen. From his last year at Haileybury onwards, he had dutifully worked at the voluntary centres maintained by school and university funds in the slums of London's East End; and each brief visit, usually at the beginning of a holiday, stirred some fleeting awareness of the miserable conditions in which millions of the Queen's subjects lived and worked. However, Childers's sense of compassion lacked consistency. He was no reformer. Unlike his late cousin, Hugh, he had no real interest in seeking to ameliorate the lot of less favoured Englishmen. So he had no eyes or ears for the subtly changing social signs of a golden era which, so far as the privileged were concerned, had almost reached its end.

Conservative and Liberal governments in turn had taken to extending the functions of the nation-state by dabbling with problems as these arose, heedless of the pernicious doctrines of Socialism which had begun to be heard in the land. Such progressive writers and thinkers as Morris, Hyndman, Bernard Shaw, Henry George and the Webbs were anathema to Childers, for whom the expansion of the British Empire continued to represent the surest recipe for every awkward economic and social problem. And the knowledge that he himself earned his keep inside the building which monitored every heartbeat of the greatest family of nations on earth was comforting to his conscience as much as to his pride.

His bachelor flat in Mitre Buildings was not commodious. He let one of its spare rooms at first to a young barrister called Wilson, though this did not preclude its use by Walter Runciman or other friends when visiting London on business or for pleasure. Childers's low opinion of the Rosebery–Harcourt parody of firm government emerges in his correspondence with 'Runcy', as he always addressed his wealthy friend. During the Whitsun recess of 1895 he spoke his mind in facetiously contrived tones:

First let me thank you for your seductive proposal for a summer cruise. It would be most pleasant, but, of course I cannot speak for certain as to my ability to join you in July. If a dissolution came about it would be all right, but the normal Session lasts till the middle or end of August; and this impotent and moribund government (to which, I believe, you lend your valuable support!) seems to take continual, fresh fizzles of life and seems determined to stick in till it is forcibly kicked out.[1]

Childers disliked the social round. Though he never begrudged time spent on duty visits to relatives, and positively enjoyed staying with his 'Aunt' Flora, a distant relative of unexpectedly stimulating and provocative views on most topics, he often pined for the open-air life and suffered from claustrophobia when obliged to spend weekends among lonely and usually trying fellow-members of the Savile Club, which he had joined shortly after settling down in London. A typical product of his generation and upper-middle-class background in his adherence to the code of gallantry regulating friendships with the opposite sex, he was perhaps untypical in viewing with abhorrence the hypocritical Victorian convention under which young men could sublimate their carnal uges so long as they were not caught. Nevertheless Childers was neither a prig nor a prude. Nor had he any homo-sexual inclinations. Shy and slightly ill-at-ease with strangers, he had charm and polish enough to respect the ordinary courtesies without giving himself away. Only at sea as a part-time sailor did he come fully to terms with his own adventurous spirit and learn the full meaning of personal fulfilment, usually alone, sometimes with others.

The logbooks in which he recorded every salient detail of his many cruises bear the unmistakable stamp of a tidy mind. Only here and there do they hint at the sea fever which raged within him until involvement in war, and finally in revolutionary politics, transformed its nature utterly. His two closest Cambridge friends, Lloyd-Jones and Runciman, being similarly addicted, took for granted the adventurous streak in Childers. Not for many years did they recognize it as the key to his deceptively quiet character.

'Just before Easter I bought an 18-foot, half-decked centreboard boat, lug and jib, very cheap and lodged her at Greenhithe, a pretty little village near Gravesend,' Childers informed Runciman on May Day, 1895.

At Easter I started off down the Thames in lovely weather about midday, on the ebb, and got to Herne Bay by that night, anchored and slept. . . . Sleeping is not exactly luxurious as the only shelter is an awning rigged up to the crutched boom but in fine weather it is quite comfortable. . . . A couple of days later Lloyd-Jones and I and another chap sailed to Boulogne. She's a capital sea boat and behaved splendidly in a rather heavy sea and a strong easterly breeze. We spent an evening of wild dissipation in Boulogne and started home next day, but what with calms, heavy showers and changeable airs of wind we took 15 hours to get back, arriving at 4 a.m. . . .[2]

This was the first of many short voyages in home waters at weekends. The longest and most exacting were reserved for the parliamentary recesses of the summer. Runciman, the shipowner's son, already had a larger, sleeker and faster yacht of his own. The *Edith* reminded Childers of a floating palace; he disliked luxurious living when afloat; but his gratitude to 'Runcy' for encouraging him to buy the 'Mad Madge', his pet name for his own first boat, *Marguerite*, was lasting.

'I have been most remiss about writing,' he scribbled one hot August afternoon, crouched over his desk in the Commons and reliving his latest outing.

It is curious to be back in town after five weeks at sea. The people look pasty. The Members, too, naturally seem queer – so many new ones and such sober, solid gentlemen planting their broad feet on the writhing scorpion of Radicalism.[1]

Even before joining the Savile, Childers had become a member of the Royal Yacht Club, a pointer in itself to his weighing of the correct priorities. From an otherwise unknown Thames boatman called Bob Eales, a taciturn, tough but patient individual whose name crops up more than once in the logbooks, he had learnt the elementary do's and don'ts without which only the most fool-hardy landlubber would ever dare put to sea. As a raw deckhand on Runciman's *Edith*, he had already picked up the rudiments of navigating and of handling a large yacht; but singlehanded cruising demanded higher skills and greater practical forethought. His first venture 'from Greenhithe to Hole Haven and thence to the Nore' remained fixed in his memory for years.

A west wind and a sluicing ebb had whirled me down Sea Reach in company with a whole fleet of Thames barges, and it was not until I was abreast of Sheerness that I realized how much of my careless fortitude was due to the companionship of these homely, motherly craft. The sun was setting in a sombre haze, the estuary broadening into vast and dim proportions, and just at this solemn moment, one after the other my dusky friends hauled their wind for the Medway, and, like heavy-winged moths, faded into gloom. It was a fearful temptation to turn and follow them, but defeat at this crisis would have been irretrievable. That thought braced my nerves for the lonely night to come. Off the East Swale I lost the ebb tide, and off Whitstable all but a faint draught of my westerly wind. There was nothing for it but to anchor in the open. It was a black night with a mist just opaque enough to shroud all lights; the barometer was inclined to fall, and a swell beginning to roll in from the east was at once a presage of head wind to come and a source of much physical discomfort; I trimmed and hoisted my anchor light and tried to sleep.

The mast whined with every roll; with every roll there were flickings and slappings of ill-tautened ropes, which I had neither the energy to pacify nor the philosophy to ignore. . . . Now, as always, however, salvation came from the cogent need of immediately doing something definite, under capital penalties. Merely to light the binnacle lamp was to find a companion, benevolent, imperturbable, indicating the direction of the wind and the lie of the land and shoals. Enlightenment on these vital points heartened [me] for the wrestle with the anchor and sails, and when once the vessel has become a thing of life and action half the battle is over. . . . Short as a child's is the recollection of those evil night hours. Keen as a child's the zest for this reward, right-fully yours by conquest. And now for breakfast!

Childers's analysis elsewhere in the same account of the motives which spurred him on are equally self-revealing:

It is not easy to explain and justify this craving to those unacquaintd with the life of the sea and accustomed to regard all sport as a social affair. Of all forms of solitude, solitude on the sea seems to most people the most unnatural and repellent. At bottom, of course, its charm for the few lies in the very circumstances which condemn it for the many; in the stark loneliness of the conflict with a formidable element, in the voluntary abnegation of all human aid, moral or physical, and in the submission of man's own faculties to a merciless ordeal self-imposed, self-contemplated. Nobody is looking on; if there is no ridicule for blunders, there is no applause for triumphs. Without a rival to vanquish or a tribunal to satisfy, save that of a man's own soul, the competitive and spectacular elements inherent in most sports are totally eliminated. Absent, too, except for rare and brief intervals, is the sense of recreation pure and simple. Body and brain are continually at high tension. Emergency succeeds emergency, and you are exceedingly lucky if one can be dealt with before the next one is on you. Often they accumulate until they produce a situation so complex that there seems to be no solution. But the rude schooling of necessity ripens capacity and sharpens the senses amazingly. It becomes a more and more fascinating exercise to see how far you can disprove the old copy-book axiom that it is impossible to pay proper attention to two things at once.[2]

Childers's vigorous individualism in his 'other life' stood out in strange contrast to the self-effacing young man going about his duties at Westminster like any other grey, nondescript flunkey of average capability and ambition.

The Committee Rooms and corridors of the House of Commons formed the ideal place in which an onlooker of Childers's sensitive, romantic if somewhat retiring disposition could sometimes believe that he might be watching history in the making. In periods of crisis, whether international or domestic, the tension and excitement of Members seemed to pervade the very atmosphere, affecting even the most blasé of his colleagues. Basil Williams's keen sense of the dramatic, counterbalanced by a grasp of important issues which eventually turned him into a respectable historian, helped Childers in time to distinguish between real and false alarms. The latter was lazing on the Riviera at the end of 1895 when the grossly ill-timed and mismanaged Jameson Raid occurred. Writing to Runciman from the Grand Hotel, Nice, he sounded a note of patriotic defiance:

I am so excited about the African business that I can hardly think about anything else [he admitted]. What a damned insolent (puppy) that Emperor (the Kaiser) is, I would like nothing better than for him to land his dirty marines in Delagoa Bay, but the whole of Europe seems to be against us, not to mention America. Lloyd-Jones is here and we spend the day in telegram-hunting and Emperor-cursing and expressing a sublime confidence in the tenacity of the Anglo-Saxon race.

Nothing could have been more dangerous at that moment than a conflict in South Africa. For Britain was in the thick of an angry quarrel with the United States where President Cleveland, maybe with an eye to the Democratic Party's electoral prospects, had invoked the Monroe Doctrine to enforce an ancient and still unresolved boundary dispute between British Guiana and Venezuela. Not only was the former Concert of Europe dead: Britain stood alone in isolation from the continental powers, being on the worst conceivable terms with Russia, France and Germany. These last two neighbours, determined not to be out-stripped in the last lap of the colonial scramble for Africa, would have welcomed the distraction of immediate armed reprisals by the two Boer republics against Britain's South African enclave. Childers, despite the blissful escapism he betrayed whenever he left Westminster on sailing expeditions into the wide, blue yonder, suddenly felt himself involved in 'the African Business'. The defence of Empire had always been a family affair. Was not one of the late Hugh Childers's sons, Spencer, serving as a lieutenant-colonel in India? Had not another son, a young naval officer, been drowned when a new ship-of-the-line, *Captain*, had un-fortunately capsized and foundered on her sea trials? The prospect of being privileged to wear uniform himself still seemed remote and farfetched. It grew more likely as the deadlock in South Africa intensified. For the repercussions had an ominous sound; and neither Salisbury nor Joseph Chamberlain appeared to be wholly in control of events.

Childers, partly under the influence of the drily critical Basil Williams, gradually ceased to think of Jameson and Rhodes as martyrs. Nor was he deceived any further by Chamberlain's obscurely statesmanlike utterances, accepting Williams's surmise that the Colonial Secretary had possibly had foreknowledge of Jameson's reckless intentions. His slow education in the anatomy of policy-making was beginning. He sought relief from the sad business of unlearning all he had once taken for granted by gulping down fresh sea air as often as he could.

By far the hardest cruise he ever undertook was the long haul across the North Sea in August 1897 on the first of six voyages of slow discovery through the narrow, sand-locked channels of the Frisian islands to the open Baltic. Increasing familiarity, year by year, with the physical hazards, the eerie scenery, the motley Dutch, Danish and German sailors and villagers he encountered gradually planted a seed of creativity in his fertile mind. The log-book shows that he sold 'Mad Madge' without regret to acquire a larger and stabler vessel. The opening entry runs: 'The *Vixen* was bought in Dover on August 1st 1897 and fitted out for crusing in the Granvile Dock.'

No sooner had Parliament risen for its summer recess that year than Childers cast off alone on 11 August, 'a cloudy, dull day with heavy showers', and set course hopefully for Dieppe. His brother Henry arrived in due course from the Tyrol, and in easy stages they proceeded through squally weather along the north-east coast of France and through the canals of Holland. 'I never began a cruise under (seemingly) less propitious conditions,' he admitted in retrospect.

To start with, no one could call the *Vixen* beautiful. We grew to love her in the end but never to admire her. A low freeboard, a high coach-house cabin roof, and a certain over-sparred appearance aloft, would unnerve the most honied tongue. In the 'saloon' [the sailor] would find just enough headroom to allow him to sit upright; and before he could well help himself, the observation would escape him that the centreplate case was an inconveniently large piece of furniture. Confronted with the fo'c'sle, candour and humanity would wring from him a sigh of pity for the crew, but here he would be comforted, for there were to be no paid hands.

She weighed seven tons and carried three tons of lead as ballast in 'small pigs'. A cutter measuring thirty feet overall by seven feet and drawing four feet, or six feet six inches with the centre-plate lowered, the *Vixen* had three comfortable berths and plenty of room for stowing stores and sails. Childers was forced to acknowledge the fact that 'we were in the habit of speaking contemptuously of her sea-going qualities, but she never justified our strictures. . . . A couple of small bilge keels make her sit nearly upright when on the ground, a feature which could be most valuable in North Germany.'

In a series of memorable, little trials, the two brothers crossed the Zuider Zee for Terschelling and onwards through a desolate seascape of long, low, uneven islands of white sand intersected by tricky channels. On 25 September, Childers logged this impression:

We saw this strange region at its best this evening, the setting sun reddening gloriously over the great banks and shining ribbons of water, and bestowing pink caresses on the distant sand hills of Rottum (inhabited, so were told, by one lonely soul who has grown fabulously rich by the export of 'sea-birds' eggs), and the feathery line of the Frisian coast. At night we sailed off into deep water.

At length, passing through the German necklace of islands, they reached Norderney and found the 'beautiful little town as silent as the grave'.

On they sailed, placidly at the end of a tug's long tow-line, through the Kiel Canal. Ahead lay the Baltic. Suddenly

the sun burst through and, unreal as a dream, after the silent expanses of the North Sea and the lonely levels of Friesland, there came the vision of a noble fiord, green hills and richly wooded banks, sloping to the blue, deep, tideless waters, where, in a long, majestic curve, lay moored a line of battleships.[2]

Henry had to leave him and return to England in mid-October, so Childers explored the fiords alone. They met again a fortnight later, as arranged, at the Canal's North Sea entrance; and after seven more weeks of braving the seething tides among the Frisian islands, they laid up the boat for the winter at Terschelling and caught the overnight steamer to Harwich. Childers arrived back at his office in Westminster on 16 December, just one day late. None of his superiors or colleagues displayed any curiosity or interest in the adventures which had toughened his body and exhilarated his soul. He had written innumerable postcards and letters to his sisters and friends, read at least a dozen books, including *Pendennis*, Boswell's *Life of Johnson*, *The Aeneid* (Book VI), *Captain Cook's Voyages*, and *Rupert of Hentzau*, a romance which had enthralled him even at bad times when the *Vixen*'s violent motion almost hurled him out of his bunk.

The following Easter, accompanied by a hired hand called Rice, Childers crossed to Holland and nosed about at will in the same bleak yet enticing reaches, this time feeling duty-bound to send a telegram warning his fellow-clerks that the Frisian winds and tides might once more delay him: but the glass rose in the nick of time, then the wind turned to help. Nobody looked twice at him when he walked into his office punctually at 11 o'clock.

Only Basil Williams could discern the satisfaction behind Childers's conspiratorial smile of greeting. For only Basil Williams took the trouble to ask him where he had been; yet diffidence again curbed the adventurer's tongue so that all his friend could extract from him was a catalogue of hilarious mishaps to which the absentminded seafarer confessed himself prone.

So Childers stood apart, always at a slight angle to the feverish world of politics which seemed to him a world overpopulated by men who had nothing but worn words and received, partisan ideals to justify themselves as guardians of British Imperialism. Not that he despised them for that; he merely wondered how long it would be before words might have to be superseded by action, ideals tested by the sabre and the rifle. In South Africa, especially, it began to look more and more as if President Kruger had deliberately embarked on a collision course with Britain, regardless of the consequences. When Parliament rose Childers laid up his boat, took counsel with the knowledgeable Runciman, and caught a slow cargo ship bound for the Caribbean. To his sisters, who had recently left Glendalough to share with him a larger flat he had found at 16 Cheyne Gardens in Chelsea, he wrote cheerfully from his cabin on the SS *West Indian*, barely one week out from Liverpool:

October 18th, 1898. It is my first long voyage, and a total suspension of posts, news, papers and all outward intercourse seems very odd.... I was nearly left behind as they started half an hour before the appointed time, and I and my luggage were somehow thrown on board while the ship was actually moving....

She is a small and very slow ship, with only room for fifteen passengers.... There is Mrs McCarthy a most goodnatured little party with perhaps a *shade* too rich a County Cork accent! And Miss McCarthy, goldenhaired eighteen or thereabouts, and a very good sort with no rot about her. We all get on very well together and often read aloud – Martin Chuzzlewit and Kipling, chess etc.... Then there's the Captain, a wiry little Welshman, flaming red, full of queer yarns and taking a great interest in foreign politics. Hearing little, as he's generally at sea, he gets me to coach him in all the contemporary questions so I am giving him a fine sound Imperial policy on the Cretan, Egyptian, Armenian and other questions; We did Dreyfus last night, from nine till eleven p.m. We go at it hammer and tongs. I always find seafaring men very interesting – their minds are clear, broad and tolerant. Besides him there is the first officer, a nice, gentlemanly young chap, the second officer whom I've seen scarcely anything of, and the third officer, an old, dour, silent, grizzled man of sixty-two, looking like some gnarled tree trunk on a blasted heath. He never speaks or unbends, except to the cabin kittens when he thinks he is unobserved; he then expands in elephantine tenderness. A strange, silent riddle of a man. There is also the purser, a dandified youth of twenty who sets up for culture, having read *all* Marie Corelli's novels.

Childers's eye for character and detail was sharp; his opinions were unoriginal. For the mind behind that eye bulged with the conventional prejudices of an upper-middle-class Englishman still basking in the patriotic afterglow of Queen Victoria's Diamond Jubilee. Nor is it difficult to understand why Childers preferred the adventure stories of Anthony Hope, Frederick Marryat and Rudyard Kipling to the lush romances of Marie Corelli. As for the bigger-than-life-size creatures who thronged the novels of Dickens, Childers could salute the genius of their creator without caring for the arbitrarily grim and unjust circumstances in which the characters worked out their several fates. He was a curious mixture, on one level blending the sophistication of a well bred, well educated late Victorian with the wide-eyed innocence of a child; and, on the level of everyday life,

proving to friends that his zest for the perils of the sea served to
offset the unadventurous chores of a committee clerk at Westminster.

Returning to his diary-like correspondence, he wrote on
1 November 1898:

Barbados is the flattest and tamest of the West Indian islands and every
inch of it is cultivated. However, as we steamed into the harbour and
the sun came out there appeared what was very like a Riviera town –
the same white, pink and yellow coloured houses and brilliant tints of
sea and land. By the time the anchor was down we were surrounded by
crowds of boats full of niggers, all yelling for our custom and abusing
one another. Then numbers of little boats, flat-bottomed, diamond-
shaped tubs, each holding two nigger boys, came along. You throw a
penny into the sea and they all dive over for it and catch it invariably
often after desperate struggles deep down. Their black, copper and
bronze skins flash in the sun and against the intense blue sea make a
beautiful sight.

Scribbling from Government House, Grenada, on 24 November
Childers informed his sisters:

I long to see Kipling's new book. It hadn't filtered over to Trinidad
before I left.... This is a wonderful land and I see stranger things
every day.... You were rather right about those introductions. I am
stopping with one now – hospitality boundless, but it is too grand and
respectable and you have to wear stick-up collars which, in the tropics,
are absurd....

> 'To the cool of our deep verandahs
> To the blaze of our jewelled main
> To the night, to the palms in the moonlight
> And the firefly in the cane'

– That is the West Indies: 'On from island unto island to the gateways of the day'. But I have only 'burst all links of habit' for two days,
getting here. Ask Aunt A.[1]

Ironically, and as though destiny sought to comment on Kipling's
admonition against vainglory in his *Recessional,* the likelihood of
an unwanted war in South Africa seemed to increase after the
Queen-Empress's triumphant Jubilee, greatly adding to the frustrations of Joseph Chamberlain. The Colonial Secretary's vision

of an Empire so closely knit in abstract terms of loyalty and sentiment, as well as in practical terms of defence and trade, as to be the biggest force for peace on earth was one which Childers instinctively shared; but other nations, France and Germany in particular, dissented through envy and because of their belated ambitions as empire-builders.

There was rejoicing in Britain over Kitchener's victory at Omdurman a few days before Childers's voyage to the Caribbean began. It meant the liberation of the Sudan and the salutary avenging of General Gordon, whom the late Mr Gladstone, if the Childers, the Bartons and all good Tories could be believed, had abandoned to the Mad Mahdi and his frenzied hordes. Suddenly the rejoicing yielded to indignant concern when a small French force, under Major Marchand, almost simultaneously reached Fashoda and hoisted the tricolor as a provocative symbol of possession. Fortunately for Childers, France thought better than to test the issue by force; he was not recalled to Westminster from the West Indies as he had first feared. However, the threat to peace grew steadily more pronounced in South Africa, where the Boers resented Chamberlain's policy of maintaining British paramountcy. For President Kruger not only believed in the sovereign rights of the Transvaal Republic; he knew beyond the shadow of a doubt that the Almighty would help him to uphold them.

Sir Alfred Milner was sent as High Commissioner to South Africa in 1897 to reconcile the interests of the ageing Queen-Empress with Kruger's. All too soon this envoy of high intelligence and rigid principle discovered the depths of Boer mistrust of Britain. If Milner's mission was intended as a fresh beginning, Gladstone's death in May 1898 seemed to sound the knell of an era. Many, including Childers, who attended the lying in state at Westminster Hall, and later watched the Prince of Wales accompany the coffin to its internment in the Abbey opposite, could have been excused for wondering whether they were witnessing the burial of Liberalism itself with the Grand Old Man's mortal remains.

Certainly the Liberal Party had failed to heal its self-inflicted wounds since Rosebery's defeat nearly three years earlier, and the Transvaal served to twist the knife in them. From his insider's vantage point at Westminster Childers observed that the Liberal Opposition was quite unable to oppose, the only common ground among its members being an overmastering suspicion of Chamberlain and all his works. It was Milner, nevertheless, not Chamberlain, whose impatience with Kruger's denial of civic rights to Europeans paying taxes in his country steadily forced the downhill pace of events. 'There is no way out,' the High Commissioner wrote to the Colonial Secretary, 'except reform in the Transvaal or war.'

Chamberlain, to do him credit, would not be rushed. He counselled patience on Milner. Then the unexpected happened. An isolated incident, as fatal in its ultimate consequences as an assassin's pistol at Sarajevo some fifteen years later, led the Uitlanders in the Transvaal, as the Europeans were called, to go over the heads of Chamberlain, Milner and Kruger and petition the Queen herself for justice. The Uitlanders to a man detested the Boer police. Shortly before the Christmas of 1898, four policemen illegally broke down the door of an apartment in Johannesburg to arrest a boiler-maker whom they suspected of assault. They encountered firm resistance. The boiler-maker cracked open the head of the leading policeman with his stick, whereupon the injured officer drew his gun and shot the boiler-maker dead. Tried for manslaughter, the policeman was acquitted by a Boer jury, the Boer judge commending them on their sensible verdict.[3] Mutual antagonism reached an intensely dangerous pitch. The Uitlanders deliberately addressed their protest to Queen Victoria, bypassing the High Commissioner, Chamberlain and the Parliament of the Transaval as a vote of no confidence in all three.

'War,' remarked Clausewitz, 'is nothing more than a continuation of politics by other means.' To Salisbury's way of thinking, as to Chamberlain's and Kruger's, war was at best a last desperate resort. The British Cabinet hesitated. The Colonial Secretary drafted a message to the Boer leader, a message wholly consistent with his conception of Britain's Imperial mission. It accepted the Uitlanders' petition. It declared that the Queen could no longer ignore their grievances. Yet its tone was mild not bellicose. Before it could be sent, a cable arrived from Milner suggesting that he should meet Kruger face to face.

Nothing positive could have emerged from the subsequent

encounter between two quite incompatible minds. The haughty, intolerant Milner was incapable of reaching any understanding with the implacably suspicious Kruger whose thickly fringed face made wits liken him to 'palaeolithic man in a frockcoat'. The Boer leader began by refusing to budge on electoral reform. 'I am not ready,' he said, 'to hand over my country to strangers.' When Kruger did relent to the extent of offering a limited franchise to the Uitlanders, Milner promptly spurned the concession, wrongly supposing that his adversary was intent only on outwitting him. Milner at once warned London to expect failure. Chamberlain replied: 'I hope you will not break off hastily.' By the time that cable arrived, Milner had called off negotiations and departed. So the Transvaal problem degenerated into an insoluble crisis.

Childers loathed the idea of war yet believed that, on balance, Kruger must not be allowed to humiliate the British Empire. The crisis imposed a minor personal sacrifice: he could not risk sailing too far away, so his cruising in 1899 was confined to a few spring weekends and one whole week at sea during the Easter recess. Even then he dared not venture further than familiar waters off the Isle of Wight.

The Liberals had lately acquired as their new leader Sir Henry Campbell-Bannerman, who owed his appointment, declared *The Times* unkindly, to the likelihood that he would 'sit on the fence, fully satisfying no section of his followers, but at least vitally offending none'. Sir Henry, nonetheless, declared that the Opposition would not at that stage support a war. The Government, for its part, cast desperately about for ways to avert one. Chamberlain's offer of a joint commission to investigate Kruger's proposals for a new Franchise Bill which would have substantially met Uitlander demands were rejected out of hand. The Boers by now were importing arms and ammunition from Germany on an impressive scale. In August, as a precautionary move, two British battalions set out for Natal; yet the entire strength of the Imperial defence forces scattered across South Africa did not exceed 12,000 men, so the Cabinet decided early in September to reinforce them with a further 10,000, mainly from the garrison in India. It was characteristic of Milner to offer the mistaken opinion that Kruger would 'bluff up to the cannon's mouth'. Chamberlain prepared an ultimatum then held it back. Finally he was roused from sleep shortly after six in the morning on 10 October 1899, to read with amazement an ultimatum from Kruger to the British. And so this needless yet somehow inevitable war began.

About a fortnight later Erskine Childers and William Le Fanu, an old Haileybury friend, went for a belated cycling trip through the Dordogne region of France. To his sister, Dulcie, he wrote with feeling from an inn at Souillac:

We get belated news (and it reads bad) of the war through the reptile press of this country which is venomously hostile to us.

Nobody in the whole wide world expected the Boers to hold out for more than a few weeks. 'It will all be over by Christmas', such was the popular sentiment, such, indeed, the official view in London. And Erskine Childers saw no reason whatever to question it. For the Transvaal and the Orange Free State between them contained little more than 100,000 people, now that the Uitlanders had cleared out more or less *en bloc*. The Boers possessed no regular army. They had no reputable field commanders. They depended entirely, or so it appeared, on a spirit of truculent solidarity to defy all odds and omens.

It was thus with a spectator's growing sense of incredulity that Childers followed the earliest phase of campaigning. The enemy began by boldly seizing the initiative, invading Cape Colony and Natal before the still small and unprepared British garrison could move to stop them. When, eventually, reinforced columns led by Buller, Gatacre and Methuen marched upcountry against the Boers, no instant confrontation took place. Reading between the lines of the unsatisfactorily bald communiqués in the London press, Childers guessed correctly that the enemy could not be lured into battle. That was not their way of fighting. Instead they were exploiting an intimate knowledge of the veldt and using their mobility as sharp-shooting horsemen to harry and outflank the advancing British. Like the American colonists in their war of independence a century and a quarter earlier, the Boers had discarded conventional methods for guerrilla tactics. These they were imposing on British troops untrained in mobility, unused to living off the land and encumbered with long, slow baggage trains.

If Childers was as discouraged as his friend and colleague, Basil Williams, by these developments, their disappointment turned to anguish and dismay in the middle of December 1899. The two men had briefly parted, Childers having caught the mail train for Holyhead a few nights previously to spend Christmas with his sisters and Barton cousins at Glendalough. There he read the accounts of 'Black Week' with feelings akin to despair. Each of the three British columns trying to engage the Boers had been humiliated in turn. Methuen, on the Monday, was pinned down by a large Boer force in concealed trenches at Magersfontein while his troops marched stolidly forward in close order; unable to extricate his men or dislodge the enemy, he eventually had to retire to a defensive position on the other side of the Modder River. As if that reverse were not enough, Gatacre's men walked into an ambush at Stormberg the following night, and within half an hour the General's force had been routed. Finally, on the Friday, Buller retired under withering enemy fire as his columns vainly attempted to cross the Tugela River, the third, inglorious setback to British arms within seven days. A note from Williams reached Childers just after Christmas: 'You should come over at once and volunteer,' it stated, bluntly. 'I've already taken steps to do so.'

The invitation was one Childers could not resist, though he dared not yet divulge to the family the true reason for his headlong decision to pack and return to London.

'A happy new century to you,' he greeted Dulcie in the first of two letters he wrote from his Chelsea flat early in January, 1900.

Things are developing a bit. I have joined the Corps and began riding drill tonight.... A battery is going to the Cape and they still want men so I have volunteered. It is quite uncertain if I shall be taken but I thought I'd better tell you. The fact is I've been longing to go out for some time. ... Don't you think it would be splendid to do something for one's country? Normally, alas, I'm an idle man on the whole, I fear, and I feel this is a chance of useful action.

Three days later, with a touch of doubt still showing, he added:

I have been selected for service subject to the medical exam, but that's the rub. It's tomorrow at 1.30. I'll let you know by wire. Heaven knows I shall be sorry enough to leave you all, but something impels me here and I feel it's right. Yet it's no good dwelling on the serious side. It's after all a splendid adventure!'[1]

The spontaneity of an incurable romantic had triggered off Childers's instant response to Basil Williams's casual reference to joining up. The latter's warning that vacancies in the special Battery of the City Imperial Volunteers were disappearing fast had clinched the matter. The CIV, an emergency offshoot of the Honourable Artillery Company, had come into being overnight in the sternly patriotic mood that succeeded 'Black Week'. The City Fathers of London, backed by many firms and individuals, lost no time in providing the cash and publicity to muster and equip the unit, particularly since the small War Office staff was swamped by the flood of volunteers pressing forward to fight the Queen-Empress's enemies. Childers's relief at being accepted for initial training as a driver in the Battery was unbounded. The strident note of vainglory in his patriotism was not unnatural. He *believed* in the Empire; as an educated child of his time he *knew* that it was great. This emotional faith helped to mitigate the disasters of 'Black Week'. Like other Britons he believed also in the virtual invincibility of the Crown's armed forces. Apart from a few desultory campaigns, most of them crowned with victory, and all fought against inferior tribesmen in India and Africa, Britain had grown accustomed to the blessings of an almost un-broken Victorian peace. An outlook of optimistic serenity, in which ill-disposed foreigners detected an air of insufferable superiority towards the rest of the human family, had come to characterize the British at home and abroad. Now that the fabric of the Empire appeared suddenly imperilled by the military efficiency of a few thousand Dutch farmers, the British promptly over-reacted. So did Erskine Childers.

Three thousand dead and wounded represented the toll taken by the Boers in 'Black Week' alone. Compared with the quarter of a million men who would be sacrificed at Passchendaele some seventeen years later, or with the retreat to Dunkirk and the evacuation of a massive British expeditionary force from its beaches in 1940, the losses incurred by the British in December 1899 must seem, now, minute indeed; but when seen in the context of the day it was plain that such losses offended Imperial pride and had therefore to be avenged without delay

The propaganda of so-called 'Little Englanders' like Lloyd George, who openly sympathized with the Boers in their struggle for freedom, struck a Tory patriot like Childers as perverse, false and treacherous thinking. In this he resembled the majority of his kind.

Stoicism and loyalty to the Imperial ideal equally caused him to shut his eyes both to the unreadiness of Britain for war and to the ineptitude of her generals in the field. Criticism of that sort appeared to him a gross form of self-indulgence. As it happened, no less a person than the Commander-in-Chief, Ireland, Field-Marshal Lord Roberts, was already critical of the conduct of the war. Two weeks before 'Black Week', Roberts had expressed his misgivings in a letter to the Secretary of State for War, Lord Lansdowne, who had been Viceroy of India during the Ulsterman's period of command in the subcontinent. The pessimistic tone of Buller's despatches had disturbed Roberts who could not resist pointing out to Lansdowne that 'the force now in the field is more than double what Marlborough had . . . or that Wellington had'. He would be more than happy, if called upon, to take over himself: 'I shall hope, with God's help, to end the war in a satisfactory manner.' The Government remembered that offer. After 'Black Week', the earlier doubts entertained by Salisbury as to the stamina of Roberts, then aged sixty-seven, quickly evaporated. The nation rejoiced at Roberts's return; so, in a more controlled fashion, did the Queen. When the little Field-Marshal called on her, she was aware that Lansdowne had told him that very afternoon the melancholy news of his son's death in action. As the Queen duly noted in her journal: 'He knelt down and kissed my hand. I said how much I felt for him. He could only answer, "I cannot speak of that, but I can of anything else."'

How eminently Victorian remains that scene. The capacity for empathy, for courage, for a measure of self-deceit in banishing depression as no fit companion for those called by the Almighty to defend the Imperial destiny, was superb. Childers joined in the general jubilation at the re-emergence of 'Bobs', the sobriquet conferred on an elderly soldier whom a nation, in its hour of trial, welcomed as the saviour of its bruised *amour propre*.

The night before the CIV battery clattered out of St John's Wood barracks at dawn to drive through the empty streets of London in a blizzard for embarkation at the Albert Docks, the officers and men of the unit sat down as guests of honour to a sumptuous banquet at Guildhall in the presence of Edward Prince of Wales. Childers felt mildly uneasy and underslept before the troopship the SS *Montfort* weighed anchor and slipped down the Thames on the morning of 3 February 1900.

'We are crowded like rats in a hamper', he wrote to his Barton grandmother after a week at sea.

Nearly all [are] sea-sick and besides that I'm 'stableman' as they call it which means duty all day. I'm sitting on a sack of bran in my little forage recess with my ink on a bucket upside down. Horses to right and left, and just beside me a half open bulwark port with a delicious glimpse of dancing blue – which, unhappily, is the highway for shooting all the rubbish off the ship, as it's the lee side. I write a diary every night which I'm sending to the girls.[4]

The rolling and pitching of the ship in the Bay of Biscay left him undisturbed. He was back in his element, if under restricted conditions. One day at the height of a particularly fierce storm an ashen-faced lieutenant approached him. 'Report to me when the horses have been watered and their feeds made up,' said the lieutenant faintly. 'Horses watered and feeds ready, Sir,' replied Childers, coming to the salute. To which he added this diary postscript that 'He turned on me a glazed eye which saw nothing.'

To while away the voyage he helped Williams to produce several editions of a ship's newspaper called the *Montfort Express*, an interesting if superficial sounding-board for the predictably conservative opinions of its editors rather than anything else; but Childers kept copies for future reference when at length the unit, with its team of horses and its four 12-pounder Vickers-Maxim guns, disembarked at Cape Town. Field-Marshal Roberts, the new Commander-in-Chief, had preceded them with his newly appointed Chief of Staff, Kitchener, by several weeks.

Special corps of volunteers were landing by every tide, not only from Britain but from other countries of the Empire. The Imperial Yeomanry, composed of countrybred men who could ride and shoot, were now being reinforced by Canadians, New

Zealanders, Australians and South Africans, whose services had been tactlessly declined at the outbreak of hostilities. With thousands of fresh men to draw on, Roberts had lost no time in playing the Boers at their own outflanking game. Compelled to evacuate their positions at Magersfontein and fall back on their base at Paardeburg, there the Boers were cut off and forced to give battle. Brave and stubborn as was their resistance for ten whole days at the end of February 1900, the large force under Kronje had no option but to surrender.

Roberts advanced again to enter Bloemfontein early in March, while a cavalry division, under French, lifted the siege of Kimberley and Buller in Natal relieved Ladysmith. The enemy had no alternative but to pull back its commandos in the face of the unslackening British advance, so that Childers feared that the CIV would reach the battlefield too late. Not for the first or last time, events proved him wrong. The Boers would go on defying the odds in the angry belief that they were defending their homes, their land and their patriarchal way of life against a tyrannical giant intent on dispossessing them; and the Boers were men of European stock. If Roberts, the victorious Field-Marshal, failed to understand that he had on his hands something more in the nature of a civil war than a punitive expedition, how could Childers, the Tory patriot in a private's uniform, be expected to do so?

Roberts's plan of campaign was straightforward and orthodox enough. By capturing the Boers' cities and sealing off their main lines of communication, he could force them to yield more swiftly. He had sufficient troops for that purpose, so he pressed on hard. The Boers, however, having been defeated once in a pitched defensive battle on a relatively large scale, reverted to the tactics of mobile guerrilla fighters who could strike unexpectedly at the British flanks and rear. Had Roberts been in less of a hurry, had he paused in that spring of 1900 and detached half his superior strength to the still unfamiliar but vital business of learning to play the enemy at their own elusive game, the South African struggle might not have dragged on as long as it did. And the bitterness which would sour relations between British and Afrikaans from that day to this might at least have been reduced. However, neither Roberts nor the War Office was blessed with such foresight. They followed the rules and applied strategic principles that had served well since the Crimean campaign. Unlike the Germans, the French or the Americans, they had been taught no new lessons of warfare. So while Roberts pushed on towards Johannesburg and Pretoria nobody, least of all perhaps the Field-Marshal himself, had any inkling that a stroke of imaginative boldness might be in order.

'We are camped in the open veldt with some militia and yeomanry,' Childers informed his sisters about a month after disembarking.

We've moved on here to Piquetherb Road, 60 miles from Stellenbosch, which is something. There are supposed to be some rebel forces about – but we know nothing. It is such a vast country and regiments are such mites in it. . . . There is a dust storm going on in a blazing sun, and the gun is poor shelter. Was the shaving brush a delicate hint for me not to grow a beard? If so I fear it may be wasted as there is no water here within a mile and a half. And no time to get it, except for watering horses.[4]

The many letters Childers wrote from the front exuded a nonchalance, an immature good humour, a candour and a stoical acceptance of conditions which were hallmarks of the Victorian gentleman and soldier. Rarely did he strike a sombre or plaintive note. Yet the very act of describing the vicissitudes of life as a volunteer in the ranks of an élitist artillery unit gradually enabled him not only to grasp what was happening around him but to start questioning the decisions of the strategists and policy-makers far above him.

Through it all he never wavered in his conviction that Britain's cause was just. But always hesitant in imputing bad motives to others or in casting blame on them, he felt compelled in the end to admit that the Boers, too, probably had justice on their side. His sense of chivalry caused him to admire an enemy who fought so cleanly, efficiently and cleverly, without counting the cost. During the six months Childers spent in the field, driving the unit's gun team from the Cape to Pretoria, far to the rear of the advancing Roberts, Childers learnt by harsh experience to appreciate the martial qualities of the Boers.

It was late April. Roberts's progress in the north had slackened

because of a severe outbreak of enteric fever among his men
'The war might have stopped altogether for all we hear of it,
lamented Childers.

I wonder if you hear more. We are under orders to go to Bloemfontein
when trains are ready. The railway seems to be in a hopeless block. I
don't think any troops are going up ahead of us.

He had not long to wait. After an uneventful rail journey to
liberated Bloemfontein, there began a steady march forward into
the bare and apparently unpeopled hinterland, still far to the rear
of Roberts's vanguard. 'The first signs of war,' the diarist noted
as they skirted the tracks of the Central Railway stretching towards
distant Johannesburg and Pretoria.

A fine iron bridge blown up, its back broken in the water, graves
trenches, barren veldt. And the strangeness of the whole thing struck
me. *Why* should men be fighting here? There seemed to be nothing to
fight for, nothing to get when you had fought.

Childers celebrated his thirtieth birthday on 25 June 1900
reluctantly rising from his sleeping bag under the brilliant stars
at quarter past four in the morning. Another short march through
desert and scrubland, then a longer ride on a troop train from a
point beyond Kroonstad where the permanent way had been
hastily repaired, brought the unit to its overnight bivouac
Childers slept like a child until his dreams were shattered by
shouting orderlies and the stars overhead vanished in the confusion of a blue and windless dawn:

Orders were shouted: 'Drivers, stand 'to your horses.' We harnessed
up at a quarter to four. Suddenly, we are in action. There was spattering
rifle fire, the chattering of a Maxim on our left flank, as we plunged
down a villainous *spruit*. We came up the other side still under heavy
fire from the *kopje* on our left. There was a mishap to my harness. My
horse had lost flesh and the girth was too loose. To my horror the pack-
saddle began to slip and turn. I had to ride holding on to the saddle
with my right hand, oblivious of flying bullets and everything because
I was full of the dread of disgrace.

This frantic half hour of blurred impressions, mixed emotions
and convulsive action would stand out in his memory for the rest
of his life: 'A load off our minds – the Honourable Artillery Company has at last been under fire.'

How odd to reflect that, as a driver, he had so much leisure, even at the height of an engagement. While enemy shrapnel burst overhead, he could stare out over the brown landscape towards distant fields, then scribble: 'Thousands of acres of rich pasture, vast undeveloped wealth. Farms few and far between.' Though he had secretly envied Williams for gaining preferment as a mounted gunner, Childers would not now have exchanged for any consideration his own job of tending horses. He loved it. The animals were hard-working, affectionate and manageable when treated intelligently and with care.

On one occasion all the drivers in the unit rode to a river seven miles from camp to practise swimming across with their animals. We stripped, off-saddled and swam them, but one wouldn't do it at all and declined to go in, in spite of half a dozen chaps goading him on,' he noted. So Childers mounted him. 'The startled beast bolted away over the veldt, carrying me naked on his broad back.'

It was impossible to separate fact from rumour in the wilderness. According to local rumour-mongers De Wet had cut the line. The Boers had got behind Roberts. They had retaken Kroonstad and massacred whole regiments. Certainly nobody knew where to start hunting for the elusive hunter. For this particular leader's skill Childers conceived a real admiration: 'De Wet is the plucky one. Now that his cause is hopeless, we have sworn to get him to London and give him a testimonial dinner for giving us the chance of a fight.'

It looked at first as if Roberts had outmanoeuvred the Boers by outmarching them. In thirty-four days, the British commander had covered the three hundred miles from Bloemfontein to Pretoria, one of the most rapid movements in military history, in view of the supply problem and the inhospitable terrain. When Napoleon marched his Grand Army from the Channel to the Rhine, it took him precisely the same period of time, and that along good roads through centres where the replenishment of resources was assured. Even Roberts's famous 300-mile march from Kabul to Kandahar in Afghanistan, some twenty years earlier, had been accomplished by a hand-picked flying column, which explained why he had needed only twenty-four days from start to finish.

The British Government, in common with others in the worl
at large, accepted the evidence that effective enemy resistance had
ceased now that Kruger had fled. What alternative had Botha
the Boers' military leader, but to parley? Peace would return once
he agreed to surrender unconditionally. This was why the un-
heeding dash and tough aggressiveness of Christian De Wet in
the Orange Free State caused Erskine Childers and his comrades
such puzzlement and exhilaration. They, too, were eager for the
fray, though De Wet had more to do than tarry and satisfy their
naïve desire to be 'blooded'. Splitting his men into three groups
then fanning out from President Steyn's new provisional capital
at Frankfort, the aggressor attacked the small British garrisons
strung along the railway north of Kroonstad. Kitchener, the Chief
of Staff to whom Roberts was preparing to hand over supreme
command, moved southwards to deal with De Wet; but enemy
activity persisted and spread, inspiring the hesitant Transvaal
leaders to reconsider defeatist thoughts of bargaining with Roberts

'It seems that General Clements has come up with a division,
Childers noted. 'They want to finish off De Wet. We are part of some
endeavour to surround him but the operation seems to get obscure
He has played this game for months – and is no nearer capture.

He knew that many foreign mercenaries, French, German
Dutch, Russians, Norwegians, had drifted in to join the Boers. He
made no mention of Major John MacBride's mounted Irish con
tingent, perhaps because he did not realize it was also in the field
He had heard Irish voices on the march; and once, visiting a camp
hospital, Childers had spent a long time with invalids from his
mother's homeland, reflecting afterwards that it seemed 'im
possible to believe these are the men whom Irish patriots incite
to mutiny. They are keen, simple soldiers, as proud of the flag as
any Britisher.'

De Wet's lightning raids never hit the same target twice, and
Childers's battery was not spared when a party of Boers crept up
unseen to within fifty yards of the tents. 'All [our] officers killed
or wounded, many gunners, horses etc.', the diarist scribbled be
fore the scattered remnants of the unit reassembled. This small
bloody incident failed to lessen his respect for an enemy leader
whose tactical ingenuity was founded on such practical routine
as thorough reconnaissance and a perfect sense of timing. Yet the

enemy seemed to bear the British no malice. Their ferocity in battle was matched by a chivalrous treatment of wounded men and prisoners after the fighting ended.

When Childers went on leave to Bloemfontein with Basil Williams, they noticed on the walls of houses printed proclamations placed there by order of the British High Command. They stood by, watching and listening, while an official intoned the words for the benefit of a silent crowd of soldiers and citizens. It was a ceremony conducted to ram home the message that, so far as the Queen-Empress was concerned, the former Republics of the Transvaal and the Orange Free State had ceased to exist. They had been formally annexed to the Crown as colonies. The scene struck Childers as oddly unreal:

A distant voice began the Proclamation of which I couldn't hear all word, except 'colony' at the end, at which everyone cheered. The flag was unrolled in a breeze. Bands struck up 'God Save the Queen', a battery thundered a salute. I was standing on British soil, not a Dutchman about.... I passed a cemetery. There were thirteen still forms in front of a gate, wrapped in the rough service blanket, waiting to be buried.

Could a proud people be persuaded by a form of words to accept the sovereignty of an alien Queen-Empress while thousands of their able-bodied kinsmen fought on to preserve their traditional way of life? Childers pondered over a dilemma which kept him awake at night. His unit had meanwhile been attached to General Paget's Brigade. Paget seemed to him a sound, approachable man, a worthy opponent for De Wet:

We trust his generalship. He seems to be one of us, a simple soldier who thinks of every man in his brigade as a comrade. What an enormous difference this makes to men in the ranks. A word of praise in one's hearing, a joking remark in a hot fight (repeated affectionately over the campfires), any little touch of nature that obliterates 'rank' and makes man and general 'chums' for the moment – such trifles have an effect on one's spirit I could never have dreamed possible.

However, neither Paget nor Roberts could reconcile Childers to the injustice of annexing the enemy's land and destroying property. He preferred to separate fact from fiction in reflecting on the fate of the individual Boer:

Many of the farmhouses are smoking ruins, the enemy, after the annexation, being rebels not belligerents. But it seems to me that such a policy uses a legal fiction for an oppressive end, for it is clear that this part of the Orange river has never been conquered....It seems too that morally, if not legally, these people are belligerents who have fought honestly for their homes and treated our prisoners humanely. Deportation overseas and confiscation of farms are harsh measures.... I hope clemency will be shown.

It was perhaps as well that Childers presently left the firing line in a Red Cross van, exchanging his dusty sleeping bag for a hospital bed in Pretoria. No sniper's bullet was responsible for this change in routine: something depressingly prosaic, a veldt sore on the sole of his foot, had laid him low, much to his disgust.

Henry Childers, Erskine's elder brother, had been serving at the front for months in a Canadian mounted infantry unit. They had exchanged a few letters, but their hopes of meeting had never materialized. Now, through an accident of war, the improbable encounter took place. Henry was dozing in bed one day when the door of the ward opened and a man in a dressing-gown hobbled in, pausing to scan the face on every pillow as he passed. Erskine stopped beside his brother's bed, then said:

'Hello, Henry. Wake up, it's me, Erskine.'

They commiserated with each other on their slight injuries, the older man's bullet wound being nothing worse, he claimed, than a scratch. When discharged, they spent a few days of convalescent leave together, wandering through Pretoria, and exchanging impressions of a war which, both agreed, had by no means ended simply because Roberts and the High Command said so. The brothers parted in mid-September 1900, Childers rejoining his battery just in time to be reviewed by Roberts, the retiring Commander-in-Chief who, in keeping with his unruffled certainty that the Boers were all but finished, was busily disbanding unit after unit of volunteers. The CIV chanced to be one of the first to be told that its task was over, Roberts duly complimenting them on their contribution to a victory which Childers stubbornly if secretly regarded as quite premature. Paget also appeared to thank them, to say farewell and to bid them *bon voyage*.

'Physically and mentally I have found this excursion into the military life of enormous value,' Childers wrote, as the troopship sailed for home.

It is something to have reduced living to its simplest terms, to have realized how little one really needs. To have learned the discipline, self-restraint, endurance and patience that soldiering demands. To have lived with, and for, two horses, night and day for many months. To have given up newspaper-reading and to have steeped oneself in the region of fact where history is made and Empire moulded.

Earnestly seeking to enumerate, like a latterday Samuel Smiles, precisely what he had gained personally from his crusading in South Africa, Childers prudently ignored the unsolved military and political problems which Roberts was intent on bequeathing to his successor, Kitchener. The fate of the Boers, however, seemed to matter little to the cheering throngs on the dockside at Southampton. The rapturous welcome lifted his spirits and momentarily drove away the cloud that hung over his conscience. When the unit's special train reached Paddington station in London, the police had difficulty restraining the wild enthusiasm of the crowds; but Childers was most touched by the comradely greetings of the Honourable Artillery Company's special contingent which turned out specially to make this a truly memorable homecoming.

His young cousin, Robert Barton, now an Oxford under-graduate, would never forget the ceremonial march of the volunteers through the City. Nor would his sisters, seated in reserved places high above the processional route.

As Childers wrote himself.

It seemed like a dream, all those upturned faces as we rode by, the roaring voices under gaslight. London was so proud of her men.... The feelings of all of us are much the same, some honest pride, stunned bewilderment at the intensity of the emotion, a deep wave of affection for our countrymen.

His last thought, thrust into the background of his mind by sheer pressure of sentiment on the triumphant day, but obtruding itself forcibly as life returned to normal, focused on that 'dusty figure still plodding the veldt, Tommy Atkins'. In spite of Roberts, in spite of the victory parade which had moved him so much, Childers was uneasily aware that the war on the veldt would not be brought speedily to an end by patriotic fervour alone.

D

4. THE AUTHOR

An element of contrivance lay behind Erskine Childers's emergence as a successful author within weeks of his return from South Africa. The contrivance was clearly not of his making. He had his sisters and perhaps half a dozen influential family friends to thank for colluding and thrusting authorship on him while his back was turned. As we have seen, the tens of thousands of words which Childers wrote in diary-letters from the front had been intended for their eyes alone. This uninterrupted war chronicle, often scribbled in pencil on any grimy sheet of paper he could find, had been passed from hand to hand exactly as he wished. Every page of it was filed away in the upstairs room at Glendalough where he had slept and worked since early boyhood. There the correspondence would remain, or so Childers supposed, until his unit came home and he could decide what to do with it. Fortunately or otherwise, that orderly plan went awry in a fashion which never ceased to alarm and amuse him in retrospect.

It would appear that the prime mover in the matter of publication was one of W. H. Smith's daughters, a Mrs Thompson, who had known and admired the young man since his years at Haileybury. She was evidently so impressed by the cumulative vividness and candour of his narrative gifts that Childers's sisters gleefully let her go ahead and publish. The problems of deciphering and editing were slight. As for the author's wishes and the question of copyright, those were naturally taken for granted. The proofs would be a nice homecoming present for him. The book itself might even sell and bring him some well-earned money. Needless to say, Mrs Thompson, the Childers girls, and the publishing house of Smith Elder, did not err in their calculations. *In the Ranks of the CIV* could not have been better timed.

Once Erskine Childers recovered from his surprise at becoming an author without consciously trying, he began to toy with the idea of composing something less slight and more considered; but the right subject would not come. So, for the present, he sat back and enjoyed the luxury of basking in a short, uncovenanted hour of fame: 'There is a third edition of *"In The Ranks"* and a lot of reviews,' he informed his great-aunt Flora on 8 January 1901.

None of the reviews are bad (except *The Standard* – 'tedious') and some very good.... Lord Denbigh, the Colonel of the Honourable Artillery Company, also wrote praising it and asking me to stay with them. Very nice considering he has no acquaintance with me.[1]

The visit to Lord Denbigh's country house near Rugby was to prove of crucial importance in three respects: first, it led to the selection of Childers in due course as joint author of the official record of the HAC's part in the Boer War; second, it put him off the idea of returning to risk his neck in South Africa; and finally it created an unexpected friendship with Denbigh which, in-directly, led the eligible Childers towards America and the girl with whom he would fall in love. Great-aunt Flora was left in no two minds about Erskine's liking for Lord Denbigh:

He is a young man with a young and charming wife and a bevy of little children.... They have a lovely red house, full of Vandycks and Rubenses and Reynoldses. From his letters etc. I got a lot of insight into the war and learnt that it *was* our special gun and ammunition that kept us back from the front. Some hidebound artillery ass on the staff objected to new-fangled guns. I say *ass* – but he was the gentleman who advised the government against adopting the gun four years ago, so his discouragement of us has a touch of unpleasant malice in it...

I have given up all thoughts of volunteering again. The Honourable Artillery Company are sending out a Yeomanry draft but there's no question of a battery. I made up my mind that nothing but a special appeal for the old battery and old members would justify me in going. It appears our coming back so soon was a result of the vanity of the late Lord Mayor [of London], who wanted all the fuss and pomp of that homecoming to occur under his own regime, and of the good nature of Lord Roberts – and doubtless of his 'war practically over' frame of mind at that time.

The death of Queen Victoria in January caused him to express the hope to his sisters that 'Granny hasn't been fretting too much' over this sad event which plunged the capital of the Empire into a period of protracted official mourning.

I'm sure she felt it deeply – she always feels so intensely about things – but she must be cheered by the thought of Henry's return. He wired on the 22nd, 'Coming home Castle line. Send £65.' Now Henry always scoffed at the idea of buying a mail passage home if he could get taken for nothing on a transport; so I'm at a loss to know what it means and can only conjecture that he married and is making the Castle trip his honeymoon! However, the main thing is that he's coming safely out of this endless, dreadful war.

Keeping a diary in the field had put a finer edge on the critical faculties of Erskine Childers. His time as a soldier had hardened him physically and mentally, without affecting his sensitive appreciation of people he cherished or causes he believed in. His faith in Britain's imperial destiny, for instance, held firm, though his mistrust of its current political champions was tinctured with impatience. In a vaguely uneasy way he was beginning to recognize that, with the demise of the great Queen-Empress, a whole epoch had somehow ended overnight.

'I'm getting sick of these acres of print about the Queen,' he admitted to Great-aunt Flora in another revealing burst of confidence.

It's all true, of course, and probably rarely excessive as euology; but it has all been said by Tennyson in his nine stanzas of exquisite simplicity and beauty, and I want nothing more. That wretched Laureate makes me swear – 'Gone and the world feels widowed' (!) gives me the shudders. The best poem I've seen was in the *Pink 'Un,* a rather disreputable sporting paper in its normal moments. I have a superstitious feeling that her death closes our greatest epoch, as [her crowning] certainly began it.

Childers, for all his protestations to the contrary, remained something of a purist at heart. Intensely patriotic, he scorned the more blatantly vulgar manifestations of patriotism, not least in some of the political speeches he read or heard. His Englishness was so natural yet so controlled that he would have gone to the stake rather than hint by the flicker of an eyelid at the shifting moods of uncertainty, exasperation and pensive hope that washed over him like the tide for months after his release from the Army. He knew that the war dragged on because of continued mismanagement by politicians as well as generals; he also knew that, short of volunteering to fight again, a decision he had already rejected, there was little he could do to help. So readjusting himself to the humdrum routine of a committee clerk's work in the Commons proved anything but easy. It consoled him to realize that Basil Williams, a more phlegmatic character than himself, felt as restless and querulous as he did. 'Ever since I came back I have been irritated and disgusted by the tone of the press and other ignorant persons towards the Boers,' he confessed in a letter to Williams from the Thompsons' Scottish estate. 'It was worth going out there if only to learn to respect them. Otherwise the excesses of the anti-Boers would have made me a pro-Boer, I believe.'

When Williams hinted that he might be returning to South Africa, not as a soldier but as an official on the staff of Milner in the High Commissioner's department, Childers could not suppress a genuine sense of disappointment:

I am not in the least surprised – only more sorry than I can say – to lose you from the office.... We two seem to have something in common which I don't find in the rest, the something that made us snatch at troopship squalors in preference to the cigarette-smoking, gossiping, bottom-warming, Bradshaw-studying life at Westminster.... Other things being equal, I would drop it if I saw a chance of more active work, but other things are not equal. My clear duty keeps me in England and I can't afford to forego the assured income for a doubtful future.

One important item which Williams left behind, still incomplete and thus in no fit state for the eyes of a publisher, was a narrative of the regiment's role in the unfinished war. Ruefully, Childers blamed himself for having stood in his friend's light by producing what was probably the only book on the topic that anyone would wish to read, let alone buy. However, he promised faithfully to look after Williams's interests; and eventually the Honourable Artillery Company invited Childers to revise and cut the manuscript, with a view to publication after the fighting ended. Meanwhile, what better could he do than keep his friend informed of happenings at home by regular letters?

'The office is just the same,' ran a typical extract.

Dicky is crouching over *The Times*, his spectacles scraping on the paper. Tupper is laying down the law on the right of succession to the [Clerks'] Table. Doyle is telling indecent stories and Colomb, Fell and Legge, are capping them. Gibbons is solemn and subdued.... I am going to drill regularly and trying to pick up some gunnery.

There were, of course, many new faces in Parliament. While the CIV had been sailing homewards, the 'Khaki Election', one of the most acrimonious contests for years, had confirmed Salisbury's Tory administration in power; but the Cabinet was largely a one-man show, with the popularity and authority of Joseph Chamberlain, the Colonial Secretary, much enhanced. Of all Salisbury's ministers, Chamberlain stood out as the only one free of blame for military setbacks or scandalous muddles over medical and military supplies. His most unsparing opponent still was the notorious 'Little Englander', Lloyd George, a remarkable orator, who gained Childers's grudging respect for the unbridled ferocity of his attacks on Chamberlain, the political hero of the hour. Had not the little Welsh Wizard neatly turned the tables on his adversary by picking up the latter's reference to 'the Transvaal, the country we created' and rejecting it scornfully as a 'Birmingham version' of the Scriptures? Nor did Childers wholly disagree with Lloyd George's repeated pleas for a serious initiative on the part of the British Government to end the unnecessary conflict with the Boers.

What tended, on the other hand, to rouse his instinctive Tory suspicion of upstarts was the aplomb with which Lloyd George used any stick to attack the tenderest part of a political foe's anatomy. Before Childers's leave ran out, the new House of Commons assembled in December, 1900, merely to discover that Lloyd George had moved the following amendment to the traditional Royal Address:

'That Ministers of the Crown and Members of either House of Parliament holding subordinate office in any public department ought to have no interest, direct or indirect, in any firm or company competing for contracts with the Crown, unless the nature and extent of such interest being first declared, Your Majesty shall have sanctioned the continuance thereof, and when necessary have directed such precautions to be taken as may effectually prevent any suspicion of influence or favouritism in the allocation of such contracts.'

As a man who had read law himself, Childers could see at a glance the damaging innuendo underlying the legalistic jargon. Here was a move calculated to cast doubt on the probity of Chamberlain and so smear his good name. In self-defence the Colonial Secretary, obviously wounded but coldly defiant, claimed that he had 'endeavoured in the whole course of my public life to be in the position in which Caesar's wife should have been – to give no cause, even of suspicion, to the most malicious of my opponents. . . . And I think it hard that after twenty-five years of Parliamentary service in the full light of day I should have to stand up here and explain to my colleagues on both sides of the House that I am not a thief and a scoundrel.'[2]

It shocked Childers less now than formerly to reflect on the lengths to which politicians would go in their distasteful attempts to score off each other; and his own deepening interest in the 'Little Englanders'' campaign to stop the war and seek an honourable peace became somewhat obsessive at times. The campaign was, incidentally, strengthened by the Cadburys' acquisition early in 1901 of the *Daily News,* the most widely read Liberal newspaper in the land, of which, ironically, Lloyd George himself was made a director. So long as the campaigners did nothing deliberate to upset the morale of the army, Childers privately wished them success. His hopes soared when it was officially admitted that Lord Kitchener, the Commander-in-Chief, had been meeting the Boers' military leader, General Botha, at Middelburg to discuss a cease-fire. The talks in February 1901 failed, and his hopes fell. For Kitchener possessed no mandate to negotiate on the question of full independence, since that issue had already been settled by force.

To Botha's demand that all burghers still bearing arms should be amnestied the Commander-in-Chief had shown sympathy, just as he had considered 'reasonable' the Boer proposal that financial grants should be offered to rebuild the multitude of devastated farms on the veldt. Joseph Chamberlain, it seemed, had flatly refused to authorize such generous terms, and the Cabinet supported him. 'The Boer proposals were preposterous,' Chamberlain duly informed the Commons. To which Lloyd George replied with blistering contempt: 'There was a soldier who knew what war meant; he strove to make peace. There was another man who strolled among his orchids, 6,000 miles away from the deadly bark of the Mauser rifle. He stopped Kitchener's peace.'[2]

The antagonism between the two politicians symbolized the divisions in the country – and to a lesser extent, perhaps, in the heart of Erskine Childers. This, he knew, was not the first time the opportunity of negotiating an honourable peace had been squandered by a Colonial Secretary who, according to Lloyd George, had resolved to show the world who really ruled South Africa. Chamberlain's outright rejection of anything short of unconditional surrender had undermined Buller's early, tentative efforts to secure an armistice, though as might have been guessed Buller's initiative was slightly premature. But if the Government had been far-sighted enough to authorize immediate negotiations after Roberts's entry into Pretoria, peace, in Childers's view, would probably have returned to the veldt months ago.

Between the venomous swiping of Lloyd George and the supercilious firmness of Joseph Chamberlain there seemed little enough to choose. The British public in the mass might detest the Boers as rebels and ruffians; but the same British public had grown tired of hearing ministerial promises to crush Boer resistance promptly. From everything Childers could glean in the corridors of the House of Commons as well as in the debating chamber itself, peace flickered tantalizingly in the distance like the will-o'-the-wisp it had once been while he, a soldier in a dirty uniform, had driven his guns for miles in pursuit of the elusive and indestructible de Wet. So for the first fourteen dispiriting months of adapting himself to civilian life the political doubts of Childers, the committee clerk, grew apace. The aesthete clashed with the realist in him whenever he pondered the indiscriminate cruelty of Lloyd George's attacks on nominal colleagues and opponents alike:

'He has been captured by the Imperialists,' the Welsh Radical said, taking a sideways swipe at the harassed leader of the Liberals, Campbell-Bannerman, 'and I am afraid that his captors have treated him as the Boers treat their prisoners: they have stripped him of his principles and left him on the veldt to find his own way back as best he can. I hope this will be a lesson to him.'[2]

There were noisy scenes at Westminster while peace still hovered uncertainly on the horizon in the late spring of 1902. One night, when Childers was present, Campbell-Bannerman accused Chamberlain of treating him with 'malignant slander, as a pro-Boer', to which the Colonial Secretary icily replied that the Liberal leader was guilty of 'malicious calumny of his own fellow-countrymen'. Only the obstinacy of the Boers, strengthened by the treachery of the pro-Boers, he declared, was prolonging a hopeless struggle. Then he referred in passing to the burghers who had formerly fought against the British and were now allied with them, and happened to mention in passing the name of their commander, General Vilonel.

'Vilonel is a traitor,' shouted the Irish Nationalist, John Dillon.

'The Honourable Member,' retorted Chamberlain, 'is a good judge of traitors.'

In the ensuing uproar, the Speaker at length made himself heard. He rejected Dillon's demand for the withdrawal of an offensive remark, ruling that the Colonial Secretary was under no obligation to retract. As Childers commented to Basil Williams the following day:

Dillon is very rabid just now. I was calling on the Matthews the other day and found there him and his wife (she was a Miss Matthew). Lady Matthew was very genial and introduced me to them as 'the Mr Childers who defended De Wet'. This annoyed me frightfully as it was as good as stamping me as a fellow pro-Boer of Dillon's. So I said: 'Yes, and I'm delighted to see Bruce Hamilton's men have captured all his stores today.' There was an awful, icy pause, and then Kathleen Matthew dragged me away to a remote window and gave me tea.

Williams's cheerful accounts of his busy and constructive days on the High Commissioner's staff struck his friend as odd and even paradoxical:

It seems bizarre to the last degree to hear of all your teeming activity for peaceful ends in Johannesburg, while only a stone's throw from you, so to speak, the war is as hot as ever.... There is a growing feeling that we are continually being kept in the dark by the authorities.

The intermittent excitements and frustrations of observing politics from within kept Erskine Childers interested and relatively well informed on developments; but an indirect effect was to make him reassess his own Unionist and Imperialist values. The disagreements between Liberals raised points of principle which touched him more profoundly than he could yet begin to admit. He could not shake off perplexity. Even when the last shots were fired and peace was imposed he felt like a traveller who had lost his bearings in a weird dream landscape where the shadows of truth remained inextricably confused with the substance. The South Africa dilemma apart, another topic began to exercise the mind of this born Unionist whose easy-going Tory faith had become infected by the bug of Radical controversy. This was the evergreen problem of Ireland, anything but a 'live' issue at this time.

'You will have heard about the fresh Liberal split, Rosebery's definite abandonment of Home Rule and renunciation of Campbell-Bannerman,' Childers wrote to Williams at the end of February, 1902.

He and Asquith are trying to form a new vigorous party but they will be more impotent than ever, I expect. I don't admire C.B. generally, but I think he shows pluck in sticking to Home Rule now – and Rosebery cowardice in chucking it. The principle it depends on is not really affected by Irish disloyalty during the war, which is Rosebery's pretext. The theory is that to satisfy their grievances will make them loyal. I'm not a Home Ruler, but I recognize that that is the principle which animates a true Home Ruler. The air is full of scandals; remounts, meat, transport. The government refuse enquiry and say it was all 'inevitable'. Millions on millions seem to have been wasted.[1]

His social life away from 'the lethargic institution', as he described the Commons' Committee Rooms, varied little from its former set pattern. Only the circle of his friends had widened, partly because of his 'double existence' as an author; but so keen was his determination to keep fit, and thus shine at the regular drill nights of his old regiment, that he cut down cigarette-smoking and vowed to give up alcohol completely. Williams could not resist expressing jocular astonishment at his friend's resolve to go teetotal. Yet from afar he noticed, too, that such acts of self-abnegation seemed to sharpen Childers's already sophisticated sense of the absurd. When the Commons' Committee had a new Chief Clerk foisted on it, in the person of Sir Courtenay Ilbert, Williams soon learnt the true reason:

It seems queer that he should have left a billet worth £3,000 to take one worth £2,000, but I believe they are raising it to £2,500 and there is the house, of course. I believe he and the Government were mutually sick of one another, as he is a Radical and was tired of drafting Tory Bills. So, to get rid of him, they offered him this – and he, to get rid of them, accepted it. The inspired observations that accompanied the notice of his appointment hinted with Pecksniffian unctuousness at the purity of the government's notices and their generosity in choosing a Radical, as much as to say: 'This is not a job, anyway!' We are the only sufferers, for an outsider after so many insiders is a severe blow.... [But] if we *must* have an outsider, Ilbert is a grand one.... I happened to have a dinner engagement there last night and we had a most amusing evening.

This otherwise clubbable man always appeared to be writing, whether in the office or out of it, though he would freeze off anyone presumptuous enough to ask on which fresh masterpiece he was working. Basil Williams knew more than anyone else, except Childers's favourite relative, great-aunt Flora, and the three sisters who shared the flat with him in Chelsea, about the precise shape and purpose of his interminable scribbling. There were several references to it, mostly dismissive and mildly scathing, in Childers's letters to Williams. The intention to write an original book, probably a novel, was already on his mind when he had sent a hasty note to great-aunt Flora from the Thompsons' estate in Inverness-shire as early as January, 1901:

I'm on a week's visit up here, shooting with the Thompsons, Le Fanu and a Miss Matthew, daughter of the Home Rule judge.... I have not begun that book yet. I forgot before coming away to get the diary of that cruise from the flat. An idea has struck me that a story, of which I have the germ, might be worked into it as a setting. Do you think that would be a good plan supposing, of course, that the story was a possible one?

His great-aunt Flora offered him every encouragement, but four months later, while enjoying the spring sunshine at Rapallo, Childers admitted to her frankly:

'I have not begun the Baltic book yet. I fear it would be no good without pictures. I also fear the story is beyond me.'

These early misgivings did not survive the winter of 1901. From time to time Williams, far away in Johannesburg, posed pointed questions and insisted on clearcut answers which he teased gradually out of his friend:

Oh, about my book which you say I have told you nothing of. It's a yachting story, with a purpose, suggested by a cruise I once took in German waters. I discovered a scheme of invasion directed against England. I'm finding it terribly difficult as being in the nature of a detective story. There is no sensation, only what is meant to be a convincing fact. I was weak enough to 'spatchcock' a girl into it and now find her a horrible nuisance. I have not approached Reginald [Smith, of the publishers, Smith and Elder] as yet.

His writing schedule forced him to curtail his yachting excursions in the summer of 1902, when he could afford to spend only a fortnight in the English Channel

with Porter and Waller, an Irish parson whom I have known since boyhood. Weymouth was our furthest point....My sisters are in Ireland and I am camping in the flat trying to finish my book. I have rather overworked at it, I'm afraid, and don't feel very fit. Reginald Smith has promised to read it when it's done but I don't feel very hopeful about it.

The steady business of drafting and redrafting had made 'all the difference to life at the House [of Commons]'. Equally it caused him 'to shudder when I think of the dreary idleness I have perpetrated in these walls'. Once the final chapter was complete, he threw the manuscript with relief at the head of Reginald Smith and tried to forget its defects of plot and style. Only the title he liked and would not hear of altering. *The Riddle of the Sands* seemed to him almost impeccable. What a pity, he mused, that the text hardly matched such near-perfection. What a nuisance too, that the publisher, in a typical fit of impatience, had tossed the manuscript back at him, advising him to cut out great chunks of it and try again.

'I had hoped to make large progress with the H.A.C. [history] but was interrupted by a demand from Reginald Smith for drastic revision of the book I sent him,' he told Williams casually towards the end of February 1903. Childers had been basking in the winter sun at St Moritz with his sisters, returning deeply tanned after a month's strenuous tobogganing and curling. He was sorry to find that his book 'displeased [Smith] in many respects. In some points he is right, I know, but in others I hold wrong; and I have concocted a compromise which I think he will swallow.'

For nights on end, until the late spring, the light burned late in Childers's bedroom-study at 20 Carlyle Mansions, the temporary flat in Cheyne Walk he had leased. His sisters helped him at the finish with the chores of correcting and checking all the rewritten sections. Then he struggled, not always successfully, to push the matter right out of his mind until publication day in May. For he was obliged to 'wage battles with Reginald over maps etc. and at the eleventh hour he has tried to wreck it by advertising it as a "novel", but by quiet persistent opposition I have managed to effect a good deal'. Childers was thus quite unprepared for the unanimous critical acclaim that greeted *The Riddle of the Sands*. Its overwhelming public reception stunned him.

The book can still best be judged as the product of a serious and creative spirit obsessed by the uneasy feeling that Britain, once the heart of a great and prosperous Empire, lay vulnerable and exposed to invasion by sea, and this in spite of possessing the strongest navy in the world. Here was the one message Erskine Childers badly wanted to shout from the rooftops. That he chose to do so not in the traditional fashion of the amateur strategist, whom none but a few experts would read, but through the medium of a light adventure story founded on simple, personally observed facts, proved a stroke of luck. In the context of 1903 it is easy to understand the initial doubts of the publisher, Reginald Smith, on first and second readings of Childers's unorthodox thesis. Even allowing for a slowly dawning awareness in Britain of Germany's development as a rival sea power, there seemed no immediate cause for concern. The chance discovery by two English yachtsmen on holiday of sinister plans to turn so unlikely a location as the flat, white, sandy wilderness of the Frisian islands into the springboard for a German assault on the unprotected east and south-east coast of England had a ring of the utterly fantastic which the publisher disliked instinctively. Because the two Englishmen in question were primarily bent on enjoying themselves while negotiating the shoals of those largely unknown and often perilous waters, the slow unfolding of the central theme grew all the more gripping in its sharp realism. For every detail of the fictitious voyage had been carefully observed and noted by Erskine Childers years before in the logbook of his own squat little yacht *Vixen*. There were the waters he had traversed with his brother Henry on their first visit to the Frisian Sands in the late summer and autumn of 1897. Even minor characters like Bartels, the friendly skipper, were redrawn from the life, the least satisfactory portrayals perhaps being those of the former Royal Navy officer-turned-German-spy and the attractive but unconvincing young woman whom the author, in his own phrase, had 'spatchcocked in' largely to placate a dissatisfied publisher's demand for a 'love interest'.

The two most finely finished characters were undoubtedly the English yachtsmen themselves, and the contrasting faults and attributes of Davies and Carruthers served to provide a low-key domestic drama, in the confined space of the *Dulcibella*, which in turn helped to hold and build up the general reader's attention from the start. Friends of Childers claimed to recognize in Davies the self-conscious, unpretentious, painstaking, versatile and occasionally unsociable likeness of the author himself. They were never so certain about the identity of Carruthers, the intolerant young man from the Foreign Office, who bore no marked resemblance to any of their acquaintances yet who ran too true to life to be either stereotype or a composite character. I myself have always tended to believe that Davies and Carruthers were subconsciously separated by Childers, like Siamese twins, from the two contradictory halves of his own complex self, with some of Henry's more obvious traits thrown in for good measure to lend a touch of verisimilitude.[3]

The book was hailed by most reviewers as an extraordinary *tour de force*. The easy style, the vivid and authentic atmosphere, the eerie yet compelling undertone of drama on the personal level broadening into danger on the national and international planes as the two English innocents abroad accidentally stumble on the key to the Riddle, these ingredients could hardly have failed to draw widespread interest in the book. It appealed to yachtsmen, of course; it appealed also to the far larger group of readers who relished a good story of detection; it appealed at a deeper level because of its solidly factual basis and lucid unsensational treatment, to an influential minority of politicians, senior Whitehall officials and military men who felt as uneasy as the author about the state of Britain's defence. Who, they asked, was this chap Childers? How had he come by his uncannily precise knowledge of the German coastline? Was it conceivable that Britain's unprotected seaboard could be assaulted and seized by an invading army from a fleet of small enemy ships as the author plainly implied? No propagandist tract could have had a more instantaneous or enduring impact.

Reginald Smith of the publishing house of Smith Elder and Company confessed at once that he had misjudged both the flair of the writer and the subtlety of his handiwork. He put through orders for several thousands of extra copies, rubbing his hands with glee. This was the second occasion within months that a book by Erskine Childers had appeared at the right psychological moment, though the new work was destined to have a more resounding success than the South African war diary of the relatively unknown gunner-driver who had earned a mere one shilling and fivepence a day for his services in the ranks of the City Imperial Volunteers.

For the next ten years Childers's book remained the most powerful contribution of any English writer to the debate on Britain's alleged military unpreparedness. To what extent, if any, it inspired the young John Buchan, a newly arrived colleague of Basil Williams in Milner's political and administrative 'Kindergarten', to try his hand at similarly striking tales of espionage, is an interesting matter for conjecture. Buchan would eventually describe one of the many later editions of *The Riddle of the Sands* as 'the best story of adventure published in the last quarter of a century. . . . as for the characters, I think they are the most fully realized of any adventure story that I have met, and the atmosphere of grey northern skies and miles of yeasty water and wet sands is as masterfully reproduced as in any story of Conrad's.' It was a description which would have left Childers absolutely furious with himself for having apparently failed in his principal aim of rousing the British public and its political leaders to a keener awareness of the dangers besetting them. In fact, his artfully conveyed message was received, understood and endorsed by influential men like Admiral Sir John Fisher, the First Sea Lord of the day, whose thoughts had been simultaneously moving along similar lines. Erskine Childers admitted as much in a post-script, dated March 1903 and hastily inserted at the back of the first edition:

It so happens that, while this book was in the press, a number of measures have been taken by the Government to counteract some of the very weaknesses and dangers which are alluded to above. A Committee of National Defence has been set up, and the welcome given to it was a truly extraordinary comment on the apathy and confusion which it is designed to supplant. A site on the Forth has been selected for a new North Sea naval base – an excellent if tardy decision; for ten years or more must elapse before the existing anchorage becomes in any sense a 'base'. A North Sea Fleet has also been created: another good measure; but it should be remembered that its ships are not modern, or in the least capable of meeting the principal German squadrons under the circumstances supposed above. Lastly, a Manning Com-mittee has (among other matters) reported vaguely in favour of a Volunteer Reserve. There is no means of knowing what this recom-mendation will lead to; let us hope not to the fiasco of the last badly conceived experiment. Is it not becoming patent that the time has come for training all Englishmen systematically either for the sea or for the rifle?

It must be borne in mind that Childers was writing nine months before the Wright brothers took off on their first tentative powered flights over the sand dunes at Kittyhawk, North Carolina, in December 1903. If the dawn of airpower would soon add a new and terrifying dimension to warfare, nobody could have foreseen such a development then. Yet allowing for the probability that both sides in a future conflict would possess primitive flying machines, the advent of airpower did not neces-sarily invalidate Childers's startling thesis that Britain could be successfully invaded from the sea, especially if the enemy were German and chose to land on the low-lying Lincolnshire coast, north of the Wash, by far the easiest approach to the industrial heart of the nation:

There is an axiom much in fashion now, that there is no fear of an invasion of the British Isles, because, if we lose command of the sea we can be starved, a cheaper and surer way of reducing us to submission. It is a loose, valueless axiom, but by sheer repetition it is becoming an article of faith. It implies that 'command of the sea' is a thing to be won or lost definitively; that we may have it today and lose it forever tomorrow. On the contrary, the chances are that in anything like an even struggle the command of the sea will hang in the balance for an indefinite time. . . . No; the better axiom is that nothing short of a successful invasion could finally compel us to make peace. Our hearts are stout, we hope; but facts are facts; and a successful raid, such as that here sketched, if you will think out its consequences, must appal the stoutest heart. It was checkmated, but others may be conceived. In any case, we know the way in which they look at these things in Germany.

The diffidence of Erskine Childers ensured that the fame he earned through this one book would never go to his head. Besides, he tended to despise most of the hostesses who sought him out as an interesting guest at their receptions, 'at homes' and dinner parties. Nevertheless, as a result of sudden, unsought acclaim, he became well acquainted with dozens of distinguished men and women whose good will he valued and whose generous praise warmed him. He could have gained easy entry to the homes of the rich and the fashionable, had he so wished; for his name was on every lip, including the lips of not a few who only pretended to have read a best-selling masterpiece for which they professed such unreserved admiration. 'I had a most interesting conversation with Lord Rosebery the other day about the *Riddle of the Sands*,' Basil Williams was informed.

He wanted to know how much was fact and talked delightfully on the various subjects suggested by the book, urged me to write again and was most kind and encouraging. As a fact I invented the whole thing, building it, though, on careful observations of my own on the German coast but I have since had most remarkable confirmation of the ideas in it. Source confidential of course and details too – but I think there is no doubt that my method of invasion – in general principle – had been worked out by the Germans.

In the social sense Erskine Childers had 'arrived'; but being a celebrity neither spoiled him nor increased his liking for what he privately mocked as 'the bubble reputation'. He said nothing about this new and not entirely unattractive aspect of life in his letters to Basil Williams who had long known of this obsession with problems of land and sea defences:

'The question of the hour is the new Army Corps,' Childers had told his friend in February, 1903, after seeing the proofs of his book through the press,

and a severe attack on Brodrick [the Secretary of State for War] was made by practically everyone except the Prime Minister. . . . Churchill made a very fine speech which I heard – epigrammatic, trenchant and yet very sound on principles and details. People say he recalled his father wonderfully, but I never heard *him* speak. He will go far, I think.[1]

People were saying similar things about Childers after the appearance of *The Riddle of the Sands*. He met Churchill through their mutual friend, Eddie Marsh. He also met another gifted young man, small in stature but sturdy and instinctively pugnacious. His name was Leopold Amery and Childers noticed that he had the same auburn-to-ginger hair as Churchill, though more of it. Amery lived practically next door to Childers in Chelsea. Already a much-travelled journalist on *The Times*, he had worked in Germany, the Balkans and South Africa; and he accepted Childers's disturbing assessment of German military ambitions and intentions. At this time Amery was full of his woes as general editor of *The Times History of the War in South Africa*. So prodigious was his energy that Amery had written the first two massive volumes himself and was now wading into the third. Milner had invited him to go out to Pretoria as his personal secretary, but Amery's committments ruled that out; so he had recommended the romantic and unconventional John Buchan to take his place. Another recent recruit to Milner's 'kindergarten' was Lionel Curtis whom Childers remembered from their Haileybury days. 'I must say I think you are perfectly right that young men, if well chosen, are what is wanted – not elderly failures from elsewhere,' Childers wrote to Basil Williams, 'and from my small knowledge of the men who have gone out it seems to me that they are exactly the right stuff.'[1]

No writer of standing can ever hope to rest on the laurels gained by a single original book. Great-aunt Flora considered that Childers ought to travel a bit and broaden his mind in preparation for a lifetime career as a man of letters. Why not, for instance, visit Greece, the cradle of Western culture, and build deliberately on the basic foundation of the classics he had acquired at school? The reply he sent her in the summer of 1903 was not promising:

I am always, I believe, at my very worse at this time of year – at my lowest ebb of sympathy and alertness – a 'finished, finite clod'. Without being insincere I cannot meet your mood in the matter of Greek things.... I feel an ungrateful, barren disciple of yours. I am not an artist (in the widest sense, I mean) and you are.... As far as artistic temperament is concerned, there is a gulf between us, but it makes no difference, thanks to you. No, I don't believe I shall ever go to Greece for fear of false, no not exactly false emotions, but of ways of thought which it is no use my following but which would then be a surface temptation to follow. I believe I want action more than anything. It has always been best for me.[1]

Short of finding the right kind of action, a further study of the organized chaos, the ineptitude, and the many instances of individual valour behind Britain's efforts to defeat the Boers was something that he would gladly settle for. Two offers came within a short space, and both he accepted conditionally. Leopold Amery wanted him as an established writer to tackle Volume Five of the South African War history. Childers had read the first two with close attention. At first, however, he drew the line at becoming a contributor himself. On a recent visit to South Africa, where he had met Milner, Smuts and other celebrities in Pretoria, Johannesburg, Cape Town and elsewhere, Amery claimed to have successfully tempted Basil Williams to become the prospective author of Volume Four; and Amery's persuasiveness gradually wore down Childers's resistance. The book was bound to be a heavy tie on his time. And though the financial terms offered seemed reasonably generous, he foresaw that the task would occupy much of his available leisure for the next two or three years at least. One stipulation Childers did insist on: the unfinished regimental story of the Honourable Artillery Company's role on the veldt must be completed first. Once Amery had accepted that, there seemed no grounds for further hesitation.

Childers's earlier chronicle of the war had consisted mainly of his own impressions, whereas this regimental account had to be baldly factual and plain. It embraced in addition the services of the small HAC infantry and mounted detachments, each of less than company strength, which had been merged with larger units. Among scores of such works then pouring from the printing presses to grace the library shelves of senior officers at home and overseas, this small volume, written jointly by Williams and Childers, was probably the most elegant in style and content. It is of negligible interest to the general reader today, and its repetitive narrative of advances, retreats, skirmishes and individual feats of bravery and endurance under fire need not detain us unnecessarily. Nevertheless, one sample of the joint authors' crisp approach to their task will suffice to show how well they wrote and how indelibly their experiences in battle were etched on both their memories.

'The weather throughout the day', they wrote of a particularly vicious fight in the hills between Lindley and Bethlehem on 3 July 1900,

was dismal, with a high cold wind, and, frequently, drenching showers of rain. At about half past twelve the enemy increased their shellfire, unmasking two fresh guns...but on the whole the fire, though heavy, was doing little damage; so little that Major Oldfield presently ordered the gunners of his battery to cease fire, and to lie down near their guns; his reason being that his ammunition was running low....

There can be no doubt that this cessation of fire gave the impression to the enemy that these four guns (which they could probably see) had been temporarily abandoned.... A detachment of Boers, numbering about a hundred, had stolen up the dead ground ahead, through the mealie fields, and were now within fifty yards of Lieutenant Belcher's section, into whose gunners they were pouring a rapid deadly fire. Major Oldfield, almost immediately, fell mortally wounded, and in such agony that Captain Budworth, after attempting to remove him, had to desist. Turning to obtain assistance, he saw that the detachment on the left of the HAC guns, and also the Australians who had been holding the rise between our own and Captain Fitzgerald's guns, had retired.... The whole ridge, therefore, with its six unlimbered guns was now left at the mercy of the Boers....

Captain Budworth managed to reach his pony, and galloped back at once to call upon the Australians to return. That he succeeded in bringing them back, and promptly too, reflects the highest credit on him, and also, it must be added, on the men he had to deal with. Who ordered their retirement it is impossible to ascertain; but it is just to say that when called upon to come back again, they did so willingly; and it is common knowledge that it requires more courage, both moral and physical, for troops in retreat to rally and face fire, than to sit tight and suffer it from the first. But meanwhile terrible mischief was being done on the ridge... Lieutenant Belcher was shot dead, and all his gunners were either killed, wounded or captured....

Fortunately, instead of pressing forwards at once towards the remaining 38th gun, and, over the intervening rise, to the HAC guns which were completely at their mercy, [the Boers] delayed to secure their prisoners and to attempt the removal of the already captured guns. This delay gave time for help to arrive....Under these difficult and perilous circumstances perfect steadiness prevailed.

Remembering that Childers and Williams had faced death together in this small, confused and isolated action, the dispassionate clarity of their retrospective account was commendable. The rest of the book followed this pattern of writing; and it confirmed Leopold Amery's good opinion of the two authors he had chosen for a less easy task.

Fate, in which Childers quietly believed, continued to smile benignly on him in various ways for the rest of 1903. The Chief Clerk of the Commons, Sir Courtenay Ilbert, not to be outdone by others who detected hitherto unsuspected virtues in the successful author, gave him belated promotion:

'I have been made Clerk of Petitions,' he told Basil Williams, tongue in cheek.

P.S. I know nothing about petitions.... It's £60 extra and I find it gives me far more work than I ever expected.... The yacht is in commission, and I have got a motor bicycle. By the way, if in order to educate the Transvaal you have to travel about much in railwayless places – get a motor bicycle. They are the greatest blessing and great fun too. Did you see about poor Herbert's mishap? He lost the King's luggage in Italy!

The unbroken correspondence with Williams provides an unblurred picture of the leisured life led by an abstemious though moderately well-to-do Edwardian bachelor, still uncomfortable in the glare of unlooked-for distinction as a writer, but nonetheless determined to enjoy success while it lasted.

There's a great scheme on for the Honourable Artillery Company to go to America this September to return the call of the Boston branch. I dismissed the notion of going myself as I dread the round of drinking and feasting which is inevitable, especially as I am a teetotaller. But I am less averse to it now, as I find Herbert is going and Budworth and the Colonel are strongly in favour of it and are trying to get the right men to go.[1]

Yet the concept of such a quaint excursion to New England also struck him as faintly ludicrous. Here was an English regiment of ancient lineage preparing to sail across the Atlantic, to land where Redcoats of George III had landed to put down rebellious American colonists, and to march through the streets of Boston with fixed bayonets like the advance guard of an army of liberation. Coming so quickly on the heels of the much-criticized war against the Boers, it promised to be an unusual if not an impertinent exercise in diplomacy. Nevertheless, Childers refrained from expressing such thoughts to the Earl of Denbigh or to anyone else. He went – and his astonishment at the cordiality of the reception was immense. As he again informed Williams:

I am alone in America with a visit or two to make but nothing particular to do – and not feeling very keen. The regiment leaves [for home] tomorrow but I always intended to stop on at leisure for a little. What a whirl it has been, an unceasing fortnight of travelling, banqueting, picnicing, speechmaking and triumphant progress and a long-drawn orgy. As for Boston, I am still in doubt as to what to make of it all. From the moment we arrived we have been fêted and raved over – whenever we turn out the whole town turns out and cheers, men, women and children, and our march after landing on October 2nd in some ways surpassed the City Imperial Volunteers Day in London. It came on me with a flash that there's a good deal more than I thought in the 'union of hearts' phrase, and in the excitement of the time [one] can set no limits to the possibilities of an alliance of the English-speaking races.... And mind you, it is the first time armed Britishers have marched through American streets since the Revolution.

As to behaviour, I believe we have got through without open scandal – mercifully, for the primitive instincts of the HAC set towards tipsy debauchery, and when champagne is perpetually flowing like water the descent to Averno is abnormally easy, especially, as our escort, a hundred members of the Boston Company ('Ancients' they are called for short) aren't noted for sobriety, celebrated as they are for many things. They are all elderly and stout.... They all wear different uniforms, some dating from antiquity, and look strangely like participants in a fancy dress ball or a pantomime.... Indeed I believe the 'Ancients' rather resent being reminded that we can fight and are visibly disappointed that we were not more their equals in age and girth.

The revelry over, Childers hired a motor-bicycle and idly drove through a New England countryside bedecked in its resplendent autumnal glory.

Each morning he would set out from the front door of the University Club in Boston, where he had taken a room. Each evening he would return, cheerful but tired, to have a bath, dine and retire early. Then fate intervened. One day, as he roared up Beacon Hill, the machine spluttered and died under him. He wheeled it to the side of the street; and, examining the engine with the experienced eye of a man accustomed to fending for himself, he straightened up and walked without a second thought to the front door of the nearest large house. A servant answered his knock. Childers enquired whether he might borrow a spanner, and presently the owner of the house, a Doctor Osgood, came to the door. On discovering that the stranger belonged to the English regiment to which Boston's convivial 'Ancients' had been playing host, Dr Osgood persuaded Childers to come inside and meet his wife and daughter, Mary, the unmarried one of their twin girls.

Childers sat opposite Mary Osgood at dinner that evening. His brain was in a whirl, his heart pounding, as he listened to her musical voice and looked into her lovely dark eyes. She was a very gentle person, far more intelligent and less daunting than the debutantes he had occasionally exchanged courtesies with at dances and receptions in London. He noticed that she walked with a limp somewhat more pronounced than his own, learning in due course that 'from the age of three to fourteen or fifteen her days and nights had been spent stretched on an iron frame because of a diseased hip'. But any shared handicap of the kind paled into insignificance beside the strong natural affinity that drew them together. Mary proved to be extraordinarily well read, despite the fact that her affliction had prevented her from normal attendance at school or university. That memorable evening with the Osgoods was the first of many. The hospitable doctor, one of the leading nerve specialists in North America, insisted on introducing his English guest to a widening circle of relatives and family friends; and wherever Erskine Childers went, Mary Alden Osgood accompanied him. Such sweet thoughtfulness and kindness did she show to others that Childers longed to be able to pay her back in kind. The pair slowly fell in love. They were seldom left alone long enough for either to declare their passion, one for the other. Yet within three weeks of his chance encounter with this girl of his dreams, Erskine Childers forgot his shyness sufficiently to propose to her. It was during one of the rare evenings they could snatch a few minutes together, and to his utter astonishment Mary Alden Osgood accepted him with a kiss. She might easily have lost him, for Childers felt himself so unworthy of her that she had virtually to coax the proposal out of him.

Fate had surpassed itself on his behalf. Here he was, three thousand miles from home; yet not a single friend, far less any member of the Childers family, had the slightest inkling of his incredible happiness and good fortune. He put that to rights by sitting down and writing to them all as soon as the wedding day had been agreed. 'I am engaged to be married to Miss Mary Osgood of this city,' he informed Basil Williams laconically. 'I met her when we had finished our trip round with the Ancients and Honourables. I am so tremendously happy, old chap. . . . We are to be married on January 5th here and shall be back in London for the session.'

5. THE REFORMER

It was a white wedding, of course, and all the more glittering as a social event for being arranged early in January, the dead time of year. Fashionable Boston turned out in strength, a bishop friend of the bride's parents officiating at the ceremony in Trinity Church, the city's largest Episcopalian centre of worship. In the unavoidable absence of Basil Williams, Robert Barton, who had recently graduated at Christ Church, Oxford, crossed the Atlantic to stand in as best man, while the youngest of Childers's three sisters, Dulcibella, brought a specially tailored outfit from London to wear as one of the bridesmaids. She also brought various articles of attire which the groom had frantically requested at the last minute, including 'besides the blue suit, my best black tailcoat and waistcoat and the best pair of town trousers you can find'.

The whirlwind romance between this upper-middle-class Englishman, already recognized as a writer of considerable talent, and the radiantly attractive Osgood girl, with the luminous brown eyes set in a small oval face, whom Bostonian gossips had long written off as ineligible because of the lameness that had dogged her since childhood, did not pass unnoticed in the society pages of the local press. Among the relatives and friends of both families the marriage gave rise to mild questionings which, for the most part, did not survive for long. The happy groom had done his utmost to dispel all doubts in advance:

'I want to prepare you for this remarkable family,' ran a revealing paragraph from one of the many letters he wrote before the American bishop pronounced Erskine Childers and Mary Alden Osgood man and wife.

They are not religious in the Christian sense but are the most deeply spiritual people I can imagine, beneath a brilliantly gay exterior and much varied cleverness.... They are utterly unworldly; and truth and beauty are the only things they really love. [The household] is perfectly simple – no luxury though they are very rich. But the house is crammed with beautiful things – and in exquisite taste. Fiske Warren [his new brother-in-law] is very nice and in complete contrast to the impulsive Mrs Osgood and Gretchen [Mary's twin sister]. He lives by reason and yet has a deep background of tenderness. He's an impassioned anti-Imperialist and spends quantities on the cause.

As for Molly, the pet name to which his wife had always answered, he would only say that 'she has more *ballast*' than the others. Into details he would not go; and it is to the half dozen intense love-letters he wrote her before the wedding that we must turn for any true understanding of the profound change which this remarkable young woman progressively wrought in him:

'I wish I could send you a poem or a wonderful story for your birthday present,' runs a typical extract from the note he scribbled to her on 13 December 1903.

I have a mad unrest sometimes to tear secrets from outward things, to overleap barriers, to find with you a new world as I have found through you a new self; to scour old territories of thought with my new eyes, find jewels in what seemed stone and dirt, paradise in what seemed desert. I wish I had never dimmed my vision. I wish, even while not knowing you humanly, I had wanted and worked for you always and unswervingly, equipped myself patiently and laboriously, kept my sword whetted and burnished, my faculties alert and blithe – so to be ready, when the moment came, to find our love a final and complete inspiration, striking vivifying fire through my intellectual being as, thank God, it does through my soul. It will, I believe.... Today my gift must be the promise when, alas, it should be achievement.... My birthday gift is just a resolve: to make my hand strong my brain clear and my soul pure, so to do my share in the climbing, take all and more my share of the stress, and give you many, many gifts by the way, acts not mere thoughts, accomplishments not dreams.[1]

Overnight, it seemed, the promising dilettante had been transformed by the fire of love into a potential crusader. For Childers's love-letters, reflecting the undying passion of youth, would continue to pour out such sentiments whenever fate or necessity separated him from Molly. Thus for the next eighteen years, until his imminent death at the hands of an Irish Free State firing squad led him to write a final, incandescent love-letter from the cell of a Dublin prison, Erskine Childers followed the uphill road to his own rarefied heights of perfection, guided by a woman whose prejudices and willpower were at once harder and more resilient than his. Being American, belonging to a proud family which could trace its descent from Anne and John Hutchinson, passengers aboard *The Mayflower*, her middle name of Alden had been borrowed from the carpenter aboard that ship, though any blood-relationship with the Aldens would not have been easy to establish. The Osgoods had fought with distinction in the War of Independence; and they laid claim to some distant connections with the sixth President of the United States, John Quincy Adams. Molly had evidently inherited also ancestral suspicions of England, despite the deeply protective affection she showered on the Englishman who had wooed and wed her.

One or two members of the older generation of Childers looked Molly over with critical eyes when the couple reached Europe. The widow of Canon Charles Childers by his second marriage detected a clear streak of waywardness in her and wished that Erskine could have been less besotted by blinding devotion for his bride. Not for twenty-three months, however, did she trust herself to speak her mind. She did so then only because her 'boy' made some mildly disparaging remarks about the Christian faith. That, at any rate, was what she read into Erskine's statement that their newly born baby boy would have to wait for his christening, since baptism was regarded by the pair as a kind of optional extra which hardly mattered.

'I cannot let a moment pass without trying to reassure you,' Childers wrote to his grandmother towards the end of 1905.

For it is not at all as you think; and it sounds strange and harsh to my ears, beyond all belief, to have it from one I love so much and who loves me so much that 'my faith has been undermined by love – Molly's and my love – instead of being deepened'. It's a very long and difficult subject to go into and I doubt if there's much use in saying very much about it because in matters of religion differences of temperament make it almost impossible for people of different faiths to understand one another's points of view. But this much I can say. My belief, in the orthodox sense, in Christian tenets...was shaken and finally overthrown long before I met Molly; and off and on, from school onwards,

I suffered the keenest intellectual misery from the change – for this reason: that while I was dissatisfied with the old faith, I had not the backbone and character to carve myself a new one, which should really represent me, my inmost spiritual nature. Well, since I met Molly I have been happy. Contact with the sweetest and strongest nature I have ever known has given me what I needed – I say this in humility – character, faith religion. I have a spiritual life such as I never knew before; and I love good, in its widest sense, as, to my shame, I never loved it before I knew her. We have a wonderful life together – and the child has crowned it all.[1]

This, of course, was the subjective judgment of a man wholly infatuated by an exceptionally charming and gifted woman. During their first five years of marriage, Erskine and Mary Childers made every effort to share their blessings with others. They led not a hectic but an even and fairly varied social life. They entertained, and were entertained. Without seeking it directly, they became an integral part of that distinctive and not uninfluential group of intellectuals who added lustre to the reviving fortunes of Liberalism in Britain both before and after the party's unprecedented victory in the election of 1906. Whereas Erskine Childers had once been content to 'drift with the tide', he could toy now with a political creed. It might serve his sceptical soul at least for a spell. For Molly had decided in her intuitive and devastatingly direct fashion that English Conservatism would no longer do: it must be rooted out of her husband's system like a diseased growth. The surroundings in which the Childers lived were well described by Erskine in a characteristically cheerful letter to his American father-in-law:

We have settled in a flat at last.... Counting a room in the basement which goes with it, it has seven rooms, excluding the kitchen etc. and servant's bedroom. We shall have a drawing room, dining room, and study, and two little rooms with a communicating door for you.... Three of the rooms look out on the extensive gardens of Chelsea Hospital – a lovely view...

We are going out a good deal and there is very little time, alas, for reading and the quiet life. But we've had some interesting parties: with the Sargants, among others (John Sargant and Henry James were there) and at the Trowers where Molly revelled in a marvellous collection of Japanese things, and we met Sir George Clarke, the ex-Governor of Australia and present member of the triumvirate who are reorganizing the national defence system and giving us a new army and War Office. I was very proud to see him going away with a copy of *The Riddle of the Sands* under his arm, which Trower gave him! Trower is President of the Navy League.... We have decided to take a fourth share in the *Sunbeam,* our old yacht with Le Fanu, Dennis and Colomb, a colleague of mine at Parliament.... This plan is for 'week-ending' principally.... I told you, I think, we decided it would be impossible to find and fit out *your* yacht this Spring as well as decorate, furnish and settle into a house, plus all the social duties of this first year.[1]

His wife enjoyed only a few weekend cruises on the *Sunbeam,* the sturdy fifteen-ton yacht, built in 1870, which Childers, accompanied by half a dozen yachting friends, old and new, had again navigated through the now notorious Frisian islands to the open Baltic in the summer of 1903. For Molly quickly became pregnant; and not until they sailed as passengers on a steamer to Norway, after the birth of their first child, a boy to whom they gave the family name of Erskine, did she resume the sailing game. Childers's American father-in-law had insisted on providing him with a specially built yacht as a wedding present, an expensive and treasured gift, fashioned after Nansen's design. The *Asgard* would carry them on wind and wave during successive holidays to some of the most distant and remote inlets of northern Europe. Molly became as keen and proficient a sailor as her husband, making light of her painful disability and apparently relishing the hazards and discomforts as much as he invariably did. Fate had sent Childers an extremely strongminded mentor and helpmate in Molly. For she it was who gently but systematically inculcated in him the lesson handed down by the noblest of the ancient Greeks that only the fearless and the best could hope to change the world by the inspiration of the example they offered to smaller, feebler men. If any wife in the Edwardian age may be said to have taught her spouse the difficult language of destiny, that lady was the incomparable Mrs Erskine Childers, the frail young bride from Boston, Massachusetts. She naturally found fault with a good deal in the stiff conventions and hollow values still fashionable in the British political establishment; and Molly was only too willing to believe that the man she loved had been born to set them right.

'It's jolly to hear you talking of political work,' Childers commented to Basil Williams on 4 March 1904.

Protection is in low water just now but the controversy has come to stay.... I am pretty sure you will find an opportunity and I will see what I can do to hear of chances. I assume you would, in other matters, be a Liberal? For, of course, there are two anti-Protection parties – the Liberals and a band of Conservatives generally known as 'Free-Fooders'. Winston Churchill, Lord Hugh Cecil etc. I shall be delighted to see you again and I only wish, though not for your sake, that we were to tramp the Committee Rooms together again. I am longing for you to meet my wife, too.[1]

Williams had lately fallen out with Milner over a point of policy, and Childers had only sympathy and admiration for his friend's principled stand against an autocrat whose affectation of omniscience he spurned. 'Milnerism' was, for Childers, almost a dirty word; though the man himself undoubtedly commanded the loyalty of the 'Kindergarten' of young administrators he had recruited, men of the calibre of Lionel Curtis, Patrick Duncan, John Buchan, Phillip Kerr, R. H. Brand, Geoffrey Robinson and W. L. Hitchens, Childers maintained that the Boers still deserved better than to have so inflexible a pro-consul lording it over them. He could not overlook the fact that Milner's rigid kind of diplomacy had contributed not a little to the outbreak and prolonging of the South African war.

Virtually without realizing the shifts that had transformed his political outlook, Childers was by 1906 a Liberal in all but name. A man in his official position could not readily subscribe, or be seen to subscribe, to the creed or the funds of any party. He refrained from doing so openly; yet the widening circle of his associates and friends recognized, or at any rate suspected, where he stood, and none better than his outspoken neighbour, Leopold Amery. A wholehearted devotee of Milner and a follower of Joseph Chamberlain in his forlorn but vigorous attempt to win the Tory Government over to the Protectionist plan for strengthening the fraying ties of Empire, Amery vainly sought to convince Childers that he was being grossly unfair in condemning these two notable visionaries. They agreed only to differ; but the differences flared into a heated row when Amery took a hand in censoring the concluding chapter of Childers's lengthy and scholarly contribution to *The Times History of the War in South Africa*.

Shortly after returning from his honeymoon, Childers had started his research for Volume Five. The brief was to describe in detail the guerrilla phases of the fighting, a slow, painstaking task which would take up much of his leisure for the next three years. In the fourth volume written by Basil Williams he found a model of clarity and precision which he resolved to emulate as far as possible: 'The more I read,' he told the author, 'the more I realize how good it is, and what an example it sets me of dignity, impartiality and sound, true insight.'[1]

In the main, the reviewers of Williams's tome thought so, too. Amery, as general editor of the series, expected still more from Childers, hence his exasperation and disappointment at what Amery took to be intrusive political bias in the final chapter on the making of peace. Curiously enough, the passage of time appeared to erase from Amery's mind any recollection of his violent dispute with Childers. In his autobiography, written long afterwards, he singled out only the virtues of the book: 'The story of that protracted fight between the mobile and the mechanical conceptions of warfare, between the heavyweight pursuer with his widespread nets and the pursued with his elusive escapes and raids, was told in full with consummate skill and with sympathetic insight by my poor, ill-fated friend, Erskine Childers.'[2]

The author, however, showed at the time how keenly he felt by disclaiming all responsibility in his preface for the sections dealing with the tortuous negotiations that preceded the signing of peace terms. 'Mr Amery, in his capacity as general editor, has largely remodelled my draft of this chapter,' he wrote, 'and, as it now stands, he is solely responsible for it.'[3]

This clash of wills tells us as much about the fast-developing crusading spirit of Childers as it does about the contrasting views and personalities of these antagonists who, despite the quarrel, remained reasonably close acquaintances until 1914. In his own impulsive attachment to the truth as he saw it, Erskine Childers was beginning to disclose the qualities of a political dogmatist himself. There was also a distinct danger of his becoming, so to speak, type-cast as an amateur strategist. For the famous author of *The Riddle of the Sands* could be just as trenchant in denouncing outmoded army weapons or tactics as he had been in exposing naval unpreparedness. Nor did he take kindly to the obstructiveness of War Office functionaries who possibly feared what Childers might write about military blundering in the recent war on the veldt: 'I am rather depressed,' he admitted to Williams, now *The Times*'s correspondent in South Africa, as late as 27 June 1906.

The people around [Kitchener] seem to be so puerile in their secrecy – varied with a little useless and unhelpful satire. I am in the midst of an imbroglio now (about Ian Hamilton) which would be exquisitely funny if it were not so exasperating.[1]

His colleagues in the backrooms at Westminster continued to poke fun at his abnormal powers of concentration. When parliamentary business was slack, Childers would scribble a short love-letter to his wife, usually despatching a messenger to deliver it and await the answer along with another large folder of military files. Then he would settle down to private work, shutting out the chatter about him and not even hearing the noisiest jokes at his expense. Basil Williams noticed, too, on his return, Childers's facility for absorbing himself entirely in his own thoughts even at his own fireside:

'He and his wife often entertained their growing circle of friends with a simple and generous hospitality in that quaint drawing room of their Chelsea flat where Childers did his writing. Here, sometimes, when only intimates were there, one would talk to his wife . . . while he would go on writing, oblivious to all the talk around him; then suddenly, when one of the boys or his wife asked him some question, his face would light up with that wonderfully sweet smile of his and he would turn round to take part in the talk like a giant awakening from sleep. When comparative strangers were there, he never for a moment neglected his company like the excellent host he always was.'[4]

Childers adored his wife and doted on his baby son, who was at last joined in the nursery by a brother, christened Robert. The combination of official duties with the pleasant drudgery of writing pleased him just as the joy of talking politics with political acquaintances of almost every shade and colour stimulated him. He was most at home, he found, with Liberals; and through Walter Runciman, already regarded as a rising star of the party, he started to nurse vague political ambitions of his own. These he kept strictly to himself. His immediate aim was to consolidate his reputation as an author; so while he rejoiced at the resignation of Balfour and his discredited Tory administration, revelling in the enormous Liberal landslide at the polls in January 1906, he ploughed on steadfastly with the seemingly interminable volume of military history.

Because it was not in Childers's character to spare the feelings either of Amery, his general editor, or of his future readers, the book by no means appealed to leaders of the military establishment on its publication in 1907. The author's purpose, clearly defined at the outset, no doubt precluded that:

Although 'regular war' and 'guerilla war' are convenient terms to denote two widely different forms of military activity, it would be a profound mistake to assume that they have nothing in common. Both pursue the same end and both are governed by the same fundamental principles.... Moreover, it is the peculiar interest of guerilla war that it illuminates much that is obscure and difficult in regular war. Just as Röntgen rays obliterate fleshy tissues and reveal the bony structure, so in the incidents of guerilla war there may be seen, stripped of a mass of secondary detail, the few dominant factors which sway the issue of great battles and great campaigns. Subjected to close analysis, one of Kitchener's combinations may be perceived to have succeeded or failed from the same causes which dictated the success or failure of Marlborough's combinations....

It is in this spirit that the guerilla war should be studied. It will be found that the qualities which make for success in it are qualities which make for success in operations of the grandest scale, and which, recognized more clearly and striven for more ardently in the early stages of the South African War, would have shortened the campaign.... Two examples will suffice. If mobility, physical and mental, strategical, tactical and individual, seemed to be supremely requisite in the effort to close with and overcome the will-o'-the-wisp partisans who continued for so long to challenge the might of their great adversary, let us not overlook the fact that the same mobility was equally requisite on the first day of the war, and will be equally valuable in any campaign of whatever sort that the future may have in store for us. If, with every day the guerilla war lasted, the rifle, in contradistinction to the gun and the *arme blanche* [cavalry], stood out more and more clearly as the weapon of decided efficacy, let us throw the light of the fact not only upon the regular war in South Africa but upon wars in general

E

and see if it does not suggest some broad conclusions as to the proper function of artillery, and as to the utility, if any, of the *arme blanche* in the conflicts of the future.

And when, to combine both illustrations, we seek to obtain in his perfection the mobile rifleman, let that ideal figure have an universal quality, transcending even the most elementary classifications. Let us draw no impassable line between horseman and infantry, but rather set both arms, each according to its own capacity and each instructed by lessons derived from the other, to pursue the same end. Above all, when the inquiry is narrowed to the special functions of mounted men, let us shake off the fetters of verbal definition, dismiss for a moment the time-honoured terminology of cavalry and mounted infantry, and, piercing to the heart of the matter, find what it is we really want, and construct, if necessary, a single definition to meet a single need. Thus, and thus only, can we reap the full harvest of military wisdom from the finest school for mounted troops that Britain has ever obtained or is ever likely to obtain.[3]

Balanced and lucid throughout, Childers's narrative was fair yet often withering in underlining the faults of politicians and soldiers alike. For that reason alone, his eloquent plea for a thorough reform of military thinking fell on deaf ears. Not for the last time in his life he would discover the counterproductive effect of arguing a case too well. Kitchener, Milner and Brodrick, the Secretary of State for War; the unnamed senior staff officers in Whitehall whose antipathy to change and unorthodox expedients had augmented the burdens of the British soldier in the field; and the sacrosanct yet moribund methods of such arms as the cavalry – all these and many more fell under his scrutiny. Of the difficult situation confronting Kitchener, the new Commander-in-Chief after Roberts's departure, he wrote:

The British aim was not merely conquest but the absorption of a free white race, a race no longer retaining the weaknesses of colonial pioneers, but firmly rooted in the soil. It was an aim unparalleled in the history of our nation. Yet it was an aim whose character and magnitude the greater part of the nation but dimly apprehended. This was not unnatural; for the relation of vassal and suzerain, which in varying degrees had existed for so long between the two peoples, had shrouded from the vision of the suzerain power the growth of a Boer national sentiment as intense as that possessed by any of the historic polities of the old world.... It was this spirit which Kitchener had to fight. The conflict bore not the least analogy to any waged by Britain in the past, save the great struggle with her own colonies in North America. But, owing to the poverty of our military literature and the narrow horizon of our general education, the history of that war had become almost a sealed book to generations of British Officers.

As Childers also stressed, Kitchener lacked the quality and numbers of trained men vital for his purpose. With insufficient mounted soldiers and insufficient horses, the British Army was badly handicapped.

The regular cavalry formed the permanent foundation; but the profound conservatism which, as in most regular armies, characterized this arm, debarred it from setting such an example of vigorous originality as was urgently needed for the conduct of the campaign. It must be conceded that to convert cavalry into mounted riflemen was a drastic and difficult change. Their training and equipment rendered them incapable of competing tactically with the Boers. The long-range magazine rifle, that final arbiter of modern combat, was unknown to them. Their manoeuvres in mass were based on shock with the *arme blanche*. Individual intelligence was not high enough for skilled skirmishing, much less for skilled reconnaissance. Something had already been done to correct these defects. The lance had been eliminated, and, when Kitchener assumed the command, instructions had begun in the use of the infantry rifle. But proficiency with this weapon is not to be won in a day; some regiments – so potent were the influence of orthodox cavalry training – took unkindly to the new methods; that subtle and sensitive quality, the 'cavalry spirit', was destroyed, and there was nothing to take its place. Hence, although the cavalry always set a fine example of discipline, bravery and endurance, and although they produced a certain number of excellent leaders, the guerilla war added but a little lustre to their achievements.... The best lessons for the cavalry were to be learnt, not from the continental wars of the [eighteen] seventies but from the American Civil War of the sixties, when men of our own race, unhampered by prejudice or tradition, attacked and solved cavalry problems on fresh and original grounds.

The policy of rounding up Boer women and putting them in concentration camps was, as he put it, quite misconceived:

The decision was taken somewhat lightly. In its primary object it failed absolutely. Far from providing an inducement to surrender, it lifted from the fighting burghers a load of embarrassment. To the British the military consequences were disastrous.

With acute insight, based on correspondence with a reluctant Kitchener in faraway Simla, Childers sketched a superbly vivid picture of the necessarily high-handed methods by which the uncommunicative Commander-in-Chief imposed his will on subordinates:

In a silent, distant room, linked up by telegraph to every post and garrison in the country, sensible of the slightest shock at the remotest extremity, the Commander-in-Chief often was better able to judge a situation than his lieutenant on the spot, immersed in the immediate object in hand, groping somewhat blindly, perhaps, in a distant and difficult region, and out of touch with the strategic point of view of the higher command. On the other hand, interference was a dangerous weapon to handle. Employed too freely, and especially in the hands of a man of powerful will and imperious instincts, it was liable to impair responsibility and personal initiative.... But was there in Kitchener's subordinates a sufficient foundation of capacity for guerilla war and of readiness to take responsibility?

Of the diverging views between Milner and Kitchener on the surest way to win lasting peace, Childers buried his prejudice against the politician and strove hard to strike a just balance. Here again, he extracted some useful, first-hand reflections from Milner before putting pen to paper:

With whom was the main responsibility for its attainment to rest? By analogy with most wars it should rest with the civil power represented in South Africa by Milner. But once again the situation was unique. No general in the past had been placed in Kitchener's position. He was fighting a nation in arms, so that the military surrender and the political surrender must, in the nature of things, be closely intertwined. His army, moreover, was, in a very peculiar sense, arbiter of the settlement. Unidentified with the fierce political antagonisms of the past, it represented the first intimate contact between the empire at large and the Boer race. Its commander-in-chief, therefore was marked out to play a leading part, perhaps the leading part, in the final pacification. Whether, from the highest political standpoint, the position was a desirable one, the reader must be left to judge. At this point we are only concerned to indicate the conditions which gave rise to it and to prepare the reader for a difference of opinion between Kitchener and Milner which, at a later stage, assumed a somewhat important aspect. Broadly speaking, the difference was that Milner, from the political point of view, favoured unconditional surrender; Kitchener, primarily from the military but incidentally from the political point of view, was content to obtain a surrender on terms....[3]

Because Childers insisted on drawing to its logical conclusion a clash of views which tended to depict Amery's idol, Milner, in a poor light, the author and his editor quarrelled; and the author's bleak interpretation was so blandly toned down that he refused to let his name be associated with the all-important closing chapter. Childers believed that the subsequent embitterment of relations between Britain and South Africa, a permanent effect of war, marking the beginning of the end of Empire, owed a good deal to the intransigence of Alfred Lord Milner.[5]

In 1866, just four years before Erskine Childers's birth, when the elderly Queen-Empress would tolerate Germany alone among the Powers as Britain's natural ally and friend, the pleasure-loving Prince of Wales had produced a startling suggestion:

'Complications could best be avoided and the general interests of Europe could best be served by an Entente between England and France,' the future Edward VII told the French Ambassador to the Court of St James.[6] Such a departure was, of course, unthinkable then and for a generation to come. So long as Victoria reigned, the memory of her beloved Albert, the Prince Consort, would sanctify all things German; and so long as Salisbury held the political reins of office there would be no foreign entanglements to hamper Britain's freedom to act in a manner that befitted the greatest imperial power ever to rule on earth. The Boer War, and the threat of European intervention, rudely ended that policy.

Europe itself had by then split into opposing camps. A Triple Alliance consisting of Germany, Austria and Italy was countered by a Dual Alliance between Russia and France. For the Austrians and Russians had each ambitions to dominate the Balkans. The Germans, linked by natural ties of language and race with the Austrians, regarded the Near East and the backward Turkish Empire as an opening for commercial expansion which would compensate them for their lack of exploitable colonies. As for the French, they loathed the Germans whose annexation of Alsace–Lorraine after the humiliating débâcle of 1870–1 still rankled. The British, to complicate matters further, had been schooled in mistrust of France since the days of Napoleon, and recent rivalries in Africa had revived the feeling. So, regardless of the lively pro-French proclivities of the new monarch, the Foreign Office in London favoured the Triple Alliance and was ready to negotiate with the Kaiser.

Joseph Chamberlain's first attempt in 1901 to obtain a treaty of understanding with Germany came to nothing. Yet Balfour's Tory administration could no longer afford to pursue the precarious policy of 'glorious isolation'. So, at last, the Francophile sentiments of Edward VII came into their own. Erskine Childers was only one among millions of men and women, on both sides of the English Channel, who doubted the wisdom of even arranging Anglo-French talks. Remembering the splenetic anti-British tirades he had both read and heard during his cycling holiday in the Dordogne on the eve of the Boer War, his doubts persisted. By 1903 Chamberlain, having failed to get his way over imperial preferences, had resigned in pique from a government already in an advanced state of disarray; but that Government's final achievement, the *Entente Cordiale*, was possibly its greatest. It was the Foreign Secretary, Lord Lansdowne, who initiated the talks; it was he who instigated the visit of Edward VII to Paris; but it was the King who got (and probably deserved) most of the credit. As M. Paul Cambon, the French Ambassador in London, remarked afterwards to a friend: 'Any clerk in the Foreign Office could draw up a treaty, but there was no one else who could have produced the right atmosphere for a *rapprochement* with France.'[6]

Where Queen Victoria had scored with her restless pen, her worldlier-wise son and heir succeeded by his imposing presence, by force of personality, and by shrewd conviction. Britain had at last openly committed herself to lining up with France against Germany. Nor did Sir Henry Campbell-Bannerman's Liberal Government shrink from extending the practical scope of the treaty between 1906 and 1908, when the British public at large were slowly waking up to the fact that Germany was the one nation from which they had most to fear. To that extent at least Childers could reconcile himself without any qualms to the *Entente*. It gratified him to think that the warnings he had spelt out so clearly in *The Riddle of the Sands* were at last being taken seriously in Whitehall. He was equally well aware of the disagreements in the Admiralty between partisans of the reactionary Beresford and of the fiercely progressive Fisher. Here again the friendship of the King enabled the redoubtable Fisher to get his way more often than not, to the relief of his admirer, the watchful Erskine Childers.

'Our only probable enemy,' Fisher wrote to the future George V, 'is Germany. Germany keeps her *whole* fleet always concentrated within a few hours of England. We must, therefore, keep a fleet twice as powerful concentrated within a few hours of Germany.'

But any radical government was bound to have other concerns besides defence. There were already too many dusty, domestic corners for the new Liberal broom to sweep clean first. Naval expenditure was cut to provide more money for overdue social reforms. Fisher wisely forbore to protest, insisting that a streamlined Royal Navy could reduce its ships and men with no real loss of striking power. A champion both of economy and of efficiency, the Admiral declared that 'swollen estimates engender parasites both in men and ships which hamper the fighting qualities of the fleet. The pruning knife ain't pleasant for fossils and ineffectives, but it has to be used, and the tree is more vigorous for the loss of excrescences.'[6]

The Royal Navy happened to be in good hands; the same could hardly be claimed for the British Army. In Childers's eyes, the minds of its military commanders were heavily blinkered. It was no doubt a fortunate hour for Britain when Campbell-Bannerman frustrated Haldane's hopes of becoming Lord Chancellor by sending him to the War Office, that grave of so many past political reputations. There Haldane, drawing on his Scottish tenacity and German education, managed to perform quiet wonders of reorganization, in spite of belonging to a party which overtly detested militarism while wanting to have an army on the cheap. As Childers knew, the Army still had no central brain, no properly trained and constituted general staff. Its shape and structure in peacetime bore no relation to its needs for war; its brigades were not formed into divisions; it lacked artillery, transport and medical units. Its second line, the militia, could not be used abroad;

and its third line, the yeomanry and volunteers, belonged to a multiplicity of local units without sufficient funds, standing, training or equipment.

What Haldane, against heavy odds, unobtrusively, gradually but effectively did was to create a general staff and rebuild the Army into a striking force of one cavalry and six infantry divisions for service overseas, to take its place alongside the French in an emergency. Officer training corps were also set up at schools and universities. On Haldane's new Army Council, and also in positions of high command, younger battle-trained officers like French, Haig, Ewart, Nicholson and Grierson were appointed; and the Committee of Imperial Defence founded by Balfour was rearranged into specialized subcommittees so that every possible contingency could be examined. Even so, Erskine Childers put his finger firmly on the one fatal flaw in Haldane's bold new model: the unwillingness of the War Office itself and of its untried General Staff to learn the lessons born of tactical blunders committed on the veldt.

Had Childers been better advised, he might have done more to assist Haldane's enlightening structural reforms by shaming the generals into rethinking their tactics. But not content with the merciless criticism he had levelled at them in his recent study of the guerrilla phase of the South African War, Childers concentrated now on further denunciations of the cavalry which he regarded as an expensive and outmoded arm on any future battlefield. Time would undoubtedly demonstrate the accuracy of his view, but nobody thanked him for being presumptuous enough to say so in two short and highly controversial books he published in 1910 and 1911. His analysis of the misuses of cavalry in *War and the Arme Blanche*, and again in *German Influence on British Cavalry*, did not excite much public interest. The military coldly ignored his appraisal. So did most of the politicians. The fact that Field-Marshal Lord Roberts, a popular hero idolized as no other British general had been since Wellington, took the trouble to write the preface to the first book, warmly supporting the author's opinions, made little difference. Childers could have spared himself a lot of hard and fruitless work by concentrating on something far less technical. Alternatively, he could have put his message across with greater success had he chosen to do so in the guise of a second adventure story as realistic and enthralling as *The Riddle of the Sands*. If only he had summoned the patience to anticipate, for example, what C. S. Forester did at a later date in his brilliant study, *The General*, the impact of Childers's polemics would certainly have been more devastating than was in fact the case. By 1910, however, he was self-employed and therefore in too much of a hurry. He depended now on his pen for at least half his income; and in his anxiety to produce books quickly, he settled for the simple, straightforward but specialized business of the military analyst.

Basil Williams has recalled 'the ardour with which Erskine threw himself into an attack on the existing methods'. Williams was too kind to add that the attack proved unavailing. Molly firmly but imprudently encouraged her husband, wrongly assuming that he was bound to succeed a second time in altering strategic and tactical thinking, no matter what the chosen form of the books he wrote. So thoroughgoing was Childers's patriotism, so untarnished his idealism, that he wrote as he felt, from a strong sense of public duty. To the instructed minority who knew that this paradoxical writer, Childers, was telling the plain unvarnished truth, no explanation was necessary; to the complacent majority who closed their minds against his provocations, no explanation was possible. The loss to literature was great. For the author could have been far better employed.

The private world Childers inhabited was a well-ordered and harmonious place. His domestic happiness never palled; the passion of first love appeared to grow more intense with time. The Childers continued to dine out with their friends and to invite them home again and again, in 'the simple, pleasant and unostentatious fashion of the best hosts and hostesses', to quote one of their number. They had no ambition to move in exalted social circles. They had little in common with political and professional acquaintances who did. For if neither Molly nor Erskine had as yet any first-hand knowledge, or any wish to acquire it, of the privations endured by millions of poor people in the slums of London and other big cities, they suffered vicariously with the under-privileged through the books and papers they read. Thus their enthusiasm for the far-reaching social legislation enacted by the Liberals was unfeigned. Edwardian society at its apex was a narrow, opulent enclosure to which no writers or intellectuals in their senses would have sought admittance. Integrity and self-respect forbade it.

The wealthy and the fashionable aristocrats were not alone, of course, in the general looseness of their morals; but, taking their cue from a monarch who had always indulged himself, Edwardian socialites set the tone and standards which the 'lower orders' sometimes thought it smart to emulate. Not so the Childers and the friends they cultivated. Molly could be tolerant of others' lapses and foibles; but her own puritan values were high and strict. Of New England stock as she was, she had discovered long ago, in the mysticism of the Eastern sages, a far more acceptable approach to the Author of Life than the teachings of Christianity could provide. Being a voracious reader, she shared the discovery with her equally tolerant agnostic husband who regarded himself as 'an eclectic', choosing the best values of every religion to create a ramshackle pantheon of his own.

Of the hundreds of surviving letters written by Childers during these serene and untroubled years, those which shed most light on his contented state of mind were the few he scribbled to his in-laws, Dr and Mrs Osgood particularly, besides the ritual love-letters he unfailingly sent his wife on her birthday. The following extracts must do service for all the rest:

We managed to have three picnics in Richmond Park under a magnificent tree we have discovered where we make tea and read and talk. It is only half an hour's run there in my little motor.... It's such splendid fun doing it that even if it is a little unconventional we do not mind. As a matter of fact nobody cares here, I think.

The generosity of the Osgoods was considerable. Occasional bank drafts for sums as large as £1,000 helped to supplement Childers's already reasonable income, and beautiful gifts of carpets, china, Venetian glass and linen were lavished on the couple while they were home-making in the early period of their marriage. But this world's goods, however magnificent, were as nothing beside the abiding strength of their magical relationship. Erskine Childers often regretted the thirty-three and a half years he had wasted before he met his wife, and on the first birthday she celebrated after the arrival of their first son, he let himself go:

Have I not seen you radiate blessings on all around you, attract like a
magnet and warm like the sun other souls in trouble and perplexity....
And now, through our love, we have wrought that awful miracle, the
creation of a soul. Conceived in love, nurtured within your loved body,
born in uttermost love, your darling head within my arms while his
little form came into the light of day – there he lies, our love incarnate.

The same ecstatic feeling radiated from the letter he wrote
exactly twelve months later, when Childers admitted that 'it
terrifies me almost to think how much I love you because of the
fear of what would happen if I lost you. I don't know where I
end and you begin.'

Yet again, looking back, he poured out his renewed gratitude
thus:

Our minds have touched at a thousand points: we have been at sea
together and we have read many splendid things together. We sail, it
seems to me, on a great tide of happiness and hopefulness.[1]

On the hard plane of everyday reality, Molly had given him
miraculous eyes through which he watched the power game at
Westminster in a fresh and harsher light. Once the place had been
no more than a theatre in which the principal characters, the
Salisburys and the Balfours, the Campbell-Bannermans and the
Asquiths, the Churchills, the Lloyd Georges, and the rest had
appeared to strut and posture and expostulate like indifferent
actors playing in an endless improvised farce. Now he viewed it
far more solemnly, without deluding himself that the farcical
elements had disappeared. Nobody had yet invented a better way
of governing the British people than through this system of
parliamentary democracy which, under the Liberals, was fostering
measures to ensure more equality and social justice than old-
fashioned Tories yet thought desirable. Molly had been urging
her husband since 1906 to become an actor instead of a stage
hand at Westminster. Nor was he wholly averse to the suggestion. But the months had slipped into years, and Childers still
seemed in no hurry to move, for deep inside himself he could
hardly have been stabler or more at peace with life. He had
ulterior designs on the self-important, largely vapid, political
world he knew and liked; but he dallied. Even those weighty
books on the shortcomings of the War Office and the failings of

the Army were, like his earlier masterpiece, *The Riddle of the Sands*, more the product of a patriot's natural sense of duty than the self-conscious offerings of a politically ambitious man seeking to draw attention to his potential merits as a future candidate for one or other of the defence ministries. In fact, as will be shown, his unworldliness in that respect would prove his undoing when the belated opportunity to enter politics arose. For this would-be reformer and crusader still had the unerring knack of standing clumsily in his own light.

6. THE CONVERT

Erskine Childers would have been the first to admit that there were large gaps in his understanding of the turbulent, swiftly changing yet unreal world as seen from Westminster. His conservative cast of mind tended to shut out problems which fell outside his own direct experience, so that nothing in the Liberal Government's accelerating programme of social reform, for example, roused him to full awareness of the squalor, disease, hunger and misery in which millions of his fellow-countrymen still lived. The slum-dwellers of East or South London, the huge standing armies of the unemployed and the underpaid elsewhere, might have been inhabitants of another planet for all the impact they made on his conscience. As for the suffragettes and their militant activities, words failed him in trying to express his genuine horror of such irresponsible, wholly unfeminine folly. His urbane indifference to the privations of the British 'lower orders', an indifference shared by many less sensitive and imaginative men who sprang from his own upper-middle-class background, can be glimpsed in this extract from a chatty letter he wrote to Basil Williams in October 1908:

Molly is beginning a course of economics and finds it enthralling. The House is rather dangerous, what with suffragette riots and a threat of unemployed invasions. Victor Grayson, the Socialist, has twice been cast out by the Serjeant-at-Arms and threatens to return with an army of the unwashed. He has been denounced publicly even by Keir Hardie and Snowden, and is earning some discredit in Colne Valley by the revelation that the only time in six weeks he appeared in the House during the last part of the last session was the day he received his quarter's salary from the party and spent an appreciable [sum] on a luncheon party to some friends, which is still (for Gargantuan splendour) talked of in reverent whispers by the waiters of the House.[1]

At the heart of Childers's casual attitude lay a firm belief in the over-riding power of Parliament to see, judge, act and gradually lighten the burdens of the underprivileged. Westminster as such continued to mesmerize him. One day soon, he hoped, his chance would come to sit on the Liberal benches himself. With well-placed friends like Walter Runciman, Charles and George Trevelyan and Eddie Marsh to counsel him, he knew that the offer of a constituency to nurse could not long be delayed. Besides, the death of Campbell-Bannerman in the spring of 1908 had resulted in a significant reshuffle of Cabinet posts. Asquith was now Prime Minister; Lloyd George had moved to the Exchequer, Churchill to the Board of Trade. For six months before these moves came about, Childers had often noticed the short, stocky figure of Lloyd George striding along Chelsea Embankment towards Whitehall in fog, rain and sunshine alike. Occasionally they had nodded to one another and walked along together, exchanging pleasantries, though the committee clerk never thought of this rising political star and temporary neighbour as anything more than a distant acquaintance. For the quick, ebullient wit of Lloyd George, even in shouting a greeting, did not captivate the correct and rather earnest Childers.

The new Chancellor was certainly an aggressive and bold individual. He did not try to disguise his intention of saving as much money as he could from armaments to spend on radical reforms for the poor and the deprived. There had already been a clash in Asquith's new Cabinet over the Army estimates, with Churchill proposing a reduction in staffs of the medical, transport, ordnance and engineering services, and Haldane firmly resisting him. The Lords, for their part, refrained from blocking the Old Age Pensions Bill, though Lord Rosebery declared ungraciously that 'a scheme so prodigal of expenditure might be dealing a blow at the Empire which could be almost mortal'. The few millions of sterling required to pay a maximum old age pension of five shillings a week were not easily or cheerfully raised in the world's richest nation. The untamed spirit of free enterprise, on which Britain's industrial and commercial prosperity had been founded, cried out still in protest against providing state doles to the elderly, the needy, the sick and the helpless.

Even so radical a reformer as Lloyd George had remarked

with menacing geniality that revenue for such purposes would
simply have to be tapped. 'I have no nest eggs,' he assured the
House of Commons. 'I am looking for someone's hen-roost to
rob next year.' After all, he had been forced to yield to Admiralty
pressure for eight of the new dreadnoughts rather than the four
he considered appropriate in 1908. Lloyd George favoured a far-
sighted, balanced naval construction plan, not a makeshift policy
which represented what he called a 'poor compromise between
two scares – the fear of the German Navy abroad and the fear
of the Radical Majority at home'.

While Lloyd George was looking round that autumn for hen-
roosts full of fresh nest eggs to finance the revolutionary People's
Budget he had in mind, the House of Lords prepared to thwart
him. The peers, five-sixths of them Tories, had already thrown
out the Liberals' Education Bill. The new Licensing Bill seemed
likely to suffer the same fate. The Tory leader in the Upper House,
Lord Lansdowne, had decreed this at a special meeting in his
London home, causing Lloyd George to declaim: 'In two hours
this nobleman arrogated to himself a position no King in England
has claimed since the ominous days of Charles the First.'

A Tory backbencher at once protested that the Welsh orator
was letting his virtuosity run away with him. Everyone knew,
said this MP, that the Upper House was 'the watchdog of the
Constitution'. The time-worn cliché brought Lloyd George,
bridling, to his feet: 'You mean it is Mr Balfour's poodle,' he
retorted acidly. 'It fetches and carries for him. It barks for him.
It bites anybody that he sets it on to.'[2]

To Childers it was plain enough that, somewhat belatedly,
Asquith's Cabinet had little alternative now but to choose the
most effective method of muzzling the House of Lords. With a
permanent, built-in, hostile majority, that body would otherwise
block all the legislative reforms of a government commanding the
assent of an overwhelming majority of the people at large. Had
not Balfour openly and impertinently boasted after the Liberals'
landslide victory at the polls in 1906: 'Whether in power, or
whether in opposition, the Tory Party will control the destinies
of the country'?

Childers's sympathies were broadly with the Liberals, though,
as we have seen, he took little enough pride or interest in their

far-reaching social innovations. Relaxing at Glendalough in the late summer of 1908, he was glad to blot out for a spell the noisy and often unpleasant atmosphere of Westminster. An unholy alliance between the peerage and the 'beerage' had resulted in a flood of petitions against the Government's Licensing Bill; and he had been obliged to handle these personally. The measure seemed to be thoroughly unpopular with the brewers, and he had no doubt that the Lords would throw it out after the resumption of parliamentary business in November. The prospect pleased him. For Childers thought it high time the peers were put in their place. It did not distress him that the Government had no immediate plans for introducing a new Irish Home Rule Bill. He could see no urgent need for one; and, at least until the last weeks of his extended summer stay at Wicklow, he believed that Ireland's peace and prosperity would best be assured as an integral part of the United Kingdom. Then suddenly, as if dazzled by a blinding vision, the views of Childers changed almost overnight. The reasons for the transformation were merely hinted at in that same letter to Basil Williams, which he wrote a day or two after his return to London.

At one point he referred to a

jolly motor tour with my cousin, Barton, through a good slice of central and western Ireland, mainly to inspect cooperative societies in which he is much interested, and in which Sir Horace Plunkett and a good many other well known people look for the salvation of Ireland. I have come back finally and immutably a convert to Home Rule, as is my cousin, though we both grew up steeped in the most irreconcilable sort of Unionism. Meanwhile, agricultural cooperation is a splendid thing and will certainly make Ireland more self-reliant and prosperous. Plunkett is a strange personality, absolutely devoid of all the characteristic Unionist prejudices, whether of creed or caste, writing copiously in that cause, and yet apparently unconscious that Home Rule is the logical outcome of all he says.[1]

As a conversion, Childers's unexpected embracing of the Home Rule cause could scarcely be compared in completeness with the mystical rebirth of Saul on the road to Damascus. For one thing, he was embracing the cause rather late in the day, so late indeed that the Irish Nationalists at Westminster could no longer be said to hold the unqualified support of the Irishmen they represented;

for another, a new ferment of 'Ireland-for-the-Irish' activity had
been brewing during the past two decades of almost uninterrupted Tory rule. By a singular irony which Childers had largely
missed, the tough measures of successive Irish Secretaries, such
as Arthur and Gerald Balfour and George Wyndham, had brought
about ordered conditions in which Irishmen could begin to progress. This had encouraged the work of land reformers like
Plunkett, political visionaries like the editor of *The United Irishman*, Arthur Griffith, and cultural innovators like Lady Gregory,
W. B. Yeats and Synge. Since the days of 'bloody Balfour's'
tenure of the Viceregal Lodge, seldom parted from his loaded
revolver, it had become clear that what his uncle, Salisbury, had
once advocated, and the realistic Parnell himself had thought
feasible, was actually coming to pass. Through those twenty
years of resolute government the Conservatives had almost
reached the point of 'killing Home Rule by kindness'. Indeed the
tranquillity enjoyed by Ireland in one generation was deeper and
more real than at any other time in the past century.

From the Ashbourne Act of 1885 onwards, the policy of buying
out the landlords was carried out until Wyndham's more ambitious Land Purchase Act of 1903. This new measure set aside
initial credits of £100 million to make possible the sale of entire
estates, thus spreading ownership to tens of thousands of land-
hungry people. The loans would be repaid by annuities over the
next sixty-eight years. A quarter of a million agreements of the
kind were completed before the end of 1908; and Ireland pros-
pered, her exports, mostly to Britain, rising to some £150 million
a year. Again, an Act of 1898 had given the country elected county
and district councils. In the context of such developments,
Plunkett's cooperative experiment promised to turn a once depressed land into a second Denmark. For the scheme's beneficent
originator and founder was also a sound businessman and farmer
who had once been a successful rancher in the United States, and
from an uncertain start in 1889 his cooperative movement took
firm root, then gradually expanded. Within fourteen years it had
800 branches and an active membership of 80,000 farmers, probably representing about half a million Irishmen all told.[3]

If Childers could not help admiring Sir Horace, he was also
impressed by his quietly efficient and industrious secretary, the

poet and painter George Russell, better known as 'AE'. Yet their shared dislike of political entanglements puzzled the Englishman. Surely, he argued, their movement would benefit if it gained the solid support of the Liberals, a party still committed in principle to offering Home Rule to Ireland? Childers argued in vain. These two Irish Protestant reformers stoutly maintained that in their country at any rate one man's faith was likely to be the next man's heresy. Plunkett had expressed this sentiment well enough in 1895 when cautiously seeking to enlist the support of all men of good will: 'We Unionists,' he had declared, 'without abating one jot of our Unionism, and Nationalists, without abating one jot of their Nationalism, can each show our faith in the cause for which we have fought so bitterly and so long by sinking our party differences for our country's good, and leaving our respective policies for the justification of time.'[4]

What Plunkett had wanted then he wanted still: namely, a patriotic truce transcending the factious rivalries between Ulstermen and their Catholic neighbours, between those who accepted the Union and those who wanted Home Rule. It did not matter greatly to Plunkett whether Ireland should have a Parliament of its own in Dublin or should carry on under the control of Westminster. Across the deep historical divide of religious and political antipathies he hoped to throw an expanding bridge. The economic self-reliance and interdependence of all Irishmen provided a common factor which might eventually serve to unite them by diminishing their mutual political and religious antipathies. Erskine Childers regarded this plan as politically naïve.

The influence of Mary Childers in quickening her husband's newfound resolve to commit himself forthwith to the Home Rule cause cannot be underestimated. She had already learned enough of the tangled and often unedifying tale of Britain's overlordship of a land which had now become her second home to resent the arrogant assumptions of the overlord. No daughter of the American Revolution could have competed with Molly in decrying the injustice of an enforced union which had outlived its usefulness. If Sir Horace had imagined that his cautious methods would rally all Irishmen in time to reclaim their lost sovereignty, then Sir Horace did not know where and who his real friends and allies were. From that autumn of 1908 onwards, Erskine and

Molly Childers set out eagerly, as dewy-eyed Home Rule converts, to speed the slow bridge-building efforts of Plunkett. The
fact that he strove earnestly to discourage them proved an incentive rather than a deterrent. The additional fact that 'AE', in
his simple mystic's way, warned Erskine Childers against im-
mersing himself in 'the bog of Irish politics' could not dampen
the convert's first fervour.

Apart from these direct personal influences, a powerful underlying element in Childers's changed outlook was the hopeful
turn of events in South Africa where, by all accounts, Boers and
Britons were busily reconstructing the ravages of war in harmony
and evolving their own system of democratic unity. It cheered
him considerably to realize that Basil Williams had begun faithfully
to record each step towards that goal as the special correspondent
of *The Times*. To Williams, who had just sailed back to Cape
Town, he wrote:

'I don't wonder you haven't enjoyed the voyage so much as that of the
Montfort, of glorious and odorous memory.... What is bridge anyway
if it isn't played on a hard-won square-yard of greasy iron deck by the
light of the stars and an inch of guttering candle? The last three weeks
of my holiday in Ireland I spent digging a drain through a bog, a
filthier and harder job if anything than mucking-out; and once or
twice I caught myself thinking over the *Montfort* and the paradoxes of
life, wondering why I had so loathed every steamer trip I have taken
before or since.[1]

As the written evidence conclusively shows, Erskine Childers's
dependence on his wife Molly, in matters spiritual and intellectual
as well as emotional, had become very onesided. Nor did it correct or right itself with the passage of time. The love-letters he
poured out were unconventional enough in their explicitness,
so much so that during the long years of her widowhood Molly
Childers took pains to edit out of them sections which seemed to
her too intimate for outside eyes. He wrote to her always when
family duties or business interests caused him to leave home
briefly; he wrote to her too during idle intervals at work, sometimes to express his longing for her presence, sometimes to admit
that, because his indifferent memory had failed him again, a
messenger would shortly arrive to pick up papers for an evening

lecture. So idyllically united were they in their relationship that a kind of instant telepathy enabled the one to read the thoughts and feelings of the other, especially when they were apart. This was no mere game of empathy between lovers: it hinged, in her case, on a fixed belief that Erskine would one day do great things for mankind.

Wherever he happened to be, Erskine Childers unfailingly wrote to his wife on her birthday, 14 December. In 1908 he told her:

I feel less need than some years to write you a long letter. The sum total of our lives seems every year, while it grows bigger and more wonderful, to resolve itself into simpler terms and to appear as a divinely natural whole.... Our two streams have united in a broad river, deep and irresistible; and we know the river must reach the ocean and cannot squander itself in any desert or swamp. Fresh waters are always encircling us: experience, joy, sorrow, effort, difficulty overcome. Little Erskine has joined us. Little Henry was with us for nine months and his spirit is with us always. The pain and sacrifice his coming meant to you are not wasted but are possessions precious to us both.... You are just the same, spending yourself lavishly not only for me but for all who love you and for some not worthy of you; always holding up noble ideals, working indefatigably for our boy and household and me, developing your own mind and capacities, and always illuminating everybody and everything around you with the rays of your bright, gentle, buoyant spirit. You conquer petty things, scorn meannesses and always take high ground. Looking quietly and clearly back, I feel to my sorrow that I have not grown as much as you this last year.... This is my fault and I must cure it.

Their second child had been born feeble and deformed, his hold on life uncertain from the start. Molly had carried him with difficulty during the pregnancy; her own rare powers of endurance, the gift she had mastered in childhood of bearing affliction without flinching, had enabled her to suffer the loss of the baby in a calm, emotionally controlled way. Her husband marvelled at it. He felt small and humble beside her; and Molly's example made him yearn for a touch of such preternatural resignation. Their God, occasionally mentioned in Childers's passionate letters, was hardly the Supreme Being recognized and worshipped by Christians. The God of Childers seemed to be a far cloudier phenomenon than that, more like a mysterious but beneficent life force inspiring men to reach higher and devote themselves joyfully to the service of their fellows.

So even was the course of their domestic existence that Childers remarked when addressing himself ecstatically to Molly on her next birthday:

The year seems to have gone like a flash, and I would grudge the speed only that I feel more and more that, whatever be the meaning of death, it cannot affect our love and unity. Somehow, I cannot tell how, there must be a harmonious end: it must all signify something imperishably good.... I have thrilled to see [you] bringing your darling influence into so many lives this last year. I think you have more vital force in you than ten thousand.

The unrolling of events in the wider world seldom excited in him the same sense of wellbeing and fulfilment. The life of Asquith's Government was shaped in the first half of 1909 by a fresh instalment of the naval controversy, in the second by the gathering political storm over the People's Budget of Lloyd George; yet Childers took remarkably little personal interest in either of these issues. His sights were fixed firmly ahead on the constitutional consequences of the expected rejection by the Lords of Lloyd George's revolutionary budget proposals.

Politics are exceedingly gloomy here [he informed Williams], and Asquith is not showing a fighting spirit.... The only bright spot about the future is that it seems certain that the Lords' veto will henceforth dominate all other issues and will be eventually modified.... The power to force a dissolution on every big Bill, or suffer the humiliation of losing it, is an absurdly tyrannical power to give to the Opposition bench, for that is what it comes to. No Government, Tory or Liberal, could maintain any authority under such circumstances....

By the way, the 'Reform of the Lords' Committee have faintly suggested a referendum for cases 'of conflict between the Houses' – a delightfully one-sided arrangement, since there are no such conflicts when the Tories are in! Meanwhile, it is an interesting psychological study to see the effect of the mere practical power wielded by the Tories through the Lords. I verily believe that a great part of the electorate forms its opinion on the *merits* of a measure by the contrast between the results of Liberal advocacy and Tory criticism – the one being nil, the other victory! 'Surely this must have been a bad measure,' reasons the man-in-the-street.

Runciman, whom Childers saw quite frequently, told him that there were squabbles within the Cabinet before the Chancellor's measures gained collective assent. The proposed land taxes, especially, stirred landowners to the depths of their acquisitive hearts: a levy of twenty per cent on the unearned increment of land values, either at death or on the sale of the property; an extra burden of one halfpenny in the pound on the value of undeveloped land and minerals; and a ten per cent reversion duty on any benefit to a lessor at the end of a lease – such swingeing reforms naturally earned the denunciations of such Liberal peers as Rosebery and Rothschild. That summer Childers had to put off his holiday. So did the Cabinet and the Commons. Forty-two parliamentary days were required to steer the Budget through, and often the House sat far into the night. The City disliked the socialist taint and confiscatory nature of Lloyd George's measures. Irish MPs deplored the new tax on whisky. The rich condemned the increase in death duties as well as the supertax of sixpence in the pound on incomes above £5,000 a year. Childers, who smoked but did not drink, felt mildly aggrieved at the token tax on tobacco, the raising of income tax from one shilling to one shilling and twopence, and the small impost on petrol and motor-cars.

'This is a War Budget,' Lloyd George had declared towards the end of an exceptionally badly delivered Budget speech. 'It is for raising money to wage implacable warfare against poverty and squalidness. I cannot help believing that, before this genera-tion has passed away, we shall have advanced a great step towards that good time when poverty, and the wretchedness and human degradation which always followed in its camp, will be as remote to the people of this country as the wolves which once infested its forests.'[2]

The fiercest and longest parliamentary struggle since the passing of the Reform Bill in 1832 did not end in the Commons until 4 November, but the Lords had still to decide the Budget's fate. Whether they would dare break a rule already 250 years old, and throw out a money Bill, remained uncertain. Childers at this point was inadvertently drawn into the constitutional uproar. He was invited to help his superior, the Chief Clerk, to draft a 'power-ful memorandum which Sir Courtenay Ilbert ... submitted to the

Prime Minister on November 16'. By then, despite the King's attempted intervention, the Lords appeared intent on wrecking the Bill: so the Cabinet were swiftly drafting an alternative package, shorn of all controversial items, to be rushed through Parliament. Sir Courtenay, advised by Childers, argued strongly against this course of action. Not only would it concede to the Upper House the right to determine what legislation the Commons could or could not pass, it would equally present Balfour with a golden opportunity to prolong the crisis: 'There are occasions when respect for the constitution must override respect for the law,' the memorandum concluded. 'This may be one of them.'

Asquith bowed to the force of the argument, but ruled that payment even of non-controversial taxes should be voluntary until the Budget became law, any revenue required meanwhile being raised by borrowing. The Prime Minister also decided to dissolve Parliament and go to the country as soon as the Lords made good their threat; and with that intention, the following resolution was drafted for a Commons' vote:

'That the action of the House of Lords in refusing to pass into law the financial provision made by the House for the service of the year is a breach of the constitution and a usurpation of the rights of the Commons.'

On 30 November, five days after the Finance Bill got its third reading in the Commons, the Lords duly threw it out. Asquith at once took up the gauntlet and requested the King for a dissolution. A general election was fixed for the New Year. Lloyd George was beside himself with delight: 'Their greed has overborne their craft,' he told the National Liberal Club, 'and we have got them.'

Childers would have put it less coarsely, but he agreed with the Chancellor that the peers had at last overreached themselves, certain Liberals in the Upper House, notably Lord Rothschild, meriting the vituperative reproaches heaped on them. Unwilling to overlook Rothschild's demand the previous summer for eight dreadnoughts instead of the four authorized, Lloyd George recalled that the same Rothschild was now refusing to pay for any. It brought back to mind the cynicism of the cruel Pharaoh who had once ordered Rothschild's ancestors to make bricks without straw, an easier task than building dreadnoughts without money.

There were many eager Liberals, including Childers, who believed that, after winning the forthcoming election, Asquith's Government would have no alternative but to curb the power of the hereditary peers for ever.

Edward VII still hoped that wiser counsels, coupled with an element of delay, might avert what he regarded as a potentially mortal blow to monarchy and constitution. So, to his credit, the King turned a deaf ear to foolish suggestions that His Majesty could refuse to create the number of new Liberal peers needed to swamp Tory resistance in the Upper House. This remained Asquith's best weapon, 'the ancient safety valve, which Lord Grey had painfully induced William IV to threaten in 1832'.

Edward VII, to buy time, vacillated in the struggle. He was old and not in the best of health. Asquith's secretary, Vaughan Nash, informed the Prime Minister, when the electoral campaigning had begun, of a conversation he had had on 15 December with Lord Knollys, the King's secretary:

'He began by saying that the King had come to the conclusion that he would not be justified in creating new Peers (say 300) until after a second general election and that he, Lord K., thought you should know of this now, though, for the present, he would suggest that what he was telling me was for your ear only. The King regards the policy of the Government as tantamount to the destruction of the House of Lords. . . .'[5]

Naturally Childers knew nothing of these high-level exchanges, nor of the restrictions under which the Prime Minister had to labour in the throes of an electoral contest of unsurpassed bitterness. He was heartened by a pledge on Irish Home Rule given by Asquith in a vigorous speech at the Albert Hall: the new Parliament, declared the Prime Minister, would be freed from that 'self-denying ordinance' in 1906 under which the Liberals had undertaken to drop the issue for the sake of unity. What with the prospect of at least 300 new peers moving up to make room for suitable Liberal candidates, and the likelihood of legislation on Home Rule into the bargain, the political career on which Childers had set his heart was drawing appreciably closer. Even the poor showing of the Liberals on polling day tended, paradoxically, to elevate rather than depress his buoyant spirits. The Government clung to power only by the skin of their teeth, with 275 seats against the Tories' 273. Yet the Irish Nationalists, who won eighty-two, and the Labour Party, with forty new MPs, were in favour of Home Rule for Ireland, so Asquith would find it harder to ignore them if he wished to hold his tenancy of No. 10 Downing Street. Childers, by now, could hardly wait to push his writing to one side and take the political plunge.

The year 1910 was the year of Halley's Comet, so called after the astronomer who identified it in the twilight of Charles II's reign. Men of a superstitious turn of mind had always believed it to be a sign of bad tidings. The comet had been sighted on the eve of the Battle of Hastings, and again when Owen Glendower's revolt in 1400 set the Welsh Marches ablaze. The Prime Minister of England glimpsed it from the deck of an Admiralty yacht *Enchantress* in the early hours of 7 May 1910, shortly after receiving a message from London announcing that Edward VII was dead.

'I felt bewildered and indeed stunned,' Asquith recalled. 'At a most anxious moment in the fortunes of the State, we had lost, without warning or preparation, the Sovereign whose ripe experience, trained sagacity, equitable judgement and unvarying consideration, counted for so much .... His successor, with all his fine and engaging qualities, was without political experience. We were nearing the verge of a constitutional crisis almost without example in constitutional history. What was the right thing to do? This was the question which absorbed my thoughts as we made our way, with two fast escorting destroyers, through the Bay of Biscay, until we landed at Plymouth on the evening of Monday, May 9th.'[6]

The Liberal Government was only just recovering its poise after four uneasy months of a mandate which voters had renewed with manifest indifference. Well might Asquith ask: 'What was the right thing to do?' He could no longer advise his critics to 'wait and see', with a testy edge to his tone. The royal funeral had to be arranged. George V, the untried and relatively unsophisticated son of the late King, had to be crowned. If Asquith, in the words of a recent biographer, 'had been in no hurry to tender unpalatable advice to the old King ... he was doubly reluctant to do so to the new one'. It would have been unseemly to demand from George V an immediate guarantee, including a promise of the early dissolution of Parliament, which could well have been extracted, though not without spirited resistance, from his father. A compromise was sought and reached. The Cabinet expressed an almost unanimous wish to hold constitutional talks with the Opposition leaders. These were promptly arranged. The talks continued intermittently from mid-June until November 1910, when the meetings broke up in disagreement.

The two sides throughout had remained far apart in outlook. There was little chance of any true or lasting resolution of the conflict between them, not merely on the rights and the composition of the Lords, but on the issue of Home Rule as well.

'The man who was primarily responsible for the failure was Lansdowne,' Roy Jenkins has written. 'Of the other principal participants, Asquith, Balfour and Lloyd George were all anxious for a settlement. But Lansdowne was a Southern Irish landlord who had never forgotten the Land League. He was determined to do nothing to assist the passage of Home Rule, and he pursued his determination with stubborn resource.'[5]

Childers's elation evaporated quickly. Could the Liberals be trusted not to sell out to the Tories? Walter Runciman and Charles Trevelyan tried to reassure him that there could never be any compromise or breach of faith on the two key matters: the undemocratic powers of the Upper House and Home Rule. Both men were astonished at the unusual strength of Childers's feelings on the subject of Irish freedom. After all, they had known him well for twenty years and had always thought of this kinsman of Anglo-Irish landlords as Unionist to the core. Runciman seemed to take the change in outlook less seriously than Trevelyan, who was seeing far more of Childers at this period through their active membership of an extraordinary Rambling Club known as 'The Sunday Tramps'.

The club had been founded in 1879 by Leslie Stephen, author and editor of the *Dictionary of National Biography*, an ex-clergyman turned agnostic, who enjoyed climbing Swiss mountains and going for long walks. With little opportunity for exercise in the vicinity of his London home at 22 Hyde Park Gate, Stephen circularized his large circle of literary friends and gathered a sufficient number who were not averse to twenty-mile marches every Sunday, wet or fine. Among early members were Leslie Stephen's current literary collaborator, Sir Frederick Pollock, a leading legal authority; the future Lord Chancellor, Haldane; Sir F. W. Maitland and Lord Bryce, the constitutional historians; the future Poet Laureate, Robert Bridges; the art expert, Roger Fry; and Sir Henry Lawrence. Younger recruits included Leonard Woolf, later to be Stephen's son-in-law, the two Trevelyans, Charles and George, Desmond MacCarthy, G. Lowes Dickinson, John Buchan, Sir John Simon, the Rt Hon. F. D. Acland, and Hilton Young, the last three being Liberal MPs; and when Basil Williams returned from South Africa to teach and write history, he was elected to the Young Tramps, the junior branch, his membership number being 45 and that of Erskine Childers 53.

What better incentive could Childers have had than the attraction of spending a whole day in the open air with companions like Williams, John Maynard Keynes, Buchan or the artist Sir William Rothenstein to keep pace with? For the time being, opportunities of sea-going with Molly had all but ceased. Her health was worrying him, not without reason. For quite undiscouraged by the loss of her second baby, Molly had become pregnant again. The fresh air, the strenuous exercise and the intellectual stimulus of his weekend walking helped him to bear his domestic troubles more calmly. According to Alun Llewellyn, a much later member of the Sunday Tramps: 'The company was designed to be a school of peripatetic philosophy. Those sworn in by the Chief Guide, under a blasted tree, were meant to combine relentless thinking with unsparing debate. . . . Childers's activity was regular, extending over thirty-four walks between the entry of John Buchan (number 36) and Stanley Baldwin (number 115). His first recorded tramp was on November 22nd, 1908; his last in mid-June, 1914.'

Only in Edwardian England, where the individualism of so many late Victorians still flourished, could so informal yet closely knit and talented a group have existed in comparative obscurity. From Windsor to Wendover and the beechwoods of Buckinghamshire they stepped out one week, to Epping Forest and the Essex flats the next, or off they would go towards the Surrey Downs near Leatherhead and the open heathland beyond Woking. The summons came in the simple form Leslie Stephen had originally devised: a postcard giving the route and the times of trains from one or other of London's terminal stations to the chosen rendezvous.

There is only one direct reference in Childers's papers to these weekend outings: 'I like the *Tramps,* in spite of George Trevelyan's seven-mile-boot methods,' he wrote to Basil Williams. 'Charles [Trevelyan] is moderate and keeps by me sometimes. They have done me a lot of good.'

Several sailors in the club took to the quiet newcomer from the Commons' Committee Rooms as if he were a long-lost brother. Until now the author of *The Riddle of the Sands* had been only a familiar name to Will Arnold Foster, Cyril Baddeley, H. Wimperis, and Kenneth Swan, all members of the Royal Naval Volunteer Reserve. They quickly put a face to the name and accepted him as one of themselves. Presently his enthusiasm for sailing enlarged 'the interests of the Company into yachting on the Norfolk Broads' in imitation of their new friend's epic feat of seamanship. Older fellow-walkers of staider views included the permanent Secretary to the Board of Admiralty, Sir Vincent Baddeley, and the permanent Secretary to the Treasury, Sir Gilbert Upcott. None of them succeeded in penetrating Childers's reserve to prise out his growing concern with the problem of Irish freedom, though the Trevelyans did learn of his impatient desire to quit the Commons Committee Rooms and enter politics under the Liberal banner. He had left it rather late, they said, and he could not deny it. For in July 1910 he celebrated his fortieth birthday in the glum knowledge that middle age had begun to close in on him.

Childers had never been in the habit of rushing his fences. In the first place he had his family to consider. As Senior Clerk to the Chairman of the Committees, he now earned in the region of £800 per annum. Then there was his sense of attachment to the small, confined yet privileged enclave at Westminster where Sir Courtenay Ilbert had always tended to spoil him. Few clerks, if any, in the six hundred years since the appointment of the first during the reign of Edward III had forsaken the work to become active politicians. The late Hugh Childers, in his typically pragmatic fashion, might have regarded the job as just a foot in the right door. Erskine had meanwhile discovered that his kinsman wholly misunderstood both the status and the traditions of this exclusive company of men who kept the wheels of Parliament well-oiled and turning.

The prospect of rising higher, perhaps in time of succeeding Sir Courtenay himself, did not come top of the list of Childers's arguments against leaving. The reverse of ambitious, he had for too long been mixing official business with the outside pleasures of sailing and writing to consider himself a candidate for the succession. So for a few months longer he hesitated, unwilling to make the break.

It was once more at Glendalough, at almost the same time of year and in exactly the same enchanting atmosphere of detachment as had led him to espouse Home Rule just two years previously, that Erskine Childers at last resolved the dilemma, with Molly's help. Her advice to him was simple and uncompromising: ideals must come before everything else. Of course he would be sacrificing his career and much else by resigning his post. Of course they would have to tighten their belts, and he would have to work far harder at his writing until he won a parliamentry seat. As they surveyed from afar the unsettled state of affairs at Westminster, where the temporary party truce seemed to be fizzling out, Childers perceived that events might force him into the fray sooner than he had imagined. By the time they reached Chelsea in October he was ready to draft his letter of resignation. The original has not survived. There was no proper filing system in the Committee Rooms, just as there were no typewriters and no girls to do the routine secretarial work. The Chief Clerk tried hard to prevent his going. He could not understand why one of his favourite young men should be so foolish and shortsighted; but nothing Sir Courtenay Ilbert could say deflected Erskine Childers from his purpose. The Trevelyans were less mystified than pleased. And Walter Runciman promised to ask at the Whips' Office whether a convenient seat might not be found forthwith.

By 10 November 1910 the desultory efforts of the party leaders to compromise on the issue of the House of Lords ended in failure. When the Cabinet met that morning they decided on an immediate dissolution. Asquith called on the King at Sandringham next day, approaching the task of obtaining the necessary 'guarantees' from George V about the use of the royal prerogative to create new peers with what Roy Jenkins has aptly described as 'considerable distaste and almost excessive delicacy'.[5] The King believed at the end of the audience that the Prime Minister would not press him for the guarantees until after the election. Only later did he discover his mistake when Asquith received Francis Knollys, one of the King's secretaries, at No. 10 Downing Street and conveyed exactly the opposite impression: 'What he now advocates is that you should give guarantees *at once* for the next Parliament.' George V was angry, but this mattered less than the likelihood that the King and his ministers were on a collision course. For Asquith would have had no alternative but to resign if the Cabinet's advice to the King were rejected; Balfour would then have been sent for to carry on the Government until after the election; and that election would inevitably have been fought with George V at the very centre of the political stage. The situation was saved by the action of Knollys who, wiser than the other royal secretary, Sir Arthur Biggs, assured his Majesty 'that Mr Balfour would, in any event, decline to form an administration'.

Erskine Childers, ignorant of these constitutional niceties, nonetheless anticipated them by entering the field. Between the last week of November and the middle of December 1910 he wrote daily to his wife from half a dozen places in East Anglia, the north Midlands, Cheshire, and Lancashire. His raw unfamiliarity with the arts of politics shone forth in almost every line. His first port of call was the Liberal headquarters in the Suffolk town of Sudbury where, he had been officially assured, local party organizers were expecting him, since they had found no suitable candidate of their own. A breakdown in communications had apparently occurred between party chiefs in London and officials in Sudbury so he departed in disgust and some discomfort across country to Shrewsbury, on receipt of a hopeful-sounding if nebulous telegram from Runciman. There his reception proved, if anything, still more embarrassing:

This is another Sudbury fiasco, only much less excusable because the local people wrote to headquarters *asking* for a candidate on Saturday. Now it seems they don't want to fight. Nothing personal to me! I know they liked me. Sheer vacillation and cowardice.... I shall decide in the morning what to do – too tired now.

After lunch next day, he wrote again:

I'm disgusted with the leaders here. I nearly headed a mutiny this morning by calling a meeting of Liberals and going along as a guerilla, but after talks with a leading Radical who had pluck, and with his agent, who is just as keen, I decided it was not humanly possible. The whole organization is rotten and the rank-and-file are dispirited.... I wired the Whips and have just heard from Herbert [Gladstone] saying he is 'astounded and sorry' but has nothing more for me.

Instead of cutting his losses, Childers moved to Rugby and the temporary home of his old friend, Basil Williams, the Liberal candidate for a rural division of Warwickshire. He was glad to be of assistance; and he chose to help Williams for as long as necessary because, in Childers's own words, the candidate had 'no permanent gentleman helper to do the things I can do'. One of the things Childers could *not* do with any verve or confidence was to make an impromptu speech. His first attempt was 'unsuccessful'. Later, after taking his leave of Williams to speak and canvass on behalf of other Liberal contenders in Cheshire and Lancashire on behalf of his influential friend, Hilton Young, he frankly admitted:

Don't imagine I am losing pluck and self-confidence if I say that I am not sure that I can make a good speaker. It is *very hard* indeed.... Conviction and sincerity are much; but technique is much, too, and memory, mental agility and humour. Every time before speaking my last thought is of you, of your splendid brain and righteous spirit burning through me and joining with mine. I am going to try hard again at Chester.

Childers kept a melancholy note of Liberal setbacks as the staggered polling results reached him. It grieved him to learn that Basil Williams, for one, had been defeated:

There's a deadweight of slow silent Toryism in that division which it will take years to move. I told him that my work there was a memory I shall not forget because he stands for the noblest type of Liberalism – would it were all quite as noble, but the provocation is great. Things were clean there, but Toryism up here is the most sordid, ugly monster you can imagine.... And I am not really bitter. I believe in my countrymen – Liberal or Tory – much too firmly. We are all right and I have

no fear for the long future, though I do have doubts about the near
and tactical future of the Liberal party.

Molly was expecting her child at any moment, and her husband's solicitude found utterance in every letter:

You said the baby had turned round. How is it now? Are you having
bad heart burn. Or is the sour milk damping it off? You are right about
our babies. They are our message and legacy to the world.

It irked and saddened him to hear so little evidence of any
positive Liberal interest in the cause of Irish freedom. From
Macclesfield he wrote:

I am appalled by the slackness up here about Home Rule. Liberals seem
asleep about it and not in the least to realize that they *must* give it
promptly or perish.[1]

The result of the election should have surprised nobody who
understood the British voter and his studious insensibility to any
political debate, however portentous, which happened to bore
him. For the second time in less than twelve months the Government sought the public's verdict on the merits of the constitutional struggle. It was given halfheartedly, an almost word-for-
word repetition of the previous indecisive result: a working
majority of 126 instead of 124, thanks mainly to the gains of the
Liberal Party's temporizing with Labour and Irish Nationalist
allies.

Childers had meanwhile come face to face with the same inscrutable phenomenon, the British voter; and the creature's
caprice equally baffled and bewildered him: 'One of the joys of this
business,' he told Molly, 'is that one meets Liberals of all classes
instead of only living in the somewhat doctrinaire atmosphere in
which we upper classes discuss our politics in London.'

Once the Parliament Bill became law, and he hoped this could
be achieved before the coronation of the King in June 1911, then
the Liberals could fortify their position as the natural party of
government. If the Lords held out then the process might take
longer. In that case his own chances of returning to the Commons
as an MP would be considerably enhanced, because Asquith
would not hesitate to invoke the royal prerogative and create at

least 200 new Liberal peers, Acland and Runciman among them. It was now, at this psychological moment, that Childers felt impelled to start writing again. His theme was new, he thought. An authoritative book on Home Rule and its tangled implications suddenly struck him as all-important. He had started to study the question at leisure in 1909.

The spur to write, and write quickly, was not applied by harsh economic necessity. On the contrary, an unforeseen incident had recently provided a welcome boost to the sales of all his previous works, *The Riddle of the Sands* in particular. In the week before Christmas 1910, at a much publicized state trial in Leipzig, two British naval officers, Captain Trench and Lieutenant Brandon, were charged and found guilty of espionage and each sentenced to two years' imprisonment by a German court. At the time of their arrest the previous August at Borkum, one of the towns in the Frisian islands immortalized by Childers's novel, the documents, maps, photographs, camera and sextant found in their possession hinted that the two officers might have been working for British Naval Intelligence.

Under interrogation, they refused to say anything about the 'Naval Baedeker', a restricted manual on the sea-coasts of various countries, or about 'Reggie', a mysterious character said to be connected with British Naval Intelligence. Their silence was understandable in the circumstances, yet Lieutenant Brandon proved less reticent when his counsel brandished a copy of *The Riddle of the Sands*. Here was a book, Brandon enthusiastically admitted, which he had already read three times. The *Daily Telegraph* correspondent in court not unnaturally deduced that Erskine Childers must know more about Borkum than the two men in the dock would ever acquire.

'Since my novel has been referred to in the trial . . . I venture to think that my impression of the episode may be of some little public interest,' Childers wrote.

So long as nations maintain armaments for purposes of war, so long, as a necessary corollary, must plans, as definite and detailed as possible, be made in advance by each nation for the eventuality of war.... In point of fact, every Admiralty and War Office has, as a recognized part of the system, an intelligence section for the collection and assimilation of the necessary facts.

F

As to the specific charges against the accused officers, Childers had no doubt whatever about their hollowness:

Captain Trench, for example, is charged with having measured depths of water while bathing at Sylt and Amrum, two of the North Frisian islands. Well, that is within the right of all bathers, whether at Eastbourne, Sylt or anywhere else. For my part, I should be content to rely for my measurements on the extraordinarily accurate and detailed large-scale charts of the German North Sea coast, published by the German Admiralty and obtainable at stationers in London, which give depths, whose accuracy I have myself tested down to the tenth of a metre.

Nor did Childers think himself unique in what he had observed on an alien shoreline: 'Travellers of all sorts – motorists, bicyclists, yachtsmen, mountaineers, scientists, economists, journalists, novelists – do, in fact, do this sort of thing every day, and in doing so promote international amity. It may seem an ugly paradox that similar studies may be directed to warlike ends, but war itself is an ugly paradox.'[7]

The fear of armed conflict with Germany haunted him less persistently now than it once had done, though for three whole months between July and October 1911 there were alarms which seemed likely to plunge Europe into war at any moment. The crisis had arisen when the Germans tried to force a settlement of their Moroccan dispute with the French by despatching a gunboat to Agadir. How ironic to think that the long Victorian peace, shattered needlessly (as Childers still maintained) by a giant's clumsy struggle with a pygmy in South Africa, now looked so illusory in retrospect. The ultimate security of Britain had come to depend on alliances with France and Russia, two nations perpetually plagued by insecurity. The hinge of British foreign policy for nearly two centuries, the isolation afforded to a people protected by the sea and a strong navy, had been broken by modern forces transcending the will of statesmen or the power of any single country. With his own somewhat grandly apocalyptic sense of history, Childers rightly felt that the French revolutionary principles of 1789 were working through to the world at large, and the terrible logic of liberty had become confused with the ideals of nationhood and racial differences. The old class-ridden world of Childers's boyhood was, he knew, fast disintegrating: so, for that matter, was the British Empire.

The expansion of the German Navy continued to be the barometer of the slow drop in Britain's military supremacy. Though the appointment of Bethmann-Hollweg as German Chancellor in 1909 had promised a respite, two years of negotiation had resulted in no agreement on 'a naval holiday'. Britain's response, inevitably, was to keep up a 60 per cent superiority in dreadnought strength and lay down two keels to every one in Germany's shipyards. The failure of Haldane's mission to Berlin in 1912 led to even more momentous results, at least one of which chimed exactly with Childers's earlier warnings: this was the basing of a Fleet in home waters and the concentration of the British Mediterranean Fleet on Gibraltar, leaving that once British-patrolled ocean to be guarded by the French. Such was the background to France's dangerous intervention in Morocco between two rival Sultans, and the equally foolhardy response of Germany in sending a gunboat called *The Panther* in an aggressive attempt to extort territorial concessions in the French Congo. The threat of war forced Britain into the open. Lloyd George, the Chancellor of the Exchequer whose political enemies had neither forgiven his pro-Boer sentiments nor forgotten his dislike of public spending on arms, offered short shrift to Germany: if Britain, he said, were to be treated 'as if she were of no account in the Cabinet of nations . . . peace at that price would be a humiliation intolerable for a great country like ours to endure'. The Agadir crisis instantly faded. Other perils to peace remained.

The Childers now had a second child, also a boy. Robert was born earlier that year in his parents' flat off the Chelsea Embankment. Erskine, the elder son, already in his seventh year, had grown into a bright, talkative and companionable child who often went walking with his father across one of the two bridges spanning the river to Battersea Park, opposite their home. The memory of those dying years of Edwardian peace stamped themselves permanently on the mind of this imaginative youngster. Some sixty years later, during his brief tenure of office as President of the Irish Republic, the second Erskine Childers declared:

'My favourite place was the park lake where we used to hire a rowing boat and row across to the island, pretending to be pirates. It was an education to be with him. For he answered all my questions, no matter how indiscreet, as though I were a grown-up. My mother adored him; and he adored her. I could see that even then. And his one regret was that she could never accompany us on our expeditions by bus to the City, or occasionally on Sundays to hear the choirs at Westminster Abbey, St Paul's, Westminster Cathedral and Brompton Oratory. It didn't matter which church we went to because my father, though quite a spiritual man, didn't hold with organized religion. We loved our home. My mother had a fine eye for finely contrasting colours, and I can still see the vivid greens and reds of the carpet and chair coverings in our drawing room.'

Erskine Childers junior was sheltered in these surroundings from the squalid world whose boundaries reared up half a mile from his home. Neither his father nor his mother, he knew, took any active interest in social problems, so that conversation about rail and coal strikes and similar disputes tended to be sparse and casual. Ireland, and the complex problem of giving the Irish their freedom, absorbed both parents to the exclusion of almost everything else except defence questions. So, when Erskine Childers senior vanished on his travels, as he did in the spring of 1911, it was to Dublin and Belfast he went for talks with leading industrialists, Government officials, 'Imperial Home Rulers', orthodox Unionists, priests and a few practical reformers like Sir Horace Plunkett:

'I have just had a long talk with Sir Horace about plans,' he informed Molly in mid-March.

He thinks it is absolutely necessary for me to go North before writing my book, though he is also very anxious for me to stay here [at the Plunkett House, Dublin] and see more ... Barber [an Ulster mill-owner] comes on Friday and ... wants to put me up and bring me in touch with the young crowd of Ulster Unionists.

Childers, on his return, scarcely lifted his eyes from the manu-script of his latest work, *The Framework of Home Rule*, until he had finished the last paragraph. He was growing more skilled with practice at sticking to what journalists call 'a deadline'. His new publisher, Edward Arnold, wanted the book for his autumn list. So the author worked away and obliged without wrecking his social life. Friends, old and new, still came regularly to dinner; and because their housekeeper lived in, just as frequently the Childerses dined out with Eddie Marsh, the Runcimans, the Arnold Toynbees, the Williamses, the Trevelyans and other intimates. Sir Courtenay Ilbert, genial and forgiving, had not struck the Childers off his guest list, despite his continuing dis-approval of Erskine's irreversible act in resigning from the Committee Office. Sir Courtenay remained unimpressed when, in May 1912, the deserter was adopted as prospective Liberal candi-date for one of the two seats at Devonport: 'MPs are ten-a-penny, and none worth the price,' he declared sarcastically.

The Lords had thought twice about defying Asquith. After the unnaturally hot summer of 1911, with temperatures in the nineties for days on end, the Government and their keenest supporters began turning their minds a little wearily to the likely shape and content of their still unpublished Home Rule Bill. Childers and Basil Williams had meanwhile been active in sponsoring and running a small society known as 'The Home Rule League', which several Liberal MPs and not a few intellectuals and writers joined. In a note to Williams from Glendalough on 15 October, Childers said:

I have been so frightfully busy with proofs etc. that I haven't had time to write.... I am awfully glad you and Buxton put together that draft Bill, because while committing the Committee to nothing you suc-ceeded in suggesting pretty clearly the advantages of the wider form of Home Rule.[1]

One factor which Childers and his friends gravely underesti-mated in their Home Rule equation was the probable degree of resistance by the Ulster Protestants and their champions, the traditionally ill-disposed Tory Party at Westminster. The rabble-rousing gifts of Sir Edward Carson, who in February 1910 had become leader of the Ulster Unionists, had yet to be tested: but friends of this eccentric Southern Irish Protestant of Italian blood, the MP for Dublin University, with his law practice, his enormous charm and the grimness of a chronic hypochondriac, took in his meaning when Carson spoke at Craigavon in September, 1911;

'We must be prepared . . . the morning Home Rule is passed, ourselves to become responsible for the government of the Protestant province of Ulster.'

No member of the Liberal Cabinet was yet solid for any Home Rule measure which would apply to the whole of Ireland, North and South. Churchill's filial loyalty no doubt explained his reservations. Had not his father, Lord Randolph, denounced Gladstone's first Home Rule Bill in advance by asserting that 'Ulster will fight and Ulster will be right', though Lord Randolph's motives were prompted by the purely political thought that 'the Orange card would be the one to play. Please God it may turn out to be the ace of trumps and not the two'? As for Lloyd George, his familiarity with the nonconformist outlook made him only too well aware of the electoral risks involved in trying to force reluctant Ulsterman to live under 'Home Rule'. The Tories, incensed and humiliated by the passing of the Parliament Bill, were bound to 'play the Orange card' once more, with a vengeance. Only Erskine Childers, romantically relying on logic, justice and historical precedent, went on idly hoping that prejudice and bigotry would not cause Asquith to weaken. His personal view of the Ulster factor was stated frankly:

It is futile [he wrote in *The Framework of Home Rule*, which appeared just in time for Christmas 1911] to criticize Ulster Unionists for making the religious argument the spearhead of their attack on Home Rule. The argument is one which especially appeals to portions of the British electorate, and the rules of political warfare permit free use of it....But it is hardly to be conceived that Ulster Unionists really fear Roman Catholic tyranny. The fear is unmanly and unworthy of them.... If I may venture an opinion, I believe that both of these mutually irreconcilable propositions – that Home Rule means Rome rule, and that Rome is the enemy of Home Rule – are wrong. Such ludicrous contradictions only help to destroy the case against trusting a free Ireland to give religion its legitimate, and no more than legitimate, position in the State.[8]

Unlike any of his previous books, this erudite and penetrating study of the Irish problem failed to exercise any influence either on the course of events or on the minds of partisans already locked in sterile debate on the rights and wrongs of the case. Yet the work remains to this day a curiosity of an exceptional kind, not merely for its readability and scholarship but again for that same eerily prophetic element that runs like a fine thread through his other works. He entertained no doubts about the difficult nature of his task in writing it:

The modern case for the Union rests mainly on the abnormality of Ireland, and that is why it is such a formidable case to meet. For Ireland in many ways is painfully abnormal. The most cursory study of her institutions and social, economic and political life demonstrates that fact. The Unionist, fixing his eyes on some of the secondary peculiarities, and ignoring their fundamental cause, demonstrates it with ease and ... passes instinctively to the deduction that Irish abnormalities render Ireland unfit for self-government.... In other words, he prescribes for the disease a persistent application of the very treatment which has engendered it.... This train of argument, so far from being confined to Ireland, is as old as the human race itself. Of all human passions, that for political domination is the last to yield to reason....

In the meantime, for those who like or dislike it, Home Rule is imminent.... And next year we shall be dealing with this problem in an atmosphere totally unlike that of 1886, when Home Rule was a startling novelty to the British electorate, or of 1893, when the shadow of impending defeat clouded debate and weakened counsel.... Unfortunately, after eighteen years the problem remains almost exactly where it was. There are no detailed proposals of an authoritative character in existence. No concrete scheme was submitted to the country in the recent election. None is before the country now. The reason, of course, is that the Irish question is still an acute party question, not merely in Ireland but in Great Britain.... In the case of Home Rule, when the balance of parties is positively determined by the Irish vote, the difficulty reaches its climax.... Not until Home Rule is a moral certainty, and perhaps not even then, do the extremists intend to consider the Irish Constitution in a practical spirit. Surely this is a perilous policy.

By drawing on his knowledge of constitutional history, especially in relation to the granting of independence to other white countries of the Empire after the loss of the American colonies, Childers managed to place the Home Rule debate in its true perspective. The experience of Canada, of Australia, and more recently of South Africa, showed how little understanding could be expected from Westminster of basic Irish needs until Irishmen and Englishmen entered into a sensible dialogue:

Within the present bounds of the Empire no lasting constitution has ever been framed for a subordinate State, to the moulding of which Parliament, in the character of a party assembly, contributed an active share. Constitutions which promote prosperity and loyalty have actually or virtually been framed by those who were to live under them.

Childers went much further than anyone else in advocating what later became known as the 'Dominion solution' of the question. What drove him almost obsessively to it was the knowledge of Ireland's physical proximity to Britain, with all the psychological, material and other disadvantages which flowed from it:

Those sixty miles of salt water which we know as the Irish Channel – if only every Englishman could realize their tremendous significance in Anglo-Irish history – what an ineffectual barrier 'in the long result of time' to colonization and conquest; what an impassable barrier – through the ignorance and perversity of British statesmanship – to sympathy and racial fusion.[8]

His plan contained no clause for the exclusion of Ulster. It embraced the whole island, North and South. Ireland would send no elected representatives to Westminster, and would retain complete control of its fiscal and financial policy. Ireland would reserve to the Imperial Parliament the power to make laws, among other things, on the Crown, on war and peace, on the Army and Navy, on foreign relations and treaties, on extradition, on treason and on titles and dignities. Writing as an idealist, a radical and a mildly disenchanted imperialist, the author finally commented:

If a Home Rule Constitution, passed into law in the heat of a party fight at Westminster, proves to be perfect, a miracle will have been performed unparalleled in the history of the Empire...

Home Rule will eventually come. Within the Empire, the utmost achieved by the government of white men without their own consent is to weaken their capacity to assume the sacred responsibility of self-government. It is impossible to kill the idea of Home Rule, though it is possible, by retarding its realization, to pervert some of its strength and beauty, and to diminish the vital energy on which its fruition depends. And it is possible in the cause of Ireland, up to and in the very hour of her emancipation, after a struggle more bitter and exhausting than any in the Empire, to heap obstacles in the path of the men who have carried her to the goal.... They will need their hands strengthened in every possible way.

Alas for Childers's romantic idealism, exquisite clarity of thought and wistfully evocative parallels with the democratic development of further-flung portions of the Empire he still faintly cherished! Those 'sixty miles of salt water which we know as the Irish Channel' were already proving too narrow to prevent the destruction of his dreams. Time itself was running out. It is only fair to add that he expected too much of his 'Home Rule Bible'; he felt it ought to be read and religiously followed. This was a mistake which converts to new causes often commit. And the consequences of failure were to prove catastrophic both for the cause itself and for the political innocent who espoused it.

7. THE ENTHUSIAST

The Framework of Home Rule only gradually became for Childers what Newman's *Apologia pro Vita Sua* already meant to the founder of the Oxford Movement while writing that classic in the white heat of conviction. The differences between the two men, the two methods and the two masterpieces need little elaboration. True, none of Childers's Liberal friends could deny the odd fact of his conversion to an unfashionable cause; but he was not yet prepared to die for it, as he would one day, with the selflessness of any martyr. For Childers's mental and spiritual apparatus, even the knowledge he possessed of his newfound creed, were far less well developed than Newman's. By mid-1912 the seven fat years of expectation, during which he had watched with mounting enthusiasm the new Liberal dawn, were slowly yielding to seven lean years of deepening disillusionment. Childers had already reached the point of no return, though recognition of that likelihood came filtering through the haze gradually and unsurely.

At the outset, from early 1912 until the spring of 1914, he behaved outwardly as if little had changed. Indeed, his faith in the good intentions of Asquith seemed to burn more brightly once the Home Rule Bill was published and launched on its stormy passage through Parliament. In missing the great parade at Craigavon, just outside Belfast, on 23 September 1911, six months before the introduction of the Bill, when Carson and his Ulster lieutenant James Craig had addressed a huge crowd of some 50,000 Orangemen and Unionists on the lawns outside Craig's home, Childers felt that he had missed nothing of any consequence. Nor did he attach much significance to Craig's grimly theatrical words of warning: 'I now enter into compact with you and with the help of God you and I joined together . . .

will yet defeat the most nefarious conspiracy that has ever been hatched against a free people . . . . We must be prepared, in the event of a Home Rule Bill passing, with such measures as will carry on for ourselves the government of those districts of which we have control.'

Childers was inclined to dismiss the affair as a highly organized piece of bluff, even while acknowledging that the naked force of religious bigotry might obstruct any immediate accommodation between Irishmen of North and South. Fortunately, not all Ulster Protestants were as prejudiced as Craig. After meetings with Andrews, Sinclair and Barber, three of several wealthy Ulster industrialists who played host to Sir Horace Plunkett and himself, Childers described them to his wife as

impressive and very narrow in a sort of way one understands and sympathizes with. Plunkett was wonderful with them – marvellously adroit, searching, candid and withal sympathetic. He avowed himself a Home Ruler of the *passive* kind, and said he would take no part in the controversy, and implored them to run their case on reasonable lines.[1]

Of extremists in Dublin and the South, Childers the outsider still knew very little except by hearsay. Perhaps here he allowed himself to be too readily persuaded by the largely apolitical Sir Horace, who had a poor opinion, for instance, of Arthur Griffith, editor of a small weekly paper of disproportionately wide influence formerly called the *United Irishman*. That Griffith and his forceful views formed a rallying point for the reviving Irish Republican Brotherhood, for disgruntled Nationalists, and for out-and-out Republicans, did not mean anything to the indifferent Plunkett. The parallels originally drawn by Griffith between the efforts of Hungarian patriots forty years previously to win freedom – emphasis on language and cultural differences as well as the withdrawal of their representatives from the Imperial Parliament in Vienna – and the attempts of the Irish Protestants in the late eighteenth century to secure legislative independence from Britain, were discounted by Sir Horace as being hopelessly irrelevant to the condition of Ireland in 1912. The resurrection of Ireland would not be achieved by such farfetched political thinking. It did not concern Plunkett that, since May 1905, Griffith's ideas had been rechristened *Sinn Fein*, a title transferred also to his newspaper. Yet neither the policy nor the weekly journal represented more, in 1912, than the sounding-board of a minority within an extremist minority; and its appeal to the Irish people appeared to Childers obscurantist and quite unreal at a moment when Home Rule was dangling at last within reach of John Redmond, the long-suffering Irish Nationalist leader at Westminster. Besides, since 1909 Griffith had been holding back deliberately in order to give Redmond half a chance.

Childers therefore felt reasonably sure, despite the ritualistic fury of Ulster dissent, that Redmond's opportunity would not long be delayed. Alas, he reckoned without the backing which the Ulster Unionists could count on from Bonar Law and the Tory Opposition at Westminster as well as from their self-chosen champion, Carson. The complacency of Childers's current mood is reflected in the breezy letters he wrote home from Dublin and Belfast in March 1912, and later from Devonport in the early summer of that year after his unanimous adoption as one of that town's prospective Liberal candidates:

Just had an open-air meeting, fairly good one, I think, on Insurance only. We find there is great interest in that...

A pleasant interlude last night a trip upriver with the young Liberals. Inevitable speech at end on bridge of steamer. I got fascinated with an Irish family – Carroll – whose baby (about the size of Bobbie), called 'John Redmond', saluted at the name and made what was meant to be a speech on Home Rule.

Like any eager candidate nursing a seat he badly wanted to win, Childers kept a wary eye on issues which weighed most with constituents who would probably be casting their votes sooner than they imagined. For the Liberal Whips had indicated, and their candidate for one of Devonport's two divisions accepted the assumption, that Asquith would seek a dissolution and order a snap election on Home Rule just as soon as the political omens were right. Then, to his dismay, the prospects of an early election receded. So Childers took time off from nursing the constituency to meet the two naval spies, Trench and Brandon, who had just been released from prison in Germany. He also took a short summer cruise with his wife, paid his customary visit to Glendalough, and returned to dance attention on the citizens of

Devonport during the chilly weekends of late autumn and winter.

'Last night was a *frost* and we were disgusted,' he reported one bleak January morning in 1913. 'No preparations, very small attendance – stony cold schoolroom hung with big, obvious texts. I spoke about Ulster. . . . Also, I think, was eloquent about Home Rule as a whole, but that wasn't reported at all. Such is fortune!' He was painfully learning the difficult arts of capturing audiences and becoming wholly accessible and amenable to individuals and deputations with grievances. In his room at the Durnford Hotel, Plymouth, where he invariably stayed, he would spend his few leisure hours writing articles for the *Nineteenth Century*, the *Western Mercury*, the *Nation* and other periodicals, on subjects close to his heart. Many of these were 'potboilers', for Childers had to keep the wolf from the door of his commodious Chelsea flat. Sales of *The Framework of Home Rule* had not been brisk. One of the compensations of a parliamentary candidate's life, he found, was the uncovenanted kindness sometimes shown by total strangers.

I had been talking to a strong Tory, a naval outfitter, quite polite and *bon enfant* but by no means Liberal. We parted and a little later I met him further down the street, evidently waiting for me. He stopped me and said: 'Are you a relative of Mr Hugh Childers?' I said 'Yes' thinking it was the old Childers' canard, but to my astonishment he said: 'I am going to vote for you – your cousin was on my ship (he'd been in the Navy) for three months in the Mediterranean. For the sake of that memory I'll vote for you.' Isn't politics queer?

Politics, he learned could also be a confusing, tedious and time-wasting business. He liked and admired Lithgow, the other Liberal candidate, but often wished the latter would respond more promptly to 'the chairman feebly applying the coat-tail brake' whenever the long-winded fellow mounted a platform. There were public scandals to bear in mind when hecklers appeared, though Childers had to admit that 'the Marconi affair has aroused little interest down here. We have not mentioned it and have not been heckled.' In his moments of despondency he felt helpless and lost without his wife to whom he confided one day in a self-deprecating note:

I only discovered my trusslessness about 4 pm today and thought you would probably observe it and send it on. I feel unhoused without it but there's no harm done. It is wretched without you and I must now go to my lonely bed without your sweet body by me.

Childers's political idealism was distinctly that of the simon-pure, somewhat ingenuous enthusiast, as another letter, written on the train from Paddington, made clear:

I am in the midst of a kind of vision – wondering how one can do most to help one's fellow-man in the exacting business of politics, wondering how we can use ourselves to the best advantage – one's brain and other faculties in the midst of issues so vast and obscure, and seeing how one can get into the soul and essence of the Devonport problem.... It's all so difficult.[1]

The couple escaped from Britain in the long parliamentary recess of 1913 to refresh their spirits aboard the *Asgard* in the seas about Germany. A young pilot of the recently formed Royal Flying Corps, Captain Gordon Shephard, joined them at one of their many ports of call. Shephard, like Childers a quiet advocate of Home Rule, was the only son of wealthy Anglo-Irish parents. An experienced yachtsman himself, he professed an unreserved hero-worship for the man who had written *The Riddle of the Sands*. Another friend on the voyage who equally relished being one of the *Asgard*'s crew was the writer and teacher Alfred Ollivant. With rare insight he afterwards described his skipper in action during a violent storm:

'The winds were contrary. We beat all down the Baltic, and, south of Christianso, ran into a gale. Some tackle broke away at the mast head and had to be lashed down. Childers, already grey, lame and the eldest of us by some years, went aloft to do it. A little figure in a fisherman's jersey, with hunched shoulders and straining arms, the wind tearing through his thick hair, his face desperately set, he tugged, heaved, fought with hands feet and teeth, to master the baffling elements and achieve his end. This is how I saw him then; that is how I shall always see him now – a tussling wisp of humanity, high overhead, and swirling with the slow swirl of the mast against a tumult of tempestuous sky.... He had [recently] written *The Framework of Home Rule*, believed in the Dominion status [of Ireland], and was standing as a Liberal candidate for Parliament. Next year he abandoned his candidature, in the main, I think, because of his disappointment at the surrender of Mr Asquith's Government to Sir Edward Carson.'[2]

Ollivant was loosely correct in that last surmise, though Childers had more practical reasons for giving up Devonport and quitting Liberal politics soon afterwards. He had never cared for the custom, still prevalent in some districts, of extorting cash from prospective candidates for local charities and other causes, including generous hospitality for people prominent in promoting such causes. At first he tried to ignore it, then he protested, and finally he explained to astonished party organizers why he must withdraw forthwith: the practice had an unpleasant whiff of the corrupt about it. The party managers offered him the choice of alternative seats, one in London at St Pancras West, the other at Kidderminster. Childers was on another visit to Belfast during the last week of September 1913 when he received the news from Liberal headquarters: 'Illingworth's [letter] is certainly nice,' he informed Molly at Glendalough,

and they evidently want to keep me.... I still have a curiously strong feeling of resistance to embarking on another constituency. I think it is partly the money question and partly the impression that I could use such powers as I have better in other ways. I fear you will think it cowardice but I believe it is not so.

His wife had become mildly critical of Childers's restiveness. She could not fathom his petulant desire to turn his back on English politics. Somewhat selfconsciously, he touched on this sore spot in the next letter he sent her:

Apart altogether from Ireland, I feel misgivings about England of the kind I told you before. Chief among them is the money question, and the feeling of being put by the Whips into situations which I should not otherwise be in.... Against this is the overwhelming desire to acquit myself well and to shrink from nothing through cowardice, and to be a credit to you and our children. Here I must be careful, for if I have been really failing rather through lack of self-confidence, as you often say, there is nothing for it but to take the bull by the horns as I did when I sailed out in the *Mad Agnes* all alone.

Significantly, it was during this same trip to Belfast that

Erskine Childers first met Sir Roger Casement at the home of Joseph Biggar, an Ulsterman and an Irish Nationalist MP:

Casement is mad about Home Rule, and has given up his official position and thrown himself wholly into it. [Captain] Jack White is very ardent, too, and is trying to get the Protestant Home Rulers together and to make them take an open stand.

It was only too plain to Molly that her husband's impetuous enthusiasms had begun to run away with his judgment. For he admitted to her virtually by return of post:

These last days I have been more and more in the back of my mind accustoming myself to the idea of giving up a political career in England. I spent most of the morning with Casement, climbing a lovely mountain just behind the town and talking. He is a Nationalist of the best sort and burning with keenness but, I fear, unpractical. That seems to be the trouble with most of the leading Ulster Home Rulers.... Nevertheless, I am beginning to think it is true, what I have always suspected, that the Carson racket is a Belfast proposition and that the Provisional [Ulster] Government is meant for Belfast only and could never gain any control outside a small radius. Oh, how sad I felt as I sat on Cave Hill and looked down at Belfast in the haze – the key to the whole of this terrible problem – and thought of its wonderful history way back and what a desperate pity it is that no resolute effort had been made for a century to win it back to Nationalism.

Even the Ulster Day ceremonial failed to deflate him. He maintained that all the martial utterances of Carson and his gang were so much empty wind. He attended the big parade at Balmoral

to see the review of the Orange hosts. What it amounted to as a political demonstration I hardly know. It seemed to me suspiciously lacking in enthusiasm and numbers, seeing it was the highwater mark of a fortnight's reviewing and alarums and excursions.... There was a very dull and silent wait of nearly two hours before the 'troops' arrived. We counted about 8,000, and you may discount all accounts purporting to give a higher figure.... Not, I should say, temperamentally a *fighting* lot. Half their number of Catholic working men, as well organized, would, I believe, best them, if they fought as they did in South Africa and as they are reputed to do in street rows here. At about 5.15 the staff came to the front on horseback, Richardson, the general, and his officers and aides (F. E. Smith conspicuous). The whole line of massed battalions then moved about twenty paces closer to the dais ... and

A cripple from childhood, Mrs Erskine Childers helped her husband
in the Howth gun-running but opposed his Irish Republican ideals
at first. (*Illustrated London News*)

An unsmiling Robert Erskine Childers, photographed towards the
end of an adventurous life when there were reasons for sad reflection
on the fate of his ideals. (*Radio Times Hulton Picture Library*)

ABOVE LEFT: Robert Erskine
Childers, aged seven (right) with hi
elder brother, Henry.

ABOVE RIGHT: At Haileybury.

LEFT: Shortly before his marriage
(1903)

OPPOSITE ABOVE: Childers, file und
left arm, at the fateful London
Conference of 1921, immediately
behind Michael Collins (seated at
centre), with Arthur Griffith (extrer
left) and Robert Barton (seated on
right). (*Syndication International Ltd*)

BELOW: Childers the volunteer,
aged 29, in the British Army during
the Boer War. (*Radio Times
Hulton Picture Library*)

Childers, the gun-runner, standing briefly on the quay at Howth, near Dublin, alongside his yacht *Asgard,* as the smuggled arms are moved ashore by Irish volunteers. Back to camera, wearing white jersey, is Mary Spring Rice, who chronicled the voyage.

Mr and Mrs Erskine Childers aboard *Asgard* in 1910 during one of their long holiday cruises through the Baltic. (*Radio Time Hulton Picture Library*)

Carson came out ... a fine figure, bare-headed, with his hooked eagle nose, sallow face and prominent chin.... He spoke then for about five minutes. I couldn't hear anything but the end – 'We will never have Home Rule'. Then the army marched past ... I expected more fire and popular excitement and more men in the ranks. The quietness *may* be due to confidence and habit ... or it may be partly due to weariness with a grand imposture.

The enthusiast's wish had become father to his thought; but Childers was obliged to acknowledge that 'there is littleness on both sides – too much of it'. What irked him most about Carson's so-called Provisional Government, defiantly set up to seize control of all Ulster once Home Rule became law, was its essentially archaic and undemocratic structure. 'It is all landlords (many peers), land-agents and employers of labour: no farmers or working men, and there is discontent among the rank-and-file.' He found this out in the course of more confidential talks over dinner with local commercial leaders. Among the guests one evening was William Young, the Secretary of Carson's provisional Government,

a charming fellow but I should say the last man for such a responsible position – and his mere presence in it strengthened my belief that P.G. is a piece of magnificent bluff....We pressed him about the Ulster Amendment to exclude the four counties. He said it was their last chance of asserting themselves and starting a revolution, but obviously uncomfortable about the implications especially with regard to the South and West Protestants. For the rest – no compromise. I found him quite ignorant of history. Talked of 1688 and missed out the whole of the 18th century. Didn't seem to have heard of Wolfe Tone or the Volunteers of 1798! Quite a child.

Nevertheless, Childers was glad to leave Belfast, the Protestant and Catholic ghettos of which he inspected, as well as 'the intermediate territory where all the fights begin'. What he saw only strengthened his faith in the urgency of Asquith's Home Rule Bill for 'an Augean cleansing of the city' where 'the extremes of wealth and poverty are appalling. I'm ... sure much of this so-called "business objection" to Home Rule is sheer fear of an uprising of labour, now held in leash by mere virtue of the religious split.'[1]

One simple reason for Childers's misreading of the increasingly tense Ulster *impasse* lay in the blindness brought about by a tolerant agnostic approach to religious divisions. It did not require a Newman to grasp the root of the matter. Anyone with a working historical knowledge of the appalling lengths to which Christian fanaticism could go might have better understood both the depth and the dangers of the current 'religious split' in Northern Ireland. It was part of Childers's misfortune that he failed to grasp its intractability. Indeed, he sent a report to Liberal Party headquarters in London, at the behest of a senior official, and in it he minimized the importance of ingrained religious bias among Ulstermen as an obstacle to Home Rule for Ireland as a whole. Familiar though he unquestionably was with the melancholy story of Anglo-Irish relations since Strongbow, conscious as he had become of what he owed his kinsman, Hugh, for disentangling so many recent and little-known fiscal and legal injustices, he nevertheless could not penetrate to the heart of a problem which Carson, Craig, Bonar Law and others were exploiting naturally and instinctively. A single episode, isolated and therefore of relative unimportance, momentarily shook him:

I had a sickening experience yesterday, a sermon by one Patterson, a Presbyterian, in a big church here – a howling tirade against Catholics and the beastliest appeal to bigotry I have ever heard. [He was] like a Mad Mullah and only fit for the Congo, calling them heathen and as good as goading his people to burn them at the stake. I hear, however, that he is a specially bad specimen of the militant divine. Lucky. More like him would drench Ireland with blood.[1]

The 'Orange Card', and everything it connoted in terms of the 'religious split', had been the trump in the hands of Unionists in Belfast and Tories in London for nearly two years already. Childers's logic worked on a higher plane, disregarding irrational factors and treating the cardinal issue of Irish freedom strictly on its intellectual merits. His awakening was thus bound to be all the ruder when it came, his disenchantment with Asquith and English Liberalism all the greater. As a seasoned Westminster-watcher, he sat back realizing that no result could be expected from the first two parliamentary circuits of the Home Rule Bill. So it hardly surprised him at all when the Lords threw it out twice, first at the end of January 1913 and again in mid-July that year. The fact that Asquith did not raise a finger to discourage the seditious provocations of the Tories, in league with their rabid Ulster confederates, did not trouble him yet. For Childers, still a reluctant Liberal candidate toeing the official line in deference to his wife's wishes, shared Asquith's wistful belief that civil strife over Home Rule was improbable because British citizens could always be counted on in a crisis to respect the authority of the Imperial Parliament. If Childers erred, he erred in highly select company.

Private conversations took place in the winter of 1913-14 between Asquith, Bonar Law, Carson and others in an attempt to reach an agreed compromise by excluding Ulster, or part of it, from the Home Rule Bill. Childers was immensely relieved by the failure of the two sides to reach a solution. From his well placed Liberal friends he gathered that the King, who had taken a hand personally in arranging these talks, was hoping for a general election and a Tory victory so that this contentious measure would be shelved indefinitely. Poor John Redmond, the hapless leader of the Irish Nationalists, who, in Childers's view, had virtually become a loyal slave of the system, clenched his teeth and accepted, in turn, first a three-year then a six-year exclusion of Ulster from the eventual operation of the Bill. Asquith had bargained, however, in vain. For Carson tossed the hard-won concession back in the Prime Minister's face: 'We do not want sentence of death with a stay of execution for six years,' he told the Commons on Monday, 9 March 1914. Not only Redmond but Childers at last felt cheated and betrayed.

The precise timing of Childers's awakening was at breakfast on the morning of 10 March 1914, when he opened his newspapers and read the previous day's parliamentary reports. He had just crossed to Queenstown to meet his American mother-in-law off a transatlantic liner; and his face was a picture of unrelieved gloom as he welcomed her ashore. On his return to London he formally asked Liberal Party headquarters to remove his name forthwith from the list of their parliamentary candidates. No longer could he serve a party which had so gravely bartered away the one cause above all others which tested its honour and its credibility. Nor did Childers shrink from explaining the reasons for his decision to Runciman, the Trevelyans, Alice Stopford Green and other Liberal friends, freely denouncing Asquith for 'spinelessness' and the Cabinet as a whole for cowardly expediency in bowing to 'Carson's bluff'. His main fear now was that the seditious example of eminent lawyers like Carson and F. E. Smith might, in the long run, sap the ordinary citizen's confidence in the stability of parliamentary government. Had not Carson, in that scandalous way of his, appealed direct to the country over Asquith's head by asking: 'Are you going to allow the forces of the Crown, which are your forces and not the forces of any political caucus, to be used to coerce men who have asked nothing but that they should remain with you? And if you are, are you going to give up, even for a moment, to a government which may be here today and gone tomorrow, the right yourselves to determine what is real liberty – and this to a Government who have refused, when asked, to appeal to the country?' This amounted to an open declaration of war, as Childers knew. What he did not appreciate was the genuine anxiety of the Cabinet that, in Ulster, warlike acts might at any moment be triggered off by the inflammatory words of Carson. Nor did he yet suppose that the loyalty of some senior British soldiers in Ireland and in Whitehall was already suspect.

What Childers grossly and completely underestimated was Ulster's will to fight. Echoing the Boers, Ulstermen were demanding the right to live in freedom; unlike the Boers, their freedom lay in retaining integral and traditional ties with the United Kingdom. Irish Home Rule was, had been, always would be, anathema to them. They had a defence force whose commander General Richardson, a retired regular officer, claimed the moral support of such eminent veterans as Kitchener and Roberts. Only when he learned that the Tories at Westminster were threatening to move an amendment to the annual Army Act did Childers succumb to despair of democracy's survival – and then only fleetingly. Bonar Law, according to Robert Blake, his biographer, sought to amend the Army Act 'in such a way that the Government would be unable to use the army in Ulster until after a general election', but decided against this course on reflecting that Ulstermen might not in the end accept the electorate's verdict if this went against them.[3]

Intelligence reports from Ulster suggested that plans had been laid by 'evil-disposed persons', as Churchill called them, to raid arms depots at Armagh, Omagh, Enniskillen and Carrickfergus. Asquith had been sufficiently impressed by these reports to appoint a special Cabinet subcommittee early in March 1914, to take appropriate countersteps. The four members were Crewe, a moderating influence, Seely, the somewhat injudicious Secretary of State for War, the impetuous Churchill from the Admiralty, and the occasionally supine Irish Secretary, Augustine Birrell. Unfortunately for Asquith, Crewe fell ill at a very inopportune moment, depriving the Cabinet subcommittee at the start of its one statesmanlike figure. Seely, needing little encouragement from Churchill, sent orders on 14 March to Sir Arthur Paget, the Commander-in-Chief in Ireland, 'to ensure the safety of Government arms and stores in the south as well as the north of Ireland'. The same day Churchill let fly at Bonar Law, the leader of the opposition, castigating him as 'a public danger . . . seeking to terrorize the Government, to wreck the Home Rule Bill, and to force his way into the councils of his Sovereign'. Churchill assured the Tory leader that there would be no yielding by the Government to the threat of armed violence; the Civil War battle of Marston Moor had settled that once and for all. 'Let us go forward together and put these grave matters to the proof,' he said.

Paget was summoned to the War Office on 18 March and told in detail by the Chief of the Imperial General Staff, Sir John French, and by Seely, Churchill and Birrell in turn, of the six contingencies (including the possible outbreak of fighting between Protestants and Catholics in Belfast, should an Ulster Provisional Government be unlawfully proclaimed) for which he must be ready to deploy troops. The consideration which weighed most with the ministers was the prospect of 'an organized, warlike movement of Ulster volunteers under their responsible leaders'. If that happened, then it would have to be met with force, and 'large reinforcements' would have to be sent from England if required. Of course, they assured the General, the worst was unlikely to happen. Precautionary troop movements of the kind envisaged would probably help to avert bloodshed. Paget strove hard to get concessions from Seely. With the help of French he partly succeeded, going back to Dublin by the night mail on 19 March 'with the assurance that officers actually domiciled in Ulster would be exempted from taking part in any operation that might take place. They would be permitted to "disappear" – disappear was the word used by the War Office – and when all was over would be allowed to resume their places without their career or position being affected.'[4]

Calling together his senior officers, Paget announced that 'active operations were about to begin against Ulster and that he expected the country to be in a blaze by Saturday'. The message had an electrifying effect. The War Office received two signals from Paget that night. According to the first, the commanding officer of the 5th Lancers had reported that all his officers except two, with one doubtful, were resigning their commissions. The second telegram was briefer but no less dramatic: 'Regret to report,' it ran, 'Brigadier and fifty-seven officers, 3rd Cavalry Brigade, prefer to accept dismissal if ordered north.'

To Seely and Churchill, it looked like mutiny at the Curragh. To Bonar Law and his friends, thoroughly briefed down to the last detail by the Director of Military Operations at the War Office, Sir Henry Wilson, an ardent Ulsterman and devoted intriguer, it appeared that Ulster was about to be treated as a 'new Poland'. London buzzed with rumours, and the newspapers naturally exploited these. Childers and his friends, particularly Alice Stopford Green, were dumbfounded by the evidence of disaffection in the Army. Asquith issued a statement to *The Times*, for publication on Monday 23 March, which was generally regarded as a masterpiece of understatement. Troop movements, he claimed, were purely precautionary. 'As for the so-called naval movements, they simply consisted in the use of two small cruisers to convey a detachment of troops to Carrickfergus without the necessity of marching them through the streets of Belfast. No further movements of troops are in contemplation.'

Hubert Gough, the troublesome officer commanding the 3rd Cavalry Brigade, stormed across to London and succeeded in extracting from his superiors at the War Office an admission that the fracas had been due to a 'misunderstanding'; the Government, he was informed, had no intention of using the Army 'to crush political opposition to the policy or principles of the Home Rule Bill' either then or when the Bill became law. Asquith subsequently drew back in alarm. He repudiated the endorsement of Gough's previous scrap of paper by the compliant Sir John French as 'a new claim which, if allowed, would place the Government and the country at the mercy of the Army'. French and Seely had no option but to tender their resignations, and both were accepted. Small wonder, in the midst of such pandemonium, that Mrs Asquith, in an emotional appeal to Austen Chamberlain, cried out from the heart: 'The first shot that is fired now, my Henry goes down and his life's work is over. *There never* was "a plot" of any sort or kind, I swear, as I wish God to help me here and hereafter.'

In spite of the so-called 'Curragh Mutiny', the Home Rule Bill got its second reading before Easter 1914; but the reverberations of the affair rumbled on for weeks after Parliament reassembled. Bonar Law promptly demanded a judicial enquiry. Asquith refused, promising instead a White Paper more informative than the first, which had been rushed out with too little preparation in a futile attempt to silence the Opposition. This second document had the opposite effect from that intended, as it turned out; the Government agreed to a grand inquest in the form of a two-day parliamentary debate to be held on Tuesday and Wednesday, 28 and 29 April.

The King meanwhile had by no means given up hope of persuading Asquith to restore peace by amending the accursed Home Rule Bill. George V proposed that the six counties of Ulster should be allowed to contract out for an indefinite period, without a plebiscite: 'Surely you could persuade Mr Redmond and his friends to go to this length for the sake of peace, which the whole country is longing for,' he wrote to the Prime Minister in the week before Easter. 'I trust that you will lose no time to renew your conversations with Mr Bonar Law and Sir E. Carson as you promised me.'[5]

Asquith who, since Seely's departure, had taken on the chores of the War Office in addition to his burdens as Prime Minister, formally acknowledged in his usual suave fashion this 'rather hysterical letter from G.R.', as he privately styled it. He was already steeling himself for the grand inquest on the Curragh incident when a disturbing telegram reached him via Dublin Castle on the morning of Saturday 25 April. It stated baldly:

'About 8 p.m. last night a large body of Ulster Volunteers Force armed with truncheons, numbering about 800, mobilized at Larne under Sir William Adair and Major McCalmont MP. They drew a cordon round the harbour and vicinity and allowed no one to pass except a few on business; police and Customs Officers particularly excluded; signals from sea had been observed and large numbers of motor cars arrived. Two steamers, believed *Mountjoy* and *Millswater*, discharged cargoes of what appeared to be arms and ammunition which were conveyed away by motor cars. Reporting fully today. Telegraph and telephone communication interrupted.'

The Cabinet could not agree on ordering the arrest of Adair and McCalmont, as Aberdeen, the Viceroy, had urged as a first priority. For four successive days the Cabinet met and finally decided cautiously against precipitate action of any kind. As the most recent biographer of Asquith, Roy Jenkins, has accurately commented:

'The pressures which pushed the Cabinet towards this retreat were typical of those which always destroyed the possibility of resolute action against Ulster illegality. The King was firmly against prosecution, of course. So was Birrell, the member of the Cabinet with direct responsibility, and so too was Redmond. The latter wrote insistently to Asquith on April 27th. He did not believe that any Irish problem could be solved by the application of the criminal law. Most insidious of all the influences, however, was the line taken by the Unionist leaders in the House of Commons.'[5]

Sweetly and unaccountably reasonable for a change, Bonar Law and Carson hinted at their belated interest in a compromise. The Cabinet, urged on by the King, drafted its own amending Bill to meet Ulster and Tory demands, introducing it by design into the Lords on 23 June 1914. The Upper House, with its huge Tory majority, rewrote the measure to suit the extremists' wishes. All nine counties of Ulster were to be excluded from the application of Home Rule, without benefit of plebiscite or mention of time-limits. Clearly another *impasse* had been reached; and the existing party machinery prevented any constitutional escape, since the original, unamended Home Rule Bill (protected by the operation of the controversial Parliament Act) would be ready

for the Royal Assent within the month, and would then apply to
the whole of Ireland.

It was at this decisive point, in the wholly contemptuous view
of Childers, that the Prime Minister suffered his final and least
defensible failure of nerve. By the use of various go-betweens,
including Lloyd George, he succeeded in narrowing down
partisan differences to a matter of simple geographical boundaries
in Ulster, or so he fondly imagined. A conference at Buckingham
Palace seemed to be the simplest method of solving the outstanding points of disagreement. The King was delighted by Asquith's
conciliatory gesture and suggested that the Speaker of the Commons, Lowther, should preside. The Buckingham Palace discussions, in which the Prime Minister, Lloyd George, and the
Irish Nationalist leaders, Redmond and Dillon, confronted
Bonar Law, Lansdowne, Carson and Craig, were solemnly opened
on 21 July. On the Unionist side at least, according to Bonar Law's
biographer, there was no expectation of a successful outcome.
Their leaders 'only attended in deference to the King's wishes'.
By that stage, an utterly scandalized Erskine Childers was on the
move.

Six weeks earlier, despairing of any honest salvaging of the
problem by a Government of which he had once hoped so much,
Childers decided to take the law resolutely into his own hands.
The 'remarkable little man' who had planned and carried out the
recent and successful gun-running to Larne, Frederick Hugh
Crawford, indirectly inspired the disillusioned ex-committee
clerk of the Commons to emulate his example in a period of
lawlessness at every level. A member of one of the oldest Presbyterian families in Ulster, Crawford, like Childers, had fought in
South Africa; earlier still, in Gladstone's last term, he had conceived a harebrained scheme of kidnapping the Liberal statesman
on the front at Brighton and marooning him on a Pacific island
with copies of Homer and the Bible, ample writing paper and an
axe for tree-felling, as sureties against boredom and idleness.
Only the reluctance of Lord Ranfurly to advance the £10,000
needed for the attempt had deterred Crawford, whose acquired
knowledge since of the international arms market had greatly
strengthened Carson's hand.

Childers, the enthusiast, shook off at last his sense of numbed helplessness. Anything Crawford could do for Ulster, in defiance of the law, he would do better for that larger Ireland which Asquith and the Liberals seemed intent on vivisecting. The Anglo-Irish patriot's concept of strict justice swept aside all the usual deterrents and restraints of commonsense. Before the last week of April 1914 he had paid little heed to the founding of the Irish Volunteers as a defensive counterpart in the South to Carson's Army of Ulster Volunteers in the North. He had vaguely heard that the Southern movement was speading fast. He also knew from Alice Stopford Green and from Sir Roger Casement that the Irish Volunteers lacked not only arms but the money to purchase them. What angered him now in retrospect was the memory of another piece of cowardice: on 4 December 1913, a bare ten days after the Irish Volunteers had officially come into being, the Liberal Government had taken fright and reimposed by decree the traditional ban on imports of arms and ammunition 'for warlike purposes' into Ireland. Only the South had suffered.

John Redmond, the Irish Nationalist leader, still held the Irish Volunteer movement in considerable mistrust but could no longer afford to ignore a force which was recruiting so many of his own supporters. He therefore invited Eoin MacNeill, its scholarly president, and Sir Roger Casement, its chief propagandist, to meet John Dillon, Joseph Devlin and himself at Westminster on 7 May 1914. Casement, whose judgment Molly Childers already suspected since she detected a 'streak of madness' in him, was also in London, living at government expense as an expert witness before a Royal Commission examining the Civil Service. The melodramatic and only partly accurate account by Darrell Figgis of his encounter with Casement and MacNeill at the Grosvenor Road home of Alice Stopford Green need not detain us unduly, though Irish writers over the years have tended to accept his testimony at face value and weave it with loving hands into the subsequent legend of Childers's gunrunning exploit. Figgis's assertion that he was involved in a plan to smuggle arms to the South even before Crawford's Larne landing sprang from a faulty memory for dates. According to Molly Childers, the Darrell Figgis version of events 'is most reprehensible, for he was making himself out to be the prime mover . . . whereas he had a minor role'. Lightning, however, sometimes strikes more than one person or object at once. And it now seems indisputable that, though many people, MacNeill and Figgis included, had long been conscious of the need for arms, the practical means of procuring and landing them were not devised until Casement, the two Childers, Mrs Stopford Green, Mary Spring Rice and several others put their heads together.[6]

The informal committee that was set up in May 1914 consisted almost entirely of Anglo-Irish Protestant Liberals sympathetic to Home Rule and ready to take risks on behalf of the Irish Volunteers. Casement served as the vital link between Dublin and London; Alice Stopford Green acted as chairman, Molly Childers as secretary. Other members or associates were Lord Ashbourne, Sir George and Lady Alice Young, Sir Alexander Lawrence, Captain George Fitzhardinge Berkeley, Mary Spring Rice, her kinsman Conor O'Brien, and Erskine Childers himself. Darrell Figgis was co-opted to the committee and, with Casement's approval, approached an arms dealer in Hamburg, Moritz Magnus Junior, for samples of their wares. Childers also accompanied Casement and Figgis one morning to the premises of a Belgian armoury firm's London agent; but in the end they settled for the old-fashioned Mauser rifles which Moritz Magnus could provide at a price.

Between them, eleven members of the London committee subscribed the sum of £1,523 19s 3d for buying and transporting guns to Ireland. Compared with the huge consignment already in the hands of the Ulster Volunteers, this could be regarded as only a token reply. The name of Molly Childers appeared high on the list of subscribers. In backing this enterprise to the hilt, she and her husband were at one. But two major hurdles had to be cleared: the first, finding a suitable ship or ships to smuggle in the arms; the second, making suitable arrangements with the firm of Moritz Magnus Junior for a bulk purchase. It was Mary Spring Rice who provided the vital spark of imagination which finally led to the use of Childers's yacht, the *Asgard*, and Conor O'Brien's *Kelpie* for an illegal enterprise as daring as it proved hazardous. Her original suggestion was that Childers should borrow a fishing smack she owned called the *Santa Cruz*. In mid-May he travelled to Foynes, on the Shannon, to examine the ship with Conor O'Brien who had already prepared designs for her conversion; but time pressed and the *Santa Cruz* needed too drastic an overhaul. Besides, as Childers informed his wife, Mary Spring Rice was 'dead against Conor having command, and says he is useless at a crisis, and that rules out *Kelpie* which is anyway too small for the purpose, except in the last resort'. But in the last resort, *Kelpie*, together with *Asgard*, it had to be. O'Brien, in fact, displayed sound sense in discussing the voyage plans after the return of Darrell Figgis and Childers from Hamburg at the end of May.

The visit to the arms dealer had gone without mishap, though the pair were obliged to pass themselves off as Mexicans, a charade which did not amuse the Englishman. This was done to still the doubts of the Magnus brothers whose reluctance to deal with prospective purchasers from the British Isles was not entirely unconnected with the recent coup of Crawford on behalf of the Ulster Volunteers. Despite these heavy preoccupations, Erskine Childers otherwise contrived to lead an outwardly conventional life, even accompanying the Sunday Tramps on walks in late May and June, and keeping in close touch with political friends at Westminster. They would never learn of his role in the forthcoming adventure, if he could help it; yet by now nothing on earth could have stopped him from undertaking it. A grand symbolic gesture was called for: Childers, the impatient enthusiast, would provide it.

In June he visited MacNeill and Bulmer Hobson in Dublin to coordinate the details of a complicated master-plan whose final success would depend on luck, good seamanship and absolutely precise timing. What Childers failed to grasp either then or for years to come was that Hobson, not MacNeill, had become the controlling influence behind the Irish Volunteers in his capacity as a member of the Supreme Council of the secret Irish Republican Brotherhood. It was Hobson, for instance, who conceived and arranged the simple tactical scheme to hold, on four successive Sundays, route marches for the Volunteers to different places near Dublin, so as to throw the police and military off the scent and allow Childers to land his cargo undetected.

It was not easy to get a reliable crew. Hands had to be selected with exceptional care in the interests of security, so Childers proceeded warily. The difficulties were borne on him forcefully over lunch at his Chelsea home one day towards the end of June. His two prospective crew hands were at table: first, Colonel Robert Henry Pipon of the Royal Fusiliers, a close friend and sailing companion of Captain Gordon Shephard, the second guest, who promptly accepted Childers's amazing proposition. Not so Pipon, who turned down the offer flat and did not mince his words in doing so.

'Childers asked us both to come and help him on his yacht to meet a German ship off Terschelling where, at sea, cases of arms would be transhipped. He was then going to land them at Howth Bay for the Irish Nationalists to show they could do what the Ulster people had done. He promised us there was no intention of using them other than as a gesture of equality. I refused. I recognized Childers as a crackpot. Something always happens to crackpots. Something always goes wrong . . . . Shephard and I knew the Childers well . . . . [They had] a little boy of nine whom they – chiefly she – wouldn't allow to be told any word of religion of any sort until he was old enough to decide freely which he considered the best religion . . . . Poor little devil! Crackpot, of course. It always comes out somewhere.'[7]

So Pipon stayed at home but held his tongue. Shephard would join the yacht at Conway in Wales, where he had laid it up at the end of the previous summer after sailing from Denmark round the north of Scotland to win the Challenge Cup of the Royal Cruising Club. He would remain aboard until his leave ran out. Molly insisted on coming, despite her disability; and so did Mary Spring Rice. Meanwhile, Joseph Biggar, with Hobson's assistance, had hired two Donegal fishermen to complete the *Asgard*'s crew. It is an interesting commentary on the natural secretiveness of the *Asgard*'s skipper that Mary Spring Rice did not discover who the mysterious 'Mr Gordon' was until she met Gordon Shephard at the local station on 3 July. In a letter to Lady Shephard, his mother, six days later from Cowes, their appointed rendezvous with Conor O'Brien and the *Kelpie*, the young aviator declared: 'Miss S.R. is a wonder. She has never been to sea before, yet she was hardly ill at all and looks and is most useful. We came round without stopping and arrived early this morning. Good weather on the whole, but head winds as far as Land's End, and then a fine fair wind up the Channel.'[8]

Since Childers, for obvious reasons, kept no log of the voyage, he persuaded Mary Spring Rice to write a detailed diary, a copy of which she gave him afterwards as a keepsake. As Mary feared, Conor O'Brien, with his short fuse of temper, cursed freely and at the pitch of his voice when *Asgard* reached Cowes far behind schedule.

'Hardly had we finished our last mouthful [of breakfast] when a loud "*Asgard* ahoy" was heard, and I dashed up on deck to be received with a torrent of abuse from Conor. Why were we so late? Why had we never written? He had spent all his money and de Montmorency [one of his crew] had gone back to Dublin. . . . If all Cowes, and Dublin, not to say the Castle, do not know of our expedition, it is a miracle. The only hope is the Government are fairly stupid. I tried my best to calm Conor down and finally he departed somewhat soothed . . . . We spent rather a harassing morning, getting our letters and sending telegrams to Figgis in Hamburg with final directions about our rendezvous and transhipment. We must have looked a quaint party, Molly and Erskine and I driving around Cowes whispering to each other, sending prepaid wires and anxiously returning to the post office for answers.'

It was the height of the yachting season, so nobody looked twice at them. If any of Childers's seafaring friends were in Cowes on Thursday 9 July, he did not run into them. They took coffee that evening with Conor O'Brien, his wife Kitty, and Diarmid Coffey, a young Dublin barrister who was sparetime secretary to Colonel Maurice Moore, the Inspector General of the Volunteers. These three, with two hired hands, comprised the crew of the *Kelpie* which had sailed down the Shannon, past the Fastnet and up-Channel, in record time. A calmer Conor O'Brien reiterated his concern at the postponement by two days of their original rendezvous off the mouth of the Scheldt, by the Ruytigen lightship: they would reach it together as things stood on Sunday 12 July, 'an appropriate date', as Coffey afterwards remarked. They were all rather tense, for they had no time left to call at Dover where, possibly, a letter from Figgis altering the transhipment arrangements might well be awaiting them. They agreed to head straight for the rendezvous.

Fairly thick fog descended on the afternoon of 12 July, and the entire crew of the *Asgard* kept watch on deck. Gingerly, Childers moved in towards shore. They spotted the lightship, but there was no sign yet of the *Kelpie* or of the tug carrying Figgis and the precious cargo. Then 'a cry from Molly revived our drooping spirits. "Conor and the tug. Do you see?" she called. "A steamer and a yacht mixed up – lying close to one another – now the tug is coming towards us . . . ." Darrell Figgis called from her deck that Conor had taken 600 rifles and 20,000 rounds of ammunition. "He's left you 900 and 29,000 rounds," he shouted. We looked at each other. Could we ever take them?'

Fortunately, it was a calm, warm summer's night. For hours on end, in a lather of sweat, they loaded the big canvas bales, one by one, each done up in straw. The guns were handed down to McKinley and Duggan, the two Donegal fishermen, from the deck of the gently swaying German tug until the *Asgard*'s saloon, cabin, passage and companion hatch were stacked high. The heavy boxes of ammunition were stowed away 'with infinite labour' wherever else spare room could be found: under the cockpit, at the foot of the companion, in the sail-lockers and in the fo'c'sle. In Mary Spring Rice's words, 'Erskine's one thought was to take everything'; and by two o'clock in the morning the last rifle and box were aboard. Gordon Shephard entertained the tug's unblinking German captain to drinks 'in what was left of the saloon', telling him in his best accent the direction in which they wished to be towed; and not long after dawn the ropes at last were cast off outside Dover. The relief of everyone over breakfast was 'tremendous . . . though the risks of discovery were now increased tenfold, and the excitement proportionately greater'.

Shephard never expressed his inmost thoughts about those hours of toil off the German coast. Like the English spies of the Frisian Sands before him, the urbane Captain Trench and Lieutenant Brandon, he had already done his own share of 'exploring', once being arrested (then released) by his Prussian hosts, who failed to scrape up sufficient evidence to indict him. A typically vacuous and futile squabble had ensued between the

Foreign Office and the Admiralty; and when the Foreign Office protested to Shephard's superiors at the War Office, he had been duly rebuked, only to be importuned unofficially by the Admiralty to carry on the good work during his leaves. Childers, though not surprised, had written it down to 'experience'.

'Our friend [Gordon Shephard] has to leave us on the 19th and he will post this,' Molly Childers wrote to Alice Stopford Green from somewhere on the high seas.

I wish I could better describe life on board to you but alas! no words can portray the peculiar fascinating savour of it – the discomfort, the glory which makes up for everything. Again and again we have been in company with the Fleet.... Were we seen at the Roetigen? Is the *Daily Mail* full of us? We dread to hear things are known. We dread that Conor may deliver his guns and talk before our date.[1]

Nothing of the kind occurred; but they were not to discover that until the *Asgard* had completed the long haul to Milford Haven. There Gordon Shephard left his fellow-adventurers at the end of an unusual leave to report back in mock-innocence to his Royal Flying Corps squadron. The letters he had written home meanwhile suggested that he had been idly cruising with friends. Childers's consistently good luck had held again when they nosed past capital ships of the Royal Navy at Spithead, and again off his former stamping ground, Devonport, where a destroyer almost ran them down in the course of night manoeuvres. Despite the overcramped conditions and the inconveniences of having to cook, wash, sleep and work among the restacked bales of weapons and immovable ammunition boxes, tension no longer gripped the *Asgard*'s crew so hard. The last leg across the Irish Sea was not the least perilous, now that Childers had parted with Shephard, the only other person capable of handling the yacht in a real emergency. Yet the thought of failure did not enter the resolute skipper's head.

'A great argument this evening as to what we should feel if Asquith in his statement today announced the repeal of the Arms Proclamation,' Mary Spring Rice recorded in her diary on Monday 20 July. '[At Holyhead] I tore open the newspaper and breathed again. I also got an Irish paper and found they had been searching all around for gun-runners, some in the Shannon, which was very disquieting, in case we had to go round there.'[9]

Had they but known it, Conor O'Brien's *Kelpie* had by then unloaded her cargo at Kilcoole, Wicklow. The landing plan which Childers had devised in collaboration with Bulmer Hobson depended on meticulously exact timing. Regardless of weather conditions, the tide would not wait for the *Asgard*, which could not tarry if for any reason the watchers on the shore at Howth and the handpicked contingent of marching Irish Volunteers failed to appear. Childers would then have to turn back, run the gauntlet of patrol vessels and head straight for the Shannon. His wife, less expert in the calculation of risks, spelled out the prepared details in her third and last deckhand's letter to Alice Stopford Green:

At 10 a.m. Sunday the 26th we lie off Lambay island near Kingstown and wait for a motor boat or, if that fails, a rowing boat, which is to come out from Howth to tell us if all is well or not. We set sail in her company for Howth Harbour where there are *vedettes* watching – men who are to behave like ordinary loungers. Meanwhile the Dublin I.V. ... one thousand strong, are to make their weekly route march out to Howth this day.... The second we are tied up, word is passed, a command given and the Volunteers fall into rank and double up the pier towards us.... We shall probably fail to get away after the guns are delivered, though we shall make a great effort to do so. If we do get away we shall sail for some English port and lay up the yacht and leave her. If we don't, they will confiscate the yacht. I don't think they will imprison us, though they may fine E. and me, in which case we should have to go to prison rather than pay.... We have never pulled any [strings] yet in our lives, but I think we will this time!

They were fortunate again in not being spotted or intercepted at Lambay Island. For the weather that Sunday was unspeakably atrocious, too rough for any motor boat to put out. It had been arranged in advance that Darrell Figgis would meet them in a hired motor boat to indicate that the coast was clear, but Figgis failed them for reasons beyond his control.

'I can remember Erskine's face and how he turned to me and said, "I am going to risk it",' said Molly, who then took over the helm so that Childers could lower the sails before *Asgard* moved in and tied up alongside the pier. Mary Spring Rice had put on a bright red skirt when she struggled out of her blankets that

G

morning. This was no brave attempt at self-adornment. As she put it herself, 'my red skirt was a signal [so] I stood well up on deck. . . . A quarter to one, up to time to the minute, and a long line of Volunteers were marching down the quay. There was "Mr Gordon" on the pierhead and, of course, the inevitable Figgis. . . . Molly and "Mr Gordon" stood by the mizzen and looked at the scene; it still seemed like a dream, we had talked of this moment so often during the voyage.'

Childers stood for a while on the little quay talking to Eoin MacNeill, O'Rahilly and Bulmer Hobson. He was then introduced to a stocky man, with a determined face, and the almost unpronounceable name of Cathal Brugha. Another stranger who did not speak to Childers but eyed him quizzically from a distance was the unobtrusive Arthur Griffith. The editor of *Sinn Fein* wore the uniform of a private; like the others with whom Childers exchanged greetings, MacNeill excepted, Griffith belonged to the Irish Republican Brotherhood. It did not cross the Englishman's mind that the guns he had brought ashore so stealthily and boldly and at such risk were now in the possession of a reviving secret society pledged to sever every link between Britain and the Ireland of their revolutionary dreams.[10] To Alice Stopford Green, Molly confided her anxieties on hearing of the breakdown of the Buckingham Palace Conference called by the King on 21 July 1914. 'We are sad about the news – the Conference, and fear it means Exclusion (for Ulster). What are our efforts for, if that happened?'

Late on Friday, 24 July, while the *Asgard* was on the last lap of her voyage, three men sat waiting in an anteroom at Buckingham Palace. The abortive talks on the Irish deadlock had been going on there all the week. Bonar Law and Lansdowne, the chief Opposition spokesman, were with Lowther, the Speaker of the Commons, ready to take leave of the King. It seemed impossible now to arrest the slide into anarchy and civil strife. Nobody knew what to expect next. Lowther's face was buried in a newspaper which he had brought with him, unread, that humid Friday morning. Suddenly he spoke, his words intruding on the thoughts of his companions. Were they aware that Austria had sent an ultimatum to Serbia? They sat up and started talking: no, neither of them had heard anything of the kind, though everyone could recall clearly that gruesome assassination of the Archduke Franz Ferdinand in Sarajevo just a month ago, and the warlike rumblings which had since been echoing round the European capitals. In that Buckingham Palace anteroom, reality had struck home belatedly from the outside world.

'We agreed,' wrote Lowther afterwards, 'that it portended something very grave indeed – how grave we did not then realize.'

Meanwhile, Erskine and Molly Childers had returned to their Chelsea home, undetected and in safety. They, too, were oblivious of the imminent danger of a world war. Only a residual sense of elation remained after the achievement of their gun-running coup. Its unhappy sequel, the killing of four people and the wounding of some thirty others in Bachelor's Walk, Dublin, where Scottish soldiers had opened fire on a crowd of civilians taunting them not long after the *Asgard*'s departure from Howth, had later horrified them both:

'Our hearts bleed,' Molly protested to Alice Stopford Green– 'We burn at the injustice and cruelty meted out to Nationalist Ireland.'[1]

The incident at Bachelor's Walk was indeed needless and bloody; but, coming as it did just nine days before the outbreak of a worldwide conflict which would witness blood-letting on a scale unmatched in the annals of the human race, both the memory and the symbolic importance to Irish Nationalists of that outrage were swiftly lost on Erskine Childers. Slipping back into his accustomed routine, he debated long and fervently with his Liberal friends in London the pros and cons of the British Government's dithering attitude to the horrendous drama in Europe. It was a question of fighting or staying out:

'As long as it was an open question, I myself was against our intervention,' Childers firmly declared to Harry Chester, a distant cousin, on 8 October 1914. By then the Anglo-Irish gun-runner was in uniform, a naval lieutenant with special duties, whom Churchill, mercifully ignorant of this specialist's leading part in the Howth episode, had summoned within hours of Britain's declaration of war. The likelihood of such an upheaval still appeared remote when Childers crossed again to Dublin, this time by boat-train, during the last weekend of peace. His heart was heavy, his temper short. The Irish Volunteers had been wrangling over policy ever since John Redmond had secured control of the movement's organizing committee; and the situation worsened with the outbreak of war. From 4 August until 12 August, as he freely admitted to Molly, Childers became embroiled in countless 'arguments all day with all sorts of people', largely because 'their fatal weakness is their utter lack of organization and money of their own.... The position is simply pathetic, comic if not tragic.' Unbeknown to the innocent Childers, the nominal leader of the Irish Volunteers, Eoin MacNeill, was being skilfully manipulated by O'Rahilly, Bulmer Hobson and other activists of the Irish Republican Brotherhood. Nor were these gentlemen likely to condone the unwarranted efforts of an Englishman to interfere with their affairs. So far as they were concerned, Britain and John Redmond were guilty of bundling the Home Rule Bill into indefinite cold storage. Any attempt by Childers to put the Irish Volunteers at the service of the Crown in a conflict which was no concern of Ireland's would be firmly resisted.

Meanwhile, the Admiralty had been trying for days to track down Childers's whereabouts. More than one urgent telegram was delivered to his London home. The First Lord, Winston Churchill, prompted by his private secretary, Eddie Marsh, still one of Childers's best friends, kept pestering the Naval War Staff to find the fellow who knew the enemy's North Sea coastline like the back of his hand. On learning that Childers was in Dublin, the Director of Naval Intelligence, Admiral Sir Henry Oliver, sent a wire 'in clear' to the Irish Volunteers' headquarters in Dublin, urging him to return at once for an interview. Molly Childers forwarded other messages of the same kind, including 'Eddie's Admiralty letter'. Given the grotesque allegation against Childers before his execution in 1922 that he had worked as a British double-agent, intent on destroying the very fabric of the new Irish Free State, it is very probable that these groundless suspicions began when Sir Henry Oliver and his Admiralty colleagues betrayed their anxiety to get in touch with him by sending urgent signals to him at the Volunteers' Headquarters, already a hornets' nest of conspiracy. What could have been more natural than for conspirators to deduce that Erskine Childers's personal involvement in Irish affairs was being monitored by his masters in Whitehall?

Childers hated leaving business unfinished; but in the end he reconciled himself glumly to the conclusion that the Irish Volunteers must be left to disentangle their own muddled affairs. The records indicate that not until the middle of August did he call on the Director of Naval Intelligence. Sir Henry Oliver passed him to Herbert Richmond, the assistant director of the War Staff's operational division, who knew Childers personally and had long admired his progressive and outspoken strategic views. All the normal formalities were dispensed with, Childers emerging from successive interviews a lieutenant in the Volunteer Reserve.

Before being ordered to report at Chatham to the commanding officer of HMS *Engadine*, a cross-Channel steamer then being hurriedly converted into the first of Britain's primitive aircraft carriers, he was found a room and a desk inside the main Admiralty building. There for three days he worked very long hours, drafting, for Richmond's benefit, the outline of a plan to invade Germany by a flank attack across the Frisian Sands. A copy of this extraordinary memorandum, written on official notepaper, has been lying for the past half century beneath a mound of less important material in one of four large trunks containing Childers's personal papers. It deserves to be quoted at some length.

Headed 'Seizure of Borkum and Juist', this individualistic battle plan noted at the outset that 'Borkum commands both branches of the Ems Estuary. Juist commands the eastern branch and would have to be seized simultaneously or subsequently.' The objects of the operation would be:

to wrest from the enemy and acquire for ourselves an important base, the Ems Estuary, with a view to (a) A close blockade of the German North Sea Coast;

(b) 'Digging out' operations by air, sea and land against German naval and military strongholds and roadsteads, e.g. Wangerong, Schillig Roads, Wilhelmshaven, Heligoland, the Elbe;

(c) Invasion on a grand scale, whether by Emden and the Ems valley to the Essen–Düsseldorf–Cologne region, in concert with an Allied advance from France, or elsewhere.

For any of these objects, an advanced maritime base with deep and secure anchorage even for the largest ships, appears to be necessary. The Ems appears to be the only suitable base of this character. . . . The ulterior objects (a) (b) and (c) could be pursued concurrently. If any of them, or the primary object itself, provoked the German fleets to decisive battle in the open, a highly important end would be achieved by that fact alone. But the defeat of the main German fleets does not appear to be a condition precedent to the prosecution of (c), an invasion in force – the greatest ulterior aim of the operations. The predominance of our naval forces and the power (conferred by the reduction of Borkum) of controlling adjacent waters, by patrols, mine-laying, mine-sweeping etc. should render invasion feasible in respect of maritime communications, even with the enemy fleets still 'in being'.

Turning his attention next to the extent of the operations he had outlined, Childers went on:

But how far would the seizure of Borkum commit us? Could we stop short with a partial command of the estuary and a blockade of the upper waters and confine ourselves to prosecuting objects (a) and (b)? Or should we find ourselves compelled to occupy Emden and some portion of the adjacent mainland, and so perhaps be led on to operations of greater magnitude still?
The answer seems to be that it would be possible to stop short at the limited aim, but it is plain the strain of maintaining the defence of the roadsteads, anchorage and island, would be severe, and security never perfect. The plan of invasion up the Ems valley, with Emden as the maritime base, seems to present the best opportunity of ending the war by a decisive stroke.

Discounting alternative invasion schemes, against the North Schleswig coast, for instance, or against Kiel and the Ship Canal, as being too difficult and dubious, Childers went on:

Large flotillas of boats would be needed, of considerable capacity and light enough draft to permit men landing from them on sand to wade easily ashore. Some should be fitted solely for carrying light guns, maxims etc....
Every effort should be made to deceive the enemy as to the point or points of landing by feints.... No attempt is made here to go into details but the following general remarks are made: [As to the] nature of sands, channels and foreshore, this subject is dealt with at length in a memorandum by the writer now in the possession of the Admiralty. (It was in the hands of the Hydrographic Office in August last.) The remarks in it upon grand strategy do not now apply, being based on different circumstances.... The sands are, for the most part, hard and

good for travelling. The beds of channels are, for the most part, mud
with muddy fringes.

The dyke which surrounds the whole mainland coast (the islands are
undyked) is not a serious obstacle but makes an excellent line of first
defence for the enemy and prevents the access of vehicles except at
points specially designed for that purpose. The country behind presents
the difficulties caused by elaborately drained land, some of it below
the level of high water, with intersecting ditches, dykes etc., and few
practicable roads or paths of any size. This class of country, with some
intervals of sand and marsh in the neighbourhood of Norddeich,
fringes the coast down to Emden....

In these circumstances, and in view of the need for the most precise
knowledge of the sand track from the islands and of the course of the
channels (which are liable to considerable change), the importance of
thorough and continuous work by aeroplanes in reconnaissance, and
the repulse of hostile aircraft and destruction of air-bases, cannot be
over estimated.

As if to demonstrate that his strategic ideas had not been conceived in a vacuum, Childers concluded by stressing his belief

that every effort will be made to make Zeebrugge and Ostend useless
to the enemy as ports, either by destruction of works or obstruction of
channels or both. It is plain that to the extent that these ports can be
used by submarines and small vessels, to that extent the advantages
won by seizing Borkum and Ems are frustrated.... It would be safer,
though not essential, that they should be impenetrably sealed before
the reduction of Borkum was begun. It is assumed that no violation of
neutrality need be involved in the operations against and up the Ems.

Such were the essential points of Childers's Memorandum on
Invading Germany. With characteristic singlemindedness, the
unabashed enthusiast appended to it this begging note to his
superiors:

The writer ventures to hope that he may have the honour of being
employed, if the service permits, whether in aeroplane work or in any
other capacity, if any of the operations sketched in this memorandum
are undertaken.[11]

They took him at his word, though it was already clear that
offensive operations on the ambitious scale he envisaged had
been ruled out for the present by the speed and thrust of the

German advance against the reeling forces of the Belgians and French, together with the six divisions of the British Expeditionary Force, on the Western Front. The military prospects looked ominous for the Allies when Childers joined his first ship, HMS *Engadine* on 20 August. Two days later, as he recorded in the war diary he now began to keep, 'our flying men, Lieutenants Ross, Miley and Gaskell, came aboard'.

He had parted from his wife sadly and not without some misgivings, though the unsolved Irish jigsaw had been provisionally relegated to the back of a feverishly preoccupied brain. If O'Rahilly, Bulmer Hobson, or even Eoin MacNeill, could have seen him on the afternoon of 22 August, shaking hands with Churchill and saluting the Commander-in-Chief, Admiral Jellicoe, when they 'paid a lightning visit' to the ship, the budding suspicions of these erstwhile comrades of the Irish Volunteers would no doubt have been reinforced.

'Being shot with volcanic suddenness into the Navy at an hour's notice is a queer experience,' he wrote happily to one of his grandmothers in mid-September, 'but I am beginning to get used to the life and to forget that I ever had a moustache or a tweed suit.'[1]

On 26 August, exactly a month after he had sailed into Howth with his illicit cargo of arms, Childers volunteered to act as the ship's intelligence officer. This was in addition to his routine duties and the specialist role assigned to him by Richmond of instructing all pilots aboard HMS *Engadine* and her two sister-ships, *Empress* and *Riviera*, in the art of navigating their crude aircraft by the stars and by any good landmarks that could be located on good maps of the enemy coast. Unfortunately his repeated attempts to obtain from the Admiralty really detailed German charts for this purpose were frustrated. Only when he visited Whitehall on leave and collected them by hand could he start in earnest. Childers was determined to go flying himself, though the decision did not rest with him. The seaplanes, he noticed, were

tractors with propellors in front, the passenger's seat forward, next the engine. He works the starting lever, 'doping' pump for flooding the carburettor [of] the 160 HP, 14-cylinder Gnome engine, and the air shutter. Also the wireless set, if there is one. The pilot's seat and all the controls, together with the mechanism for dropping bombs and torpedoes, are aft. The compass is in the pilot's compartment.... The atmosphere on board is one of cheerful optimism. It would be ridiculous, though more accurate perhaps, to call it pessimism – so sanguine and jovial is the anticipation of a certain doom in our gimcrack pleasure boat with its popguns and delicate, butterfly planes. But indeed no human being can forecast our destiny because the whole enterprise is new in war: an incalculable experiment.

Overburdened as he liked to be, Childers settled down to acclimatize himself by memorizing a variety of codes and signalling procedures. The 'whole thing', he confided to his diary, 'is practise, practise, practise'. Often, in the ship's wireless room, he would listen to the uniformly dismal war news from 'Poldhu [in Cornwall], Paris and Germany. Poldhu is sometimes true but always dull and two days behind the newspapers, Paris always false and Germany ridiculously so.' Early in September, the ship left for a stretch of ocean some twenty miles off Tynemouth to hunt for floating enemy mines – 'a strange alternative to the partridge shooting now just in season and rather *infra dig,* we think'. It was here that Childers experienced his first taste of flying, with a boyish officer called Ross as pilot.

At first I found my observing duties extraordinarily difficult, my glasses being perpetually clouded with oil splashed from the engine, my neck cricked with the strain of holding my head braced against the hurricane of wind from the propellor and the deafening noise.

On his next trip, Childers accompanied Lieutenant Gaskell. Twenty miles out, directly above the minefield, engine failure forced them to land on the heaving surface of the ocean, trusting to luck that they would not be blown instantly to smithereens. They bobbed about. Darkness fell. With no water and only a bar of chocolate to share between them, they tried moving gingerly away on one back-firing engine towards the faint smudge of afterglow in the west where the Northumberland coastline lay. The hours dragged slowly by. They took turns as their bodies grew cramped and cold to watch and to doze. Three ships passed close by without spotting them, then at two o'clock in the morning a fourth vessel approached:

This time we decided that at all costs we must get across her bows.... so we started up the engine. It back-fired violently, flames shot out and a fire began to burn inside the carburettor. I crouched down close to the air shutter, which was open, and succeeded in blowing it out. We shouted with all our might, fired shots, and, reckless of matches, burnt sheet after sheet of a signal pad as flares. To our joy, we saw her stop.

She was a Swedish cargo ship. She took the plane in tow and the two exhausted men aboard, handing them over at breakfast time to a tugboat captain off Hartlepool, whence they were hauled back to the Tyne. The destroyer patrol to which they were attached strove to improve the search-and-destroy techniques by sending instructions that seaplanes must take off and land by the mother-ship, not from shore.

With the solitary exception of Childers, the flying men were young, irreverent and boisterous. So nobody questioned the right of this grey-haired man, already in his forty-fifth year and therefore well above qualifying age, to risk his neck unnecessarily every time orders came through to lower the aircraft from deck to ocean and soar off into the unknown. His companions respected him for his love of the sea and his profound knowledge of its more vicious ways, and gradually learning to accept him as one of themselves, the disparity of age counted for less and less as the weeks went by. Childers could never wholly unburden his mind to any of them, so he had to carry his recurring political anguish about with him like a secret affliction. To Alice Stopford Green he once poured out his heart in an unusually frank letter which, to evade the censor's attention, he must have posted on one of his occasional visits to the Admiralty. Thanking her warmly for keeping in close touch with Molly, he went on:

She has kept me posted as far as humanly possible on Irish developments and you can realize how anxiously, and alas sadly, I have watched them ... the petty imbecility of the pro-German intrigue, bound to peter out either in summary arrests or in ridicule and another era of Irish impotence and disunion; then the weaknesses and blunders of the Redmond party, only too obvious but deriving very far back from the lifeless, unfruitful political machine which their nationalism has tended to degenerate into – redeemed much, so it seems, by what Molly tells me of Redmond's exertions, and successful exertions against betrayal by the Government whose inability to read Ireland intelligently has aggravated the mischief. Now there seems to me not a shadow of doubt as to which party to support, namely Redmond, though I can't recall the contrast with the thrilling days when we hoped so much of MacNeill and his men as representing (so we thought – and I think still) the most vigorous and unsullied nationalism in Ireland. I am afraid their incapacity, and this financial mess strikes me as ugly, if proved; and the disastrous descent into a kind of anaemic treason sets the crown on it.

On one related matter, that of recruiting Irishmen as volunteers on the Allied side, Childers could sympathize with the dilemma of MacNeill, a man in whose 'absolute fundamental integrity and single-mindedness I shall always believe'. As he put it:

I don't think any power on earth can educe any *large* Nationalist force for the European war independently of the existing Irish regiments and normal recruiting for them. The compelling motive is lacking, especially with Home Rule as yet only a scrap of paper and ready to be repudiated by the next – that is a Tory – Government. My friends say – 'But what a chance! If they send out a strong brigade and do splendidly and shame the Ulstermen, their cause is won forever. No one would dare refuse them any Home Rule they wanted.' Plausible, but human nature is not made that way. Cavour's Piedmontese brigade in the Crimea is not a true parallel.[1]

It was socially disconcerting for Childers to run into yachting friends of yesteryear, now wearing the uniforms of Admirals, or of senior officers only slightly less exalted. For if he had a weakness, it was the natural Victorian inclination to touch his forelock to lesser men set in authority over him, however stupid or unimaginative they might be. When HMS *Engadine* was signalled back from her fruitless mine-hunting exercises off Tynemouth, preparations began in earnest at last for offensive action. Yet Childers's relief was clouded by doubts he could not bring himself to express about the proficiency of his junior colleagues, the naval airmen. Some bomb-dropping practice at Calshot in mid-October proved an utterly inadequate rehearsal for 'the real thing': an expedition along with *Riviera*, one of the sister ships, to the north German coast. The operation was fortunately cancelled at the last minute. Its object was clearcut. The six available seaplanes were to have been hoisted out before dawn on 25 October and 'to fly forty-nine miles with the first light to a point nine miles south of Cuxhaven and three miles inland on the Hanover coast to drop bombs on some Zeppelin sheds reported to have been recently built near the village of Cappel'. Commodore Reginald Tyrwhitt had led his protecting screen of cruisers and destroyers to the appointed rendezvous; and while Childers was collecting survival gear to stow aboard his aircraft, he 'found to my intense disgust that my revolver cartridges were flat-nosed dum-dums, a fact I hadn't discovered, not having opened a packet before. I should like to see the responsible person shot and his carcase sent to the Germans as a proof of bona fides. I resolved to throw all away and go unarmed.'

His wrath quickly fizzled out. Instead, frustration set in. For only one of the seaplanes succeeded in taking off; the rest, after various mishaps, had to be hauled back aboard. Childers thought the whole 'fiasco' absolutely 'maddening'. His diary received the impact of his splenetic feelings as well as his calmer reflections on the cancellation of a mission on which 'quite a substantial fraction of the Navy was employed'. Next time, he vowed, the thing would have to be better managed. Because of appallingly savage weather, the raid was cancelled again on 21 November. By now Childers, with the approval of the *Engadine*'s skipper, was instructing the flying men aboard her and the *Riviera* in the rudimentary skills of navigating and observing from the sky. In his own words: 'My idea is to show very clearly every sea-mark that can be sighted and identified by the seaplanes en route to their objective.... Also to give all information possible as to the character of the land.' The Childers Chart, based on the German originals, became the Bible of aircrews on both ships. There were moments of exhilaration, too, at news of the dashing exploits of others: 'It was pleasant to hear in the evening', Childers laconically recorded on 24 November, 'that some naval airmen in land machines had succeeded in dropping bombs on the Zeppelin sheds at Lake Constance.'

Where brave pathfinders had led, they soon must follow; yet nobody (least of all, perhaps, the Germans) expected any hostile raid on Christmas Day, 1914. *Engadine*, the 'flagship' of the two British seaplane carriers, had been joined at Harwich early in December by a third vessel, *Empress*: 'All are Dover–Calais boats', noted the indefatigable diarist, 'under the command of our captain', who, after a conference at the Admiralty, asked Childers 'to prepare another lecture for the pilots'. During those long days

of intense planning, the two men more than once discussed together with animation that larger project drafted by the shy
Childers for seizing a Frisian island and invading the German
mainland. By now, he presumed, it was gathering dust in some
Sea Lord's in-tray. Not all the conversation was of war and
strategy. Another diary entry reads: 'A talk with the captain
about German coast and Rosicrucianism, and a long and heated
argument with Miley [a pilot] at dinner about matter and space
and infinity and the "limits" of knowledge.'

Then they put to sea again as part of Tyrrwhitt's task force,
once more heading for the enemy coast. When the navigation specialist had briefed the pilots and observers for the last
time, Flight-Commander Kilner of the *Riviera* said suddenly:
' "Childers, you ought to be flying with us." I said: "I'm longing
to do so, and have asked to do so, but understand no passengers
are allowed." At the end Kilner said: "I have a 200 HP Canton
Short which will carry us both with ease. Get leave from your
skipper and come with me. Robertson (my skipper) will agree." '
After some hesitation, *Engadine*'s Captain reluctantly gave permission.

There was, perhaps, just a touch of *Boy's Own Paper* heroics in
the tone of Childers's diary narrative at this climactic point. A
little elderly he might be for joining in such an enterprise on the
first Christmas Day of the war; but no middle-aged Englishmen
of his upbringing and instincts could have resisted its clamorous
appeal. Besides, the response was expected of him; and he had
never been a man for half-measures:

I began the day badly, waking with a guilty start at – when? 6 a.m. An
hour and a half late. I shall never foreget my horror and despair. The
quartermaster was abject. He had forgotten to call me before – on this
day of days.... I leapt into my boots, trousers and jacket, tumbled all
my gear, lying ready laid out, into my bag, donned helmet and goggles,
seized charts and rushed to the upper deck.... The dinghy was lowered.
...The sea was calm under a heaving swell. *Engadine* towered above
my cockle-shell. The dark shapes of *Riviera* and *Empress* could be seen
not far away, and of *Arethusa* [Tyrrwhitt's flagship] and some destroyers, and at intervals on the surrounding sea the dim, spidery
forms of planes at rest, expanding their wings and preparing for
flight.... I strained my eyes for Kilner. The hoarse hum of an engine

was heard in the direction of *Empress*. 'Row like blazes' I shouted to
my men and out we went to meet the plane.... 'Is that you, Kilner?'
I called, 'Is that you, Childers?' was the reply. We sculled up to the
port-side float and I jumped on to it, saying 'Happy Christmas'. 'Same
to you' came back from the pilot's seat. The dinghy sculled away ...
I was groping in the dark for places to stow things ... trying first and
foremost to fix the compass. Impossible – no place whatever. All I
could do was place it on the sloping floor between my feet in their
sea-boots, where it was useless.... The second most important thing
was a place for the chart. None. A wretched little dash-board and a
tiny table with no rim upon which nothing at all could be placed with
safety. I had to hold the chart.... Greedy for every minute of preparation, I was busy with little arrangements when Seaplane 136 began to
leap from swell to swell with resounding bumps. One final leap and
she was free....

The miscalculations and disappointments of the next three
chilling hours fill twenty-seven whole pages of the diary. The
frustrated perfectionist raged inwardly at what might have been,
and would rage on helplessly:

A saffron dawn was in the east between great grey wreaths of cloud
and morning mist ... below us, my first experience of that unnatural
inversion, but the day here was distinctly clear.... I looked for Heligoland: there sure enough it was in the south west, a grim grey cliff
wreathed with clouds but gaining definition as we proceeded.... Three
other seaplanes could be seen flying far below us ahead and astern, like
children's toy-models with their yellow, red-ringed wings.... We saw
one or two trawlers but the first thing of note was a message from
Kilner to me drawing attention to the fact that one of our seaplanes
had alighted and was damaged.... A moment later we sighted two
German torpedo-boats steaming from Heligoland towards the dis-
abled seaplane. (We fear it was Hewlett of the *Riviera* and hoped the
Germans picked him up alive.) ... I strained my eyes for marks. We
had been flying nearly an hour and I wanted a definite lead. I had
already passed a message to Kilner to ask him to fly lower.

They made their landfall by two beacons as familiar to Childers
as old friends, and re-set course for the target. Crossing the foreshore, he quailed at the enveloping murky haze which seemed to
turn the land below dark brown:

At the same time, by double-fatality, Kilner passed to me 'Engine failing' and I could hear it misfiring badly and [see it] losing height.... Presently a little road appeared beneath, then suddenly, the spire of a church, then a village which I took to be Cappel. Then the railway.... In any ordinary light we should, by this time, have easily sighted the sheds.... We now circled for a bit, searching for a clue, but then Kilner turned south west....Engine-trouble rendered it imperative to return to open water....

Over the Schillig Roads and between the Jade and Weser estuaries lay

quite a considerable fraction of the German fleet.... I had not given a thought to hostilities when suddenly, just audible above the boom of the engine, I heard a slight report and saw a puff of brown and dirty white smoke directly in front of the machine. We were under fire.... It did not seem remotely possible that any shot would hit us, though some came near, and one could take one's notes undisturbed.... Meanwhile what about our own bombs? I had supposed that Kilner must have dropped them on the German warships and sent a message asking him but he said 'No'.

It was 10.15 on Christmas morning when they reached the escorting squadron of destroyers, picked out the *Riviera*, with her 'special black pendant' visible, and clambered aboard. No seaplanes had been destroyed or damaged by the enemy, though three had to be abandoned; and days passed before it was learnt that Hewlett, the missing pilot, had been rescued by a Dutch ship. Childers maintained that the operation had not only been unsuccessful but blatantly counterproductive. Not one bomb had hit a single enemy target, and nobody had even located the Zeppelin sheds whose existence at Cappel he suddenly began to doubt. Worse still was the discovery that while the British seaplanes had been flying towards the enemy coast a Zeppelin and several aircraft had crossed in the other direction to attack the group of escorting British cruisers, destroyers, submarines and carriers. Fortunately no damage or loss of life had been inflicted by the Germans either.

The agonizing post mortem Childers conducted with himself in his diary continued until the task-force returned to Harwich; and when he read the euphoric reports of the raid in the press, based on a sensational communiqué from the Admiralty, his disgust knew no bounds:

The papers dotted all the i's and crossed all the t's, hinting at great achievements which it had not been thought wise to publish, giving biographies and photos of all the pilots. All this is thoroughly bad, but unfortunately thoroughly characteristic of the Naval Air Service, which has done the same with its land pilots and motor car officers in the land campaign, and, I understand, sickened the whole army with the bombastic advertisement of the exploits of airmen. It is the worst possible thing for these young pilots – already a somewhat spoilt and privileged class and suffering in efficiency on that account.... Experience has shown that the risks of flying are considerably smaller than those of fighting on *terra firma*. On this very day the all-too-familiar, long, grim list of killed and wounded in the trenches, half a page of close print, made me well-nigh blush for the outrageously exaggerated *réclame* of these seven youths who, I firmly believe, don't want or need the puff, but are only human if they are harmed by it.... No, it is all wrong.

Yet other morals lingered long after his bottled-up fury had subsided. The evidence of Childers's fluctuating states of mind is startling in places. So precise and careful in weighing every particle of relevant information, so rigorous in distributing blame impartially between himself and others, he appeared altogether too fond of quietly picking away at the scabs on his own conscience. This was his only outlet, his one form of self-indulgence.

The psychology of the air is a very curious and interesting study. Kilner himself – this is the crucial point – did not know where he was, that is, from his own observation. He was relying on me for navigation and I am pretty sure that the psychological effect on himself, though he was probably quite unconscious of it, was to make him too ready to abandon the search prematurely.... Such a state of mind is quite consistent with complete personal bravery.... But it is also consistent with that slap-dash, careless temperament almost universal among pilots.... I am twelve years older than him. I was acting, not as a passenger, but as an intelligent observer. I knew the topography as he did not know it ... I should have shown stronger initiative, urged, almost insisted on, a more thorough search for the sheds, whatever the risk. Well, I did not do so. Why?... I can't honestly remember any physical fear.... I have not that particular physical tendency (no credit to me).... I think I have sometimes almost an exaggerated respect for rank and professional acquirements, apart from age and standing. The decisive factor was that I myself gave way to the temptations of the flying temperament.... Fog, engine-trouble – where are those wretched sheds? How the devil can we ever see them in this light? And the blessed engine may stop any moment. Rotten, bad luck, but not our fault. I'm not responsible anyway. Kilner has the engine and controls it. I haven't even got a compass.

Having squeezed the topic dry, Childers, the visionary and enthusiast, turned his gaze from the past to the present, then to the future:

From the cold, military standpoint, the contest may perhaps be declared a draw, though it must not be forgotten that it had a distinct moral effect in heartening and encouraging our people whatever effect it had on the enemy. Finally, there can be no question about the extraordinary technical interest of the Christmas engagement. It marks a new era in war; the first regular battle between the ships of the sea and the ships of the air. We are fortunate to have witnessed this remarkable event which is but a foretaste of a complete revolution in warfare.[12]

8. THE ILLUSIONIST

Early in January 1915 Childers went home on a week's leave. The joy of his reunion with Molly was unconfined; but two whole days were scrupulously squandered on informal talks with Captain Murray Sueter, the Chief of the Admiralty's Air Department, who let him ransack the dusty recesses of the Admiralty for sets of German ordnance maps of the enemy's North Sea coastline, which, Childers knew, had been mislaid there. Besides, his wife was fully preoccupied with voluntary work which kept her away all day. As honorary secretary of a committee concerned with the welfare of Belgian refugees, she put in longer hours at Crosby Hall, Chelsea, than most civil servants and munitions workers. In the evenings they sought to escape from the dark shadows of war which, with its mounting toll of death, destruction, sorrow and uncertainty, had begun to alter not only their sense of perspective but the pattern of their lives.

On one essential Erskine and Molly Childers were wholly agreed: they must soldier on to the end, spiritually side by side, and ensure the liberation of every small defenceless country. The conflict had no other justification. If Belgium happened to be the original test case, the ultimate freeing of Ireland, unsatisfactorily left suspended in mid-air at the outbreak of hostilities by Britain's political leaders, did not come far behind. Lieutenant-Commander L'Estrange-Malone, the new skipper of the *Engadine,* was an Anglo-Irishman himself; and there were two or three others aboard the three makeshift carriers. Yet to none of them could Childers, the quiet, meditative patriot, disclose what he felt about the uncertain fate of Ireland.

From Sueter Childers learnt little that he had not already surmised. The Chief seemed 'much pleased by the Cuxhaven raid', but the pleasure was shortlived. On hearing from Childers that the bombing might have been less of a fiasco if the pilots and observers had been able to pinpoint the targets, Sueter first bridled then authorized a thorough search for the missing charts which his visitor eventually unearthed. What, Childers next enquired, had happened to that scheme for invading Germany? The naval air chief would not be drawn, merely professing ignorance. Such wish-fulfilment as Childers nursed was not so wide of the mark in those dark January days of 1915. Churchill's subsequent authoritative version of events makes that abundantly clear. Five months earlier, on 19 August 1914, 'I had', wrote Churchill, 'with the consent of the Prime Minister, entered into communication with the Russian Government with the object of directing attention continuously on the strategic aspects of the Baltic.' Since then the struggle to contain the German armies sweeping into France, the saving of Paris, the race of both sides to the sea and the opening phases of indecisive trench warfare from the English Channel almost to the Alps, had led to its postponement. But the plan received what Churchill called 'a powerful impetus from the arrival at the Admiralty . . . of Lord Fisher' in place of Prince Louis Battenberg:

'It was our turn now. The initiative had passed to Britain – the Great Amphibian. The time and place were at our command. It was for us to say where we would strike and when . . . . The First Sea Lord was deeply convinced that the command of the Baltic, and the consequent letting loose of the Russian armies upon the whole of the unprotected Northern seaboard of Germany would be a mortal blow . . . . Lord Fisher . . . was still favourable in principle to the attack on Borkum, but like everyone else he realized the momentous character and consequences of such an operation. . . . Within a week at the latest of the island being in our possession, much more probably while the operation of landing was still in progress, the whole German Navy must have come out to defend the Fatherland from this deadly strategic thrust . . . .'[1]

On 7 January 1915, when Childers had given up trying to sound out Captain Murray Sueter, Churchill obtained, with Fisher's support, 'the provisional approval of the War Council to an enterprise which the Admiralty had been hesitantly considering for at least seven years'. Clearly *The Riddle of the Sands* and its paradoxical lessons had not failed in its true purpose. A senior officer was actually appointed by Churchill in the late autumn of 1914 to prepare for an amphibious attack on Borkum; but Admiral Lewis Bayley never got much encouragement from the Naval Staff. In fact, the invasion scheme finally lapsed because of 'a steady and palpable reluctance' detected by Churchill among his professional advisers, 'which grew as the details of the problem came into view, and which manifested itself by lethargy and a complete absence of positive effort'. However, not until February 1915 did it become sadly plain to Erskine Childers that Borkum would remain intact in German hands.

On returning to Harwich after his leave, Childers received an invitation to dine aboard the battle cruiser *Arethusa* with Tyrwhitt, the flotilla commander. His fellow-guests included L'Estrange-Malone, two seaplane pilots and the local submarine commander, Commodore Roger Keyes. Most of the conversation ranged over the raid on Cuxhaven; but Keyes, 'a less robust more intellectual type than T.' talked with animation about the work of his submarines which were 'constantly in the Bight having amazing adventures and also at the mouth of the Ems. He thought a seaplane-submarine enterprise quite feasible.'

Twice in late January the Tyrwhitt armada escorted the carriers to the enemy coast, its orders being to repeat the air assault of Christmas Day with greater accuracy and determination. Twice, owing to appalling weather conditions, the mission had to be cancelled. Childers, accustomed as he was to this routine, could scarcely conceal his impatience. L'Estrange-Malone cheered him up. He returned one night from a conference at the Admiralty with the exciting news that a larger ship, *Ben My Chree,* was being refitted at Barrow-in-Furness. She would shortly be joining her sisters on offensive missions to enemy territory. It was almost too good to be true; but Childers's intuition warned him that he would not see the Frisian coast again:

'I feel in my bones that everything is indefinitely posponed, if not abandoned...', he confided to his diary, and the feeling was quickly confirmed. The *Ark Royal*, another aircraft carrier, forthwith received secret instructions to leave for the Mediterranean. *Engadine, Empress* and *Riviera* went into dock for improvements, sailing round the south coast from Harwich to Liverpool past many familiar landmarks. Off Falmouth, Childers noted, on

9 February: 'I felt as though I were on a yachting cruise. Of course the whole trip was crowded with memories of last summer's tremendous beat down-Channel and over to Ireland in weather which, for two days at least, was worse than any we had now, though most of it was much finer.'

HMS *Engadine* was consigned to 'the wreckers', and Childers's poignant sense of bereavement yielded to one of gratification, when he inspected HMS *Ben My Chree* before renovations were complete. The cramped and untidy conditions in which, aboard *Engadine*, he had been expected to compile intelligence reports, act on signals, and prepare the pilots' maps, had not been endured in vain. Thanks to L'Estrange-Malone's studiously exact notes, an enlarged operations room, fitted with lockers and ample working surfaces, had been constructed. The new ship's observer-instructor and intelligence officer stayed to supervise the finishing touches in his own fussy, half-querulous and half-apologetic fashion. The carrier, *Ben My Chree*, it appeared, would not be reinforcing Tyrwhitt's battle group for a combined assault on Germany by sea, air and land. What a later generation of men learnt to call 'the second front' was being moved, for undisclosed reasons, more than a thousand miles away to the shores of the eastern Mediterranean. Murray Sueter at the Admiralty proved as enigmatic as ever in breaking the news unofficially to Childers at the Admiralty in the middle of March 1915. Neither man was fully conversant with the divided counsels and spirit of indecision in the War Council which had caused the plan to attack north Germany to be finally abandoned. That these continuing disagreements were already eroding the alternative plan to turn Turkey's flank through combined operations in the Dardanelles not even the most perspicacious of ministers could as yet foresee.

Being a small cog in the Admiralty's vast and complex machinery, though one well primed with strategic views of his own, Childers knew nothing of these squabbles. Had he done so he would undoubtedly have sided with the imaginative Churchill against the immovable obstinacy of Fisher, the ageing First Sea Lord, against the well-remembered, autocratic self-sufficiency of Kitchener, and against the feebleness of Asquith in the War Council's chair. Any bold and doughty fighter, whose single aim was to defeat the enemy by taking the unexpected but calculated risks, would be Childers's man every time.

On 19 February 1915, before Childers knew what was afoot, British and French warships opened their bombardment of the Turkish outer forts on the shores of the Dardanelles. Aircrews from *Ark Royal* strove to direct the firing. In Churchill's words, 'our seaplanes in those early days were neither numerous nor very efficient, [so] the coordination of the gunnery and the observation, though based on sound principles, was in practice primitive through lack of experience'.[1] A 'second front' so far away seemed foredoomed to failure. For the War Council in London, swayed by Kitchener's magisterial unwillingness to act decisively, could not agree on assembling an army to land and exploit early naval successes. Childers, painfully watching these ill-planned moves from afar, correctly surmised that soon he would be quitting the cold, grey, northern seas for the unknown perils of the eastern Mediterranean. Confirmatory orders to sail with *Ben My Chree* reached him in May.

The chief of the Royal Naval Air Service in the Middle East was Colonel F. H. Sykes, who until recently had been acting head of the slowly expanding squadrons of the Royal Flying Corps with the British Army in France. Sykes had first gone out to see for himself the limited opportunities and massive difficulties in a sprawling and gravely undermanned theatre of war.

'All naval air units', he reported, 'should be more centrally grouped and closer channels of communication should be opened between them and the naval and military headquarters.' Sykes also recommended an immediate increase in the number of aircraft at his disposal – 'a minimum of thirty-six, as well as eight submarine scout airships'.[2] By the end of July Childers had gradually become acclimatized to the torrid atmosphere of an exotically beautiful and hazardous seascape. The moment for renewed adventure was at hand.

How ironic it was, he reflected, that Ian Hamilton, one of his personal champions when Childers's prewar polemic against the misuse of cavalry had been published, could not break out of the tight cordon that hemmed in his infantry on the beaches of Gallipoli. The Turks were holding fast, repulsing with heavy losses every attempt to dislodge them. On 6 August, in a last determined effort to loosen the stranglehold, Hamilton put 20,000 fresh troops ashore at Suvla Bay by night. Secrecy and surprise were crucial; and as if to emphasize the point, the pilots aboard *Ben My Chree* took off on a diversionary bombing raid against port installations at Sighajik about twenty miles south-west of Smyrna. French naval forces in the area controlled this curiously tangential exercise which initially deceived the enemy. Hamilton's reinforcements secured a good foothold on the Suvla beaches but unaccountably delayed their advance, in spite of an almost total lack of opposition. Childers and other flying observers in *Ben My Chree*'s seaplanes received official praise afterwards for their prompt, accurate but increasingly doleful reports to Hamilton and his staff. There were, nonetheless, some small, incidental compensations. Twice in the hot month of August the careful spotting techniques developed by Childers enabled his best pupil, Flight-Commander C. H. K. Edmonds, to score direct hits on enemy supply ships in low-level swoops and send them straight to the bottom.

The air space above and behind the Turkish lines was vast: the machines which Colonel Sykes could call on to control it were too few. Seldom were there more than twenty serviceable aircraft available at any one time, none being wholly reliable in performance. True, the enemy had no machines whatever to begin with, so to that extent air superiority rested with the Allies. Yet no matter how meticulously Sykes pored over tactical ideas for assisting Hamilton's land forces pinned down on the inhospitable shores of Gallipoli, and however hard Childers might concentrate on dinning perfectionist techniques into the seaplane pilots, the puny naval air service lacked the strength to turn the enemy's Mediterranean flank by bombing or reconnaissance. Exciting and risky as nearly every sortie proved to be, tangible results were usually negative. For that very reason, the persistence of Childers as instructor and morale-raiser invariably impressed Sykes at Naval air headquarters.

When Bulgaria declared war on the Western Allies in October 1915 it seemed only a matter of time before the Allied expeditionary forces, on whose eventual triumph Churchill's vulnerable reputation and ministerial future depended, would be forced to leave Gallipoli. The Bulgars quickly overran Serbia, unblocking the strategic railway line that crossed Central Europe from Berlin to Constantinople and ensuring a flow of fresh war supplies to Turkey. The Admiralty in London instructed Sykes to interrupt that flow by attacking the key railway bridge across the Maritza River in Eastern Thrace. Characteristically, Childers broke regulations by going on that abortive raid as navigator in one of two Short seaplanes which accompanied a single land-based aircraft handled by the experienced and intrepid Wing-Commander Samson. Each of the three aircraft carried two 112-pound bombs, and Samson's machine had to be fitted with an extra petrol tank for a round trip of nearly 200 miles over land and sea. The leader released his bombs from a height of only 800 feet, missing the target by a few yards. One pier of the bridge was so severely damaged that rail traffic was interrupted for weeks. Edmonds and Dacre, diving low in turn, succeeded only in hitting the track. Childers enjoyed the ride but wrote off the mission as another experiment that failed. For the Turks at once brought in anti-aircraft guns; and the intensity of their fire denied him and the other observers that first, unrepeatable chance of directing their bombs at the bridge with unruffled precision on the next five abortive sorties to a now heavily defended target. The evacuation of British, Australian and New Zealand troops started at last on 19 December 1915, in accordance with Hamilton's instructions. For two whole days Childers and his fellow-observers kept patrol overhead until the army re-embarked at Anzac, Suvla and Cape Helles, virtually without loss:

'Never was the paramount importance of command of the air more triumphantly vindicated than on this occasion,' declared Colonel Sykes in an access of euphoria which several subordinates, including Childers, did not wholly like or share. As the latter noted in the war diary: 'It was melancholy to realize through maps, charts, trench diagrams etc. the prodigious amount of time, money, labour and life wasted over the attempt to force the Dardanelles.'[3]

Would the verdict have been different if the War Council, prodded by a unanimous Admiralty, had plumped instead for that invasion of the north German coastline on which Childers's extravagantly audacious heart had been set? It is extremely doubtful; in any case, by early 1916 the prospect of a long war of attrition was one to which Erskine Childers, in common with many other serving officers, had learnt to resign himself.

One late January day in 1916 *Ben My Chree* received orders to sail with her seaplanes on deck to Port Said. There she was joined by her refitted sister ship, *Empress,* as well as by two smaller carriers, *Anne* and *Raven II.* Their duties, even their status in the local and strangely overlapping system of command, were 'unclear' to begin with. Then, with acceptance, came a happy interlude of overwork. Overland reconnaissance of the desert approaches to Egypt through Syria, southern Palestine and Sinai became a daily routine, coupled with bombing attacks on Turkish camps and depots along the way. The High Command feared that an enemy invasion of Egypt could not yet be ruled out, though Childers regarded this as a 'colossal bluff' that bore no relation to strategic realities. Part of his task now lay in proving it. So he set out to become an expert in another sphere, that of aerial photography. His consistently low opinion of the Sea Lords and their bureaucratic aides spurred him on. None of the newly arrived carriers, he noticed, not even *Empress,* had a single trained intelligence officer aboard, far less any accurate maps or charts. As for the single-seater Schneider machines which were sent out as replacements, these he decried as typical products of the carelessness and ignorance of the so-called experts: 'They are really useless on this station, though the truth has not yet dawned on the Admiralty people who continue withholding Sunbeams and every other sort of two-seater – the only machines of the smallest use out here. It takes a year or more – a war one might say – to ram the simplest truth home in high quarters.'[3]

As usual he was less ruffled in the heat of action. Once, when L'Estrange-Malone sailed west of Alexandria to frighten off hostile Senussi tribesmen in their desert encampments beyond Bardia, Childers and his pilot, Edmonds, could not locate the ship after completing their photographic mission. They were forced to land on a hazy sea when their petrol ran out and the machine died on them:

The port wing rose high in the air and Edmonds shouted 'Run out on the wing' which we both did and she righted.... In another minute the tail began to sink and the floats rear up vertically so that the whole of the observer's seat was submerged. Edmonds stayed where he was on the end of the wing, knee-deep in water, I nipped back to the floats and stood on the crossbar between them, dry except for my feet.

Drifting out to sea, the two men clung on until a fishing boat picked them up and slowly towed the sinking seaplane to *Ben My Chree*. Then 'we reported to the captain and the general. I was bitterly disappointed at the loss of twenty-nine negatives – all good, I'm sure, as conditions were perfect.'

He was luckier on flights over Palestine and Sinai. Up to this point in the war no photographic evidence of Turkish dispositions had been obtained, largely because nobody as hard-working and businesslike as Erskine Childers had bothered to organize facilities in a command shared by too many commanders, each jealous of his own narrow preserve.

'We sail tonight', wrote Childers on 29 January, 'to carry out flights to Beersheba and the railway northwards.' Later that same day, they circled low over the town's outskirts, Childers failing to persuade Wright, his pilot, that the danger of being hit by rifle fire at 800 feet was almost negligible.

All we did was to make one circular sweep south of the town then home again. However, we did obtain some important results: verjfying the fact that the railway does not go beyond Beersheba, though the railway embankment and a light construction railway alongside do: that the bridge across the Wady al Saha, a splendid viaduct, is uncompleted; that 200 or more loaded camels were leaving the town for Auja by the direct road; that there is a large number of troops at Beersheba on both sides of the Wady and big barracks, shown in half a dozen photos; that the approaches to the town from Gaza are entrenched for many miles out (photo); that three hitherto unreported bridges exist, two of them near on the Gaza road, one of them being broken or uncompleted as well as one of the deviation bridges on a loop at this point so that traffic is blocked. (Two trains standing – photos). We flew back very low over Gaza and I gazed in rapt admiration at a beautiful mosque and courtyard, showing an exquisite pale green colour, with delicate fretted arches and porches. Wright made, as always a beautiful landing.

This man of forty-five had once worn spectacles for reading. Yet so well did he combine long-sightedness with an uncanny ability to single out and identify every feature of the desert landscape, recording it on film as he went, that L'Estrange-Malone and Sykes and the new Flag Officer, Admiral Wemyss, heaped more and more responsibility on him. Childers did not mind. On the contrary, he wanted planners to study 'the other side of the hill' and deduce what was going on far behind enemy lines. In due course Allenby and his forces would reap full advantage by smashing through those lines and advancing to Jerusalem with comparative ease. As for Childers, the rugged contrasts of the panoramic scenery below invariably captivated him. On another reconnaissance, this time with Dacre at the controls, he saw his first kibbutz:

I was much struck by what I took (rightly as it turned out) to be a Jewish colony, just north of a river. A splendid wood, densely planted, the only one I have ever seen in the East, make it a large area of beautifully cultivated land ringed by an enclosure and skirted by a mile long avenue of trees. These lead to what I should call a model village laid out in regular streets, each house with its garden – a garden city indeed, with large separate farm buildings. Behind it, as we faced the sea, ran a dazzling golden belt of sand-dunes, and beyond the vivid blue ocean.

Again, above the plain that stretched inland beyond a straggling village, which is today the city of Tel-Aviv, to the ridges of the Judaean escarpment around Jerusalem, Childers watched unfolding beneath him patterns of variegated life and colour which drew out the instant philosopher-poet in him:

The country is a paradise of fertility: vast orange gardens around Ludd [Lydda] and distant Jaffa, and nobly cultivated land everywhere. South of Ramleh the scene gradually changes until the railway is winding through a vast wilderness of barren hills and plains seamed by deep river beds now full of water and in colour, for the most part, a deep chocolate. There is a big bend inland at the southernmost point – and here the scene is infinitely desolate. It would have been more so, but for the thin ribbon of metalled civilization below us, with its great arched bridges fretted and dazzling white against the gloomy background. As an engineering work the railway filled me with admiration. To think of war in connection with it seems paradoxically irrelevant. It is an enormous feat of industrial development linking Egypt with the rich region of Palestine, and war or no war – it is a permanent asset of immense value.[3]

The seaplane he cherished as a new species of magic carpet. It was also, he recognized only too well, a potentially revolutionary weapon of war, though the unseemly rivalries between the two separate air departments in Whitehall, each squabbling interminably with its neighbour for scarce raw materials, engines and designs to equip the rival air forces of the Army and Navy, had temporarily blunted the sharp, business end of airpower. None of these distant animosities seemed to matter much in the untroubled skies above the Red Sea and the tideless Mediterranean. For there the Fokker scourge was still unknown. Childers did photograph an airfield with new hangars and parked fighters at Beersheba on 7 March 1916. But until that date only the mischance of a sniper's bullet could foil a trained observer or cause a mission to end in disaster. The airpower problem began to concern Childers personally from the day a signal arrived unexpectedly from the Admiralty, recalling him home to join its intelligence branch. As L'Estrange-Malone put it: 'You can help us better than anyone. You know our needs.'

The mails had always been slow, and the restrictions of censorship which Childers applied fairly and rigorously to everyone, himself included, often made him long for home. Molly's daily letters had kept him abreast, during those months of separation, of ordinary, familiar matters: her unsparing work for the refugees, the difficulties of food rationing, the progress of Erskine, their elder son, at his preparatory school from which he would soon go to Gresham's, a place they eventually chose in preference to Eton or Harrow because the headmaster, G. W. S. Howson, seemed to both of them a paragon of liberal open-mindedness. Sometimes, after scanning the grim lists of casualties in the newspapers, Molly would mention the name of a friend or distant relative killed, wounded or missing in action; then the insane costliness and messiness of war as a means of defending human liberties would cast him into the depths of despair. So tight-fitting, however, was the mask of self-deprecating composure he habitually wore that none of his fellow-officers, none of the skilled men under him, ever caught him off guard:

'He was very strict but very understanding,' declared one seaman who voiced the common view. 'Should any of the lower deck put anything in their letters of which he did not approve, the man would be persuaded to write another letter. He would even go so far as to write another letter himself for that man – but woe betide the offender if the error was repeated.... I once heard him tick off two young sub-lieutenants who were attached to us for a while and I never heard the English language spoken so fluently yet without a single swear-word. He was a bit abstemious and drank only port at dinner. In spite of his being censor, the lower deck thought well of him and all respected him.... He was invariably out for the underdog.... What drove him on to take the personal risks he took in the sky mystified everyone. For when I knew him his sight was bad, his hearing none too good, and he had been crippled in the South African War [sic].'[4]

According to Colonel (later Major-General Sir Frederick) Sykes: 'When Childers was under me our chief difficulty was to prevent him taking flights out of turn. On two occasions when he crashed into the sea it was found that he had no business to be on that patrol at all.... He was a biilliant officer and utterly fearless.'[5]

That brilliance and fearlessness did not go unrewarded, much as Childers tended to undervalue the quality of his work and the virtues that drove him on. When L'Estrange-Malone recommended him for a gallantry award, both Sykes and Admiral Wemyss endorsed the recommendation. Not unil 21 April 1917, by which date he had added to his credit a string of daring deeds just as long again, was it officially announced that 'the King has been pleased to give orders' for conferring the Distinguished Service Cross on Lieutenant (now Lieutenant Commander) Erskine Childers, 'in recognition of his services with the Royal Naval Air Service for the period January–May 1916. During this time he acted as observer in many important air reconnaissances, showing remarkable aptitude for observing and for collating the results of his observing.'[6]

But his heart was heavy on the bleak winter day he eventually limped into Buckingham Palace to receive his decoration from George V. The momentary pride he felt when his turn came for a perfunctory exchange of words with the monarch weighed little beside the indignation still simmering below the surface of Childers's vulnerable, idealistic mind. He could not, and did not,

blame the King for the renewed woes of Ireland. He did condemn
the King's shortsighted ministers and their advisers, just as he
deplored the self-sacrificing folly of Irish extremists for having
acted on the age-old rebel adage that England's difficulty must
always be Ireland's opportunity. He had only just returned home
from the Mediterranean to enjoy a few days' respite from the
stresses of fifteen months' flying when an unbelievable event
plunged him into the depths of gloom. When he first read the
news of the armed uprising by a small force of Irish Volunteers
in Dublin on Easter Monday 1916 Childers was torn by conflicting emotions. How could MacNeill, a man of integrity if ever
he knew one, have lent the authority of his name to such a hopelessly ill-timed and utterly quixotic demonstration of defiance?
What possible advantage could there be in proclaiming an independent Irish Republic if the ringleaders and their followers
represented only themselves?

Such an instant response was natural if not unique; undoubtedly
many other well-informed English Liberals shared it. Yet as
Easter Week 1916 slowly passed, as British reinforcements,
equipped with artillery and superior weapons, blasted out the
shrinking pockets of rebel resistance in the heart of Dublin,
Childers's feelings slowly changed. No longer did he question the
dubious ends to which the Mauser rifles he had personally smuggled into Howth had been put by the conspirators, once it became plain how callously the British commander, General Maxwell, treated the captured rebel leaders, some of them quite unknown to Childers. There was O'Rahilly, shot down while
making a run for it down Moore Street from the burning Post
Office building, a man he had met only once. There was also the
crueller case of James Connolly of the Citizen's Army, so badly
wounded that he had to be propped up in a chair to provide an
easier target for the firing squad. Major John MacBride and the
eccentric Countess Markievicz, whose life was spared, Childers
had also briefly encountered; the rest were total strangers to
him.

The self-styled Commandant-General, Padraic Pearse, had
written prophetically just a year previously in an otherwise forgotten play: 'We thought it a foolish thing for four score to go
into battle against four thousand, or maybe forty thousand.' To

which the hero had replied: 'And so it is a foolish thing. Do you want us to be wise?'

Pearse, the mystic playwright; MacDonagh, the lecturer in English; Joseph Plunkett, the minor poet; Eamonn de Valera, the mathematics teacher; Edward Daly, the nephew of an old Fenian of the 1867 rising; the veteran IRB leader, Tom Clarke, and his colleagues Sean MacDermott and Edmund Kent (who had adopted the Gaelic name of Eamonn Ceannt) were rebels of whose very existence Childers had been unaware. He correctly assumed that men far more ruthless than MacNeill or Bulmer Hobson must have manipulated the breakaway Volunteer movement with near-suicidal success: yet the ingenuous Childers neither then nor later connected any of the rising's leaders with the plottings of a reformed Irish Republican Brotherhood.

What swung his sympathies slowly to the other extreme was the cold-blooded ruthlessness of the British courts-martial that followed the surrender of the last batches of insurgents: in the words of Roy Jenkins: 'Part of the trouble was that, with martial law proclaimed throughout the country and the civil administration in practical dissolution, the military were given an almost free hand.... Lord Wimborne [the Viceroy] thought the policy of retribution by execution was carried too far, but he hardly knew what was happening until it was over. The Cabinet was also a little nervous, but decided, on May 6th, that General Maxwell must be given discretion in individual cases.'[7]

Asquith, unable to find the right man to replace Augustine Birrell as Chief Secretary, crossed to Dublin and shouldered the burden for a while himself. After investigating what Maxwell had done, the Prime Minister concluded 'that on the whole, except the Skeffington case, there have been fewer blunders than one might have expected with the soldiery for a whole week in exclusive charge'. True, public opinion in Dublin and elsewhere reacted strongly against a rebellion which was bound to collapse. Yet reprisals alienated that same opinion and inscribed more than a dozen new names to the roll-call of Irish martyrs. Then there ensued the public trial for treason of the wretched Sir Roger Casement, Childers's prewar associate, who had been arrested on Good Friday, after being put ashore in Ireland from a German submarine. Alice Stopford Green, Childers's main source of inside information, confessed herself appalled at the grotesque lengths to which Casement had been willing to go as a crusader for Irish freedom. The correspondence between them had begun in 1904. Until Mrs Green found him out consorting with Imperial Germany to secure the Kaiser's active support for the cause, the pair had been in the habit of addressing one another in mock-heroic terms, such as 'My dear Knight of the Island' and 'My dear Woman of the Three books'. Some of Casement's letters to her had been intercepted by the Foreign Office, inducing Birrell, who knew the lady, to comment: 'I don't know where she stands in the hierarchy of treason but I should put her *low down*.' Birrell's estimate was just. Alice Stopford Green's correspondence with Casement had ceased once she realized his wild aim. She expressed 'profound and heartfelt sorrow' at what he had done, but in her charity thought him misguided rather than wicked.

Childers spent much of that agonizing summer of 1916 inside the Admiralty. He was thus well placed to watch the stage-managing of the public drama at the Old Bailey which, as in the cases of the rebel ringleaders whom General Maxwell had executed, enabled Casement to win the unlikely crown of martyrdom. No evidence exists to suggest that Childers knew anything of the fantastic plan, apparently concocted by Captain Reginald Hall, Chief of Naval Intelligence, to capture Sir Roger before he could set foot on Irish soil: a suitable yacht was to be chartered to a German-speaking American owner, put in charge of a British captain who would pretend to be an emissary for Casement and set off cruising to the west of Ireland, where, in the end, the wanted man would fall unawares into the trap. Indeed all the necessary elements, owner and skipper and yacht, were provided; then the *Sayonara* sailed away towards the sunset on its voyage to nowhere. Nothing, of course, came of this improbable piece of melodrama, which coincidentally 'sounded like a parody of *The Riddle of the Sands*', to quote Casement's latest biographer, Brian Inglis, 'except that Childers' plot was by contrast credible'.[8]

Mrs Green's efforts to enlist support, first, for a proper defence of the accused, then for a reprieve after the predictable death sentence had been passed, proved unavailing. Well might Molly Childers add her name to the list of distinguished signatories of the petition organized by Sir Arthur Conan Doyle, alongside the names of Arnold Bennett, G. K. Chesterton, Galsworthy, Jerome K. Jerome, Sir James Frazer, H. W. Massingham, C. P. Scott, A. G. Gardiner, G. P. Gooch and a score of others. Her husband, the prisoner of his own voluntary contract to serve King and country for the duration, was certainly not at liberty to do so. Childers felt impotent, angry and frustrated. While he would readily have endorsed Casement's own verdict on the Dublin judicial killings that 'the shot Irishmen will now take their places beside Emmet and the Manchester Martyrs in Ireland, and beside the heroes of Poland and Serbia and Belgium in Europe, and nothing on earth can prevent it', he also felt as deeply as did George Bernard Shaw that the British Government behaved idiotically in allowing the law to take its inexorably stern course. In a letter to Asquith, Shaw presumed that the Prime Minister had no wish to turn Casement into a national hero: 'There is, however, one infallible way in which that can be done; and that way is to hang him. His trial and sentence have already raised his status in nationalist Ireland; but it lacks the final consecration of death. We urge you very strongly not to effect that consecration.'

On 30 August 1916 Casement was hanged. The effect on opinion in the United States could scarcely have been worse. In Ireland, of course, Casement became a martyr. Even in England the reverberations of a bad decision continued rumbling on for years.

On returning from Dublin in the middle of May, Asquith tried ineffectually to remove the Irish Home Rule Bill from cold storage. He appointed Lloyd George to act as a mediator between the interested parties after the Welshman's refusal to become the new Chief Secretary for Ireland. To begin with, the exploratory talks went well, much to everyone's surprise. Redmond and Carson, those prewar antagonists, were in complete agreement on a settlement which would have meant immediate Home Rule, the Six Counties being excluded until the end of the war when an Imperial Conference would determine the best permanent solution. No sooner were these terms published, however, than a storm of Tory recrimination burst over Asquith's head. The Coalition Government, itself the cause of Redmond's hopelessly

H

exposed position, seemed for a few days to be on the point of disintegrating.

The principal diehards now were not Ulstermen but Southern Unionists like Walter Long and Lord Lansdowne; and it was the latter, 'a moderate on many issues but always a cold and determined extremist on anything touching his position as a Kerry landlord', in the discerning phrase of Roy Jenkins, who finally killed the initiative. To the consternation of his colleagues, Lansdowne rose to speak for the Government in the Lords and emphasized that the exclusion of Ulster must be a permanent feature of any deal and that the rest of Ireland should be governed by a tightened version of the Defence of the Realm Act.

On 24 July, just ten days before Casement went to the scaffold, Asquith informed Lady Scott, a frequent confidante, that he considered Redmond was 'trying to kill the whole thing', adding, 'in fact, it's dead'.[7] The Prime Minister did not err. Bitterly divided among themselves, the Irish MPs at Westminster recognized finally that they no longer represented their own people. The ground had once more been cut from under their feet, so that, in Asquith's judgment, they had 'nothing to suggest but despair'. Wimborne was sent back as Viceroy to renew a decrepit and discredited system of direct rule, thus ensuring that the abortive Sinn Fein coup of Easter Week had not wholly been in vain.

Childers's maternal forbear, Thomas Erskine, that unusual Lord Chancellor of England who had made a virtue of upholding the rights of the underdog, deeply shocked the Establishment of his day when, in 1796, he condemned 'the uncontrolled licentiousness of a brutal and insolent soldiery' during his unanswerable defence of the case of Thomas Stone. One of Thomas Erskine's lineal descendants, Robert Barton, shocked Childers not long after Easter Week by resigning his British Army commission and cheerfully damning the consequences. A regimental officer sent to Dublin when the Irish rebels were on the point of surrendering, Barton could not stand the merciless treatment meted out to most of them and acted in accordance with his conscience. Childers failed to dissuade this favourite cousin of his from taking so rash and damaging a decision. In hinting jocularly that the next worst thing that could happen to Robert was his 'conversion to *Sinn Fein*', the older man struck uncomfortably nearer to the truth than he could have realized. The latter's conversion to a movement at which Childers looked askance was not long delayed. Yet the two men did not fall out; their affection for one another ran deeper than passing differences over political loyalties. At least they could and did agree that the faintheartedness of Asquith had once more prevented a settlement of the Irish problem.

It was still Childers's belief that Redmond and his Irish Nationalists, who had struggled for decades to earn independence by constitutional means, deserved better of their countrymen than did the rebels of Easter Week. He did not, however, despise the mystical concept of the dead Padraic Pearse that only through the blood-sacrifice of martyrs could the seeds of liberty grow.

What he deplored was the total mismanagement of the rebellion, quite apart from the twisted motives of those mysterious men who had instigated it. Hardened by the repeated risks he had so often courted in a total war for liberating *all* small nations, Childers's fastidious mind still shrank from foolhardiness, from mindless destruction and from wanton or ostentatious bloodletting. Perhaps, in the process of taking risks, his formerly keen political insight had been dulled a little. Certainly he was no longer so well informed about Irish affairs as he had once been.

Little is known in detail about the three months he spent at the Admiralty in the first half of 1916. For Childers always dropped the practice of keeping a diary while billeted comfortably at home. The exact nature of his duties in the Naval Intelligence branch are therefore obscure, a regrettable omission from the biographer's point of view. For when his political assassins accused him towards the end of his turbulent life of having worked, in effect, against Ireland as a double agent in the pay of his British masters, they were reading the very worst into the bare facts of his service career. Nor should that surprise anyone. No former naval officer, notably one who had been openly recalled from Irish Volunteer Headquarters in Dublin shortly after the outbreak of war by the then Chief of Naval Intelligence, and who subsequently worked on the staff of that man's successor, the enigmatic Captain Reginald Hall, could fail to attract the suspicions of rumour-mongers, or the ultimate vengeance of the IRB.

Reluctant to 'hang about' the Admiralty, mainly shuffling papers, Childers pulled strings to escape; and, with Herbert Richmond's help, he was soon posted for training to one of the Royal Navy's new coastal motor-boat depots.

On 13 December 1916, writing the customary love-letter to Molly from Queenborough, the naval air station outside Felixstowe, he declared:

Another birthday away from my beloved but not so far this time.... Last year I remember writing to you from Mitylene and all that I said then seems poor and inadequate: so it is now. But I love to repeat my old familiar vows and credo and lay my flowers on the blessed altar and say that I only count my own years since our meeting, that they were wasted and null till you came and made life significant and sacred and the whole world full of meaning – 'setting the rose of beauty on the brow of chaos'.[9]

His wife had long accustomed herself to his compulsive and romantic urge for adventure. She understood it; and, for the sake of their two young sons, she hoped and prayed that the mysterious life-force which sustained the universe would not be brutally withdrawn from him in the chaos of war, either above or on the sea. Molly claimed to have an unerring sixth sense which warned her whenever he was in mortal danger. It did not forsake her during the eventful five months from March to July 1917. By then Childers had resumed his war diary. 'So at last after thirteen months I have been on a *war* enterprise with the CMBs. No luck however.'

He had grown weary of playing bridge, arranging fixtures and charts in his office at the back of a hut close to Dunkirk's breakwater, hearing about the difficulties of former flying colleagues stationed at First Wing Headquarters not far away, and generally idling away precious time. Since navigating the leading coastal motor-boat of a group of six from Queenborough to Dunkirk, atrocious gales and wintry conditions had ruled out all operations. Then fine, calm weather returned with rumours of plans for 'a great bombardment of Zeebrugge'. Ungrudgingly recognized as the most experienced navigator in all three divisions of the fast

little coastal craft, with their powerful if sometimes undependable
engines, Childers made up for lost opportunities when regular
night patrols were resumed. They had orders to lie in wait for
unwary German destroyers or submarines entering or leaving the
heavily fortified harbours of Ostend and Zeebrugge; and for
three months the imperturbable Lieutenant-Commander Childers,
who swore that he preferred flying to sailing, bore an extraordinarily charmed life, as these random excerpts from his diary
amply testify:

April 19th...Calm weather. We just missed a submarine off Z: it submerged as we were about to fire. We went twice to within a mile of the
Mole. Nothing else of much interest. The trench lines of Nieuport are
like a firework show with star-shells and searchlights. No. 13 tried to
torpedo a patrol twice off Ostend but missed.... The bombardment
was cancelled at the last minute – like all Bacon's things.

Vice-Admiral R. H. Bacon was the operational controller of all
ships and aircraft at work in the Dover–Dunkirk sector. Erskine
Childers seldom disguised his philosophic contempt for the man.
Bacon seemed to model himself on the excessive caution preached
by the new First Sea Lord, Sir John Jellicoe; and Bacon, who had
small faith in airpower, equally discouraged torpedo and coastal
motor boat commanders from trailing their coats too pro-
vocatively in pursuit of the enemy's iron-clad prizes.

April 22nd. At 2.30 a.m. we were called and tumbled hastily out.
Howard [the Divisional commander] said the Huns had bombarded
Dover and that we were to try and cut them off but that it was too late
to go to Zeebrugge.... I cursed myself for not having recommended
dashing straight for Zeebrugge at thirty knots to cut the Huns off.
Against orders, true, but I doubt if the Commodore and Howard
realized or remembered that we could, if need be, get to Z. in one hour
and ten minutes....
April 26th. In the afternoon asked by Fellowes [Squadron Commander of First Wing] to go for a reconnaissance trip with him over
Zeebrugge in a De Havilland 4.... Rose to 20,000 feet. Cold intense. A
beautiful day and splendid view. Six destroyers in Zeebrugge by the
mole and submarines etc. in Ostend. Heavy anti-aircraft fire but no
serious danger. Interesting to see them attempt a regular barrage off
Ostend but we dodged it. When down, I tore off in a car to Dunkirk,
just in time to snatch a bite of dinner and start on Zeebrugge patrol

with Number 8 boat and Number 2. Off Ostend we three times saw red and green signals – Verey lights or recognition lights. Rushed over to search and found nothing: a bewitched feeling we had....I believe I must be the only person who has been to Z twice in one day, both by air and water.

News had belatedly reached him from the Admiralty that 'I was given the DSC for Mediterranean services in RNAS. Year's delay unexplained. I don't deserve it anyway.' The award did serve to remind him that he must get back to aerial observing, his first love in this strangely unreal war. Then Vice-Admiral Bacon sent for him personally, having learnt that Childers had been four miles above Ostend in a Short seaplane one night, instead of aboard a coastal motor boat skippered by a Lieutenant Welman who persisted in the absurd claim that he had scored a direct hit on a destroyer off that port. Childers arrived expecting a wigging!

May 11th, Dover. Saw Admiral at 9 a.m. He questioned me about the explosion I had seen in the sea plane on the night of April 30th – May 1st when Welman torpedoed the destroyer. He is sceptical about W's story – very unjustly I think....He specially asked about the colour of the explosion, saying that of a torpedo ought to be red. I said what I saw was a warm orange.

Bacon happened to be one of many senior naval officers who respected Childers as a writer and on that account tended to overlook his intense individualism as a junior officer. Nevertheless, Bacon would not let him go back to seaplanes because he thought more of Childers's proven seamanship than of his enthusiasm for air observation. Not until early July, after completing nearly thirty pointless runs to and from occupied enemy harbours on the Belgian coast, after enduring enemy bombardments by night and day at the Dunkirk base, and after flying on a number of un-authorized attacks himself, did he at last receive his clearance. In response to a signal from his own obstructive Commodore, asking when Childers might rejoin the air service, the following curt replay came back:

'He has nothing whatever to do with the CMBs.'

'Words fail me,' the diarist scribbled in an outburst of fury. 'Which is the worst – the impudence or the inefficiency of the thing – I cannot say.'

It was perhaps too much to expect that a creature of orderly habits with a mind as tidy as Childers's should suffer without protest the insensitive bumbling of uniformed jacks-in-office whose lightest whims carried the force of law. To which these heavily braided gentlemen might well have retorted: 'Whatever makes any hypersensitive and gifted man in his forty-eighth year want to go on recklessly dicing with death like an unthinking youngster half that age?' The Admiralty, to be fair, contained not a few high-ranking officers who occasionally conspired together to protect Erskine Childers as far as possible from his incomprehensible lust for adventure.

The Commodore shamed him a little by saying at a farewell dinner in his honour that the elderly Childers never ceased to work 'full out'. Did he deserve such praise? On reflection that night, the diarist believed that he did: 'I know this is so,' he wrote without false modesty, 'for I have been on more service stunts with the boats than any other officer, though I have had disproportionately bad luck in meeting the enemy.' As for the younger, hardier specimens who often pulled his leg, while looking up to him as an exemplar, he told them simply why he had always 'felt a little bit of a father' to them.[3]

The protective gentlemen at the Admiralty were no doubt mildly relieved when Lloyd George intervened in July 1917, and helpfully headed Childers off for them. Molly had been hinting obliquely for some time that 'something interesting' was 'in the wind'. She had recently been seeing a good deal of Sir Horace Plunkett; and Sir Horace was angling for Childers's temporary secondment from the Navy to serve on the secretariat of a special Irish Convention which, it appeared, the Prime Minister intended shortly to summon. This somewhat clumsy and conditional attempt to gather together all interested parties, so that, by encouraging them to talk, a watered-down version of Home Rule could be agreed on and implemented at once, was as far as the wartime coalition Cabinet would allow its new leader, Lloyd George, to go. It is an interesting fact that today, nearly sixty years later, only the specialists can recall the confused and inconclusive deliberations of this ill-starred constitution-making body.

That it failed to produce even an agreed majority report should surprise nobody, so deeply divided were the delegates among themselves. Yet as a milestone in Erskine Childers's political development, that same, half-forgotten Irish Convention of 1917–18 proved to be of cardinal importance.

Saw Sir Graham Greene and Commodore Payne, the Fifth Sea Lord, at the Admiralty [Childers noted on 27 July], and was told I was to go to Dublin as an assistant secretary to the Convention. To receive my pay as before. To wear civilian dress, if I wished. I asked Payne to be sure to send a relief for me (to the seaplane base).... He said he would ... I left by 8.45 night mail for Ireland full of hope and joy at the prospect of being useful to Ireland at this crisis.... M. is to follow me over. How soon depends on her health and her refugee work.

Childers at once decided to accept the offer to stay with Diarmid Coffey, the witty young lawyer whom he had met briefly at Cowes when the crews of the two gun-running yachts, *Asgard* and *Kelpie*, had anchored there on their outward journey to German waters in the summer of 1914. When Molly eventually joined her husband she at once noticed his vacillating moods of cheerfulness and despondency. Coffey, who was also serving on the secretariat staff of the Convention, did not give too much for its chances, partly because Sinn Fein had merely sent an unofficial observer. His name was Edward MacLysaght; and he became a frequent visitor to Coffey's home in Harcourt Terrace. Rightly or wrongly, Molly Childers felt that Erskine paid too much attention to the strange and unacceptable political opinions which this frequent visitor to Coffey's home never tired of expressing with calm and charming moderation.

MacLysaght grew attached to Childers, though he found it 'faintly embarrassing' to sit hour after hour watching Erskine holding hands with his wife on the couch where, with her disability, she usually held court. It wasn't as if they were a pair of young lovers! 'It seemed to me that Molly had undue influence over him, not only politically but in other ways. Our main topic was naturally the Convention and politics, but we talked about other things, too, and Erskine often brought the conversation round to his yacht, in which he went sailing whenever practicable on the Shannon. I regarded him as an Englishman who showed an intelligent and sympathetic interest in Ireland. None of us then thought an Irish Republic to be a realistic aim – the British Empire, after all, was at its zenith – and Childers obviously favoured his own solution of Dominion Home Rule.'[10]

As for Childers's view of MacLysaght, one flattering entry in the diary refers to him as 'a very interesting young man – landlord – Sinn Feiner though not official enough of one to prevent him coming under the Sinn Fein boycott of the Convention. Much depends on him, for he is practically their unofficial spokesman. He thinks Dominion Home Rule will satisfy them and all other information is to that effect, but this assumes an absence of trouble in the country and the good sense of the Castle.'

Unrest was certainly brewing at this time. Eamonn de Valera, the leading survivor of the Easter Rising, was again in the public spotlight. Among 117 Irish prisoners recently amnestied by the British Government as a goodwill gesture, the former commandant of the last rebel unit to surrender had stood as a Sinn Fein candidate in July 1917 against Redmond's nominee at a by-election in East Clare, and soundly defeated him. De Valera's campaign manager had been Eoin MacNeill, another newly released prisoner. Childers chose to ignore the victor's declaration that the voters of East Clare had demonstrated their faith in complete independence for Ireland. For by now he was coming to grips with some of the immediate difficulties placed in the path of that ideal goal by others.

With one half of his mind he feared that 'for all we know the Castle, in its blind, irresponsible way, may – working on reports of police, spies and informers – be trying to wreck the Convention or just blundered on in a muddle. That is the curse of this horrible system of martial law and secrecy.' The allusion here was to the sudden arrest of several minor Sinn Fein leaders. With the other half of his mind he suspected that the differences between extremists inside an otherwise representative talk-shop, to which he had been recruited for his rather rusty constitutional expertise, might turn out to be irreconcilable. For Redmond's back was pressed hard against the wall. Having pushed the limit of concession beyond what was acceptable to his critics in 1914, and again in 1916, the Irish Nationalist leader had no room for man-oeuvre left. His credibility, too, had all but evaporated; if he tried to placate Ulster further, it would almost certainly vanish without trace. Yet, with Carson and other dependable Tory supporters helping to maintain Lloyd George in office as Britain's war leader, the Ulstermen at the Convention felt confident enough to offer Redmond nothing. The Nationalist leader's sole hope lay in wooing the Southern Unionists who did not want a partitioned Ireland largely on the grounds of self-interest.

The Prime Minister, in a letter to Redmond on 16 May 1917, had warned him in advance that 'the choice of alternatives has been narrowed down'. Lloyd George was able to offer two things only: either a Bill for the immediate application of Home Rule to Ireland, excluding the six counties of north-east Ulster, 'such exclusion to be subject to reconsideration by Parliament at the end of five years'; or 'a Convention of Irishmen of all parties for the purpose of producing a scheme of Irish self-government'. The snags in each of the two schemes still seemed irremediable to poor John Redmond. Childers, in his own moments of euphoria, which tended to dwindle as weeks quickly spread into months, still duped himself into believing that the Dublin Convention would put flesh on the bones of his own skeletal plan of Dominion Home Rule and thus convince a sceptical Prime Minister that Irish unity must be preserved at all costs because the needs of Ireland dictated it and the majority of representatives at the Convention desired it.

By mid-October, a note of bitter realism had crept into his letters and diary entries:

HMS *Convention* is still afloat [he informed his sister], Constance. I cannot say more. Irish situation intensely interesting. Folly of government inconceivable. Difficulties for Convention very great.... It is lovely to have Molly here [at Glendalough] and little Bobby, I have just been digging an underground dwelling with him – with tunnels, chambers, stable etc. I was not thinking of the war but I suppose some instinct made me do war-work! God knows, the whole world may be living underground some day!

On 2 November, after setting out in detail the efforts of sub-committees to iron out their differences, he commented:

The crux came on the fiscal question. Ulster refusing any concession
to fiscal autonomy, declining to put forward any constructive suggestions or even to state roughly how far they would be willing to go.
They were in fact unwilling to give Ireland taxing powers of any sort.
... Plunkett meanwhile composed an address or letter ... saying that a
crisis must not develop, that political or sentimental arguments must
be separated from business arguments and the latter discussed seriously,
and finally that a break-up of the [steering] Committee of Nine would
not upset the Convention which would continue to work on and, if
no agreement was possible, present a majority report.

Shortly before Christmas Childers drove in a blinding blizzard
to spend another weekend at Glendalough, an 'Easter rebel' to
whom he gave a lift helping him to dig the vehicle out of more
than one snowdrift. 'Bob [Robert Barton] is still a very keen
Sinn Feiner,' he confided to his diary. 'We had long talks. He
thinks Sinn Fein will accept any agreement of the Convention
and use the Parliament as means to obtain more...'
Plunkett's unenviable task as chairman took a steady toll of the
old man's limited stamina and almost excessive patience. Like
Childers, he kept his fingers crossed while seeking some
semblance of compromise in the welter of conflicting views.
Their hopes were extinguished early in the New Year of 1918.
Plunkett's final submission to the Prime Minister, on which the
Chief Secretary, Lord Southborough, and Childers put the best
face they could, underlined the refusal of the wrangling Irish
delegates to yield an inch. When, in February, Plunkett warned
Lloyd George that breaking-point had been reached, the latter
invited a small, representative group of the disputants to Downing
Street. Neither the Prime Minister nor his ministerial colleagues
could persuade them to budge. In a firm and carefully considered
letter to the Convention, through its chairman, Lloyd George
re-emphasized the urgency of concessions 'on all sides. It has been
so in every Convention, from the USA to South Africa.' But the
advice fell on resolutely deaf ears.
On 5 April, the Irish Convention adjourned *sine die* after eight
months of wrangling. 'Perhaps', declared Plunkett in a masterly
example of understatement, 'unanimity was too much to expect.'
For he failed to persuade the unruly delegates to sign an
agreed majority report, the Ulstermen and a splinter-group of

Nationalists deciding to enshrine their intransigent dogmatism in separate addenda. The final document on which Childers burnt much midnight oil ran to 176 pages, hardly an appetizing dish to set before a busy Prime Minister then faced with catastrophic military problems in France, where the Germans had broken through the Allied lines in March, inflicting heavy losses on the British. Childers was caught between the sorrow he felt for Ireland and his anxiety to get back into uniform. He had done his best to help Plunkett, but the best was not good enough to win over inflexible men of dogma.

'While, technically, it was our function to draft a constitution for our country,' declared Plunkett, 'it would be more correct to say that we had to find a way out of the most complex and anomalous political situation to be found in history – I might almost say fiction.'

The deadlock, unbroken to the last, could be summed up in two words: Ulster and Customs duties. As Plunkett put it:

'The Ulster difficulty the whole world knows: but how the Customs question came to be one of vital principle, upon the decision of which depended the amount of agreement that could be reached in the Convention, needs to be told.... The claim for Dominion Home Rule was concentrated upon a demand for unrestricted fiscal powers. Upon this the Nationalists made a strong case...and to obviate any serious disturbance of the trade of the United Kingdom, the Nationalists were prepared to agree to a free trade arrangement between the two countries. But this did not overcome the difficulties of the Southern Unionists, who on this point agreed with the Ulster Unionists. They were apprehensive that a separate system of Customs control, however guarded, might impair the authority of the United Kingdom over its external trade policy.... Neither side was willing to surrender the principle; but both sides were willing, in order that a Parliament should be at once established, to postpone a legislative decision upon the ultimate control of Customs and Excise.'[11]

The new Irish Parliament would have consisted of a House of Commons of 200 members and a Senate representing commerce, industry and labour interests, the Churches, the county councils, the universities and the peerage. The Nationalists offered a guaranteed forty per cent of all Commons' seats to the Ulstermen who, refusing to consider nominated membership, remained cool towards any scheme for extra representation by direct election. With a concluding note worthy of the desperate salesman, Plunkett declared that 'a larger measure of agreement has been reached upon the principle and details of Irish self-government than has ever yet been attained. Is it too much to hope that the scheme embodying this agreement will forthright be brought to fruition by those to whose call the Irish Convention has responded?'

The question, of course, was academic and entirely rhetorical. Even if Lloyd George and his colleagues had not been grappling with one of the gravest military crises of the war, it is doubtful whether Plunkett's report would have merited such handsome treatment. As it was, a distracted Prime Minister quite naturally chose to ignore it.

Childers, lost for so long in the storm-clouds of theory, returned to earth with a bang during the third week of February 1918. Sir Horace, who had business in Whitehall, asked him over to advise. Weeks before, Molly had anticipated the worst and gone ahead to reopen the flat. She had fully expected the Convention to fail. Besides, she had arrears of her own war-work to make up. This random selection of extracts from Childers's diary during the week he spent at home plainly illustrates the bewilderment of someone reawakening to the drab realities of life in a country grimly struggling for survival in the fifth and darkest year of a conflict that seemed to have no ending:

February 17th. Sunday at home. I wrote to Tyrwhitt who had sent me a nice letter speaking of big operations coming and that I should be useful.

February 18th–22nd. I stayed in London as there was no work in Ireland....Wrote a memo for Plunkett.... He is unquenchably optimistic but I gather that the situation has not changed for the better and that Carson refuses to help.... Food very scarce. Controls and ration cards on meat, sugar, butter and coal. Had to go on my knees to the coal-controller as we had nearly used all we were entitled to up to October 1st! He gave us eight tons....There were three air raids this week, a bomb falling on the east wing of the Royal Hospital (killing five people) about three hundred yards from us on the 18th, breaking some of our windows by concussion. No panic among the children or servants.... Long talk with Molly on the future, if Convention fails – whether to make Ireland or England a home? Nothing settled. Must finish with Navy and war first.

That truncated entry hid a world of hurtful uncertainty. For Childers had his first open disagreement with Molly on the subject of his own tangled and opposing loyalties. She was quite positive that his loyal duty to England must take precedence over his protective feeling for Ireland. Their children were English. He must think of them before jumping to rash decisions. She had originally turned her back on America for his sake; now he must make a similar sacrifice for all their sakes. The idea of settling in Ireland did not appeal to Molly. She had grown extremely attached to England, especially an England at war. Erskine listened intently to her reasoning but could not wholly accept it. Her clinching argument, to the effect that because his roots and his friends were English he could contribute more to the Irish cause by remaining in England, was one he particularly disliked. The stubborn streak in him suddenly came to the fore. They let the question drop for the present, agreeing not to discuss it again.

After her husband's tragic and premature death, Molly sorted out his papers in her own arbitrary fashion. One regrettable piece of editing which she insisted on perpetrating was to expunge from the many intimate letters they exchanged almost every reference, direct or indirect, to this absorbing and revealing quarrel. Subsequent events showed that Childers won the argument when it came to the point of decision, Molly reluctantly abiding by his judgment. If it was in character for this strong, resolute woman so to 'cook the evidence' as to mislead members of her own family, quite apart from posterity, it cannot be said that Erskine Childers's oblique and guarded allusions to the dispute were wholly out of character either.

What helped to turn his heart to stone in the deadly month of April 1918, was the Government's decision to rush through an emergency Manpower Bill extending conscription to Ireland. To a diary already crammed with some 30,000 words on the recent barren Convention business in Trinity College, Dublin, Childers added this revealing note:

[I thought] the war might be over before the Convention ended but subsequent events destroyed this hope and for some time past I have roughly estimated October 1919 as the end, when the full weight of American assistance will have had time to crush Germany. It is a terrible thing to say but the hopes of Ireland now as for the last 700 years depend on the pressure she can exert on England. The crisis is approaching now and the English Government characteristically is pursuing an insane and criminal course in trying to coerce Ireland even at the moment when it is offering Home Rule. . . . The sands are running out. . . . Alas, a large part of Ireland is in a grave condition, under military law, with opinion stifled; the young men almost hopelessly estranged from Britain and not merely willing but anxious to die – not on French battlefields but in Ireland for Irish Liberty.[3]

Of course, Molly Childers would have been upset by such gloomy and nihilistic introspection. Disloyalty of the sort hardly squared with the progressively pro-British sentiments of this energetic and ardent American lady who had lately been thrilled to receive a letter from Buckingham Palace, advising her of the King's wish to confer on her the MBE for outstanding services to the Belgian refugees in England. A somewhat acrimonious exchange of letters between Robert Barton and Molly emphasized how much she deplored Irish recalcitrance:

'I don't believe you when you say that "England has more gleanings of righteousness than any other nation," ' Barton told her brusquely. 'She has more hypocrisy.' Nor could Barton resist teasing her about the award: he could not understand how 'people holding your ideals are still willing to accept and rejoice in "Empire orders" ', since 'Empire and freedom are terms which deny one another. I now know that England is no more fighting for freedom than Germany is, perhaps less.'

Writing separately to his cousin, Childers, about this time, Barton ended a lengthy and harrowing account of the apprehensive atmosphere in Ireland with these dry words: 'I fear Molly will be dreadfully disappointed that Ireland cannot convert England by godly means. I think they'll have done well if they live up to their determination not to strike until they are attacked.'[12]

Childers was for once glad to leave home and resume his intelligence work in the new Royal Air Force. The service had come into being, appropriately, on 1 April 1918. Sir Godfrey

Payne, whom Childers had consulted off and on, ordered him at once to Felixstowe. There he found everything 'higgledy-piggledy' on the intelligence side – 'a big job to get it in order'. Hugh Trenchard had touched off a first-class political upheaval by resigning as first Chief of the Air Staff within a month of accepting that office, after a furious row with his inefficient Minister, Rothermere; and Childers's former boss, Sykes, moved into Trenchard's vacant place: 'I wrote congratulating him and saying I would be glad to help him if he wanted me.... Poor fellow, he is making a troubled start.' In due course Sykes sent for him and asked whether Childers would care to write the history of the recently born RAF. Childers gracefully declined. He wanted proper war work, preferably a job with a whiff of danger in it. Not until the late summer was this wish gratified, and then not by Sykes but by that formidable man of action, Trenchard, who summoned Childers unexpectedly to the headquarters of the Independent Air Force at Autigny, near Nancy, in September 1918.

The past four summer months had been frittered away in a frenzy of activity, much of it useless. He had been scandalized by the continuing strife inside the Air Ministry, where personal animosities between the partisans of Sykes and Trenchard interfered with routine business and were matched only by the more ancient rivalries between former War Office and Admiralty branches in the new third service. It cheered him immensely when the call came to join a bomber group at Bircham Newton, in Norfolk, though no bombers had yet arrived on the huge, half-finished airfield with its sprawl of empty new huts. His two reliable friends along the endless corridors of the Cecil Hotel, apart from the preoccupied Sykes, were a Colonel Davidson and a Lieutenant Colonel J. D. Boyle; and it was the considerate Davidson who advised him to fly out in a Handley Page machine to consult with Trenchard:

'Paris looked gorgeous from the air,' he noted. 'We flew over the eastern suburbs, the Sacré Coeur a great landmark with its fine façade high up at Montmartre while, of course, the Eiffel Tower could be seen long before any sign of the city was visible.'

The Handley Page was being ferried to one of the airfields from which the squadrons of Trenchard's so-called independent bombing command took off night and day in the first, largely unsuccessful campaign in the history of warfare to strike at German industrial targets from the sky. At Autigny Château, the command headquarters, Childers spent four days studying procedures and had three separate interviews with the tall, shrewd, gruff man who controlled an enterprise extraordinarily impressive in its potential scope. He was still more impressed by the craggy personality of Trenchard,

a bluff man, unintellectual I should think but with great driving power and energy. He did not anticipate our starting operations till November at earliest, possibly January. Otherwise he appeared to me unduly optimistic, talking lightly of Berlin and seeming to think the machines will rise to 17,000 feet *with bombs*.... A long talk of which I took careful notes. The main points were (1) that he wished me to have the same system of intelligence in Norfolk.... (2) that we were to communicate directly, not through the Air Ministry.... (3) that we were to interchange information, I dealing with all objectives north of latitude 52, [Major] Paul [Trenchard's intelligence office] with those south of it.... (4) that the first objectives to concentrate on were (a) Westphalian towns and (b) Wilhelmshaven and Kiel.

Childers next arranged with Major Paul the precise details of 'our relations and communications', visited both Wings to check their methods of coordinating meterological and other information, marvelled, in passing, at their keenness and efficiency, and was firmly snubbed by Trenchard on seeking permission to fly with one of the squadrons on an operational flight over Germany. In Paris on the homeward journey he paid two calls: the first 'to the Bon Marché to buy safety pins etc. for M.', the second to the French Army cartography department 'to get an invaluable French catalogue of maps'. The writ of that iron man Trenchard might run unquestioned around Nancy; but Bircham Newton happened to be so far off that Childers was still quite confident of guiding a Handley Page crew all the way across to the enemy heartland as navigator.

Much remained to be done before 27th Group, to which he had been officially assigned as intelligence officer, could pretend to be ready for action. In Childers's view, there was no violent hurry: the turn of the year would be time enough, he thought, since, as has been explained, he firmly believed that the war would drag on until the end of 1919. On 18 October he wrote in his diary: 'To Air Ministry at 10. The news is a special stunt a fortnight hence to bomb Berlin with the first two machines. I am to do maps and intelligence here.' On 22 October he noted: 'Majors Darley and Digby, the two pilots, came up and spent morning over maps.' At Trenchard's instant behest, the mission had to be put off because 'we are to wait for the next moon which means about the middle of November and do the thing in a thorough and well prepared way, after proper tests of the machines'. By then, too, all crews would have the large-scale maps on which Childers had been frantically labouring.

'The question of crossing Holland in raids on Germany has been raised,' he wrote towards the end of October, 'and to my great regret [Colonel] Mulock [the station commander] and of course the pilots were strongly in favour of it. I hoped Trenchard would turn it down but not so. The answer was a "smile". It is utterly unsportsmanlike and immoral.' Equally unsportsmanlike, if not quite so immoral, was Trenchard's simultaneous and rigid ban on operational flying by all staff officers, Childers included: 'This is very disappointing as in joining the Group I intended to take up active service.... I had put in an urgent claim to be allowed to go on the special flight, feeling I had a right as intelligence officer.'

The aircraft in which the privileged few would take off on one long and perilous hop to the German capital were huge Handley Page machines, the first four-engined bombers in the world, and the last of their size and power that Britain would build until 1942. Childers registered his dissatisfaction with the design when Darley took him up one day on a short practice flight. The facilities for navigation, he discovered, were 'very bad. No room to handle maps in the front observer's cockpit and practically none in the seat next to the pilot.... an amazing thing in a machine with fourteen hours' endurance, after four years of war.'

Political development early in November brought about a fresh change of plan. Austria sued for an armistice. Her once mighty empire broke up after 'the liberation of Bohemia and other states'. This, Childers narrowly observed, 'made it possible for machines starting from Prague to bomb Berlin from a distance of only 150 miles and for our machines to land if they desired in

Bohemia'. But could the necessary maps be begged, borrowed or stolen from official sources? No. Yet maps were found and provided by Childers's assistant who collected these from a friend when the 'Air Ministry and War Office both declared that there were none to be got in London'. At last, on 10 November, orders came through that Berlin was to be attacked by aircraft of the 27th Group that night:

I had a last talk with pilots and observers at noon but a little later it was settled that the raid could not begin that day....It was just as well as the night was a very bad one with rain and strong wind, in spite of a good forecast by our meteorological section.

The entry in the diary for 11 November stated laconically:

The orders were for a start in the afternoon, but at eleven o'clock [we were] called to fire stations and addressed by the Colonel who said the war was over and the armistice signed. There was a great cheer....

For Childers, one more war mission remained. The Air Ministry summoned him next day and 'offered me the job of reporting on bombing damage in Belgium'. While awaiting the full team of draughtsmen, photographers and general handymen assigned to him, Childers turned a lofty nose at the uninhibited rejoicing of people in the streets: 'Mafficking in London each day since the 10th – a rather sordid business: hordes of flappers and young soldiers rioting vacuously. Bonfires in Trafalgar Square. No sign of national dignity.'

When he left Victoria station with his new colleagues for Dover and Dunkirk, Childers felt colder, wearier and more decrepit than he considered any reasonably fit man of forty-eight had any right to feel. Was it simply a reaction to the exhilarating strains of war, or a sickening presentiment that the era of peace might not yet have dawned, despite the collapse of Germany and her allies? Childers could not decide; but he did recognize that the time for shedding old illusions had certainly come.

9. THE HOSTAGE

Directly Erskine entered the front door of their Chelsea flat, shivering in his greatcoat and RAF uniform, Molly realized that her husband was far from well. His hands trembled. His face had a drawn, emaciated look and a ghastly pallor. He sweated profusely, while trying as usual to dance attendance on her, but would not hear of letting the family doctor call. Long after their normal bedtime he was still talking about plans for a future which, Molly feared, he might not live to see. Next morning he did not get up, nor the morning after that. Childers had fallen victim to the lethal influenza epidemic then ravaging Europe, and sheer carelessness had produced complications. For the best part of a month he hovered between life and death in hospital. As his wife acknowledged afterwards: 'It really was touch and go.' She knew how heavily he had drawn, throughout the war years, on dwindling reserves of nervous energy; and the pleurisy that set in 'very nearly killed him'. Only an extremely tenacious will to live pulled the patient slowly through. Childers still had work to do, so death must wait. That work, she foresaw, would have to be for Ireland, probably in Ireland.

Of course, it takes two to make so far-reaching a decision. Molly was still opposed to his severing every tie with England. The cause of Irish freedom, she insisted, could best be served by their staying together in London. The private papers covering these early months of 1919 show that Molly's gradual surrender to his wish resembled the loving folly of a mother intent on humouring the whim of an ailing, wilful child.

When Erskine had recovered sufficiently to sit up in his dressing-gown, he felt too weak and listless for work. The doctors, in any case, were quite adamant that he should rest, preferably in the country, otherwise they could not answer for the consequences.

The harrowing bouts of coughing that convulsed him at night sounded suspiciously tubercular to Molly. In the way of many lifelong invalids, she probably possessed far too much superficial knowledge of human ailments for anyone else's good. Early in March she packed him off to Glendalough for a lengthy convalescence, and the couple at once resumed the wartime habit of corresponding every day. From these letters it is possible to trace the converging influences which conspired like the fates to change the direction of their lives. In Molly Childers's soulful words: 'This was a period of tremendous mental and spiritual development for us both as we gradually became ready to give ourselves to Ireland. You will notice that we both still think ourselves as British or English: Erskine may still use the word "us" in that way.'[1]

She remained behind, not only because both their sons were now at school in England but because her voluntary work for Belgian refugees had not automatically ceased with the Armistice. If at the outset Molly tended to use this as a convenient excuse for putting off the evil day of accepting her husband's once unacceptable ideals, she deserved credit for gently dissuading him from doing anything rash or irretrievable until they had thought out all the practical effects dispassionately and openly.

'I think about our future', Childers wrote on 22 March 1919:

and at present the idea is gaining strength in me that I should work in Ireland. It is far the less easy course in every way and it is for that reason I think that I feel impelled towards it. But my mind is torn in different ways.... I cannot see that what is right for me is necessarily right for you.... Nor do I find it easy to imagine the boys as being properly educated here or in their right milieu.

His wife replied philosophically by return of post:

I think and think of what you wrote of choosing what is hard because it *is* hard.... I would ask you not to choose on such a ground. You see I am involved, and the boys.... Precious, I ask you not to let this motive have any influence with you. Remember how untrustworthy it has proved. This very thing in you very nearly made our marriage impossible: you thought the harder way the right way and that you must deny yourself me. Of course there will be sentiment in it. But sentiment must be one with reason, or it will not last.... If Ireland's national freedom is a great enough reward to effort, if we are willing because we see it is the way in which we can *effect* most good – then there could be no question of its being a sacrifice and we should go to it of divine necessity, as a lover goes to his true love, as a mother dies for her child.

Childers could not emulate such flights of feeling. Always coming like an unwelcome intruder between them, native reserve held him back when he tried to analyse himself clinically on paper.

I understand what you say so wonderfully that if there is necessity there is no sacrifice, though I find it hard to reduce the whole matter to 'pure reason' because, as I said yesterday, reason cannot forecast the future, and any human plan made must be dependent firstly on impulse – when you yourself speak of the 'divine necessity' is not that what you mean?

Not all the letters reflected this abstract concern for the future. Childers's illness had left him short of energy and breath, and still subject to those uncontrollable fits of coughing which disturbed the Glendalough household at night. He made light of his troubles, nonetheless, and brushed aside expert advice. The best medicine, he contended, was the delectable pure air of the Wicklow hills, and the mountains of eggs, butter, cream, cheese and even porridge he ate. 'I am ashamed at the way we live,' he acknowledged. 'It seems wicked to eat it all with you not here.' He worked at intervals on his final commission for the Air Ministry, that much deferred bombing report.[3] He also spent an increasing period each day digging and weeding the garden paths. Then the wholly unpredictable happened. Robert Barton, who had been returned as the member for West Wicklow to the illegal and unrecognized Dáil in the general election of December 1918, was suddenly arrested by the British authorities in Dublin. This thrust on his cousin, Childers, the main responsibility for supervising the management of the estate. It also aroused his slumbering anger. At once the Englishman's passionate caring for Ireland overflowed into his letters home. A speech by Lloyd George at the end of March drew this typically scathing comment:

George interesting, but his view of the strategical importance of Ireland to England is pure 'Prussianism' (this noun is absurdly out of date). It completely justifies Germany and Austria in the war; more than justfies them, for the strategical importance to them of the Balkan and other states was much greater than that of Ireland to us. It makes me despair a little when minds like G's have not begun to move fundamentally. Why do we abuse the Tories? I don't know. Perhaps I am unfair because you say he is sympathetic about Ireland. He cannot have it both ways.[2]

The regular coming and going of weekend visitors to the imprisoned Robert Barton's country residence rekindled Childers's old obsession with Irish politics. He had promised Molly to seek impartial counsel on their unresolved personal dilemma from wise and disinterested friends like Diarmid Coffey, Edward MacLysaght and the poet AE (George Russell). Eagerly he did so: and though all the while sedulously striving to suppress his own desire, he had to tell her their verdict was that Ireland would benefit if the Childers family decided to settle permanently on Irish soil. The process of his rapid alienation from England had started in earnest. For the abnormal political condition of Ireland both exasperated and bemused him. He had been wandering about Belgium, measuring the destructive effects of tactical as opposed to strategic bombing, when the results of the so-called 'Coupon Election' had been announced not long before Christmas 1918. Any momentary sense of elation he had experienced then on reading of Sinn Fein's political triumph had drained away during the months of illness and recovery. Now the bridging of intervening gaps in his political knowledge had been rendered simple.

Ever since the failure of the Irish Convention, and Lloyd George's glib assurance that conscription would not be imposed on Ireland until a measure of Home Rule was applied, Childers believed that the Act of Union had died of inanition. The untimely threat of calling up Irishmen for military service in April 1918 had simultaneously killed the hope of reconciling the Irish people to any prolonging of the constitutional agony. Sinn Fein's electoral victory at the end of 1918 was thus a foregone conclusion. For most of the Irish Nationalist MPs had left Westminster in protest seven months previously, never to return, and many had since joined hands with Sinn Fein.

De Valera, now the acknowledged as well as self-proclaimed leader of his people, took it on himself to preserve the Irish

Republic born in the Easter rising of 1916. As A. J. P. Taylor has pithily expressed it:

'The British government, with curious indifference, actually completed attendance at the Dáil by releasing all Irish prisoners from British jails in April, 1919 (apparently because they feared that some might cast discredit on their jailers by dying from influenza)....The Dáil behaved as though the Republic were in full being and the British no longer existed....The original Sinn Fein was non-violent. They intended simply to disregard the British authorities and put them on the shelf, as the Hungarians, according to Arthur Griffith, had done with the Imperial Austrian agents between 1861 and 1865. The old secret society, the Irish Republican Brotherhood, decided otherwise. At its discretion, the National Volunteers, organized before the war, were reconstituted in January, 1919, as the Irish Republican Army under the command of Michael Collins a former post office clerk who had fought in the Easter rising – a command somewhat disputed by another fierce republican, Cathal Brugha. The IRA plunged into war against the British without waiting for authority from the Dáil, or indeed ever receiving it.'[4]

This historian's concise assessment clarifies in an almost dismissive way issues which were somewhat obscure at the time. For an army of some 50,000 British soldiers was stationed in Ireland, reinforcing the flagging efforts of the Royal Irish Constabulary to impose the law. The Dáil's defiance of Westminster and Dublin Castle proved on the whole as constructive as that of the underground Irish Republican Army, pledged to serve the Dáil, became necessarily destructive. Childers himself, now living with Irish relatives who supported the Republican ideals of de Valera and Arthur Griffith, found his sympathies agonizingly divided. Pro-Irish he had been for a decade, but pro-Republican or pro-de Valera he certainly was not at this early stage. He stubbornly held that any future settlement with Britain must be on the lines of the Dominion solution he had long advocated.

He thought of himself still as a free-thinking Liberal in politics. Nor did his repeated railing against Lloyd George's hypocritical stance as the world champion of democratic rights, who rejected Ireland's rightful claim to self-determination, set him apart from his old radical friends in England. Men like Kenworthy, Maclean, the Trevelyans, Wedgwood Benn, a former air force colleague, and even the hardheaded Runciman, all these opposed the expediency of official policy towards Ireland, while continuing to question Sinn Fein's needlessly provocative response. For the Irish were behaving as though the writ of Dublin Castle no longer ran in their land. Republican courts were superseding the existing courts; and alongside Sinn Fein's administration of justice, separate machinery for levying taxes and reforming the land purchase system was also being set up. Partly because 'The Troubles', as they were locally called, tended to bypass Glendalough, a rural oasis close enough to Dublin for the Bartons' highly placed Republican friends to call regularly, the political re-education of Erskine Childers proceeded apace.

'For myself,' he informed his wife, in a typically candid bulletin on his current state of mind,

I have been growing more and more to dislike compromise, which only builds on the work of the idealists, and to thirst for whole ideals where the creative work is accomplished and whence all the splendid inspirations of the past arise – all the great messiahs, earth-movers. The best architects of compromise render their teaching palatable to a generation which as often as not has crucified the teacher. This is a great work – this assimilation of fine things in the face of tremendous opposition from the vested interests, but it has its ugly side often: it is apt to taint and warp the mind, to paralyse imagination and generous instinct, and too often to end in utter sterility. I think some master-minds can do it nobly. For too many it is mainly a coward's refuge. Of course, there are two distinct classes of compromiser: the Conservative who has the sense and courage to meet halfway an ideal he does not like because he knows resistance will hurt his people, and the 'liberal' (for short) who is in natural sympathy with the ideal but holds it impossible of accomplishment without qualification or is just afraid to back it unqualified. Now we belong to the liberals in everything and I think that is why I myself fight shy of compromise.[2]

At Eastertide 1919, before Childers had fully recovered, the chance arose to put such noble preaching into practice. He responded with a fearlessness that brought him favourably to the notice of de Valera, Griffith, Collins and the Sinn Fein leadership, though that was not the idealist's prime aim. In securing a writ of *habeas corpus* for an unknown youth named Connors, whom the police had apprehended and were holding incommunicado as a likely witness in a case of armed robbery they intended to bring against person or persons unnamed, the Englishman demonstrated both to Molly and himself what he really meant by dislike of compromise. 'Sinn Fein won't act officially so I am instructing in the case,' he told her. The Dublin Castle authorities took note, then hesitantly drew back. So did Childers's critics in England when Tim Healy accepted the brief and pressed it to a triumphant end in court. Whatever had come over the man, they wondered: such quixotic behaviour was ludicrous. Had Erskine gone mad?

'So glad you are pleased about my winning the case,' he wrote to Molly on 12 April. 'It really was important and probably puts an end to this persecution of children.' Offhand and guarded replies by ministers inevitably followed the occasional questions Childers planted on Kenworthy, L'Estrange-Malone and other receptive Liberal MPs at Westminster. His wife, for her part, was resigning herself slowly to the inevitable, particularly after learning why both George Russell and Alice Stopford Green upheld Erskine in his wish to stay. Their pretext was

steady, thoughtful, creative work is required here – utterly lacking owing to the political violence – economic especially. I found that neither, curiously enough, seemed to think an absolute breaking of English ties necessary, and both were against official membership of Sinn Fein or any definite party organization as being inconsistent with the best intellectual work. I questioned this, for the sake of argument, on pure lines of expediency in winning an end – and we reached no decision....

And, rather offhandedly, he wrote again. 'I'm forgetting everything now and I can't remember if I told you I had a few words with de Valera...'

Barton, now on the run, had introduced him to Michael Collins, who at once was captivated by Childers: so Collins lost no time in introducing him to the leader de Valera, and de Valera as it happened, also took to him at first sight. The Dáil's President would later acknowledge that the quiet Englishman was 'the model of all I'd wish to have been myself'; but now he merely wondered whether more use could not eventually be made of Childers's willingness to serve. It was a changeable spring season that year; and the convalescent had to nurse his uncertain health. Yet he drove himself on to write topical polemical articles:

I *must* tackle those essays now. I see they have persuaded the League to act definitely to exclude the Irish Question from its scope.... Your idea about Dominion Home Rule coming through self-determination is exactly what I have been thinking and saying myself. It's the only way. Quite possibly it would happen not so much from [the] generosity of [the] Irish as from [the] absolute necessity of squaring Ulster.

Childers returned home to London at the end of April 1919 and spent a few weeks in his old haunts, eking out a living by occasional journalism, and renewing old friendships. When an official letter arrived at the end of May from Sinn Fein head-quarters in Dublin, inviting him back for urgent talks, nothing could detain him further. Cross-examined on his return by Griffith, Collins, Desmond Fitzgerald and others, he emerged a little bewildered by the proposal they had put to him:

Upshot of the matter is that they want me to go to Paris and I think I had better try to do so.... Bob [Barton] is rather against it, fearing the centre of gravity may shift to London or Ireland and I should be landed, but I could always come back of course.... Sinn Fein very keen about the propaganda question.

His letter provided conclusive proof to Molly that her husband was implacably determined to offer himself up as a hostage to fate.

Whatever may have been Arthur Griffith's reservations about the motives of this improbable Anglo-Irish volunteer, whom he would one day have some cause to criticize if not condemn, Collins clearly had none. To do Griffith justice, he could think of nobody better qualified than Childers in that summer of 1919 to publicize the Irish case at the Peace Conference in Paris. Two Irish envoys, neither of them trained in the arts of publicity, were already there. And when Childers joined Sean T. O'Kelly and the lawyer, Gavan Duffy, early in July 1919, both men were overjoyed to see him.

We dined at the Café de Paris to celebrate my arrival. ...We sat on for a long time, smoking and talking. I have not altogether got the hang of the thing yet. . . . They seem to think that so far from the peace having finished things a new phase of possibilities is opening. . . . I am appalled by the cost of living here. They say, truly I think, that it is necessary for them to keep up a certain state and have proper rooms to see people in. The salon costs £6 a day. Duffy was apprised of my expenses being paid and my hotel account is part of theirs. He makes light of it, says that. . . funds are ample. I think I shall have cheap meals out as much as possible and let the hotel expenses rip.

For the next ten weeks Childers did his utmost to gain the ears of French, British and other diplomats as well as prominent French journalists. His efforts proved quite unavailing. Though he could produce no evidence to support the suspicion, he assumed that the local British propaganda machine had managed to warn off some and poison the minds of others. Childers called on one editor after another; but the chief executives of *Le Temps*, *Figaro*, *Débats* and a succession of other journals listened politely and could promise nothing. They were all, so he said, 'as nervous as old women about offending England'.

With the help of an introductory note from Mrs Sidney Webb, he at length encountered members of the British delegation, notably Philip Kerr and Lionel Curtis, the latter a contemporary at Haileybury. It distressed Childers that 'a nice fellow' like Kerr should bring up 'all sorts of so-called European parallels where the Conference is splitting off minorities, but had to admit that Bohemia is his only real parallel to Ireland and that there they are *including* the German Ulster'. Curtis upset him even more and proved 'much more reactionary than Kerr'. He

seemed impervious to the idea that it is other than an intellectual exercise for constitutional experts, like South Africa and India (in both of which he has taken a large part), and obsessed by the partition idea and of aiming at a solution through UK devolution. I have rarely seen the English – hypocrisy is quite the wrong word – impenetrable egotism in such an insolent, anti-Irish form. But he is really honest and single-minded, and all in all we had some fairly useful talk after the first half-hour. . . . So hard it is to develop force in such a situation. One speaks on behalf of a helpless country. Hectoring is useless.

Childers's own helplessness increased as other members of the British delegation paid court to him socially, then poured ice-cold water on his burning ideals:

Pressed, they care nothing about anyone's freedom in Europe and regard the whole thing as a means of curbing Germany. I have a kind of blind fury sometimes at seeing these cultured, cold-blooded, self-satisfied people making careers out of the exploitation of humanity and crucifying the Christs with a *bon mot* or a shrug. Meanwhile I smile and argue good-temperedly.

It was no easy assignment. Nor could it last. For Childers's anomalous position with the unofficial Irish envoys caused comment, much of it disparaging. He continued to dash off press articles, most of which appeared in print, but was 'horrified to see in the *Irish Independent*, in leaded type, a statement quoted from the *Chicago Tribune* that Lloyd George entrusted me with the solution of Home Rule in 1917!...It makes me look such a fool.' He had not felt so badly since the press had stupidly tipped him in that same year, 1917, as the likeliest candidate to fill the vacant post of Under-Secretary for Ireland. He was not sorry to shake the dust of Paris from his feet on 4 August, the anniversary of the outbreak of the recent world war whose bitter fruits were manifestly so much to the perverted taste of the victors. Had Childers not stood at his hotel window to watch the vast, glittering military parade down the Champs-Élysées on Bastille Day? Had he not meditated on the grim holocaust of blood, treasure and sorrow symbolized by the endless columns of troops, so that some lines from Goethe's *Faust*, referring to the 'shrill agony of mankind',[2] had tripped involuntarily off his pen when he wrote his daily letter to Molly? How glad he was to go back to her and prepare for their last family holiday together in England, by the sea at Worthing.

Molly had not finally yielded. She would put no firm date as yet on the completion of her refugee work. 'These partings are just like the war all over again,' her husband complained on returning alone to Dublin. Until he found a suitable house, Childers for a while stayed as the guest of Alice Stopford Green at 90 Stephen's Green. His service gratuity had reached him at last; and Molly acquiesced with his express wish 'to invest £500 in the Republican Loan'. When he visited Sinn Fein headquarters to report on his fruitless efforts in Paris, it was the acting President Arthur

Griffith who thanked him, then promptly urged him to go back. 'The Chief', as everyone called de Valera, was on a controversial tour of the United States, successfully raising money from the large Irish-American community in the main cities and unsuccessfully trying to secure official recognition, on his own terms, of Ireland's claim to independence; so the decision on Childers's role as a publicist lay with Griffith, whom the Englishman found a more puzzling and even less communicative person to deal with than 'the Chief'. The news that Sean O'Kelly had eagerly written 'suggesting that I go to Paris in a month's time' was disconcerting. Childers promised to think it over. What he most longed to do was help Desmond Fitzgerald and Patrick Gallagher in rebuilding the movement's propaganda department, which had recently been raided and virtually cleaned out by the military. It was, he thought, 'a dastardly dodge to silence legitimate propaganda and business. It makes me howl.'

The mind of Arthur Griffith remained a closed book to Childers. Indeed, until the two men eventually clashed over what the Englishman considered to be fundamental points of principle, they saw comparatively little of one another. Michael Collins, as generous and warmhearted in accepting comrades as he could be coldblooded and ruthless in disposing of enemies, defended Childers against all comers, not excluding Griffith and the fiery Defence Minister, Cathal Brugha, undoubtedly Collins's most vitriolic critic and rival inside Sinn Fein. Allowing for the selective processes of hindsight, it is not unfair to quote the judgment of Piaras Beaslai, a dutiful disciple of Collins, whose intuitive mistrust of Erskine Childers ran very deep: 'Collins', he wrote, 'conceived an entirely exaggerated estimate of the character and abilities of Childers, and this proved one of the fatal mistakes of his career.'[5]

A word which occurred more than once that autumn in the steady stream of Childers's letters to Molly was 'desolating'. It summed up his sense of personal inadequacy as he cycled round Dublin, househunting by himself. Prices had soared, and because evictions of tenants without notice seemed to have become the vogue in the prevailing atmosphere of lawlessness, he had to suffer in silence both the abuse of the tenants and the bottomless cynicism of various estate agents he visited. No ideal home for his beloved Molly, commanding a fine view of the Wicklow hills and conforming to Childers's demanding specifications of spaciousness and accessibility, was immediately forthcoming. In the end he had to rent a furnished house, greatly to his wife's relief: 'The six months will enable us to find what we want to buy,' she assured him. For at long last she had consented to come. 'Don't worry any more about the house....Maples say we must be out of this flat on December 18th.' A farewell treat lay in store for him. It reconciled Molly to the difficult break:

What do you think has happened? Our Chelsea friends, all your and my friends and all my work friends, whom you don't know, are planning a big fête or rather Chelsea party to say goodbye to us....Basil [Williams] came to tell me, and his description of the way people feel about you made me nearly cry with joy....Old Lady Courtney [is] one of the plotters – and Lady Lyttleton....It's to be at Crosby Hall because no other place is big enough.

Their Chelsea neighbours, of course, were greatly mystified and not a little grieved at the decision of the Childerses to turn their backs for ever on England. Only Basil Williams understood that a compulsive streak of the Byronic in Erskine's complex nature was driving him adventurously towards the shoals of Irish revolutionary politics, as inexorably as it had driven him into the Admiralty and the Royal Air Force in wartime, so that those who crushed the weak should not prevail. That war had been fought for one purpose: the freeing of small nations from bondage, and Childers's unsparing conclusion was that in the case of Ireland Britain had betrayed her trust. Molly's attitude proved much more of a conundrum to Williams. All he knew was that it had changed perceptibly since the summer of 1919. The turning point had come when a former colleague of Williams and Childers in the Clerk's Office at the House of Commons had met Molly and Erskine, by appointment and at her instigation: but all his earnest pleading to dissuade Erskine from taking so irreversible a step was in vain. The appeal had fallen on deaf ears, particularly that part of it which dwelt on the dangers of being misunderstood by Englishmen and Irishmen alike. It was the least of the considerations that could have deterred him, and Childers said so politely. Molly had ceased resisting there and then.[6]

Neither she nor her husband chose as yet to calculate the heavy odds against them. They shut their minds to such trifling details, ignoring not only the probability of being regarded as eccentrics or worse by old friends in England but the equal likelihood of being scorned and mistrusted by newfound comrades in Ireland. An aura of legend still enveloped the name of Erskine Childers in Dublin because of his valorous role in running those guns to Howth in the high summer of 1914, thus making the abortive Easter rising possible; but there were influential Irishmen in the secret conclaves of Sinn Fein who wondered why the same Erskine Childers, until lately an officer in the Crown forces, appeared to be so anxious now to turn his coat. The man's motives invited misconstruction. The man himself would obviously have to be watched rather closely – just in case...

Molly acclimatized herself amazingly quickly to life in a city divided against itself. She, the American Anglophobe who had slowly become so ardent an Anglophile that the prospect of abandoning her many English friends had led to a temporary rift with Erskine, found no difficulty in gradually reverting subtly to type. Had not her ancestors risen with George Washington against the British in similarly disadvantageous circumstances and fought on until American independence was won? Between the good British people and their wicked rulers Molly Childers never failed to draw a real distinction: the former she continued to love and admire, for the latter she had nothing but contempt. She held court to her husband's friends and colleagues, dazzling them with her intelligent and well-informed comments on affairs. She had a notably soft spot in her heart for Michael Collins, encouraging him to read her favourite books and taking comfort from his obvious affection and regard for Erskine. Arthur Griffith relented only to the extent of not insisting that her husband should return to Paris, for in all conscience there was enough work in the Sinn Fein publicity department to keep everyone busy.

Almost a year before, standing at a window of his London club with Basil Williams to watch President Wilson drive past,

Childers had declared scornfully: 'A weak, vain face. He will do nothing.' Childers's elder son, another Erskine who one day would move into the Viceregal Lodge at Phoenix Park as President of the Irish Republic, was with his father that day and never forgot the words either. While Eamonn de Valera was in the middle of his transatlantic tour, vainly striving to rouse American opinion against the refusal of Wilson to recognize Ireland's claims, Childers was just beginning to direct his specialist skills to influencing public opinion in Britain. Under Desmond Fitzgerald he reorganized the office in his pedantic, somewhat fussy fashion because, in his judgment, it badly needed to be reorganized:

Nothing struck me more, when I first got insight into the publicity department, than the failure of the political side to take definite responsibility for the Army and its work – a fatal failure because the propaganda of the enemy was that the Army was a 'murder gang' and it was only by insisting that it was waging a legitimate war of defence and by basing propaganda on that principle that one could meet the torrent of defamation. Griffith was undoubtedly responsible for this curb on propaganda. How far Collins opposed or conceded to him on this point I do not know. It was only after de Valera returned from America late in 1920 that the issue was made clear and the civil administration, officially and in its use of propaganda, took entire responsibility for the actions of the Army.[7]

This significant extract from a contemporary note, written by Childers one weekend at Glendalough, underlines the tensions existing between rival and, in some cases, temperamentally incompatible ministers during de Valera's lengthy absence. He knew, for instance, that Collins, a man of flexible outlook and prodigious energy, was at loggerheads with his technical superior, the Defence Minister, Cathal Brugha. A manufacturer of church candles who kept a wary eye on his business interests while handling, unpaid, his official portfolio, this simple, exceedingly tough little son of a Yorkshireman (his original name had been Charles Burgess) strongly resented Collins's high-handed interference as Director of Intelligence, Minister of Finance, and Adjutant-General of the underground army, with what Brugha judged to be his own exclusive preserves. The latter, a confirmed Republican and militarist diehard, thought little of his sub-

I

ordinate's resilient tactics, still less of the meretricious glamour surrounding his name. As for Arthur Griffith, the acting President and a man who disapproved of needless bloodshed, Childers wrote with acute insight:

Griffith had, of course, always represented a moderate element. And Sinn Fein, which he founded, was originally a pacifist organization not standing for out-and-out independence but for national self-reliance. ...Both he and Sinn Fein had been dragged irresistibly into the Republican movement after 1916 – he and it would have perished. politically otherwise – but even in effecting the union, the revised con stitution of Sinn Fein had to contain verbal loopholes for those who would not be bound to the doctrine of complete independence. With the establishment of the Republic, with Sinn Fein as its semi-official political organization, these loopholes were almost forgotten; but it is certain that Griffith, although Vice-President of the Republic, and during de Valera's long absence in America the Acting President, was never at heart a true Republican and had little sympathy with the militant party and the war of Independence.[7]

That war, in which Childers now felt himself to be fully involved, may be said to have begun in January 1919, 'with the declaration of independence in the first Dáil'; but its escalation on the very day of his wife's arrival in Dublin was clearly marked, regardless of the fact that Childers himself had no hand whatever in the escalation. Brugha had originally pointed out to the Volunteers that, as the army of a government lawfully elected by the Irish people, they were entitled 'morally and legally when in the execution of their duty to slay the officials and agents of the foreign invader'.[7] Nevertheless, it was Collins whose total commitment and breathtaking speediness of response to daring opportunities raised both the pitch and the tempo of the increasingly bloody underground struggle. It proved to be a pure coincidence that an attempt on the life of Lord French, the Viceroy, took place on 19 December 1919, when the Childers couple were being shown over their furnished rooms. By then, the whole of 'G' (Detective) Division of the Dublin Metropolitan Police had been 'killed off, intimidated into impotence, or induced to lend Sinn Fein secret help'. The Royal Irish Constabulary, subject from the beginning to social ostracism, were obliged by mid-1920 to give up all pretence of carrying out their duties in Southern Ireland. The force withdrew in self-defence to barracks in the larger towns. This, in addition to widespread competition from the civil and criminal tribunals of the Republic, led to the wholesale desertion of the British courts. Childers, to demonstrate his own Republican convictions, assumed the extra responsibility of serving as a temporary judge in Wicklow. Apart from his propaganda work, he was also appointed an active director, unpaid, of the newly founded Land Bank presided over by his cousin, Robert Barton. For her part, Molly readily accepted Collins's offer to become a trustee of the Republican Loan to which ordinary people in their tens of thousands were already subscribing out of their meagre savings or hard-won earnings. Thus Childers's sense of identification with, and partial fulfilment in, the cause of Irish freedom proved real enough; but British retaliatory measures grew steadily more severe, especially when the Auxiliaries, all volunteers who had served as officers in the British Army, were despatched from England to fill the badly depleted ranks of the Royal Irish Constabulary and the notorious 'Black-and-Tans' were unleashed in country districts.

'Take a typical night in Dublin', Childers wrote in one of several special articles which A. G. Gardiner, editor of the *Daily News*, had commissioned him to write.

As the citizens go to bed, the barracks spring to life. Lorries, tanks and armoured searchlight cars muster in fleets, lists of objectives are distributed, and, when the midnight curfew order has emptied the streets – pitch-dark streets – the weird cavalcades issue forth to the attack. Think of raiding a private house at dead of night in a tank whose weird rumble and roar can be heard miles away! The procedure of the raid is in keeping, though the objectives are held for the most part by women and terrified children. A thunder of knocks: no time to dress (even for a woman alone) or the door will crash in. On opening, in charge the soldiers – literally charge – with fixed bayonets and in full war-kit. No warrant shown on entering, no apology on leaving, if, as in nine cases out of ten, suspicions prove groundless and the raid a mistake. In many recent instances even women occupants have been locked up under guard while their own property is ransacked. Imagine the moral effect of such a procedure on the young officers and men told off for this duty! Is it any wonder that gross abuses occur: looting, wanton destruction, brutal severity to women? If challenged, I am ready to give chapter and verse to substantiate all these charges.

Such articles, and there were many, produced a steadily mounting effect of shock and dismay among his Liberal friends in
England. Those who knew him personally or by repute accepted
his version of events, while deploring his role as the sophisticated
mouthpiece of terrorists who shot first and seldom stayed to ask
questions afterwards. Nevertheless, coercion would not pass
for long as a substitute for policy; and so a deepening sense of
revulsion, spreading outwards like ripples on the face of a pond,
started to work against the coercion strategy, approved by an
otherwise preoccupied Lloyd George, for settling the Irish Problem once and for all. As Childers had warned in the same article.

This Irish war, small as it may seem now, will, if it is persisted in,
corrupt and eventually ruin not only your Army but your Empire
itself. What right has England to torment and demoralize Ireland? It
is a shameful course, and all the more shameful in that she professes to
have fought five years for the liberty of oppressed nations. But her
own oppression of the Irish nation will react disastrously upon herself.
The reaction has begun.[8]

The colleagues at his Harcourt Street office, talented young
men such as Frank Gallagher and Robert Brennan, marvelled as
much as did visiting journalists at Childers's singleminded
concentration. If any man could convert other Englishmen to
see the error of their ways, that man must surely be someone
so amply endowed as Erskine Childers with honesty, enthusiasm
and an unquenchable thirst for justice. To others he might
remain an alien and a somewhat sinister man of mystery. But to
these, as to the absent de Valera and the ubiquitous Collins, he
stood out like a star, a paragon of self-effacing idealism and
integrity. Desmond Ryan, who worked at the time for the
Freeman's Journal, a daily newspaper of independent views whose
capricious proprietor already suspected Childers of being a
British spy, had only praise for this English convert to the
Republican cause:
'It was a pleasure to work with this courteous person who
never spared himself. The man had a spell. It was possible to feel
that as you watched him walking from his house fronting the
Wicklow Hills....A burning faith and noble indignation were
implicit in every line of his denunciation of military rule in

Ireland, and after I read this testament I always admired and believed in the man who had written it. Dublin was unmoved for the most part. What had Erskine Childers told Dublin that Dublin did not know already?'

He did not care a straw whether the cynics misjudged him. It consoled him greatly that by June 1920 he had succeeded in acquiring a suitable home of his own at 12 Bushey Park Road, with plenty of living space for Molly and her mother, and rooms to spare for the two boys when they came home from school. It also mattered much to him that the writ of *Dáil Eireann* ran right through the land all the way from the Ulster border to the wilds of Kerry, Clare and Mayo. As Desmond Ryan noted, Dublin wags might laugh at the dignified letter of complaint which Childers wrote to the press when, in the course of a sudden night raid on his house, 'some young pup in a second lieutenant's uniform had dropped a cigarette on his best carpet. Janey, was that all he had to vex him? Jesting and doubting Dublin had no time to listen to the chord that was vibrating in the heart of this noble man limping past the trees of Terenure, his worn features and searching eyes alight with an otherworldly fire. Some strange faith was graven on his furrowed features and mirrored in the thoughtful and ardent look as he pushed his bicycle along Bushey Park Road, a bundle of papers beneath his arm and all his journeys through the clouds and wrestlings with the oceans plain to any eye but a Dublin wit at a loss for a new epigram.'⁹

Perhaps the superseding of the King's writ almost everywhere outside Dublin and Ulster moved Childers more than anything else. For it was his privilege to inform the outside world of the underlying reasons. To quote Lord Longford:

'Testimony in favour of the new courts was astonishingly general. Lord Monteagle praised them, the *Chicago Tribune* praised them, the *Manchester Guardian* and the *Daily News* praised them, the *Daily Mail* praised them; even the *Irish Times* had no complaint to make of them, and plenty of fun to poke at their supplanted rivals.... Department of Finance, Defence, Trade and Commerce, Agriculture, Home Affairs, Local Government, Labour and Propaganda were established. Sweeping Sinn Fein triumphs at the local elections of January and June, 1920, confirmed national support for these organs.'¹⁰

But the twelve months from July 1920 to June 1921 witnessed an all-out attempt by General Macready's forces to smash these working instruments of an illegal administration which Lloyd George and his Tory colleagues refused to recognize or come to terms with. The arrival of thousands of ex-servicemen to swell the ranks of the undermanned police, and their kitting-out with khaki uniforms, black caps and belts because of an insufficiency of regulation RIC outfits, ushered in a veritable reign of terror. The Black and Tans, so called after a famous pack of hounds in the Limerick region where the first company of these oddly attired recruits set about their task, tried to enforce their will by arbitrary and often brutal methods. Reprisals against them instantly began. In September 1920 the Restoration of Order in Ireland Act was passed at Westminster. Even the imposition of martial law on eight Irish counties in December and January 1920, and the wanton destruction of houses and property belonging to any person thought to be 'implicated in or cognisant of' outrages against the Crown forces, failed to deter Collins and his underground units from hitting back with equal or greater vigour. One foreseeable result of this nihilistic orgy was the dislocation of the Republican machinery of government and the imprisonment of not a few leading politicians, including Robert Barton, who this time was sentenced to ten years' penal servitude for 'incitement to violence'. Not long after de Valera's secret return from his American tour, the Minister of Propaganda, Desmond Fitzgerald, was also put behind bars. Without hesitation, the President offered the vacancy to Childers who accepted it towards the end of February 1921. The appointment displeased among others, no less a person than the Vice-President, Arthur Griffith. According to the watchful Beaslai:

'This was irregular, as Childers was not a member of the Dáil.... Arthur Griffith ... held that, while a struggle with England was being waged, it might be permissible to use an Englishman's help but that it would be dangerous to put an Englishman in an official position of trust. Apart from this, he distrusted Childers whom he considered, to use his own phrase, "a disgruntled Englishman", who had taken up the Irish cause through irritation against his own country.'[5]

Before the close of 1920, regardless of the terrible turmoil in Ireland, the Lloyd George administration had succeeded in putting on the Statute Book its own hurried and belated attempt to secure a settlement by constitutional means. Sinn Fein, of course, rejected instantly and outright the new Government of Ireland Bill which Lloyd George had originally intended as 'a real contribution towards settling this most baffling of problems'. The measures envisaged the establishment of two Parliaments, one for the North and the other for the South, with restricted powers. Neither government would have jurisdiction over foreign policy, defence, external trade, Customs, police or even the Post Office, though at a later date the two separate assemblies would be amalgamated into a single all-Ireland Parliament and Government. The debates at Westminster undoubtedly showed, as the Bill went through its progressive stages, that partition was not Lloyd George's intention; but partition became the inevitable consequence, given the strong pro-Ulster bias of Bonar Law and others in a predominantly Tory Cabinet. Craig and his Ulster Unionist friends, after much heartsearching, reluctantly accepted a scheme, which they had never asked for or seriously considered before, as the lesser of two evils. Even Ulster Home Rule was something alien to them, cherishing as they did the traditional ties with Westminster and the Crown. Nor could they be expected to welcome a plan which permanently reduced the area they would rule from nine counties to six.

All this constitution-making amounted to no more than ostentatious window-dressing; and from the outset Childers impressed on his Sinn Fein associates that they must disregard it. On the other hand, the fear nagged away at the back of his mind that Ulster, once reconciled to this new state of statutory isolation, might choose to become a permanent Protestant enclave. When de Valera returned secretly from the United States towards the end of 1920 Childers admitted that the prospect gravely worried him. Should not Sinn Fein, he wondered, use the electoral machinery provided under the Act for its own ends? The only positive element in the measure which respected the concept of unity was the proposed Council of Ireland, which would comprise twenty members from each Parliament, and would have the power to coalesce the two Parliaments without direct reference to Westminster. That element seemed to Childers worth preserving, though so many other imperfections riddled the New Act that he doubted whether anything at all could be salvaged easily from the wreck.

For the present, Lloyd George felt obliged to dispense with statesmanship until 'the murder gang', led by Michael Collins, had been cornered and throttled. Unfortunately, he was invariably provoked by opposition, though the instruments for his punitive purpose were futile in a liberation struggle, with no holds barred, which would come to be regarded during the next half century as the prototype of a whole series of others from Egypt and India to Palestine, Cyprus, Aden and colonial territories throughout Africa. The intriguing *Whitehall Diary* of Tom Jones, the secretary to successive British Prime Ministers in the nineteen-twenties and thirties, has vividly portrayed the difficulties, the hesitations and the temperamental doubts of Lloyd George, his colleagues and his advisers, after the formal decision was taken in the spring of 1920 to bring Sinn Fein and Collins's 'murder gang' ruthlessly to heel. Having allowed an Irish-American deputation to visit Ireland and move freely through the country before publishing a report which damned the activities of the British military administration, Lloyd George brazenly sanctioned a more intense campaign of repression. It was a bad miscalculation, for it pushed the mass of ordinary Irish citizens into the arms of the very leaders he sought to isolate and destroy.

It was not insignificant that J. I. Macpherson, later Lord Strathcarron, resigned his post as Chief Secretary for Ireland in April 1920 because, being a moderate Home Ruler, he could not abide the contradictions of the Government of Ireland Act which cut the political ground from under his feet. On the advice of the War Office, in particular of Sir Henry Wilson, the unpleasantly bigoted Chief of the Imperial General Staff, General Tudor took over policy, while the ironclad and oversanguine, Canadian-born, Sir Hamar Greenwood replaced the unhappy Macpherson.

Despite these outwardly determined and aggressive moves, we are offered an unusually graphic insight into the British Government's inward quandaries by Tom Jones, who took notes at a crucial session of interested Cabinet ministers, with members of the Irish Executive in attendance, on 31 May 1920. Apart from Lloyd George and Bonar Law, Greenwood and Macready, others present included Winston Churchill, Lord Curzon, Lord Birkenhead and Sir John Anderson, the recently appointed Joint Under-Secretary to French, the Viceroy or Lord-Lieutenant. During the meeting Churchill outlined his own ideas for the successful recruiting of 'a special force of 8,000 men' (the future Auxiliaries) to make good the deficiencies of the RIC. He also reminded the Prime Minister that 'you agreed six or seven months ago that there should be hanging' for men caught and convicted of murder:

'What strikes me,' said Churchill, 'is the feebleness of the local machinery. After a person is caught he should pay the penalty within a week. Look at the tribunals which the Russian Government has devised. You should get three or four judges whose scope should be universal and they should move quickly over the country and do summary justice.'

The Irish, Attorney-General, Denis Henry, then commented: 'When that was put to the judges some months ago they did not want to touch it.'

To which Churchill retorted: 'Shows all the more need for extraordinary action. Get three generals if you cannot get three judges.'

For once, Greenwood expressed genuine perturbation:

'The real difficulty about Ireland,' he admitted, 'is not so much the big issue of putting down crime as the inadequacy and sloppiness of the instruments of Government. We can only rely on the Navy, military and RIC. The Dublin police cannot be relied on, nor the Post Office nor the Civil Service.... The vital point is to deal with the Thugs, a number of whom are going about shooting in Dublin, Limerick and Cork. We are certain that these are handsomely paid, that the money comes from the USA, that it is passed through Bishop Fogarty (of Killaloe) and Arthur Griffith by means of cheques issued to Michael Collins, the Adjutant-General of the Irish Republican Army.'

At this forthright condemnation of his allegedly slack rule, Lord French bridled. 'I do not quite agree with the Chief Secretary,' he said. 'In my view the mischief originates with the Irish

Volunteers and unless you knock them on the head you make no progress.'[11]

French, the crusty, ancient and not altogether successful ex-general, was right for once, too, in his diagnosis, as Childers would readily have agreed had he been either a fly on the wall or the English spy some ill-natured Irishmen already imagined him to be. Not until May 1920, when Brigadier-General S. P. Crozier was appointed Commandant of a freshly recruited Auxiliary Division composed of nearly a thousand ex-British Army officers sent over to support the Black and Tans in the name of law and order, did it dawn on Sinn Fein's Anglo-Irish Minister of Publicity that a darker chapter in the annals of repression had been authorized by a British Cabinet unable to improvise anything better.

Throughout the summer of 1920, in fact, ministers were at odds on the merits of two opposed policies. Such painstaking advisers in Dublin as John Anderson, the Under-Secretary Alfred Cope, his energetic assistant, and J. O. Wylie, the Lord Justice to the Government of Ireland, tried to convince the Cabinet's Irish Committee that there were alternatives to the blood-curdling 'policy of thorough' advocated by Sir Hamar Greenwood and that unabashed Ulsterman, Sir Henry Wilson. The majority favoured firmness, a policy of 'kicks before kindness', at any rate so long as Macready had the superiority in men and weapons required to subdue the gunmen. So nothing constructive emerged from the deliberations in London. Churchill's inbred bellicosity helped to tip the balance. Similarly Balfour, the veteran hardliner and ex-Chief Secretary of Childers's golden youth, backed the militarists' argument: 'At the heart of Sinn Fein the real ideal was a separate Republic', he stressed, 'and nothing would be got by seeing their leaders but humiliation.'

Anderson, Cope and Wylie, with sources of information that reached them circuitously, sometimes from inside the Sinn Fein movement itself, might be as sympathetic to the case for Dominion Home Rule in Dublin as Childers had once been and as Tom Jones now was; but Lloyd George would not be deflected until the Government of Ireland Bill had become the law of the land. Bonar Law's brooding presence probably stiffened the Prime Minister; Tom Jones suspected as much on 31 January 1921. For heedless of the signs that Americans were growing increasingly critical of Britain's excessively harsh treatment of the Irish, an indirect consequence of President Wilson's humiliating reverse in the recent election in the United States, the Tory leader still preferred to let his long-standing prejudices guide his thinking.

'Coming along the passage with B.L.,' wrote Jones that night, 'I told him that I felt intensely about the Irish business and that the ghastly things that were being done were enough to drive one to join the Republican Army. In effect his answer was that coercion was the only policy: that in the past it had been followed by periods of quiet for about ten years: that that was the most we could hope for from the present repressions, and that he had come to the conclusion "that the Irish were an inferior race".'

The periodic visits of Lloyd George to the Supreme Council in Paris to redraw the map of postwar Europe served only further to delay matters. Nevertheless, this distraction alone can hardly explain away the scandal. Indeed the personal responsibility of the Prime Minister for failing to grasp the Irish nettle can best be gauged by considering the following brief sentence taken from a lengthy lunchtime conversation between Anderson and Jones on 15 February 1921: 'I said B.L. was one of the most persistent opponents of conciliation and had greatly influenced the PM throughout. Anderson agreed that he was worse than Carson but that the PM was the person really responsible for the policy of reprisals.'[11]

Ironically, in that same month, Brigadier-General Crozier, the Commandant of the Auxiliaries, resigned in protest against official sanctioning of inhuman methods of repression, later writing to *The Times* in favour of an early truce. Reared in a staunch Irish Unionist household, Crozier had believed in the British Empire and fought for it longer than Childers; indeed, as a young officer he had formed part of a British square in a battle against Hausa tribesmen in West Africa. Having been thwarted by Macready and Tudor in his efforts to discipline insubordinate Auxiliaries, Crozier suddenly began to discover virtues in Sinn Fein as well as vices in British policy. Childers met him a few times and thought him somewhat unbalanced, a compliment which Crozier duly reciprocated. In the latter's eyes the Sinn Fein Director of Publicity was simply a fanatic and an eccentric.

Hamar Greenwood's blind faith in reprisals should surprise and scandalize nobody. For the Chief Secretary was a tough optimist, and his optimism continued to mislead the Cabinet, including a largely absentee Prime Minister, a point correctly divined by Childers and one with which he made skilful play both in the *Irish Bulletin* and his propaganda abroad. He kept no personal diary in those days, only an enormously detailed daily catalogue of the individual murders, woundings, lootings, burnings, hangings, floggings and other atrocities committed, or allegedly to have been committed, by the Crown Forces and their IRA adversaries in times and places which he took infinite pains to check and specify.

Scrutinizing this litany of horror some fifty-five years afterwards still has the effect of turning the stomach. One can well imagine how deeply it must have scarred the spirit of Erskine Childers as he compiled it, though rarely did he permit himself even a marginal comment. The grisly register also exhibits the unsparing pace at which he still drove himself. Dublin remained his base, but he travelled at frequent intervals, mostly by rail or road, to towns throughout the country on Land Bank, publicity or White Cross business, this last-named philanthropic enterprise enabling him to renew an old friendship with David Robinson, the fearless and flamboyant companion whom he had first run into at Glendalough during school holidays from Haileybury. Robinson, badly wounded in the 1914–18 war, had been awarded the Croix de Guerre with palm and DSO for gallantry in action with his Canadian tank unit.

Only once did Childers cross the sea to England, and that was in February 1921, on a compassionate visit to his cousin, Robert Barton, whom he visited in his cell at Portland Prison and found proudly wearing the shaven crown and the rough, broad-arrowed garb of a convict.

'When Childers was appointed Dáil Director of Publicity', noted the critical Beaslai, 'I was appointed Army Director of Publicity for the purpose of concentrating with him on the military side. All information with regard to the IRA or military matters passed to him through my hands. This brought me into close daily association with him and gave me a good opportunity of observing his character and abilities. In view of Collins' high opinion of his capacity, I was amazed at the impression of fussy, feverish futility he conveyed to me. He displayed the mind, outlook and ability of a capable British civil servant, but no adequate appreciation of the situation with which he was dealing. I formed the opinion, reluctantly, that he carried weight as an outsider, with an English-made reputation, which he could not have carried on his merits, had he been an Irishman in the movement for years and finding his own level.'[5]

De Valera, for one, did not share that unfriendly judgment. Nor did Michael Collins, though it must be added that the Dáil's Finance Minister had acquired the insidious habit of following double standards. A basically warm, loyal and generous human being, he would nonetheless stop at nothing, morally, if a foul deed might promote the cause for which he unwearyingly schemed and fought and lived, never counting the cost to himself. When, for instance, the Cork No. 1 Brigade of the IRA executed an elderly Protestant woman, a Mrs Lindsay, for informing, the local commander did not bother to tell Collins, far less notify him of his intentions in advance. Mrs Lindsay had been taken from her home and shot as early at February 1921. Some three months went by before an embarrassed Childers consulted Collins, in all innocence, about the IRA's policy in capital charges against women. As it happened, a second case had meanwhile arisen, the case of a certain Kitty Carrol who had apparently been put to death in turn for ignoring a Republican ban on the distilling of illicit whisky:

'Shall we', Childers asked Collins on 2 May 1921, 'say (a) the execution of women spies is forbidden, and that Kitty Carrol was not killed by the IRA? or (b) Kitty Carrol was killed in contravention of orders by the IRA, and that (c) Mrs Lindsay is now in prison for giving information to the enemy?'

Childers had been kept in blissful ignorance of Mrs Lindsay's execution seventy-nine days previously, largely because Beaslai, his IRA colleague, had not thought it worth while mentioning so trifling an incident. For his part, Michael Collins, hoping that the matter would quickly be forgotten and that Childers's embarrassment would subside, deliberately ignored the Dáil Director of Publicity's request for a prompt answer. Both men were aware of the Englishman's meticulousness and overriding passion for justice. Characteristically, Childers pestered the overworked Collins until, bit by bit, he extracted the nasty truth from him.[12]

A special Enabling Act was rushed through Parliament that spring to allow the former Lord Edmund Talbot, who had become Viscount Fitzalan of Derwent, to succeed French as Lord-Lieutenant of Ireland in late April 1921. As Fitzalan came of an ancient Catholic family he was debarred from holding viceregal office on grounds of religion. However, Lloyd George, who at last had taken to playing a double hand of cards in the Irish game, saw and seized the chance of appointing the first Catholic to occupy the Viceregal Lodge since Tyrconnel's day. The move was a straw in the new wind of change.

The arrival of the new Lord-Lieutenant made not the slightest difference to the 'policy of thorough' which Macready was determined, with the unqualified blessing of Greenwood, to pursue to the end. March 1921 had been the worst month so far for intimidations and murders, and there was much desultory talk in Downing Street and the special Cabinet Committee on Ireland as to whether the forthcoming polling in the South, under the Government of Ireland Act, should be deferred or accompanied by a temporary truce. Events were left to take their own course.

'The decision is to let the elections go on,' Tom Jones informed Bonar Law, then on holiday in Cannes after his recent but only temporary retirement from active politics through ill-health. 'In Ulster there will be bloodshed, and in the South the Sinn Feiners will be returned without contests. They will refuse to take the oath and the Government will have to decide whether to try some form of truce of Constituent Assembly or Crown Colony. Meanwhile no General will name a date when murder will cease and the Chief Secretary [Greenwood] has dropped his optimism of six months ago and now talks of pacification in years rather than months.... The tenacity of the IRA is extraordinary. Where was Michael Collins during the Great War? He would have been worth a dozen brass hats! Can't you get him to spend a weekend with you in France unofficially? I'm sure the PM has a secret admiration for him and his hands are no bloodier than those of the Angora butchers [Turks] we entertained lately, and his cause is quite as good. He'll be canonized some day.'[11]

Meanwhile the labours of Childers the arch-propagandist, visible in embryo on every line of his carefully filled ledgers, had been succeeding better than he knew. Dublin Castle had long been wary of his subtle influence; and the growing suspicions of John Anderson and Alfred Cope were slowly but systematically confirmed by events. Perhaps his greatest single coup was the slow moulding of American press and Congressional sympathies against the excesses of British military rule and in favour of the Irish struggle for freedom. It was a task in which he was assisted considerably by his wife. All the ammunition fired off by Senator Robert La Follette of Wisconsin on 25 and 26 April 1921, in support of a joint resolution declaring that 'the independence of Ireland ought to be recognized by the United States of America', had been industriously provided by Childers. The words of Asquith, G. K. Chesterton, Lord Bryce, Lord Grey, Lady Frances Balfour, Lady Robert Cecil, General Sir Hubert Gough, Major General Sir Frederick Maurice, the Archbishop of Canterbury, and two former Liberal ministers, Charles Masterman and Walter Runciman, had been carefully gathered and duly transmitted to Washington. These were among the many notable witnesses whose written or spoken criticisms of a bankrupt British policy echoed round the Senate on Capitol Hill, thanks to Childers.

It was the pressure of adverse world opinion as much as anything which forced Lloyd George and his reluctant Tory colleagues abruptly to change course; and in the later admission of one of them, Winston Churchill, 'No British Government in modern times has ever appeared to make so sudden and complete a reversal of policy'. History has largely borne out that verdict. The Irish election went forward in late May, 128 candidates being returned unopposed. Only four of them, the Independents who sat for Trinity College, attended the Parliament prescribed by the recent Government of Ireland Act; being unable to form a quorum they adjourned, never to assemble again. Erskine Childers was duly elected Member for Wicklow West on 23 May. At once he took the oath of allegiance to the new Dáil, along with others who had either escaped imprisonment or been released.

Thereafter the Castle authorities kept a closer eye on him, yet still appeared unwilling to arrest him on any of the usual trumped-up charges they might so easily have brought. In fact Childers 'went on the run', in his own words, after the Auxiliaries raided his home in Terenure on the night of 9 May 1921. Molly managed to conceal beneath her corsage some papers which would have incriminated other leaders, while the armed men were banging at the door with rifle-butts. When they rushed into the room where she half-sat, half-lay, on her couch, Molly baited them gently, watching them ransack the drawers of her husband's desk. They impounded material he was preparing for the current issue of the *Irish Bulletin*, and at once arrested him and his assistant, Frank Gallagher. Molly watched both of them being manhandled into the lorry below and driven off into the night. A bare month previously Childers's office in Molesworth Street had been stripped bare of its records, files and equipment, the Dublin Castle authorities betraying a healthy respect for his handiwork by issuing forged numbers of the *Bulletin* on the impounded printing press. No doubt he had been on the 'Wanted' list since that earlier raid.

'We were both taken to the Castle,' Childers noted.

From there Frank was sent to Wellington barracks. I was put in an underground cell but to my immense astonishment was called for in an hour, taken to an officers' sitting-room and given a cup of tea. After a long wait in another room, Arthur Cope came and told me I was to be released. I insisted that F.G. (who passed under another name) must be released too and this he agreed to and sent officers to get him out. The disgust of the officers at the whole business....was amusing, but Cope was adamant. While waiting news of Frank, Cope tackled me about Dominion Home Rule for fully an hour and a half and we went at it hammer and tongs....When the Colonel eventually reported that Frank had been released, I left the Castle myself, Cope effusive in his manner and actually carrying my valise out of the gate for me![7]

A reference to Childers's partial immunity from the full rigour of the law was made by General Macready on 15 June 1921, when the Commander-in-Chief, Ireland, visited London to present a paper 'of the most ensanguined hue', in Balfour's descriptive phrase, to the special Cabinet committee on Ireland. According to Tom Jones, who was present, Macready did not conceal his personal belief, which Anderson evidently shared, that coercion as a policy would 'land this country in the mire'. What the General objected to was half-heartedness: 'De Valera, Arthur Griffith [and] Erskine Childers ought to be tried for treason and the law should be allowed to take its course.' By then Griffith had been interned once more. De Valera and Childers remained at liberty. Hamar Greenwood, who made it clear that he disagreed with Macready on several points, 'held that apart from de Valera – he had not opposed the arrest of members of Dáil Eireann and agreed to the arrest of Erskine Childers whom Anderson characterized as "very mischievous"'.[11]

A typical sample of Childers's 'mischief' had been intercepted by Macready on 21 July, and forwarded immediately to the Prime Minister. It proved to be 'an extract from a letter which is understood to have been sent to the American State Department and to embody the views of Arthur Griffith and Childers on Dominion Home Rule for Ireland'. The extract spoke for itself, and the core of it disclosed the unmistakably fluent style of Childers:

Any hope I might have of Dominion Home Rule as the beginning of a settlement in Ireland would entirely depend on the character of the Act. If there were a host of safeguards for 'British Supremacy' and if there were oaths of allegiance, or any series of tricks and traps, half measures, delays in time and limited powers, such attempts would surely for ever wreck any project of Dominion Government and make the situation worse for England than it is now....I do believe in the good sense and clear judgment of the Irish people, and that a settlement is attainable. The trouble is that England, like a nursery governess in a dispute, insists first of all in standing on her own dignity – and when there is no dignity to stand on, what must happen? Sinn Fein cannot be asked for any provisional promises nor for any consent to an English Bill. It can be asked to work a good act in being. The new position would be that Sinn Fein would then be bargaining with their own countrymen.[7]

By then, as it happened, Lloyd George had been purposefully toying with the trumps in his own pack of peace cards for almost a month. A stream of emissaries had been descending on Dublin since the end of April when Lord Derby stayed at the Shelbourne, under the pseudonym of Mr Edwards, only to be fended off, with magisterial aloofness, by an indifferent de Valera. Then, in May,

Sir James Craig gallantly permitted himself to be conveyed by the IRA to a secret rendezvous on the city's outskirts for exploratory talks with the President of the Dáil. The talks came to nothing, partly because each of the two principals had been given to understand by the ingeniously devious Alfred Cope that the other wished to meet him. A meeting between de Valera and Smuts proved equally vain. 'This particular peace-move business has been on for some time,' de Valera reminded Collins. 'The reply I have sent through other channels is that if they send a written communication addressed to me directly and not through intermediaries they will get a reply.'[5,10]

Nevertheless, the role of the persistent Smuts in utilizing the channels kept open between Dublin and London by Cope, the Under-Secretary at the Castle who had formerly worked as a detective in Customs, did yield positive results in the end. The South African leader lunched with King George V and persuaded him to appeal publicly to all Irishmen when opening the new Northern Ireland Parliament at Stormont towards the end of June 1921. Various hands worked over the wording of the appeal, including those of Edward Grigg, Lionel Curtis, the King's Secretary Lord Stamfordham, and Smuts himself. Nor did the monarch leave it at that. He was speaking, as he admitted, 'from a full heart.... I pray that my coming to Ireland today may prove to be the first step towards an end of strife amongst her people, whatever their race or creed'. And the monarch later impressed on Lloyd George his personal desire for some constructive move.[13] The personal letter which de Valera had been awaiting was drafted, redrafted and finally sent. It invited the President of the Dáil to attend a conference in London with Sir James Craig for the purpose of exploring the possibility of a peaceful settlement. Any colleagues he might wish to accompany him would be welcome. De Valera replied formally that he was consulting such of his colleagues as were not in prison, a hint which expedited the early release of Griffith, Barton and E. J. Duggan, a solicitor who had taken part in the 1916 rising; but the Irish leader insisted that no settlement could be expected on the basis of a partitioned Ireland.

In this uncompromising allusion to Ulster we can unquestionably detect the hand of Erskine Childers. In fact, so strongly did he feel on the subject that he sought out de Valera alone and eloquently stressed the dangers of embarking on any negotiations with a Prime Minister as untrustworthy as Lloyd George. Unless the British Cabinet accepted the *de facto* existence of the Republic and its right to arrange safeguards for Ulster in an all-Ireland Parliament, there would be no point in accepting the invitaticn. Courteous but stiff, Childers persisted until de Valera grew irate and dismissed him with the cold words: 'If that's all you have to tell me, you're of little use to me.'[14]

It was Smuts again, as Tom Jones had indicated, who impressed de Valera still more strongly with the contrary argument at a further meeting that took place in Dublin on 5 July. To refuse the invitation, he warned, 'would be an awful blunder'. Significantly perhaps, Childers was not asked to attend. Only Arthur Griffith, joined later by Barton and Duggan, were present. Smuts assured Lloyd George and the Cabinet that his words had considerably 'shaken' them, 'all small men, rather like sporadic leaders thrown up in a labour strike. De Valera had done most of the talking: "We want a free choice," he said. "Not a choice where the alternative is force..." The choice should be limited to a Republic or Dominion status and it should be put to the vote. I said I had lived under both systems and worked them. The old Transvaal Republic was a limited Republic bound down by the London Convention.... We fought a three-year war over the limitations and my country was reduced to ashes. If I can give you any warning it is to avoid that fate. I said – supposing a Republic is out of the question, what about Dominion status? Will you accept that? They said such an offer had never been made to them. If made it would be a very serious matter and they would use their Republican machinery to submit it to their people. ... De Valera continually harped on the crime of partition. I said that the Ulster Parliament was not a partition of Ireland and that they ought to be thankful for it as conciliating Ulster.... De Valera said that my reading of history was hopelessly wrong.'[11]

The Cabinet agreed, on the strength of Smuts's report, to call a temporary truce in Ireland and to meet the Southern Irish alone, leaving Craig out. 'Let them talk themselves to the death,' advised the smooth South African when Lloyd George declared that he was not 'looking forward to meeting them with any satisfaction'.

The most mortifying phase of Erskine Childers's ordeal was about to begin. No longer could he immerse himself entirely in his propaganda work, conscious only of an enemy whose heinousness and inhumanity it was his agreeable business to expose as a matter of duty:

Publicity was hard and delicate at this period in the new and strange atmosphere of peace, with the necessity of avoiding excessive partisanship and at the same time of keeping up our principles. I was able to get the principle definitely established that the *Irish Bulletin* was the official organ and all public communications from the President – correspondence with Lloyd George, etc.... – came through it.... I was attending meetings of the Ministry at this time and vividly remember one held at a country house south of Dublin. It must have been about July 8th, when for the first time I heard words spoken which implied a possible weakening on the Republican issue. Collins' words especially struck me – something to the effect that it might possibly be necessary to pass through a Dominion phase and Mulcahy's rather pessimistic words about military prospects. But there was only a general discussion – no vote – there was uncompromising talk from several Ministers, notably, of course, Cathal Brugha, so that the painful impression passed temporarily from me, I think mainly for the reason that I could not yet seriously grasp the idea than an abandonment of the Republic was possible, least of all by a man such as Collins who was a unique hero to me.

It was at this time, too, that I first realized de Valera's difficulties in handling the diverse elements in his Ministry and his extraordinary skill in doing it. That there was a cleavage was clearly apparent: a personal antipathy between Collins on the one hand and Cathal Brugha, Minister of Defence, and Austin Stack, Home Affairs, on the other. With Collins Griffith came to be ranged and also Mulcahy, the Chief of Staff.[7]

De Valera eventually crossed to London on 12 July, accompanied by Griffith, Barton, Stack and Childers, and met Lloyd George alone four times between 13 and 21 July. After each session the President called his colleagues together to tell them what had been discussed. It quickly become obvious to everyone that the British Prime Minister would not move beyond the offer of Dominion Home Rule. Childers noticed once more the reaction of each member of the delegation. After the official proposals were submitted in writing on 20 July, Stack sided with de Valera, Barton and himself in rejecting them outright as a betrayal of the Republic, while the Vice-President, Griffith, hedged with a diplomatic suggestion that the terms deserved to be studied more closely.

The sketchy diary notes which Childers hurriedly resumed contain a lighthearted entry relating to the delivery of the British terms late at night:

At 10 p.m. I and Bob being half-dressed, messenger appeared and said in hoarse whisper: 'Sir James Craig and the Prime Minister'. Tableau. Bob's face a study. Hasty dressing by him. I, who had not heard, maintained my *déshabillé*. In came Sir Edward Grigg and Tom Jones (who said he was Secretary to the Prime Minister). Tableau. And much laughter all round. They brought LL.G's proposals and a message from the King.[15]

Despite Lloyd George's blandishments about the chair awaiting Ireland as a full and equal member of the Imperial Conference, and his jesting at the Gaelic rendering of 'Republic' by a word that meant 'Free State', de Valera could promise nothing. For that relief, at least, Childers was able to return to Dublin with a lighter heart.

The impression left behind by the Dáil's Director of Publicity was that of a rigid, unsmiling but courteous man who seemed most anxious to avoid any unnecessary fraternizing with old friends. Winston Churchill's private secretary, Edward Marsh, whom Childers had instructed in the rudiments of fly-fishing during their carefree days at Cambridge, had sat facing Childers in the Cabinet Room when the Irish delegates first arrived for the formal opening exchanges, and before de Valera accepted Lloyd George's proposal to talk things out man to man.

'Seeing Marsh again for the first time after so long, seated on the opposite side of the table, he [Childers] showed no flicker of recognition.'[16] This, as he freely admitted to Molly, was a studied decision; and in a similarly defiant mood, he had agreed to accompany Barton and David Robinson to church on their first Sunday in London. 'To St Paul's in top hats (David, Bob and I) for service at 10.30. Put in the stalls. Mistaken for Craig's party. No publicity value in this stunt.'

The differences between the men of inflexible Republican principle and the minority of appeasers in the Dáil ministry appeared to widen perceptibly during August and early September while Lloyd George and the President haggled by letter over fundamentals. Very adroitly, de Valera kept the initiative firmly in his own hands as far as possible, consulting his ministers only when this became unavoidable. Childers was asked to help, for instance, in drafting the various replies. He did so gladly. Lloyd George picturesquely described the process of treating with de Valera as not unlike 'trying to pick up mercury with a fork', on hearing which his Irish antagonist wryly commented: 'Why doesn't he use a spoon?'[10]

In all the fifteen letters and telegrams which passed between the two leaders, de Valera would not accept Britain's superior claim to restrict in advance the framework of Ireland's political freedom. Nor did he welcome implied or explicit threats. Childers himself ridiculed in the *Irish Bulletin* a policy of threatening war if Ireland refused 'as a free Dominion to join voluntarily a free association of free nations'. Here lay the nub of the ingenious if over-subtle distinction which de Valera now seized on and developed as his own – the distinction between Dominion status, which Lloyd George was apparently ready to offer, subject to certain limitations, and 'external association' which, in de Valera's judgment, was the furthest step towards compromise which the Irish could dream of taking. Unfortunately for him and Childers, not many of their colleagues could see the point of that fine distinction. The Dáil simply wanted talks to start. For the Irish people wanted peace. Fitzalan sent a secret message to Britain's Prime Minister on 20 August: 'Out of the whole Dáil,' he declared, 'six held out against acceptance. Only three of these, viz., Mulcahy, Childers and a name something like Burgas [*sic*] carried any weight, and these will accept the decision and give no trouble....Childers' wife is an American, a chronic invalid and intense hater of England, but she has not got the money she is credited with. Dymont [the retiring American Consul] says on the money point she is confused with a sister who married a man of wealth.'

Reporting again just eight days later, Fitzalan was able to reassure Lloyd George still further:

'You will probably get an intimation the end of this or early next week that they will be glad to come over and see you.... They have left Childers out of the Government altogether. This is good as he was dangerous, and I believe they make no secret that this is the reason, though they excuse it by saying that he is overwrought. The only two now of any importance whatever who are fighting are Mulcahy and Burgess, both of whom will submit to the majority.'[17]

The friendly American Consul had got his inside information from Desmond Fitzgerald, whom de Valera at once recalled as Minister of Publicity in Childers's place at the instigation of Arthur Griffith. The President, however, insisted on inviting Childers to serve as Secretary to the London delegation, 'knowing that it would be impossible to find in the Dáil anyone so qualified for the position.'[18]

This mark of de Valera's personal confidence touched him. He had recently been upset, not so much by the increased querulousness of Griffith as by the President's overt and skilful humouring of his deputy, especially during the long-range written exchanges with Lloyd George. Once, in his diary notebook, Childers tersely noted that the President had chose to send his own 'macaronic' reply instead of the blunt words he had composed himself. Yet even the sop of being appointed Secretary to the delegation did not pass unchallenged, the Dáil voting for Irish-speaking staff only, but the President overruled their decision. Of far more crucial importance was the choice of delegates. Not only would they be acting as plenipotentiaries, but they would be so treated from the start by the British. The Sinn Fein Cabinet fully expected de Valera to go, and voted accordingly. He refused, using his casting vote to thwart his colleagues and recalling the failure of President Wilson who had gone to Versailles in similar circumstances. De Valera's resolve to stay at home filled Childers with dark forebodings. Brugha, Stack and Collins in turn had also each declined to go, Collins being finally prevailed on to change his mind and accompany Griffith. Barton, Gavan Duffy and E. J. Duggan were then selected as men well fitted to co-operate harmoniously with the two principals. It is interesting now to remember, in view of their subsequent hostility to the terms accepted by the delegation as a whole some three months later, that de Valera, Stack and Brugha each had the chance of negotiating but found good reasons for not doing so. Nobody can rebut the verdict of Longford: 'that tragic consequences flowed from de Valera's absence both friends and enemies of the Treaty would agree today'.[10]

John Chartres, an Anglo-Irish barrister and constitutionalist who had served during the 1914–18 war in the intelligence branch of the Ministry of Munitions, was selected to assist Childers in the secretariat. Tom Jones noticed, when the two Anglo-Irish secretaries came to see him on 10 October, the day before the London talks opened, how 'very stiff and most cautious in all their utterances' Childers and Chartres were. 'Took them to see Hankey,' Jones added. 'Hankey had last met Childers on a boat at Gallipoli. Hankey said the PM might want to bring Grigg into the conference whereupon Childers suggested at once that it might be necessary to bring a third on their side to keep the balance equal. I remarked that secretaries were not plenipotentiaries and Hankey offered to stand down.'[11]

Downing Street, Childers observed, was lined with 'cheering crowds' on 11 October as he walked along with the Irish delegates to the main door of No. 10 just before Big Ben boomed out the chimes of eleven o'clock. Inside, the British Prime Minister, his face alive with a welcoming smile, shook hands with each of them and spoke briefly to the polite but enigmatic English secretary whose notoriety as Sinn Fein's arch-propagandist had preceded him. Childers's feelings were mixed but well masked. The two delegations took their places at the long table in the Cabinet Room: and after the opening statement by Lloyd George some preliminary sparring ensued between him and Arthur Griffith. Childers, seated directly opposite Tom Jones on Griffith's left, listened intently and avoided the roving eye of Lionel Curtis, whom he had last talked to in Dublin when rumours of a truce were thick in the air. The mobile countenance of Lloyd George and the solid, heavy jowls of Birkenhead, who sat next to the British leader, fascinated him. Would such men yield an inch? he wondered.

The hint of an answer came when Lloyd George dwelt on 'the limitations imposed on us by public opinion behind us'. It was Griffith's cue to remind the British delegation in a mumbling, half audible voice: 'We, too, have our limitations. We feel that from the days of Pitt onwards it has been the policy of this country to keep Ireland in a subordinate position.... As to procedure, we are in your house and will follow your suggestions.' It was decided, for a start, that Hewart, the British Attorney-General, would redraft the first five of the seven proposals set out in Lloyd George's original offer so that Admiralty, War Office and Air Staff could be fully consulted. By a curious coincidence, reflecting the reluctance of both British and Irish delegates to anticipate the worst and least soluble difficulty, there was no mention whatever of the seventh proposal: namely, that 'the powers and privileges' of the Ulster Government should be 'abrogated or diminished' only with Ulster's consent.

Clearly this contest of wits and wills and tactics would continue until one side or the other weakened or surrendered at least one of its entrenched positions. Childers wished that the negotiating scope of his colleagues had been less ambiguously defined by de Valera. They were plenipotentiaries on paper only. The term scarcely applied to men obliged to refer back to the President, to the rump of the Cabinet, and to the Dáil every amended proposal and every disputed point. This was the cumbersome method which had been adopted in a vain attempt to secure nominal equality with the British.

In his current diary-notebook, he scribbled on 13 October:

Subject: Trade. 12–1.30. A deal is possible here but I fear we missed a chance of getting completely free hands. [He did not elaborate. As chief Secretary, he took no direct or active part in any proceedings except Defence on which, exceptionally, he could if so minded upset all the calculations of Churchill, Beatty and their advisers by sheer strategic logic. His chance came that same afternoon:] At 3.15 conference at Colonial Office – Beatty, Churchill, Mick [Collins], me and Dalton. They are not as stiff as we thought.

On the following day, he entered the bare remark: '11–1.30. Subject: Ulster. No progress.' He had expected none. The agreed tactics of the Irish delegates were to explore every other possible avenue of progress first and, if it came to such a pass, break on Ulster last. When Griffith reminded Lloyd George in passing that there were 'two ways of annoying the ordinary working class

Orangeman: to speak respectfully of the Pope and to call him an Englishman', the Prime Minister retorted: 'That makes your difficulty less. I talked this over with Lord Carson and he is confident they will come in if you do not bully or deny them. They are pugnacious people with a touch of the Scotch about them – which is a very stubborn race.' Then Collins, Gavan Duffy and Griffith weighed in, one after the other, accusing the British Government, in effect, of having perpetrated a vivisection of Ireland which the Irish people alone could rectify by peaceful means. Lloyd George confessed how glad he was that de Valera had ruled out force as a weapon to coerce Ulster: 'It would break in your hands,' he insisted. 'Mr Collins shakes his head. He knows Ireland, I know Great Britain and the Empire. It would resolve itself into a religious war.... Until agreement you must allow the present arrangement to stand.'[11]

The parties remained far apart on Ulster, so much so that towards the close of the fifth session on 17 October Tom Jones pushed a note in front of the Prime Minister. It carried the terse message: 'This is going to wreck settlement.' By now de Valera had sent over his own interpretation of the critical Ulster clause. The North, he contended, should give up the 1920 arrangement and voluntarily enter an All-Ireland Parliament in Dublin. Alternatively, Ulster might retain its own legislature and special powers, provided that overriding authority were transferred from London to Dublin. Collins warned Lloyd George: 'We are prepared to face the problem itself – not your definition of it.' And Lloyd George hit back: 'It is not our definition but our compromise ... to get out of a problem which wrecks every Bill. ... In the main the Nationalists accepted it in 1914 and 1916. They had our credentials then and you have them now. Don't father this compromise on us.' The argument went round and round and petered out in deadlock. On Ulster, at any rate, the Irish delegation stood intact and at one.

The arrival next of de Valera's so-called Draft Treaty A, advocating external association with the British Empire rather than proffered Dominion status, brought Childers into a head-on clash with Churchill over the duly amended Defence clauses. Britain's Colonial Secretary described the document redrafted by Childers as one of 'marked ability'; but it amounted to a 'reasoned rejection of every one of our points and to a claim of neutrality for Ireland.... I regard this as a mortal blow.' The debate, when joined, produced what the cool but implacable Childers called 'a great flutter'. He understood the difference between being free and being foreign, pressing it home vigorously.

'Ireland, an island with a maritime frontier, is to be denied responsibility for her own naval defence' merely because she happened to lie sixty-one miles off Britain. 'Supposing,' he said in an aside to Beatty, 'that Ireland were not there. What would you do then?' The doughty Admiral paused for a moment, then swiftly countered: 'Ah, but she *is* there.'[7] Both Churchill and Beatty refused to accept that the denial of naval defence rights was a denial of Irish freedom. On 21 October, with becoming gravity, the Prime Minister told the Irish delegates that

this situation cannot be prolonged. We must know where we are.... A formidable document has been put in by Mr Collins [the Childers defence paper] which challenges the whole position with regard to what is vital to our security against attack.... Is the communicating link of the Crown to be snapped for ever?

Then Collins tentatively broached the question of 'a new form of association' with Britain and the Empire under the counter-proposals listed by de Valera in his document Number 2. The British did not rise to the challenge. Instead, Lloyd George asked Griffith to have ready in writing, 'for our next meeting', the new Irish counter-proposals, answering each of the three key points he had raised. The vital session took place on the afternoon of 24 October. It was the last which Childers attended in person as secretary. For that evening, he noted in some puzzlement, there was 'at 6 p.m. a private meeting of Lloyd George and Austen Chamberlain and Arthur Griffith and Michael Collins'. This had been apparently contrived by Collins himself, with the help of the ubiquitous Alfred Cope. Well might Erskine Childers privately resent 'the great mystery' surrounding this procedural departure. For as Tom Jones remarked in his diary, without attempting to put too fine a point on it, Lloyd George wanted 'to exclude Childers, believed by Britain to be the most extreme'.[11]

Rarely did Erskine Childers turn off the light in his office at 22 Hans Place, the London headquarters of the Irish delegates, until two o'clock in the morning. He had no social life whatever. His hands were too full. Edward Marsh he continued to ignore, the sole friends of former days whose occasional invitations to dinner or drinks he accepted being Basil and Dorothy Williams, J. L. Hammond, G. P. Gooch and Lady Courtney. The Williams thought he looked and sounded distraught and incredibly tense. This was not the Erskine they had once known and still loved; only when his drawn features relaxed momentarily into the old, familiar smile did they feel a little more at ease with him.

Every day, sometimes twice, he wrote home to Molly. Not once did he dream of using the telephone, a self-denying ordinance followed religiously by every member of the Irish delegation. Puzzling as the practice may appear now, it was understandable then. What more natural reflex could there have been after the recent reign of terror, when eavesdroppers abounded and no mechanical device of the kind could be trusted by the few Irish leaders who were not behind bars? This rooted allergy to ringing up Dublin on official or private business proved ineradicable. That it hampered their work and finally destroyed the harmony between delegates will shortly become abundantly clear.

'The 30th was here a very critical day, perhaps the most critical for Ireland of all days in centuries,' he informed Molly. 'I cannot speak to you about it...and I was up till two this morning with J.C. [Chartres] as a result.' In a pitying reference to the pro-British outlook of his American mother-in-law, who was by then living permanently with Molly, he added: 'My tears burn to think that she cannot today recognize her own creative effort, for two strong souls are nobly engaged.'[2] With their invariable endearments and only fleeting hints of actual or looming crises, Childers's letters to his wife refute the frequent allegation that, as Secretary to the Irish delegation, he used her as a kind of secret *poste restante* through which confidential reports on the changing loyalties of individual delegates could be passed on to de Valera. On the contrary, an occasional note of impatience with the President's aloof high-handedness can be detected here and there in this highly personal correspondence.

In accordance with agreed procedure, the President received

regular communications from Griffith, the delegation chairman, on day-to-day developments, as well as copies of all documents drafted by Childers and the small staff at Hans Place for the British. These, together with de Valera's replies, were carried to and from Dublin by special couriers. Fortunately for historians of Anglo-Irish affairs, Childers, in his sedulous manner, kept for his own files nearly all the original drafts, some typed, others in his own handwriting, besides most of Griffith's original pencilled letters and notes, many of them heavily altered in the Chairman's sloping handwriting. After 24 October these alterations had to be wrung from Griffith by Childers often and at the cost of bitter argument and deepening misunderstanding, the Englishman henceforth assuming the self-appointed role of watchdog to the Irish delegation. Even a comma out of place, let alone a loose phrase which the British might twist for their own nefarious purposes, stirred him to criticism. His small suite of adjoining rooms upstairs became a kind of gladiatorial arena in which the adversaries cut and thrust away ferociously at one another in the interests of what Childers deemed to be Republican orthodoxy.

The advantage now lay with Lloyd George, though the British Prime Minister still felt that negotiations could easily break down on the two major stumbling blocks of Ulster and the Crown. From a distance he admired and feared the pervasive influence of Childers. In a bitter-sweet allusion to him at a later date, Lloyd George spoke of his 'slight figure, his kindly refined and intellectual demeanour', adding for good measure the words: 'brave and resolute he undoubtedly was, but unhappily for himself also rigid and fanatical'.[19, 10] With Childers isolated, at least during formal sessions, from the reasonable men, Griffith and Collins, who happened also to be the principals, a way round the two outstanding obstacles to agreement might yet be contrived. After all, had not both Griffith and Collins assured Tom Jones of their willingness to meet him and Austen Chamberlain 'at any time and on any topic'? Indeed, Jones minuted on 26 October that copies of the next set of British proposals must be shown 'in advance' to Griffith and Collins so that as much agreement could be secured before these 'got into the hands of Childers'.

Jones also complained about the studied ambiguities in Childers's drafting which, he said, caused 'great trouble' and amounted to 'a war of technicalities between me and Grigg. I phoned the memorandum in Welsh to the PM! And then sent it by train.' But Lloyd George did not like what he read either at first or second sight. 'Well, Mr Jones,' he said on 29 October, 'you may tell these gentlemen that in my opinion they are just playing with us, just fooling us.' The naval paragraph would not do, to begin with. Nor did it mollify the British Prime Minister to learn that 'unfortunately Childers was their scribe and the meticulous qualifications were no doubt his'.[11] The 'further Reply' prepared by the Secretary to the Irish delegation led to another *impasse*. Only as the result of private talks between Griffith and Lloyd George, and again between Collins and Churchill, were the verbal misunderstandings cleared away – if just temporarily. For Lloyd George's double dilemma now lay in trying to entice Ulster to the conference table without antagonizing the predominantly Tory members of his Cabinet. Both sides, in other words, faced formidably complex difficulties, though Childers could hardly have cared less about the political problems of Lloyd George.

What the latter required from Arthur Griffith immediately was a personal letter of assurance on the three fundamental points of Crown, Empire and Defence. Griffith artlessly put pen to paper on 1 November; but Barton, Duffy and Childers rejected his draft on grounds of principle and content, urging him to rewrite it. 'He refused at first,' Childers noted, 'then agreed – and finally consented to sign as Chairman.' Only at the third attempt did Griffith satisfy his critics. The letter gave Lloyd George enough leeway to approach Craig, the Ulster leader, and ask for some token gesture of conciliation and compromise; but Craig, relying on the sensitivity of diehard Tory opinion shortly before a meeting of Conservative representatives at Liverpool, proved utterly unyielding. It looked almost certain that by the end of the first week in November the Irish delegation would pack their bags in the knowledge that they had been wasting their time in London. And if the break did come on Ulster, Lloyd George loudly asserted, though not loudly enough to be overheard, then he would resign. 'I shall go out,' he said. 'I will not be a party to coercing the South.'

If only Childers had been more in the confidence of Tom

Jones, Edward Marsh, Edward Grigg and Lionel Curtis, he
would have been better placed to give his own colleagues informed and sensible guidance on the next step. However, Griffith and
he were by now scarcely on speaking terms, while Collins chose
to ignore the repeated angry outbursts at Hans Place and maintained his outward air of inscrutable calm. Childers noted in his
diary that Griffith had met Tom Jones privately on successive
days, 11 and 12 November, and had been shown Craig's implacable reply to the British Prime Minister's overtures. According to Griffith, Craig had been guilty of 'a gigantic piece of bluff'
which would be called by holding a plebiscite in the North.
Neither Griffith nor Collins liked the alternative idea, which
Jones had thrown in casually, of a boundary commission for
Ulster. For though it might save Lloyd George's face and avert
the need for his resignation, it also sacrificed the principle of
Irish unity; and for Collins and Griffith that unity still remained an
essential precondition of any settlement. It was Lloyd George who
suddenly found himself on the wrong foot, uncertain whether he
could stay on as Prime Minister yet unwilling to go until pushed.
Coercion of the South, whose delegates had offered some real
concessions, seemed to him quite unthinkable. Coercion of the
North by Westminster could not be realistically considered either,
thanks to the terms of the 1920 Partition Act. Lloyd George was
in a trap. Then Arthur Griffith innocently, and without troubling
to tell Childers or even Collins of the action he had unwisely
taken, swallowed the proposal for a Boundary Commission.

What happened was this. On the afternoon of 12 November, at
the London home of Sir Philip Sassoon, Griffith went through
Craig's reply, line by line, with Lloyd George, who cunningly
extracted from him a promise not to oppose the Boundary Commission proposal in view of the approaching and critical Liverpool
meeting of the Tories. The political survival of the Prime
Minister and all chances of a settlement equally depended on it.
Had Childers been informed, he would certainly have protested
vigorously, not only to Griffith but to Tom Jones and to Lloyd
George himself. Certainly there would have been no suggestion
afterwards that Griffith's word-of-mouth assurance constituted
a solemn and binding pledge, put down in writing at once by
Jones and later pulled out of the files like a magician's rabbit from

a hat and flourished as a secret guarantee committing the entire Irish delegation, the President, the Dáil and the Irish people in perpetuity. It was the kind of legerdemain in which Lloyd George instinctively specialized. If it incidentally smacked of dishonesty, then Griffith must also be reproached for his extraordinary naïveté.

The British delegation, released from the trap, were free at last to present their draft treaty, including fresh safeguards for a separate Ulster. Its delivery at 22 Hans Place resulted in the most acrimonious wrangle yet between the appeasers, led by Griffith, and the militants, inspired by Childers. The Irish delegates dissected the document clause by clause. The Secretary said that these proposals brought Ireland willy-nilly into the British Empire. As it happened, de Valera took the same uncompromising view as Childers. He wrote to remind Griffith briskly: 'There has been so much beating about the bush that I think we should now get down to definite business and send them as far as possible our final word.' But what was the final word to be? On it the choice of war or peace in Ireland would depend. For hours on end Childers concentrated on preparing a full reply to the British terms, pretending when it came to the point of distributing it that Robert Barton was the author. To such petty deceits and subterfuges were they all reduced. Even so, the Chairman of the Irish delegates quickly lost his temper:

A.G., insolent to me about altering drafts. Attacks me about *Riddle of the Sands*. Says I caused the European War and now want to cause another. I said I stood on the strategical case in both instances.... I protest and virtually threaten resignation. He climbed down.

Then, in a further outburst,

Griffith broke out about allegiance, saying he was willing to save the country from *our* war – personally willing. He implied that he was willing to tell LL.G. this, but Robert Barton put it to him then he said No.[7]

The climate grew stormier inside the delegation while the drafting and redrafting continued. The two factions had become virtually irreconcilable. Collins, though quiet and usually friendly, invariably took Griffith's side, as did Duggan, against the Republican dogmas formulated by Barton and Duffy with the guidance of Childers and Chartres. Lloyd George did not care much for the dry, precise, finely written yet curiously intransigent tone of the Irish reply to the British draft treaty, which reached him on 22 November. In the presence of Austen Chamberlain, he instructed Tom Jones to tell the Irish that 'the document filled him with despair'. Tell them also, added Chamberlain, that he personally felt 'let down'.

As the editor of the Whitehall diary summed up the situation: 'The Irish reply had been a hotly contested one, and in a sense represented the maximum concessions which Griffith could extract from Duffy, Barton and Childers. Yet it had been insufficient; and if Tom Jones had carried out his mission as instructed, the conference must have broken up there and then.' But Jones was not so easily defeated, for he interpreted his watching brief much more broadly than did Childers his. Instead of handing in an ultimatum from the British, he drew from Griffith and Collins the fear lurking at the back of their minds that, if they simply put everything down in black and white, 'it would be tantamount to giving the PM a blank cheque'. The two men promised Jones that they would go away and reconsider the tone of the Irish reply. At a further meeting they had with the Prime Minister, arranged by Jones on 23 and 24 November, several misunderstandings were gradually cleared up.

Lloyd George afterwards commented scathingly on the presence of Barton, the foil and the cousin of Childers: 'Why did they bring that pipsqueak of a man with them?' he asked. 'I would not make him a private secretary to an Under-Secretary.' Of course, the absent de Valera still kept prodding the delegates from Dublin. If semantic distinctions failed to move Griffith and Collins, they moved the President deeply. The Crown as a symbol must not be accepted, he warned, nor the oath of allegiance. He had already tried to rally them with the sharp reminder: 'We're all here at one. If war is the alternative, we can only face it and I think the sooner the other side is made to recognize it the better.' That letter had caused every delegate at Hans Place to bridle. Momentarily they forgot their differences. Were they plenipotentiaries or not? By what right did the President seek to curb their freedom of discussion? The irony of it all did not elude Childers. It was, he had noted, 'a memorable scene'.

K

Presently the partisans were at each other's throats again. When the Secretary drafted a paper simply to demonstrate how many concessions the delegation had been forced to make, without getting anything tangible in return, Griffith at once exploded. The paper was meant for internal consumption only; but that hardly mattered now.

'Ireland's full claim is for a Republic, unfettered by any obligation or restriction whatever,' the Childers broadside began. It concluded: 'Out of the ten paragraphs of the proposals, Nos 1 and 7 are the only ones which do not make concessions from this position.' Not unnaturally, Griffith accused the writer of working might and main to prevent any peaceful settlement. Childers demanded to see the accusation in writing, whereupon Griffith cooled down and said he was sorry. In the perspicacious verdict of Longford: 'Childers, the old Committee Clerk of the House of Commons, was prone to a formalism, strange to Ireland and, in the eyes of Griffith, ridiculous.... It has been said, and not by enemies of Griffith, that behind these trifling exasperations lay a genuine and growing suspicion that Childers was no honest friend of Ireland. Be that as it may, there is no doubt that Griffith saw in Childers, with his rigid limits on the verbal scope of the bargaining, an obstacle not much less menacing than the British themselves to a satisfactory settlement.'[10] Barton and Duffy knew otherwise. Yet even they felt that Collins and Griffith deserved better than to be provoked petulantly on points of propriety rather than of principle.

Left high and dry outside all conference discussions, the Secretary normally passed the time debating constitutional niceties with Tom Jones, Edward Grigg, Philip Kerr, Geoffrey Shakespeare or Lionel Curtis. He remained unaware of the extent to which these advisers, as well as the ministers they served, had already gauged how deep were the dissensions inside the Irish delegation. Nor did he surmise how resolutely Lloyd George would play on it. On 1 December, another urgent meeting of the delegates was convened in Childers's room, this time to discuss the finally revised British draft treaty and its sombre implications:

'I want to hear all points of objection,' said Griffith, 'so that nobody can say afterwards that all arguments were not fully heard.' Childers listened in silence to the others criticizing the

Ulster Boundary Commission proposal, the trade and financial
clauses. He spoke only on the defence clauses, and Griffith
'flared at me for often before having said the delegation was
going back on July 20th. I said on this occasion I had criticized
on defence only. Michael Collins, instead of backing me up, said
he thought I implied a wider criticism and refused to withdraw
when I asked him. M.C. made a ghost of an apology after the
meeting.' The isolation of Childers, inside as well as outside the
Irish delegation, was complete. The effect showed in a diary comment he scribbled late that night as he mused glumly on the fact
that Griffith and Collins were 'utterly unable to compete with the
English crooks and their skilled draughtsmen'. Defeat now stared
him in the face:

Cope urged me to support peace (outside the Cabinet Room). Continual
going and coming of people – Churchill etc. I thought of the fate of
Ireland being settled hugger-mugger by ignorant Irish negotiators –
and A.G. in genuine sympathy with many of the English claims....
Redraft came at 1 a.m. A.G. muzzy with whisky.

Childers feared at that awful moment that nothing and nobody,
not even de Valera, could now save Ireland from humiliating surrender at the conference table. If it crossed his mind that he had
become a hostage to fate himself, he was too tired and disillusioned to care.[7]

Childers did not sleep a wink during the journey from London to
Dublin on the night of Friday, 2 December 1921.

Off the Skerries the steamer accidentally collided with a fishing
smack. Three men were drowned. The ship picked up the sur-
vivors and turned back dead slow to Holyhead. An exhausted
Secretary arrived just in time for the President's Cabinet meeting
which all delegates attended. Cathal Brugha created 'an unpleasant
scene' almost at once by asking why Griffith and Collins had
attended all sub-conference sessions. Was it at the request or the
direction of the British? 'M.C. angry but contained himself,'
Childers noted.

De Valera said he would not accept allegiance to the King and would
reject the document. Griffith said he *would* – to prevent war. Collins

difficult to understand – repeatedly pressed by Dev but I really don't know what his answer amounted to. Barton said he would not. Duffy ditto. Duggan same as Collins. I spoke only on defence, pointing out that these proposals left our status lower than that of a Dominion.

The Irish Cabinet resumed its emergency session at 5.30 on the evening of 3 December: 'Went through documents with suggested amendments.... After meeting he handed me written formula.... All this amendment business was too hurried, but it was understood by Barton, Duffy and me that amendments were not mandatory on delegation, only suggestions.'

The confusion of minds degenerated into further heated and prolonged disagreement when the delegates returned in haste to London and debated how they should proceed. At 22 Hans Place there were 'sneers and bluster' from Collins when Childers set to work again on revising the British terms as, he claimed, de Valera had decreed.[20] Copies were taken down to Whitehall by Griffith, Duffy and Barton for what seemed likely to be the conclusion of the whole sordid, muddled and sorry affair. For Collins had forthwith refused to go; and Childers sat outside the Cabinet Room, lost in thought as usual:

At 6.5 pm [on 4 December] Duffy whispered to me 'C'est fini.' Communiqué drafted. We left. In the car Barton said to Griffith: 'Well, I admired the way you stuck like a bulldog to the Ulster issue. It may be all for the best yet.'

Would Griffith stick to his guns and 'break' on Ulster? Would he resist to the death? Childers doubted it. He had become even less popular during the past traumatic week, rushing out, for the edification of the two principals, another of his spiky and provocative papers entitled 'Law and Fact in Canada and Ireland'. He was determined to ram home the point that, with Dominion status, even an all-Ireland government must remain a British colony because of the country's physical proximity to Britain and because of a spiritual alienation rooted in seven centuries of oppression. The paper was so succinct that Griffith grudgingly accepted it, and even passed it across to Lloyd George.

In law: Canada is a subordinate dependency.
In fact: Canada is by the full admission of British statesmen equal in status to Great Britain and as free as Great Britain.

In law: the British Parliament can make laws for Canada.
In fact: Canada alone can legislate for Canada.
In law: The British Government can veto Canadian Bills.
In fact: It cannot.
In law: The Crown has supreme authority in Canada.
In fact: The Crown has no authority in Canada. It signifies sentiment only.
In law: There is an Oath of Allegiance to the Crown in Canada.
In fact: The Canadian owes obedience to his own constitution only.
In law: The Governor-General is the nominee of the British Cabinet only.
In fact: He is the joint nominee of the Canadian and British Cabinets.

Nevertheless, the wily British Prime Minister had taken the wind out of the sails of everyone, notably Griffith, with the soothing suggestion that the Irish could insert 'any phrase they liked' to ensure the same position for the Crown in Ireland as in Canada. Why at this eleventh hour? wondered Childers. Why not at the outset, all those tormented weeks ago?

Collins reluctantly went to see Lloyd George privately on the morning of 5 December when it seemed to Childers that the Conference had irretrievably broken down. Then the last, fatal round of exchanges began. Seated outside the Cabinet Room in Downing Street through much of the afternoon, evening and small hours of 5–6 December 1921, Childers knew in his bones that the pass was being sold within. Like a stern intellectual Titan, regardless of jarring personalities or individual antipathies, he had made a last supreme effort after dinner on 6 December, to restate the minimum terms that were consistent with Ireland's rights, as the President had required. Griffith, Collins and Duggan in turn had refused to touch it: 'Let those who want to break present it,' they countered. Barton and Duffy had responded at once: they would deliver it themselves to Lloyd George. At that point Griffith had relented.

In his private talk with Lloyd George on the morning of Monday, 5 December, Collins had derived the firm impression that Ulster would be 'forced' into an All-Ireland Dominion by means of the Boundary Commission to which, it now appeared, Griffith had pledged his colleagues some three weeks before without informing any of them. Yet no Irish delegate could overlook the dramatic warning issued to Griffith, Collins and Barton by Lloyd George about teatime on 5 December; nor could Childers, who noted: 'Our reply must be ready by 10 pm. Document to go to Craig by special train and destroyer. LL.G. showed the alternative letters – one in the event of our refusal. They directly threatened war. I sat outside reading Lincoln.'

The emotional climax at Hans Place was reached on the night of 5 December. In its abrupt, staccato style, the diary of Erskine Childers recaptures the tense atmosphere perfectly:

Re-draft came. Meeting of delegates 9 pm. Final discussion. A.G. spoke almost passionately for signing. It seems the other side insist *all* delegates shall sign and recommend Treaty to Dáil. Monstrous document. M.C. said nothing. Bob refused to sign and G.D. Then long and hot argument – all about war and committing our young men to die for nothing. What could G.D. get better? etc. etc. G.D. murmured quietly, Bob shaken. Asked me out, and I said it was principle and I felt Molly was with us. Suddenly he said: 'Well, I suppose I must sign.' I stopped him and said: 'At least you only did it under duress.' We then went back in and [he] said he would sign under duress and solely because if he didn't the country would get no opportunity to decide. A.G. then said *he* would say they signed under duress – and if they refused, tell them to go to the devil.[7]

Gavan Duffy, the odd man out, at length said he, too, must sign the agreement as it stood. The very mention of Molly's name, so Barton admitted to a mutual friend of ours in after years, accounted for his unexpected decision to spurn the advice of his cousin at this, perhaps the most dramatic turning point in both their lives.[21] It seemed to Barton in a flash of resentment that Childers had been acting throughout like a man under the spell of his absent wife, focusing his mind intently until it responded exactly as Molly's would have done, while damning the consequences for everyone else. It was too much. What better reason could there have been for inducing Robert Barton to break that spell and follow his own conscience like a mature adult? After all, he was a plenipotentiary – on paper, at least.

Barton's decision still grieved and troubled Erskine Childers as he sat quite still, trying to imagine what was going on behind the heavy Cabinet Room door. Already that day the rug had been dexterously pulled from under Griffith's feet when Lloyd George

had reminded him of the so-called pledge which the Irish delegation's Chairman had freely given him on 12 November.
Griffith had been foiled in his intention of breaking off negotiations at this, the weakest link in the British chain of argument,
whereas the shadowy concept of external association seemed to
have impressed nobody at all on either side, except Childers,
Gavan Duffy and possibly Barton. The Irish had thus been robbed
of their one likely bargaining counter. Back they had gone naked
to the conference table at 11.15 on the night of 5 December 1921,
ready to sign away their essential rights, as Childers saw them:

My chief recollection of these inexpressible, miserable hours was that
of Churchill in evening dress, moving up and down the lobby with his
loping step and long strides and a huge cigar like a bowsprit, making
him a very type of brutal militarism.[7]

The Lincoln biography Childers was reading had been thrust
aside. He could no longer concentrate.[22] Another hour and
twenty minutes ticked away before the stenographers, scurrying
in and out, tidied up the few small, insubstantial alterations in
the Articles of Agreement for the signature of delegates on both
sides. Lloyd George had not missed the brooding presence of
the hunched figure waiting without, in this his own great hour of
triumph:

'Outside in the lobby,' he told the world later, 'sat a man who
had used all the resources of an ingenious and well-trained mind,
backed by a tenacious will, to wreck every endeavour to reach
agreement: Mr Erskine Childers. At every crucial point in the
negotiations he played a sinister part. When we walked out of
the room where we had sat for hours together, worn with toil
and anxious labour, but all happy that our great task of recon-
ciliation had been achieved, we met Mr Erskine Childers outside,
sullen with disappointment and compressed wrath at what he
conceived to be the surrender of principles he had fought for.... I
never saw him after that morning.'[19]

The appearance of Lloyd George after the signing ceremony
left no such lasting mark on the Secretary's mind. Nor did Childers
notice Hamar Greenwood walk out with Michael Collins, still
less overhear the banter between them:

'You had us dead beat,' Greenwood was told by the leader of

Ireland's violent, underground resistance to the Black and Tans. 'We could not have lasted another three weeks. When we were told of the offer of a truce we were astounded. We thought you must have gone mad.'[23]

Childers himself was beyond speech when Arthur Griffith chattered ecstatically in the car on the way back through London's lamplit squares to the darkened house in Hans Place:

'We are on top of the wave,' intoned Griffith. 'We'll never get such terms again.'[7]

Historically, events proved Griffith right. Nor had the sharp eyes of Lloyd George deceived him as he caught that parting glimpse of the pale, taut features of Childers, the Englishman who bore all the signs of a man who had already given himself up as a hostage to fate.

10. THE REBEL

As he lay thinking in the death-cell, Erskine Childers felt no anger, remorse or fear. Nor did the approaching dawn of his own execution day serve to concentrate his mind more wonderfully than usual, in spite of Dr Johnson's hackneyed dictum. Too many brave men had gone to their deaths already. One more, his own, would make little difference. A creature of habit, he had put his affairs in order expeditiously and without fuss. He had then settled down calmly to spread over the remaining days and nights that inordinately long and poignant farewell letter to his crippled wife Molly. The authorities had rejected requests that she should visit him; so, with the docility of a perfect hostage to fate, he had accepted the cruel decision without self-pity. A saint might have envied him his serenity. None of the elemental emotions to which mortals are prey in similarly hopeless predicaments appeared to touch him. Even the maddening and once haunting sense of bewilderment at the steady collapse of his dreams had gone. This had dogged him intermittently for eleven months, ever since Arthur Griffith first savaged him in the Dáil during the bitter debate after the London Treaty by publicly damning him as 'an Englishman'. The memory no longer hurt him. Without the prospect of a heaven or a hell to absorb him, without the ritual comforts of a religious faith to sustain him, Childers could look death straight in the eyes. He had conquered any uncertainty he may have once had about this, the last enemy.

Like some latterday Aristides the Just, he did not really mind dying; his task was done. All he asked for was paper, pen and ink to reassure his wife that nothing had changed. Thus he communed with a strong woman whose destiny had become indissolubly bound up with his own. The prison guards and their commandant increasingly marvelled at him. So did the doctor, who examined him perfunctorily the night before his execution. As for Edward Waller, the Protestant clergyman who was his oldest Irish friend, how could he ever erase the recollection of their final walk together to the yard where the firing squad stood at ease until Childers had shaken hands with each man and given an agreed word of encouragement as the signal to open fire. This contrary victim of the Irish Civil War had purged the guilt falsely imputed to him by official propagandists. His innocence cried out for vindication. Yet in a country renowned for immortalizing its heroes who had sacrificed their lives for freedom through seven hundred years of persecution and oppression, no odder or more controversial candidate for belated inclusion in the roll of Irish martyrs could have been conceived than the enigmatic Erskine Childers, the 'damned Englishman' of whom one Dublin friend remarked, with devastating realism, that it was 'his sniff of disdain which got him killed'.

Childers's very Englishness, the air of indefinable superiority which, according to critics, he exuded like a smell that stank in good Irish nostrils, had not been the least of his handicaps, the greatest being his temerity. By embroiling himself recklessly in a family feud, he had been predictably treated as an intruder whom either side would cheerfully have hounded down without much regard for the civilized niceties. The fact that it was the Irish Provisional Government of Cosgrave, the natural heir of the late Michael Collins and the late Arthur Griffith, which caught, summarily tried, then shot Erskine Childers out of hand as an example to other hardline Republicans, does not invalidate the point. An Irish patriot by intellectual conviction, he failed to win in his lifetime the complete trust of more than a handful of his adopted fellow-citizens. The consistent exception among the leaders was Eamonn de Valera, now a victim of circumstances like himself, throughout those turbulent eleven months that followed the dashing of Childers's hopes at the London Conference in December 1921. From Hans Place he had taken home a litter of unsorted papers and several copies of the signed Agreement with the British, which he disowned but was unable to reject; then characteristically Childers had become a man marked down for extinction. It is questionable whether anyone, least of all himself, could have done anything to stay the inexorable hand of fate. Having settled for the part of a hostage, he did not tilt or rail against his expected doom. What did astound him were the far-fetched calumnies noised abroad by his detractors in their final vicious campaign of character assassination. That deliberate process he found harder to understand than to forgive. For Childers remained to the end the incorruptible, lionhearted yet slightly diffident and casual English gentleman he had always been, in spite of the doctrinaire Republican sentiments he professed.

Ironically, it may well have been an estate-worker at Glendalough who informed on him, disclosing to the authorities the fact of his presence. He had worn himself out on a cross-country trek of nearly 200 miles to reach the place that had always been home to him. David Robinson had returned with him. When the detachment of soldiers in their green uniforms had charged up the staircase to his room on the first floor, Childers could easily have escaped. Instead he had confronted them, unpinning from his braces the small, pearl-handled revolver which Collins had once given him as a keepsake in happier days. A maid had thrown herself between him and his assailants calling out: 'Don't you dare touch Mr Childers.' He would almost certainly have pulled the trigger in self-defence otherwise. It did not occur to him that his capture in possession of a lethal weapon would rank as a capital charge, and that the military court would be bound to find him guilty, whether he chose to recognize its legality or not.

The usurpers wanted to make a public example of him. In their haste to rush Robinson and Childers to a cell, first in Wicklow, then in Dublin's Portobello Barracks, the search-party removed no papers. Childers had been writing in a small exercise book when the crash of rifle-butts and the warning cry of a woman's voice disturbed him. I came across the unfinished document, a clear and extraordinarily moving *apologia* for his life and work in Ireland since 1920, lying loose and at random in one of four large trunks containing a vast assortment of family and personal records. Its significance proved elusive until the context gradually indicated precisely when it was composed. The pencil he used could as usual have been sharper. The handwriting was shaky but legible enough. The story, with its repeated reflections on points of political theology which still mystified him, broke off in mid-sentence. Fortunately the manuscript lay undetected during subsequent raids on Glendalough House, and an extra copy was eventually made by Robert Barton. Because of the oblique light it throws on the enigmatic mind of Erskine Childers at the time of his arrest, one section of the document must be quoted at length. In response to the key conundrums which had been puzzling him for months, namely why so many unlikely Irish patriots veered round, first to welcome the Truce, then to accept the British offer of Dominion Status, Childers wrote:

I do not suppose that there can be any doubt now, though I, for one never suspected it at the time, that matters had gone much further, and that at the time of the Truce there were already in existence a group secretly determined to accept Dominion Status – a group composed of the majority of the Supreme Council of the Irish Republican Brotherhood. It is common knowledge that the nature of this body eventually determined the issue, but when its decision was actually come to I do not know and probably no one outside the Supreme Council of the secret society itself knows. Collins dominated the Supreme Council which included also Mulcahy, the Chief of Staff, O'Sullivan, the Adjutant General, and in fact a majority of the Headquarters Staff of the Army. I myself, except for some very vague gossip, was wholly ignorant of this powerful undercurrent at the time, and through my ignorance lost the clue to much that followed. The same must have been the case with all those who were not of the IRB, and this accounted for such mystification and bewilderment. Through it all Cathal Brugha's obstinate opposition to anything even suggesting compromise stands out clear in my memory. De Valera had immense difficulty in keeping together a team which included him, Griffith and Collins, and his chief difficulty consisted in getting Brugha to go forward at all; but he succeeded with his wonderful personal authority founded on crystal integrity of character and a temper almost utterly devoid of all pettiness and bitterness – all the time suggesting by degrees and slowly building up the conception of a modified course, relinquishing the naked demand for an isolated Republic (simple international recognition and nothing more) and substituting the idea of a Republic as independent as before but in free external association with Britain.[1]

As de Valera, Brugha and Griffith did not belong to the IRB, leaders so prominent had to be individually humoured. Griffith had reached the position of desiring a compromise peace with Britain before the IRB accepted the military necessity; so the continuing obstructiveness of the other two had to be challenged systematically. The scales thus belatedly dropped from Childers's eyes. He saw only at the twelfth hour the Machiavellian realism underlying the ambiguous attitude of his former friend Michael Collins, not only in London but later when the divisions that had rent the Irish delegation there spread far and wide and progressively. The Cabinet had split, then the Dáil, then the country. Everything seemed to have moved in accordance with the IRB's secret masterplan. Their one big miscalculation had been to suppose that true Republicans, whether among de Valera's supporters or among senior Army officers, would follow Collins like mindless sheep. Bred in the short traditions and narrow loyalties of any revolutionary force, the Irish Republican Army had split in a deeper and more ominous way, bringing the spectre of civil war appreciably and inexorably closer. Erskine Childers, regarded by the IRB as its most formidable adversary next to de Valera, had been unable to prevent the campaign to destroy his good name. Arthur Griffith had helped to start it by petulantly and publicly denigrating Childers as an English double agent. His military talents were presumably at the disposal of the irregular troops deployed against Government forces in the South and West: so repeated acts of sabotage, which inflicted untold misery and loss on a new nation struggling to survive, could readily be blamed on this convenient English scapegoat. The provisional Government, far from denying such preposterous rumours, had sought to propagate them by calculated innuendo. It had served the purpose of ministers like Cosgrave, Mulcahy and the pugnacious Kevin O'Higgins, as it had once served the purpose of Griffith and Collins, to let Irishmen and others believe the impossible.

Having unravelled the truth and traced to source the otherwise inexplicable chapter of accidents which had brought vengeance on him, Childers ceased to worry. His conscience was clear. He awaited death calmly, indifferently, without bitterness. He had solved the hardest part of the riddle: the aims of the conspirators. The bizarre irony of this temporary liaison between the IRB, the Free State authorities and the British, however much it might be formally discounted in Whitehall or in Dublin, no longer troubled him either. It had a wild logic which might have appealed at one time to Childers, the dogmatic logician; but time was running out fast for Childers, the intractable rebel condemned to die for a technical offence by a court he steadfastly refused to recognize.

All the tormenting discords of the London period fell neatly into place now. Whether Arthur Griffith ever perceived the complex pattern of Michael Collins's role mattered no longer. What counted then was that Griffith's pacific instincts and moderate views had coincided perfectly with the tortuous means to larger ends of 'the Big Fellow', as Collins was popularly known. Besides, both men were already in their graves, as Childers would soon be himself. The grisly civil war had taken an early toll of them, Collins from a ricocheting bullet in an ambush, Griffith from a sudden heart attack brought on by overstrain and the burden of worry. Had Collins lived, he might have achieved his desperate secondary aim of reconciling the pro-Treaty and anti-Treaty forces, especially in an army which had once been the obedient tool of the Brotherhood. The effort of living simultaneously on three separate planes had proved too much even for 'the Big Fellow'. Childers had continued to admire and respect him on the personal level, even after discovering why Collins had trimmed tactics, ideas and behaviour to suit the shifting requirements of the Brotherhood. What a topsy-turvy world it was where gifted men had to conform to the orders of secret masters and yet pretend to be acting solely on their own account! Whether Collins, had he survived, would willingly have spared the life of Childers must remain a matter of conjecture. Splendid antagonists as they were, little trust remained between the Englishman and Collins, who shrewdly anticipated the dark future in two notes to his Hampstead friend, John O'Kane, at the end of the London talks:

'The advice and inspiration of C. [Childers] is like farmland under water – dead. With a purpose, I think – with a definite purpose. Soon he will howl his triumph for what it is worth.... will anyone be satisfied at the bargain? Will anyone? I tell you this – early this morning I signed my death warrant. I thought at the time how odd, how ridiculous – a bullet may just as well have done the job five years ago.'[2]

Curiously enough, Arthur Griffith's animosity had once appeared far more calculated than anything Collins or the Brotherhood could have contrived to blacken Childers's reputation. The drama of the marathon Treaty debates was past history now; but Childers, looking back, remembered only too sharply the acrimony of the exchanges. It had been a shock to find how many supporters of the Treaty were ready to stand up and be counted in the Dáil. The vote on 7 January 1922 had shown that they outnumbered de Valera's followers by sixty-four to fifty-seven. Griffith, elected President in de Valera's place, had declared that 'the Republic of Ireland is going to remain in existence until the Free State is prepared to have an election. I do not want any obstruction.... Within the next three months we are going to have the heaviest task ever thrown on to the shoulders of Irishmen.'[3] At that point Childers had risen impetuously in his place to enquire icily whether Griffith would care to outline the new policy. Though out of order, he had stood waiting for an answer, ignoring loud and hostile shouts. The hostility hardly astonished Collins's disciple, Piaras Beaslai:

'There was something particularly irritating in the spectacle of this English ex-officer, who had spent his life in the service of England and English Imperialism, heckling and baiting the devoted Griffith, with his lifelong record of unselfish slaving in the cause of Ireland – answering Griffith's moving appeal with carping criticism. Griffith, usually so stolid and unemotional, lost his patience. He rose, like a sleeping lion roused, and declared – "Before this proceeds any further I want to say that President de Valera made a statement – a generous Irishman's statement – and I replied. I will not reply to any Englishman in this Dáil." "What has my nationality got to do with it?", asked the ultra-rational Erskine Childers. Banging the table furiously, Griffith repeated.

'"I will not reply to any damned Englishman in this assembly!"

'"I am not going to defend my nationality," said Childers, "but I would be delighted to show the President privately that I am not in the true sense of the word, an Englishman."'

The offer was not accepted. Griffiths had far more onerous problems on his mind.

On Saturday, 14 January 1922, the sixty-four members of the Dáil who had voted for the Treaty assembled in the Mansion

House with the four Trinity College representatives of the dead-letter Southern Parliament created in 1920 by Britain's Government of Ireland Act. There, without oratory or ceremony, they elected the Provisional Government. Its chairman, significantly, was Michael Collins. For it had been thought judicious not to complicate life needlessly by offering a second hat to Arthur Griffith who retained the style and title of President of Dáil Eireann. It was the last ghostly link with the dying Republic and as insubstantial as the smile of the Cheshire Cat in the new constitutional confusion. The Irish Republican Brotherhood, according to the conspiracy theory which alone made sense at last to the calm mind of Erskine Childers, had managed things competently so far. Alas for their careful plotting, the Irish Republican Army foiled them. For the Army next split roughly down the middle, with units generally following the pro- or anti-Treaty attitudes of their commanders. Because the Army had begun to occupy barracks and depots all over Ireland as the British forces evacuated them, the stage was set that doleful spring for a head-on clash between the rival forces. De Valera and Childers were bound to be blamed for it, though the charge would not bear serious examination.

'His [de Valera's] anti-Treaty attitude undoubtedly gave a coherence and a political point of focus to anti-Treaty opinion in the country,' Robert Kee has written with dispassionate precision. 'But anti-Treaty opinion inside the IRA, which was to bring about the civil war, organized and consolidated itself independently. It looked not to de Valera but to its own leaders.'[5]

It needed only a spark to set the country ablaze. For the military leaders who rejected the Treaty also repudiated their allegiance to the Dáil, yet still swore to defend to the death the mystical and largely notional Republic. They meant business. On 13 April their Commander-in-Chief, Rory O'Connor, occupied and set up his headquarters in the Four Courts of Dublin, a highly symbolical move. With him went Liam Lynch, Ernest O'Malley, Sean Moylan and other veterans of the common struggle against the British. 'If the Army were ever to follow a political leader,' O'Connor told the press, 'Mr de Valera is the man.' But O'Connor reiterated that the Republican faction of the Army had no formal links with any politician. Childers had then received an unexpected visit

from the rebel general, as his wife would one day remind de
Valera:

How well I remember that day...when Rory O'Connor told Erskine
and me that he had acted without consulting you or even informing
you of what was planned. He made his reasons clear...Mulcahy had
broken his promise made in the Dáil to maintain the Republican Army
as it was, until an election should decide the Treaty issue. The Army
Convention had been cancelled when Griffith and Mulcahy learned
from the resolutions forwarded by Army units for the agenda that 85
per cent of the men were anti-Treaty. Only the Army itself could deal
with such a situation. Rory had himself summoned the Convention.[6]

The trail of broken promises, of angry men and of confused
corporate bodies like the IRA responding by taking the law into
their own hands, had led, as everyone feared, to catastrophe,
chaos and bloodshed. Collins had striven helplessly to hold the
two armies apart and find some compromise formula of recon-
ciliation. For the gathering turmoil in the South had not gone unnoticed in the North where Craig stood ready to defend Ulster
with a force of 25,000 paramilitary A and B Specials, a force used
first to cow the Nationalist Catholic minority within Ulster's
borders by the use of emergency powers. Serious rioting broke
out in Belfast when contradictory explanations of the Boundary
Commission clauses in the London Treaty heightened the prevailing uncertainty, Collins claiming that Lloyd George had
promised him one thing and Craig retorting that Lloyd George
had promised him virtually the opposite. How typical, Childers
reflected. The British Prime Minister had prudently held his
tongue, first when taxed with it and again when sectarian killings
in the North began to multiply. Events in a partitioned Ireland
continued to interact upon each other with tumultuous effect,
Collins's toleration of Rory O'Connor's defiant stand inside
the Four Courts inciting Ulstermen to further direct action
against Catholics in their midst. By the middle of June 264
people had been killed in the six countries since the signing of
the London Treaty, 171 of them being Catholics.

In his dilemma Collins sought out de Valera who was as
anxious as himself to avoid civil war in the South. A general
election was due in June 1922, to give democratic respectability

to the Provisional Government and the new constitution then being prepared on the basis of the London Treaty. After talks between the two rival leaders, an electoral pact was agreed: the old Sinn Fein party would stand as one political organization on a single voting panel, the candidates being distributed in proportion to the pro- and anti-Treaty voters in the Dáil the previous January. The pact also provided that a Coalition Government of five pro-Treaty and four anti-Treaty ministers would take office after the election. The announcement caused alarm and indignation in London as well as Belfast. The evacuation of British forces from Ireland was suspended; and Churchill warned that if a newly elected coalition government tried to establish a republic in defiance of the Treaty, then 'we should no more recognize it than the Northern States of America recognized secession'.

Watching the unfortunate Collins struggling to extricate himself from a trap of his own devising, Childers had hoped against hope that the electoral pact would not be broken. He felt doubly betrayed, therefore, on 16 June when Irishmen went to the polls. For on the very eve of the election, Collins had spoken in Cork and advised Irishmen to vote, not necessarily for the Sinn Fein panel, but for the candidates of their choice: 'The country must have the representatives it wants,' he said. 'You understand fully what you have to do and I call on you to do it.' When the results were declared on 24 June, Childers lost his seat to an independent. The manipulative talents of Michael Collins, great as these might be, seemed to the defeated candidate thoroughly despicable. De Valera, successful at the polls, waited in some doubt for an invitation to join a new coalition Government. He waited in vain.

Just two days after Childers was rejected by his disillusioned constituents in Wicklow, a political murder with grave consequences was perpetrated in London. Sir Henry Wilson, the former Chief of the Imperial Staff, whom Craig in Belfast had recently appointed as his military adviser, fell riddled with bullets in the doorway of his London home as two unknown Irishmen opened fire at short range. The sense of outraged horror in Britain was aggravated by the fact that the attackers were self-confessed members of the IRA. The British Government imputed the crime to the anti-Treaty Republican forces of Rory O'Connor, in the Four Courts; they were wrong, of course; and Collins 'knew he was on strong ground' in 'demanding proof'.[5] For, though impossible to prove, the distinct probability remains to this day that Collins had tacitly sanctioned the killing, if not at that inopportune moment then during the earlier struggle against the Black and Tans.

The immediate impulse of Lloyd George and his colleagues was to order General Macready in Dublin to blast Rory O'Connor and his henchmen out of the Four Courts; Macready, more practical, countered with the reminder that nothing would serve better to unite the pro- and anti-Treaty factions against the vestigial British garrison. So Collins and Griffith received an ultimatum from London instead; they must do the blasting themselves, as befitted the newly re-elected leaders of the Provisional Government. Poor Childers, a bemused and purely passive onlooker, suddenly realized that events had got out of hand.

Michael Collins could no longer hold back. The British would certainly have intervened forcibly had he temporized further. When the men of the Four Courts requisitioned sixteen cars from a Dublin garage, and the officer in charge of the raid was duly arrested by pro-Treaty forces, Rory O'Connor had retaliated by kidnapping one of Collins's generals. It was at 3.40 a.m. on 28 June that Collins sent O'Connor an ultimatum; unless he evacuated the Four Courts in twenty minutes, the stronghold would be attacked. There was no reply. At seven minutes past four that morning Childers stirred in his sleep at home. He could hear the distant thunder of artillery. The bombardment had begun, with the help of two field guns borrowed from the obliging Macready. Erskine Childers, on learning the bare facts, knew that civil war had broken out. For two days the shelling continued until the building was reduced to a blazing ruin and O'Connor with most of his staff surrendered. But other points in the centre of Dublin had meanwhile been occupied by anti-Treaty forces, and for more than a week there was serious skirmishing until practically the entire side of O'Connell Street opposite the one still scarred by the 1916 Easter Rising had been demolished. By 5 July sixty people, including Cathal Brugha, lay dead; a further three hundred were wounded. The time had come for Childers to consider moving out before Collins's agents came for him.

As an open and unrepentant propagandist against the Provisional Government and the Treaty, he could expect no quarter. In any case, for at least three months he had suspected that Arthur Griffith would not rest until Childers, whom the President had publicly accused of working against Ireland, was safely behind bars. So he packed a few belongings, consulted his friend de Valera, and disappeared from home. His duty to the mystical Republic rather than any apprehensions about his personal safety prompted him to leave. Perhaps he might be able gradually to live down Griffith's recent venomous assertion that Childers, the 'damned Englishman', was nothing but a secret agent in the pay of the British.

The President had gratuitously uttered that second, damaging insult in the Dáil before the end of April. The press in Ireland and all over the English-speaking world had repeated it, and nobody understood better than Erskine Childers that mud thrown by so eminent a figure as Griffith would be sure to stick. As the injured party he had risen immediately to rebut the charge, but was ruled out of order. For nearly six trying weeks, until Cathal Brugha managed on 5 June to gain a hearing in the Dáil for a resolution censuring Griffith, Childers was denied the opportunity of speaking in his own defence; and when he did, Griffith had been inconveniently absent. Re-reading that speech by Childers, no detached critic today could find fault with its dignified restraint. Recalling the President's sweeping statement that 'I was an Englishman who had spent all my life in the British Military Secret Service... qualified later by something he said as to my work as an Intelligence officer which was not very distinct', Childers had said:

Now there can be no point in making that charge at all, unless he had the implication in it that my position and connection here were in someway dishonourable; that in opposing the Treaty as I have opposed it I was acting not only in English interests but in some disreputable way, I suppose, as some secret agent of England.

He had then mentioned his past and recounted exactly where and how he had spent it:

I have human understanding enough to realize that he may have felt
deep resentment at my opposition to the Treaty in London....I can see
him completing, as he thought, the crowning achievement of a life
spent in brilliant and imperishable service for Ireland and regarding me
as an interloper and an Englishman and feeling bitter.

Childers wanted to 'dismiss it from my mind and regard it as a
closed chapter', if only Griffith would offer a simple expression
of regret. But handsome apologies were too much to expect in
such times of theological rancour.

Cathal Brugha, now dead, had been kindness itself, of course.
'God forgive me', Collins had remarked during the ensuing exchanges when de Valera reminded everyone that it was none
other than Collins who had originally brought Childers to his [de
Valera's] notice and introduced them. The Englishman had later
written to thank de Valera for intervening so warmly on his
behalf:

When all is said and done, my antecedents did of course make my *use* of
the Cause infinitesimal enough by comparison with those whose
sacrifices and sufferings *made* the Cause – did make me much less of an
asset than I might have been had I come to the truth sooner. So all the
more I value the faith and confidence you placed in me from the time
of our first meeting....[I] would rather cut off [my] hand than weaken
or injure the noblest of all Causes, or you, the greatest leader of a
great Cause I have ever met.[6]

It was the last letter Childers ever sent to 'the Chief', who
reciprocated in full, not only by continuing to regard the Englishman as a national asset but by describing him in words that
sprang from the heart after the Englishman's death as a 'Prince
among men'. Not unnaturally, Griffith and his disciples continued
to think of Childers as a national liability best wiped out, then
quickly forgotten.

'On the day of the death of Collins,' wrote Frank O'Connor, 'I
was on a hillside ten miles from the place of ambush and in the
company of Sean Hendrick and Erskine Childers. We did not
know of the death of Collins until we read of it in the papers.'
By then (22 August) Cork had fallen without a fight and some 500

men on both sides had been killed in desultory and half-hearted guerrilla actions which bore no relation to warfare as Childers knew it. Yet the removal from the scene of a leader who might somehow have separated and pacified the combatants, halting the almost casual slaughter and destruction on both sides, had roused an instant resolve for revenge among the new men in Dublin. The frustration of Childers as the would-be propagandist of the armed Republican cause in the South began to tax his patience to the limit, as the few surviving letters he smuggled through to Molly testify.

The isolated position of Molly herself was anything but easy. The authorities kept a close watch on the house at 12 Bushey Park Road; and what had once been a refuge for men on the run, as well as a salon for visiting journalists and enquiring politicians, became an unsafe place. The influence which, it was said, Molly exerted over her husband, the authorities regarded as sinister and excessive. Certainly Mrs Mary Alden Childers was filled with a passionate enthusiasm for the Republican cause. She continued to work clandestinely for it, saddened and disillusioned as she unquestionably was by the chapter of treacheries and misfortunes which had scattered to the four winds the once united champions of that cause. She had schooled herself to put away all ambition for the sake of the husband she loved. The polemical books he might have written had they stayed in England, the novels which leapt up at her from the closely written pages of the illuminating war diaries he had kept, would never be published now. For the man of action, the adventurer ready to die like a chivalrous crusader of old for his high ideals, had ultimately triumphed over the man of letters. In any event he would earn the gleaming laurels of a martyr if the worst befell him. Of that Molly remained absolutely convinced: 'We do not belong to ourselves,' she assured him.

'I don't know when I can get this to you,' he had scribbled with a blunt pencil early one morning before decamping for 'the front'.

I had a wakeful night in a chair after finishing today's issue of the [Republic] of [Ireland] at 1 a.m....The news is sad and bewildering for the moment. I am trying to get out the [paper] twice or once every day and have succeeded so far but material is becoming difficult. If it fails, I will of course join up.

Childers did not 'join up' either then or later. No Republican commander wanted him in Dublin or Cork or anywhere else. They preferred their own native Irish warriors. So he persevered with the self-appointed uphill task of creating publicity throughout July: 'Note all your propaganda points,' he wrote to Molly.

Is *The Times* reaching you? Censorship in English papers is heavy. How would it be to order cuttings about Irish War from the news cutting agency? Expensive, I know, but very valuable. Could you send me two pairs of *thick* socks and three more bolsters?

Shortly before vanishing and reappearing in Cork, Childers had a snatched conversation with his cousin, Robert Barton, who was, he reported, in the

depths of depression and hopelessness....Says we can't do anything. ...Dev, I think, has collapsed....Frank [Gallagher] and I furious and fear a general cave-in. Trying to get them to form a nominal Government and at least act strongly. No *one* leader, alas....Dev says we should surrender while we are strong, I believe. Have not seen him.[6]

Nor did Childers again set eyes on de Valera until the latter, dressed in the rather untidy uniform of a private, accidentally encountered him at a brigade headquarters to the west of Cork several weeks later. By then the pro-Treaty forces, better led, better armed and better disciplined than the Republican, though inferior in numbers, had pressed into service a number of small ships to land troops behind enemy lines, cutting communications and capturing Cork, the country's second biggest city, almost unopposed. Griffith had meanwhile collapsed and died of heart failure in Dublin. Confident of swift victory, Michael Collins then visited the liberated city of Cork and sallied forth in an armoured car to inspect the terrain west of it, only to meet his violent death in that ambush near Crookstown on the road from Bandon. 'This supremacy of tragedy', Childers had termed it mournfully. The Provisional Government's well orchestrated propaganda did not actually pin the responsibility directly on de Valera or Childers; only whispers to that effect were allowed to circulate. Was it not G. K. Chesterton who shrewdly wrote that 'twice one is two, twice two is four, but twice two is twenty-two if you know the way to score'?

Childers was almost continuously on the move from the end of August until his capture. He took no part in the planning or conducting of any military action. The letters to Molly, his business manager and sole remaining link with scattered Republicans like Frank Hogan in Dublin, ceased altogether after his portable printing-press fell over a hillside and sank into a bog. He had been somewhat premature in telling his wife, in a note from Republican headquarters at Clonmel: 'I am more and more convinced of the value of the *Poblacht*', the southern edition of which he wrote and edited as often as was practicable. 'They have lived on it here in the south, fitting it into the *Cork Examiner*, but supply is precarious and may be wholly cut off.' Again he complained: 'The lack of communications is desperate.... Don't even know Free State news. I have made strong representation at HQ about necessity of daily couriers.'

To veteran soldiers like Childers and his old friend David Robinson, instinctively impatient as both were of the prevalent slackness and inefficiency, the conduct of hostilities by local commanders on both sides had a strangely farcical quality: 'No organization', he admitted. As to his own non-combatant role:

Am labouring hard to improvise but have not responsibility.... It is a chance whether I stay longer – my duty, I think to try and get something done if I can, but no use beyond a certain point.... I stick on in the obstinate determination somehow to galvanize these people into life, but it may fail at any moment.... Picture me in a remote cottage without even a bicycle, trying to arrange this kind of thing![6]

There was much more in the same vein of deepening scepticism and gloom. The impression he left on the minds of others was mixed because, being utterly English, Childers hugged his frustrations and forebodings to himself. Sean O'Faolain, Sean Hendrick and the youthful Frank O'Connor had conceived a lasting respect and admiration for him since their original chance meeting with him in Cork:

'Our first glimpse of him was disappointing,' O'Connor wrote. 'He came down the stairs of the Victoria Hotel, limping and frowning; a small, slight, grey-haired man in tweeds with a tweed cap pulled over his eyes, wearing a light mackintosh stuffed with papers and carrying another coat over his arm. Apart from his

accent, which would have identified him anywhere, there was
something peculiarly English about him.... His thin, grey face,
shrunk almost to its mould of bone, had a coldness as though life
had contracted behind it to its narrowest span; the brows were
puckered in a triangle of obsessive thought like pain, and the
eyes were clear, pale, and tragic...Later Childers's friend, George
Russell, asked me if I thought he was taking drugs. I was certain
he wasn't, but I knew what Russell meant.'

Frank O'Connor saw much of Childers from then onwards at
and behind the arbitrarily fluid front line. They ate together with
Liam Lynch in the officers' mess at Fermoy, Liam 'looking like
the superior of an enclosed order in disguise'. The books with
which Childers whiled away the sleepless small hours were not
to his young assistant's taste. O'Connor was passing through his
Dostoevsky and Walt Whitman phase and had no time for boys'
adventure tales by Fennimore Cooper or Buchan. It was at Butte-
vant Barracks in September that O'Connor witnessed the
reunion of Childers and David Robinson – 'another "damned
Englishman" but of the sort I get along with'. The future Irish
writer, who had aspirations at that time to earn fame as a local
war correspondent, watched Childers one day go out to survey
the nearest enemy positions. The English observer had to cross
a railway bridge covered by machine guns. The Republican
officer in charge ran for cover, as did Frank O'Connor, but
Childers walked coolly across, studying the country and apparently unaware of danger. 'This, of course, was partly the attitude of the professional soldier who always knows by instinct
when and where to take cover but there was also an element of
absent-mindedness about it.'

That night, in the great hall of Achill Towers, the headquarters staff sat smoking and poring over their maps. It would
have been demeaning to consult any English ex-officer about
tactics, so Childers sat, unconsidered, on a petrol tin by the open
door, scribbling away at despatches which might never reach
their destination. Once more, at Macroom, Frank O'Connor
noticed the perfect understanding that existed between Childers
and Robinson until the latter hinted to his English comrade that
he had no business to remain any longer at the front. For the
Free State authorities were clearly determined to capture, try and

execute Childers for tremendous, barbarous and wholly mythical feats of arms which he had never been in a position to commit because the Republicans preferred to plan and fight their own muddled battles.

Robinson had then concocted his hare-brained scheme for smuggling Childers to France in a fishing boat, but the Republican headquarters' staff would not hear of it. In any event Childers would have refused to go. The Dublin newspapers, fed by official propaganda went on printing fantastic tales of the daring raids which Childers had seemingly schemed and led.

'I'll never understand this country,' Frank O'Connor overheard him complain after twice failing to witness a battle through falling fast asleep over his work-table and not being roused. 'I thought I was going off to a bloody combat and instead I found myself in Mick Sullivan's feather bed in Kilnamartyr.'[7]

Robinson, more cavalier and vigorously outspoken, had undeniably been leading a column of sorts, just as he had earlier commanded what passed for a Republican cavalry unit until Republican strategists abandoned any idea of organized frontal warfare. To Molly Childers, a woman he feared as much as he idolized, Robinson wrote a cheerful letter (undated) not long before the two men left the countryside of West Cork to walk and cycle all the way back to Glendalough:

'Erskine and I are going into a show together tonight merely as spectators...so Erskine said "I must send a despatch to Molly, why don't you send her a despatch?",...I need hardly say very few of us have either his mania for work, his power of concentration or the capacity to accomplish things. And so we are not always so sympathetic to him as we ought to be [since] we still retain a liking for food and sleep which apparently don't count with him....We are much amused by the reports which appear in the papers – in no case has there been any foundation for any of them. In one case, something I did was put down to him – I think the local people thought that the only person with an English accent in the Army must be he. It irritates him as he thinks the people here *mind* their victories being credited to him, and no doubt they are published with that object, but of course nobody gives a damn.'[8]

The Republican officers in the field found Childers's unaffected drawing-room manners definitely offputting at times. Once, as Diarmid Brennan has testified, Childers 'attended a meeting of column leaders in a farmhouse at the back of beyond when the campaign's end should have been as obvious as Big Ben to a Londoner, yet the same old guff was being spouted as in Hitler's bunker. Childers got up dreamily and inquired politely where "the toilet" was.... The others stared at him. Then one got up, winked at his companions, and led Childers out to the rear exit where nothing but an ebony blackness of fields stretched out to a starry sky. "You want the toilet," said the guide. "Well, here it is." "Where," asked Childers, gazing round him, bewildered. "From here to the bloody horizon," was the reply.'

Sean O'Faolain, now an old man, has never forgotten the melancholy spectacle of 'this highly talented man ... moving quietly among the Southern IRA officers who knew nothing of his career and service to Ireland and completely underestimated his abilities. I once heard one of them say patronizingly, "Childers, you ought to be given some kind of Army job. You would make quite a good adjutant." '

Childers experienced a sense of mild revulsion when the belated news reached him that the new Dáil, the third to meet since the creation of the vanishing Republic, had assembled for the first time on 9 September 1922. An irregular trickle of newspapers still came by courier from Dublin or Cork. They were invariably a week out of date. Unlike de Valera, he no longer had any political standing. This irked him just a little, for it had not escaped his attention that the British Government was embroiled in a dangerous quarrel with Kemal and his Turkish forces of liberation at a place called Chanak on the once-familiar shore of the Dardanelles, and there were already signs of mutinous discontent among Conservatives in the British Cabinet. If only de Valera could take advantage of it, the true Irish Republic might yet be resurrected and saved. Unbeknown to Childers, de Valera was already on his way to Dublin for an abortive meeting with Mulcahy, his erstwhile Chief-of-Staff, in the home of a Dr Farnan in Merrion Square:

'Couldn't find a basis', de Valera wrote tersely in his diary. 'Mulcahy was looking for a basis in acceptance of the Treaty – we in revision of the Treaty.'[9]

Childers had already noticed without special interest that William Cosgrave had been duly elected President in place of the late Arthur Griffith, promising to 'implement the Treaty, enact the Constitution, support and assist the National Army, and ask parliament if necessary for any powers thought necessary to restore order'. That promise had an unpleasant ring, perhaps; but no more so than Erskine Childers could have expected. Cosgrave's choice of ministers, apart from Desmond Fitzgerald in charge of Foreign Affairs, included the energetic Kevin O'Higgins at the Home Department, Ernest Blythe, a tough Ulsterman, made responsible for local government, and the inevitable Richard Mulcahy who now combined the portfolio of defence with the command of the Free State forces, in the manner of the late Michael Collins. In itself the reshuffling of the ministerial pack to produce so powerful a team of emotionally detached and younger men augured badly for the Republicans; and before Childers had decided that his negligible usefulness as the breakaway Army's chief publicist in the South had ended, Kevin O'Higgins spelled out an unmistakable message of warning. The Dublin Cabinet, said O'Higgins, carefully glossing over the ministerial disagreements which had preceded their collective decision, would tolerate no longer the guerrilla campaign of destruction: 'The life of this nation is menaced,' he told the pro-Treaty Dáil. 'It is menaced politically, it is menaced economically, it is menaced morally.'

That being the case, the Cabinet had agreed to confer emergency powers on the National Army which would set up its own courts and inflict severe penalties, including death, on men convicted of possessing firearms, ammunition or explosives, 'without proper authority'. Childers was stunned to see himself described by the Home Affairs Minister as the 'able Englishman who is leading those who are opposed to this Government...steadily, callously and ghoulishly on his career of striking at the heart of this nation, striking deadly, or what he hopes are deadly, blows at the economic life of the nation'. If O'Higgins really believed that, he would believe anything. Yet Childers suspected that belief and disbelief no longer counted.

'I don't think any of us hold human life cheap,' O'Higgins had concluded, 'but when, and if, a situation arises in the country

[and] you must balance the human life against the life of the
nation, that presents a different problem.' With his sharp legal
brain, O'Higgins drew the distinction clearly and concisely, foreseeing that Ireland would otherwise be 'steering straight for
anarchy, futility and chaos'.

The Dáil had voted by forty-eight votes to eighteen in favour
of giving the National Army the extremely stern powers sought
for it by the Provisional Government; but to Childers, as to most
Republicans, it amounted merely to another illegal usurpation, as
meaningless and hollow as the offer of an amnesty on 7 October
to all Republicans who surrendered their arms before 15 October.
In the last issues of the well written but poorly printed southern
edition of *War News*, the editor poured his scorn on the counterproductive nature of these measures.

The casuist in O'Higgins had largely convinced the politician
that this unspeakably intransigent English ex-officer deserved to
die. Had not Griffith originally denounced him as a spy? Did not
the military reports from the turbulent South and West repeatedly
mention an Englishman as the accepted master-mind and chief
tactician responsible for numerous acts of sabotage? The rough
notes left by Childers, describing what he did and where he went
between late September and early November, are innocently
devoid of references to military activity or involvement. His last
journey, in fact, took him by circuitous side roads to the Cable
Station at Valencia, off the coast of West Kerry; but his mission
was not to blow it up, as his detractors afterwards alleged.
Instead he had simply discussed with the officials how best he
might make use of their facilities to transmit his war despatches
to the United States.

De Valera's fragile success in persuading the Republican Army's
executive to give conditional backing to an alternative underground government headed by himself may have been the immediate reason for Childers's sudden resolve to leave the fighting
zone and return to Dublin, via Glendalough. The Republican
cause, he realized, had long been in a bad way; it needed a
constitutional framework, as its recent proscribing by the Irish
Catholic hierarchy in a vehement pastoral letter belatedly emphasized. Needless to say, Childers, with withering courtesy, had
exposed the bias and expediency of the bishops, hardly a diplo-

matic gesture at a moment when their Lordships were condemning those who 'have chosen to attack their own country as if
she were a foreign power'.

'It was in the Coole Mountains, between Dunmanway and
Macroom, that Erskine produced the last issue of his paper',
according to his friend and part-time assistant, Sean Hendrick.
The loss of the printing press clinched the matter. Childers informed Hendrick that he intended to collect all his papers, notably
those on the Treaty negotiations, and prepare them for publication. David Robinson, nevertheless, believed that Erskine was in
urgent need of medical care, and even mentioned the likelihood
of 'an operation' before there could be any question of his
writing books or of trying to help de Valera. At local headquarters Childers announced that he had finished with propaganda,
adding that he would gladly serve in any other capacity:

'One of the officers threw up his hands in horror and said
something like "that wouldn't do at all. My God, if the Free
State troops down in Dunwanway heard you were with us, they
wouldn't give us any peace, night or day."'

So Robinson set off with Childers for Glendalough on 25
October. The bare outline of the itinerary, with coded initials for
the real names of places and people, survives in the Childers
Records. With customary disregard for prudence, David Robinson wrote down for his own use as much as he could remember.

'Erskine had a bicycle but I had not....However, HQ said
they would get one for me. It did not turn up till half an hour
before we started. The saddle was held on with string, the
pedals were crooked in their sockets, and there were no brakes.
We started at 6 p.m. following a horseman to show us the way to
Dublin....The next day we travelled on and had to hide in a
field at night while a lot of Free State troops passed us. By this
time my boot had completely worn through from using it as a
brake [then] the pedalling arrangement broke. In the neighbourhood of Slieveanamon in Tipperary we came to a big hill so I
told the others to clear the course. Unfortunately a drain had been
cut at the bottom and having no brakes I could not stop. I was
hurled along the road and picked up unconscious and carried
into a house the owner of which, our companion told us, would
be friendly; but they were not and we had to go on. Eventually

I was taken to Liam Lynch's house at midnight where ... a
relation of Liam's looked after my shoulder which had been hurt.'

After abandoning their bicycles they travelled by night,
mostly on foot. The trek lasted a week. At Curraghmore, Childers
and Robinson crossed the river in a flat-bottomed boat and found
refuge in Wexford with two old ladies. A hired car provided by
Republican well-wishers sped them further towards their destination, and as a precaution they tramped the last few miles through
woods, across fields and up hillside paths, arriving at Glendalough House after dark on 3 November to find that Robert
Barton had been imprisoned again in Mountjoy jail. David
Robinson, aware of the danger to Childers, insisted on prowling
round the estate at all hours, 'with Miss Barton's pistol in my hip
pocket', to enable his friend to rest and start his writing. For
there were Free State troops in the vicinity, and only when
neighbours reported that the troops had marched off towards
Dublin did Robinson decide to relax his vigilance.

'I had hardly closed my eyes when I heard Miss Barton rushing
down the corridor. She said the Free State troops were in the
house. I ran to the hall and saw them at the end of the stairs. I
shouted to them "Is Captain Byrne there?" as he had been a
friend of Bob Barton's and was the only man who knew the
layout.... He then came forward. I asked him what he wanted
and he said "We've come to raid the house." They continued to
advance up the stairs. Miss Barton joined me and asked him
where was his warrant. "This is no time to talk of warrants," he
said, and struck her with a rifle. At that moment Erskine appeared
from his bedroom nearby with a little souvenir revolver Michael
Collins had given him. They seized him. I suddenly realized that
the nozzle of Miss Barton's revolver was sticking out of my
pocket; and as she would never have forgiven me if the Free
Staters had taken it, I rushed down the backstairs and put it in a
saucepan in the kitchen and gave the ammunition to a little boy.
I went back and joined the group. Then I was arrested.' It was
the early evening of 10 November 1922.[8]

It had helped Childers to bear the tedium of waiting by playing
elaborate games of chess with David Robinson, using torn-up

strips of paper for moves across the matching squares they had carefully chalked out on the floors of their adjacent cells. A convenient hole at floor level enabled them to communicate. The devil-may-care cheerfulness of David was a comfort. Childers had been roughly treated at first, then the detectives and armed guards began to behave civilly towards him. He did not complain. Robinson did enough complaining for them both. Childers's flickering sense of indignation, feeding the stubborn faith in Republican ideals for which he was happy to die, flared up fitfully when Free State ministers had sought to justify in the Dáil their decision to execute four unnamed prisoners on the very day of his own summary and grotesque court-martial. As they provided him with newspapers as well as pen and ink, he could savour the appalling hypocrisy of their sentiments. Mulcahy had stuck to general policy; 'We are faced,' he said, 'with eradicating from the country the state of affairs in which hundreds of men go around day by day and night by night to take the lives of other men.' Ernest Blythe, who once upon a time had written inciting the Republican Volunteers to kill policemen as an act of patriotic virtue, now described Republicans as mostly criminals; only the sternest methods would suffice, he said, to put down the 'conspiracy of anarchy'. It was, however, O'Higgins who accounted for the executions in a quite specific way:

'If you take as your first case,' he said, 'some man who was outstandingly active or outstandingly wicked in his activities, the unfortunate dupes throughout the country might say, "Oh, he was killed because he was a leader," or, "He was killed because he was an Englishman..."' The implication could not have been plainer or more ominous. Childers's momentary anger did not endure. Death, he now realized, stared him fully in the face.

His elder son and namesake had received compassionate leave-of-absence from Gresham's, his English public school. The prisoner formally requested permission to see the boy for the last time, especially as the authorities would not allow Molly to visit him. In the death-cell the father begged Erskine junior to promise him two things:

'The first is this,' he said. 'I want you to shake the hands of every Minister in the Provisional Government who's responsible for my death. I forgive them and so must you, Erskine. The second will apply if ever you go into Irish politics. You must not speak of my execution in public.'

It is a matter of record that this sixteen-year-old youth, destined to become President of the Irish Republic over half a century later, kept trust with his father's wishes.[10]

Official confirmation of Erskine Childers's death at the hands of a firing squad in a bare yard beside Beggars Bush Barracks, Dublin, on 24 November 1922, produced a spate of reasonably predictable reactions in Ireland and elsewhere. A handful of his English friends had vainly hoped that the new Tory government of Bonar Law might mediate to save him; in fact, as the official records indicate, not a finger was raised on Childers's behalf.[11] Nor was this surprising. The outside world saw no reason, as yet, to disbelieve the worst accusations against him; only the few who knew Childers best would have quarrelled with Churchill's description of him at the time of his capture as a 'murderous renegade'. That he had turned into a quiet fanatic none could dispute. Yet the shrewdest as well as the kindest analyst of his acquired fanaticism was Alfred Ollivant, the companion who had sometimes sailed with him in their salad days:

'His intellect was the least of him, and its limitations his ultimate undoing. He was first, foremost and all the time a mystic, though probably an unconscious one who would, I think, in the days when I knew him best, have defined himself as an agnostic. Nobody could be with him and not feel his spiritual apartness. He lived in a cloud of dreams and ideals remote from the world. His feet were on earth, but his head was certainly in heaven. He was one of those practical mystics of whom Lord Rosebery wrote many years ago that they were the most formidable of men. Had his mind been as good as his heart was big he would have been one of the great world forces of our times. But the eye of his intellect was obscure and growing, so it seemed to me always, obscurer. You can see it in that noble and pathetic apology he wrote when lying under sentence of death. The good democrat had become merged in the dogmatic pedagogue. At the last it was no longer the will of the Irish people he sought but what he believed was good for the Irish people. In this dual phase, his judgment proved as faulty as his purpose remained pure and his courage high. Some will-o'-the-wisp seemed to

L

possess his brain and lead him ever forward over bogey-haunted quagmires to his inevitable doom.'

The verdict of Herbert (H.A.L.) Fisher, a former Liberal minister who had cherished Childers personally while helping to plan the downfall of the Republican movement during the Black and Tan period, was broadly that the victim had somehow seemed predestined for some such violent end: 'I doubt whether the counsel of friends – and E.C. had many warm and devoted friends in England – could have saved them [Molly and Erskine] for they were impervious to advice and resolved to go on their own perilous way.... All through history the miseries of mankind seem to me to have been chiefly due not to a particularly low standard of behaviour but to the vein of recklessness in human nature which is the substance of tragedy. I suspect that element was an essential part of his character, but there may be something too in an explanation given to me by one of his English friends that he was thrown off balance by the nervous strain of aviation in the war.'

In the straightforward view of one ex-Royal Navy comrade, Will Arnold Foster, Erskine's shouldering of the Republican standard had been quite out of character:

'I could not understand in the least,' he confided to Flora Priestley, 'how he could have persuaded himself – either intellectually or morally – to fight with force against the will of Ireland in this last year. But it is dreadful to think that if only Englishmen had not been so blind and slow in giving Ireland such liberty as she used to claim, Ireland might now be using his wonderful gifts and his burning love of her.... The waste – Lord; And to think how little time ago I was walking with him and hearing him talk still as a Dominion Home Ruler.'

No power on earth could have saved a zealot so willing to lay down his life for a cause which he had embraced from the outset with unswerving fanaticism. It is said that Diarmid Coffey obtained leave from his Free State unit to seek a pardon from President Cosgrave for his former colleague of the gun-running and Irish Convention days, but that Childers, whom he visited in prison, would not hear of accepting any conditional favours. It had, as ever, to be all or nothing. As for Sir Horace Plunkett, that kindly, wise old man laboured feverishly, too, to win a stay of execution, pleading with the Provisional Government for the condemned man's deportation on parole 'if he would give his word'; or in the final resort 'as a prisoner-of-war if he did not see his way to refrain from further active opposition'. Plunkett's petitions went unheeded. How could ministers be expected to make an exception of Childers, when they had conspired to make an example of him *pour encourager les autres*? Even the Master of the Rolls had to be openly rebuffed for the sake of the Irish nation. So Childers's fate was sealed by what Basil Williams has termed the 'uncompromising sternness' of captive and captors alike. For his part, Plunkett could not abide 'the talk of treachery, of instability and the rest. It is simply disgusting.' Indeed Sir Horace believed with the poet, George Russell, the gentle AE, that Erskine would have done better to let his genius flower, to the greater good of England and Ireland, outside the maelstrom of Irish revolutionary politics. Yet the perceptive Sean O'Faolain has quite independently endorsed AE's half-mystical perception of Childers as a man whose end already lay in his beginning. 'He was,' O'Faolain said, 'what the Russians call a "fatal" character and the shadow of his doom was over him from the first.'

EPILOGUE

More than half a century has passed since the body of Erskine Childers was laid to rest. The scars and wounds of the Civil War in Ireland are not yet healed. A residual bitterness remains. That martyr's crown which Molly, his loving but inflexibly determined wife, willed for her husband until she died on New Year's day 1964, is still denied him by many a sceptical Irishman. For after repeated outrages, interal convulsions, and many a fine, pseudo-theological splintering since his execution in 1922, an irreconcilable rump of the old Irish Republican Army, whose cause Childers served with selfless devotion, continues to loot, kill and maim wherever its partisans roam. Their weapons have become more sophisticated; their brutality and nihilistic political aims continue to appal all civilized men. Ulster, whose passionate divisions the intellectual Childers failed to grasp, is only one of their battle-zones. Old hatreds persist not far below the surface to the north and south of the border in partitioned Ireland; and on such hatreds the lawless gunmen thrive to this day.

There have been some positive achievements also. Thanks to common sense, goodwill and the loosely evolving nature of the British community of nations, the Republic of Eire was steadily and progressively hewn out of the 1921 Treaty which Childers opposed. 'External association', the hair-splitting, alternative formula for which Childers died and his mentor, de Valera, suffered disgrace and temporary eclipse, ceased to be an unacceptable dream and has long been a fact of Commonwealth life. Britain's unavailing efforts to transform the Ulster legacy of Lloyd George have already cost her dear. It is for the historian rather than the biographer to sit in judgment on those constitutional compromises which enabled, first Lloyd George and Arthur Griffith, then Stanley Baldwin and William Cosgrave, next Chamberlain and de Valera, and various their successors, on both sides of the Irish Sea, to buy a little more time without managing to redeem outright the long and terrible heritage of Anglo-Irish history.

It was not the love of glory which impelled Erskine Childers to play out his tragic role as a would-be Anglo-Irish liberator. Idealism, tempered by the fearsome logic which has converted many a Byronic dreamer into a remorseless partisan, helped to unmake him. His last phase was the worst. A blinkered visionary who chose action out of preference, he utterly failed to perceive that the substance of Dominion status, for instance, 'might mean all, and perhaps more than all, that the name of Republic could give', to quote the words of his oldest friend, Basil Williams. A rare mixture of opportunist and perfectionist, of intellectual and compulsive adventurer, Childers's potential greatness was marred by an ungovernable tendency to stand in his own light and thus confound even those who knew and loved him best. So the gifted writer became the doctrinaire propagandist whose virulent logic caused his enemies to ascribe to him bloodthirsty feats of which so chivalrous a man was wholly incapable. Erskine Childers belonged to that select company of courageous but misguided human beings who do not mind taking wrong turnings. A man of outstanding but unfulfilled promise, he was – in the immortal phrase of Antoine de St Exupéry, another pioneer-aviator whom Childers spiritually resembled – 'rich beyond dreams, but doomed'.

NOTES

PROLOGUE (pp. 13–27)

1 Frank O'Connor, *An Only Child* p. 165 *et seq.*
2 Childers correspondence.
3 Childers papers.
4 Private information to author from Ernest Blythe.
5 The prison commandant at Beggars Bush Barracks, Sam Irwin, acknowledged how 'Bravely' Childers faced death, adding: 'I cursed the fates, the frailty of the leaders, the stupidity of man, or whatever it was, that brought the country to this pitch of barbarity.'
6 Words attributed to Frank MacDermott by Lord Longford, Desmond Ryan *et al.*
7 George Russell ('A.E.') to Molly Childers.

CHAPTER 1: THE BOY (pp. 29–48)

1 Letters of Robert Caesar Childers contained in family papers.
2 *Dictionary of National Biography*, vol. 10, p. 248.
3 Dr Arthur Ransome, *The Causes and Prevention of Phthisis*, Milroy lecture, 1890, p. 135.
4 Robert Barton's notes to author.
5 Childers correspondence.
6 Letter from H. S. Arkwright to author.
7 Testimony of Ivor Lloyd-Jones and others.
8 Private information to author.
9 The Headmaster's Book, Haileybury.

CHAPTER 2: THE DABBLER (pp. 49–70)

1 Robert Barton's notes to author.
2 Childers correspondence.
3 Spencer Childers, *The Life of Rt Hon. Hugh C. E. Childers*, vol. 1, p. 8 *et seq*, vol. 2, p. 236 *et seq*; see also John Morley, *The Life of William Ewart Gladstone*, vol. 3, pp. 235–6.
4 The late President Childers to author.

5 Christopher Hassall, *Edward Marsh*, p. 47.
6 Letter to the late President Childers from H. F. McClintock.
7 Basil Williams's short memoir on Erskine Childers.
8 *Queen Victoria's letters, 1886–1901*, vol. 3, p. 387.

CHAPTER 3: THE ADVENTURER (pp. 71–97)

1 Childers correspondence.
2 Childers logbooks.
3 Rayne Kruger, *Good Bye Dolly Gray*, pp. 45–6.
4 This and the following quotations in this chapter are from Childers's Boer War diary letters.

CHAPTER 4: THE AUTHOR (pp. 98–120)

1 Childers correspondence.
2 Frank Owen, *Tempestuous Journey: Lloyd George, his life and times*, p. 108 *et seq.*
3 Hammond Innes, the author and amateur sailor, is one notable critic who endorses this opinion. See his introduction to *The Riddle of the Sands*, Collins Classics edn, pp. 14–15.

CHAPTER 5: THE REFORMER (pp. 121–40)

1 Childers correspondence.
2 L. S. Amery, *My Political Life*, vol. 1, p. 162.
3 Erskine Childers, *The Times History of the War in South Africa, 1899–1902*, vol. 5, preface p. 11 *et seq.*
4 Basil Williams's short memoir on Erskine Childers.
5 Of more than passing historical interest in themselves the personal letters Childers received from Kitchener and Milner obviously hardened the author's heart against the partisanship of Leopold Amery as general editor.
6 Virginia Cowles, *Edward VII and His Circle*, p. 119 *et seq.* See also Sir Frederick Ponsonby, *Recollections of Three Reigns*; Sir Sidney Lee, *King Edward VII*; and *Les Origines Diplomatiques de la Guerre 1870–71*.

CHAPTER 6: THE CONVERT (pp. 141–69)

1 Childers correspondence.
2 Frank Owen, *op. cit.*, p. 162 *et seq.*
3 Keith Feiling, *A History of England*, Macmillan, 1950, p. 1030.
4 Childers papers. This extract is from a contemporary declaration by Sir Horace Plunkett.

5 Roy Jenkins, *Asquith*, p. 202 *et seq.*
6 Asquith, *Fifth Years of Parliament*, 1926, pp. 87–8.
7 Erskine Childers, *The Daily News*, 29 October 1910.
8 Erskine Childers, *The Framework of Home Rule*, p. 184, also introduction p. 14 *et seq.*

CHAPTER 7: THE ENTHUSIAST (pp. 170–209)

1 Childers correspondence.
2 Alfred Ollivant's short memoir of Erskine Childers in the *Atlantic Monthly*.
3 Robert Blake, *The Unknown Prime Minister, the Life and Times of Bonar Law*, p. 174 *et seq.*
4 A. P. Ryan, *Mutiny at the Curragh*, p. 121 *et seq.*
5 Jenkins, *op. cit.*, p. 316 *et seq.*
6 F. X. Martin, *The Howth Gun-Running 1914*, p. 28 *et seq.*; this is probably the most dependable Irish account.
7 Letter of Colonel Henry Pipon. Written after the event and unearthed in the Childers papers.
8 The letters of Gordon Shephard.
9 The *Asgard* Diary of Mary Spring Rice.
10 Despite the secretiveness of Erskine Childers, none of whose Liberal friends knew in advance of his gun-running plans, news of its success seems to have spread among them afterwards. For instance, G. M. Trevelyan wrote this complimentary note to Childers from Ambleside: 'So you worked better than you knew when you smuggled those rifles. Without that, Redmond would be on no equality with Carson at this crisis, and his offers to England of help would have been impossible for him to make at least so effectively. You have not lived in vain.'
11 Childers Memorandum on Invading Germany, 1914, a copy of the original on the files of the Admiralty.
12 The Childers Great War Diaries, parts 1 to 3.

CHAPTER 8: THE ILLUSIONIST (pp. 210–43) –

1 Winston Churchill, *The World Crisis 1911–1918* (Odhams reprint), vol. 2, p. 479 *et seq.*
2 Extract from Colonel F. H. Sykes's appreciation to Murray Sueter at the Admiralty.
3 Childers Great War Diaries, parts 4 and 5.
4 Private information to author.
5 F. H. Sykes, *From Many Angles*, p. 171.
6 Extract from official citation in the *London Gazette*, April 1917.

7 Jenkins, *op cit.*, p. 396 *et seq.*
8 Brian Inglis, *Roger Casement*, p. 285 *et seq.*
9 Childers correspondence.
10 MacLysaght's personal notes and testimony to author.
11 *Report of the Proceedings of the Irish Convention*, Dublin, HMSO, 1918.
12 Robert Barton's correspondence.

CHAPTER 9: THE HOSTAGE (pp. 244–96)

1 Molly Childers's notes.
2 Childers correspondence.
3 Official survey by Erskine Childers of the effects of allied bombing. No copy of this has been found in the family papers, but see H. A. Jones, *War in the Air*, vol. 6.
4 A. J. P. Taylor, *English History 1914–1945*, p. 154.
5 Piaras Beaslai, *Michael Collins and the Making of a New Ireland*, vol. 1, p. 270. *et seq.*
6 This episode was confirmed to the author by Sir Barnett Cocks.
7 Childers Irish notebooks.
8 Childers's articles were reproduced as a pamphlet, *Military Rule in Ireland*, 1921.
9 Desmond Ryan, *Remembering Sion*.
10 Frank Pakenham, *Peace by Ordeal: negotiation and signature of the Anglo-Irish Treaty, 1921*, p. 41 *et seq.*
11 Tom Jones, *Whitehall Diary*, vol. 3, p. 17 *et seq.*
12 Robert Kee, *The Green Flag: a history of Irish nationalism*, p. 707.
13 On 22 June 1921, the day of the King's speech at the opening of Stormont, de Valera was arrested and almost immediately released through the intervention of Alfred Cope much as Childers had been a month earlier.
14 Testimony of the late President Childers to author.
15 Childers Irish Diaries.
16 Hassall, *op. cit.*, pp. 487–8.
17 Fitzalan correspondence with Lloyd George (Lloyd George papers).
18 Words used by de Valera in the Dáil, June 1922.
19 Article by Lloyd George in *Daily Telegraph*, 23 December 1922.
20 Margery Forester, *Michael Collins: the lost leader*, Sphere Books, p. 247 *et seq.*
21 This 'mutual friend' is famous but must remain anonymous.
22 Geoffrey Shakespeare spent some time also gossiping with Childers about *The Riddle of the Sands*: see his autobiography *Let Candles Be Brought In*, See also Forester, *op. cit.*
23 Amery, *op. cit.*, vol. 2, p. 230.

CHAPTER 10: THE REBEL (pp. 297–323)

1 Childers Irish notebooks.
2 Rex Taylor, *Michael Collins*.
3 Dáil proceedings.
4 Beaslai, *op. cit.*, vol. 2, p. 354 *et seq.*
5 Kee, *op. cit.*, p. 733 *et seq.*
6 Letter from Molly Childers to de Valera.
7 O'Connor, *op. cit.*, p. 168 *et seq.*
8 David Robinson's letters and notes.
9 Longford and O'Neill, *Eamon de Valera*, Gill Macmillan, p. 199.
10 Testimony of the late President Childers to author.
11 The Lloyd George and the Bonar Law papers.

SOURCES AND REFERENCES

Books

In the Ranks of the CIV, Smith, Elder, 1900
The HAC in South Africa (co-author Basil Williams), Smith, Elder, 1903
The Riddle of the Sands, Smith, Elder, 1903
The Times History of the War in South Africa, vol. 5, Sampson Low, Marston, 1907
War and the Arme Blanche, Edward Arnold, 1910
The Framework of Home Rule, Edward Arnold, 1911
German Influence on British Cavalry, Edward Arnold, 1911

Pamphlets

Military Rule in Ireland, Talbot Press, Dublin, 1921
The Constructive Work of Dail Eireann, Talbot Press, Dublin, 1921
Who Burnt Cork City? (co-author Alfred O'Rahilly), 1921

Periodicals

Irish Bulletin (later *Poblacht na h'Eireann*), 1920–2
Poblacht (war bulletin), June–October 1922

Sources of quotations

I wish to thank authors and/or publishers for permission to quote from the following:
AMERY, L. S., *My Political Life*, 3 vols. Hutchinson, 1951–5
BEASLAI, PIERAS (Piers Beasley), *Michael Collins and the Making of a New Ireland*, 2 vols. Harrap, 1926
BLAKE, ROBERT, *The Unknown Prime Minister: The life and times of Bonar Law*, Eyre and Spottiswoode, 1955
CHILDERS, SPENCER, *The Life of the Rt Hon. Hugh C. E. Childers*, 2 vols. Murray, 1901
COWLES, VIRGINIA, *Edward VII and His Circle*, Hamish Hamilton, 1956

FEILING, KEITH, *A History of England*, Macmillan, 1950

FORESTER, MARGERY, *Michael Collins: The lost leader*, Sidgwick and Jackson, 1971; Sphere Books, 1974

HASSALL, CHRISTOPHER, *Edward Marsh*, Longman, 1959

INGLIS, BRIAN, *Roger Casement*, Hodder and Stoughton, 1973

JENKINS, ROY, *Asquith*, Collins, 1964

JONES, TOM, *Whitehall Diary*, 3 vols., Oxford University Press, 1969–71: vol. 3, *Ireland 1918–25*

KEE, ROBERT, *The Green Flag: A history of Irish nationalism*, Weidenfeld and Nicolson, 1972

KRUGER, RAYNE, *Good Bye Dolly Gray*, Cassell, 1959

LANDRETH, HELEN, *The Mind and Heart of Mary Childers*, Boston (privately published)

LONGFORD, 7TH EARL OF (Frank Pakenham), *Peace by Ordeal*, Sidgwick and Jackson, 1935

LONGFORD, 7TH EARL OF, and O'NEILL, T. P., *Eamon de Valera*, Hutchinson, 1970

NEESON, EOIN, *The Civil War in Ireland 1921–23*, The Mercier Press, 1970

O'CONNOR, FRANK, *An Only Child*, Macmillan and Pan Books

OWEN, FRANK, *Tempestuous Journey: Lloyd George, his life and times*, Hutchinson, 1954

PAKENHAM, FRANK: *See* LONGFORD, 7TH EARL OF

RYAN, A. P., *Mutiny at the Curragh*, Macmillan, 1956

RYAN, DESMOND, *Remembering Sion: A chronicle of storm and quiet*, Arthur Barker, 1934

SYKES, MAJOR-GENERAL SIR FREDERICK, *From Many Angles*, Harrap, 1942

TAYLOR, A. J. P., *English History 1914–45*, Oxford University Press, 1965

TAYLOR, REX, *Michael Collins*, Hutchinson, 1958

Other sources

ASQUITH, H. H. (1st Earl of Oxford and Asquith), *Memories and Reflections 1852–1927*, 2 vols., Cassell, 1928

BEAVERBROOK, 1ST BARON (W. Maxwell Aitken), *Politicians and the War*, 2 vols., Butterworth, 1928 and 1932
    The Decline and Fall of Lloyd George, Collins, 1963

BELL, J. B., *The Secret Army: A history of the IRA 1916–1970*. Blond, 1970; Sphere Books, 1972

BIRKENHEAD, 2ND EARL OF (F. W. F. Smith), *F. E., 1st Earl of Birkenhead*, Butterworth, 1933: vol. 1, *The First Phase*

BOYCE, D. G., *Englishmen and Irish Troubles: British public opinion and the making of Irish policy 1918–22*, Cape, 1972

CALLWELL, MAJOR-GENERAL SIR CHARLES E., *Field-Marshal Sir Henry Wilson: His life and diaries*, 2 vols., Cassell 1927: vol. 1

CARTY, JAMES, *Ireland from the Great Famine to the Treaty, 1851–1921*, Fallon, 1940
   Bibliography of Irish History 1912–21, 2 vols., Stationery Office, Dublin, 1936–40

CHURCHILL, W. S., *World Crisis 1911–18*, 6 vols., Butterworth, 1927–31; repr. in 2 vols, Odhams, 1939

COLVIN, I. D. and MARJORIBANKS, E., *The Life of Lord Carson*, 3 vols., Gollancz, 1932–6

COOPER, A. DUFF, *Haig*, 2 vols., Faber, 1935–6: vol. 1

CRAWFORD, F. H., *Guns for Ulster*, Graham and Heslip, Belfast

CROZIER, F. P., *Ireland for Ever*, Cape, 1932; repr. Portway Reprints, 1971

ENSOR, R. C. K., *England 1870–1914* (*Oxford History of England*, vol. 14), Oxford University Press, 1936

FIGGIS, DARRELL, *Recollections of the Irish War*, Benn, 1927

GALLAGHER, FRANK, *The Anglo-Irish Treaty*, Hutchinson, 1965

GOUGH, GENERAL SIR HUBERT, *Soldiering On*, Arthur Barker, 1954

GWYNN, DENIS, *The Life of John Redmond*, Harrap, 1932
   The History of Partition 1912–25, Browne and Nolan, Dublin, 1950

GWYNN, STEPHEN, *The History of Ireland*, Macmillan, 1923

HAMMOND, J. L., *Gladstone and the Irish Nation*, Longman, 1938

HEALY, T. M., *Letters and Leaders of My Day*, 2 vols., Butterworth, 1928: vol. 2

HORGAN, J. J., *Parnell to Pearse*, Browne and Nolan, Dublin, 1948

HYDE, H. M., *Carson*, Heinemann, 1953; repr. Constable, 1974

JONES, H. A., *War in the Air*, 3 vols., Clarendon Press, Oxford, 1928–31

LAZENBY, E., *Ireland a Catspaw*, Boswell, 1928

LEE, SIR SIDNEY, *King Edward VII*, 2 vols., Macmillan, 1925–7

LESLIE, SHANE, *The Irish Tangle for English Readers*, Macdonald, 1946

LLOYD GEORGE, D., *War Memoirs*, 6 vols., Odhams, 1933–6

LYONS, F. S. L., *The Irish Parliamentary Party 1890–1910*, Faber, 1951

MACARDLE, D. M. D., *The Irish Republic: A documentary chronicle 1916–23*, Irish Press Limited, 1937

MACREADY, GENERAL SIR CECIL F. N., *Annals of an Active Life*, 2 vols., Hutchinson, 1924

MARTIN, F. X., *et al., The Howth Gun-running and the Kilcoole Gun-running 1914*, Browne and Nolan, Dublin, 1964

MIDDLETON, 1ST EARL OF (W. St John F. Brodrick), *Ireland – Dupe or Heroine*, Heinemann, 1932

MORLEY, JOHN, 1ST VISCOUNT, *The Life of William Ewart Gladstone*, 3 vols, Macmillan, 1903: vol. 3

NICOLSON, SIR HAROLD, *King George V: His life and reign*, Constable, 1952

O'HEGARTY, P. S., *A History of Ireland under the Union 1801–1922*, Methuen, 1952

O'MALLEY, E., *On Another Man's Wound*, Rich and Cowan, 1936 *Les Origines diplomatiques de la guerre 1870–71*

PONSONBY, SIR FREDERICK, *Recollections of Three Reigns*, Eyre and Spottiswoode, 1951

RANSOME, ARTHUR, *The Causes and Prevention of Phthisis*, Milroy Lecture 1890, Smith, Elder.

RIDDELL, G. A., 1ST BARON, *Intimate Diary of the Peace Conference and After, 1918–23*, Gollancz, 1933

SCOTT, C. P., Diary (British Museum)

SEELY, J. E. B. (1st Baron Mottistone), *Adventure*, Heinemann, 1930

SHAKESPEARE, SIR GEOFFREY, *Let Candles Be Brought In*, Macdonald, 1949

SHEPHARD, G. S., *Memoirs*, 1924 (privately printed)

ULLSWATER, 1ST VISCOUNT (J. W. Lowther), *A Speaker's Commentaries*, 2 vols., Edward Arnold, 1925

VICTORIA, QUEEN, *Letters 1886–1901*, John Murray

WHITE, T. DE VERE, *Kevin O'Higgins*, Methuen, 1948

YOUNGER, CALTON, *Ireland's Civil War*, Muller, 1968

INDEX

Compiled by Gordon Robinson